WORLD AFFAIRS
National and International Viewpoints

WORLD AFFAIRS

National and International Viewpoints

The titles in this collection were selected
from the Council on Foreign Relations' publication:
The Foreign Affairs 50-Year Bibliography

Advisory Editor
RONALD STEEL

The JEWS in the SOVIET UNION

BY

SOLOMON M. SCHWARZ

ARNO PRESS

A NEW YORK TIMES COMPANY

New York • 1972

Reprint Edition 1972 by Arno Press Inc.

Copyright © 1951 by The American Jewish Committee
Reprinted by permission of Syracuse University Press

Reprinted from a copy in Syracuse University Press

World Affairs: National and International Viewpoints
ISBN for complete set: 0-405-04560-3
See last pages of this volume for titles.

Manufactured in the United States of America

∾∾∾∾∾∾∾∾∾∾∾

Library of Congress Cataloging in Publication Data

Schwarz, Solomon M
  The Jews in the Soviet Union.

  (World affairs: national and international viewpoints)
  Includes bibliographical references.
  1. Jews in Russia--History--1917-   I. Title.
II. Series.
DS135.R9S36 1972   914.7'06'924   72-4298
ISBN 0-405-04589-1

THE JEWS IN THE SOVIET UNION

The JEWS
in the
SOVIET UNION

BY

SOLOMON M. SCHWARZ

Foreword by ALVIN JOHNSON
President Emeritus, New School for Social Research

SYRACUSE UNIVERSITY PRESS

Sponsored by The American Jewish Committee
Manufactured in the U. S. by American Book–Knickerbocker Press

Designed by Meyer Wagman

Preface

WITH THIS VOLUME the Library of Jewish Information of the American Jewish Committee completes the first half of a study, begun in 1948, of the situation of the Jews in the Soviet Union and its European satellite countries. The aim has been to obtain the first organized body of knowledge, based on a critical examination of all available sources, on the Communist attitude toward Jewish problems and the effect of the Soviet system on Jewish life. This is in line with the policy of the Committee to study and make available the facts about the civic and political status of Jews in the contemporary world.

The undersigned, who was charged by the American Jewish Committee with the direction of the undertaking, welcomes this opportunity to acknowledge the invaluable assistance rendered by the Committee on Library, Research and Publications of the American Jewish Committee, under the chairmanship of Salo W. Baron, Professor of Jewish History, Literature and Institutions in Columbia University, and by the special sub-committee it set up to advise on this study; by A.R.L. Gurland, who served as translator from the Russian as well as research and editorial consultant; and by Martin Greenberg, who edited the manuscript. Meyer Wagman of Kurt, Volk, Inc., served as typographical consultant. Mrs. Effie Solis-Cohen prepared the Index, and Miss Dora Cohen and Mrs. Estella Weckstein of the staff of the Library of Jewish Information rendered useful technical assistance.

MORRIS FINE, *Director*
Library of Jewish Information
of the American Jewish Committee

Foreword

by ALVIN JOHNSON

WE MAY RECALL the time when it appeared to us that whatever wrongs and cruelties strained the record of the Soviet government, in one point at least it represented a great moral advance over the fallen Tsarist regime. The Communist leaders proclaimed an end to all policies of persecution of religious, racial, and national minorities.

It is generally acknowledged that the way a society treats its minorities is an important index to its character, and that the official attitude towards the Jewish minority, far from being a matter of exclusive Jewish interest, is of key significance. The Soviet system has put forth extravagant claims in this respect, asserting not only that it has secured complete equality for all minorities, but also that it has assured all national groups the right to full self-determination. As for the Soviet Jews, the Soviets have claimed to have extirpated the very roots of antisemitism and racial prejudice, and to have solved the age-old Jewish problem in an exemplary fashion.

The Jews of pre-Soviet Russia were in effect a minority nationality, with a language of their own, Yiddish, an extensive and able Jewish press, an elaborate system of education, and a notable national culture. They expected with the advent of the Soviet system to be given full freedom to develop that culture, like any other minority group.

All these hopes have turned to ashes. Reports coming from behind the Iron Curtain describe the liquidation of all independent Jewish organizations and institutions, and the complete destruction of Jewish communal life. The Yiddish press has been abolished, the Yiddish schools have been closed. Birobidzhan, proclaimed a national home for Soviet Jews, is a failure; few Jews remain, and there is no autonomous Jewish life in the "Autonomous Region," Zionist activities are banned, and no Jews can receive exit permits for emigration to Israel. The younger generation has been educated to abhor the religion their fathers held sacred. Recent reports describe violent propaganda against "Jewish nationalism" and "Jewish cosmopolitanism," extensive purges among the Jewish intelligentsia, the resurgence of discrimination in government service, and growing popular antisemitism, often exploited by the ruling circles for their own political purposes.

vii

In the present volume these facts are corroborated beyond doubt and carefully analyzed by Dr. Solomon M. Schwarz, an authority on Soviet Russian affairs and one of the best equipped and painstaking of research scholars. Dr. Schwarz analyzes the entire history of the Soviet theory and practice in regard to the Jewish question: the Bolshevik minority practices in general and their application to the Jewish problem; the forced Sovietization of Jewish institutions; the early development and later decline of Jewish cultural life; the roots, extent and manifestations of resurgent antisemitism.

The experience of minority groups under Soviet dictatorship has made it clear that there can be no freedom for them under a totalitarian dictatorship. Totalitarian systems permit no individuality, no free or autonomous developments to any group. Minority cultures cannot develop without a certain degree of freedom; but the totalitarian regime does not tolerate such freedom. The cultural freedom of most minorities has been reduced to the right to repeat the Communist propaganda and to praise the leader in their own language; in the case of the Jews, whom Lenin's theory does not consider a nationality, even this right has been gradually withdrawn. Under despotism, all citizens suffer the loss of freedom; but the members of minority groups suffer doubly, both individually and collectively. This truth is again confirmed by the careful analysis of the fate of Jews under totalitarian Communism.

No real security for the Jews existed anywhere before the rise of western democracy, which gradually liberated them from political disabilities and abolished all official limitations upon their economic life. Only under democracy have the Jews been able to build up great and prosperous communities, to maintain the integrity of their religious and social customs, to develop a rich and fruitful communal life, and to defend their rights wherever they might be threatened. Only where the freedom of the individual is securely established, where the government can be criticized and changed by the people can there be, in the long run, security for religious, social, or national minorities.

Author's Note

M Y ENDEAVOR has been to base the two studies making up the present work as much as possible on Soviet sources—newspapers, periodicals, books, and other publications in Russian and Yiddish. But since Soviet publications are subject at every point to official control, and since independent evidence is scarce, getting at the truth requires an intricate process of reconstruction from fragmentary data and indirect clues. The method necessarily resembles that of the archeologist, who pieces together the picture of the past from incomplete and scattered facts. There is this differences, however—the Soviet Union is not buried in a remote antiquity, so that the student of Soviet life may at least occasionally test his findings against the testimony of living witnesses.

This book is the result of two year's labor undertaken at the instance of the American Jewish Committee. It has profited from criticisms and suggestions made by an advisory subcommittee of the Library of Jewish Information, consisting of Professor Nathan Reich of Hunter College, Professor Solomon F. Bloom of Brooklyn College, Herbert Solow of *Fortune* magazine, Professor Koppel S. Pinson of Queens College and Avram Yarmolinsky of the Slavonic Division of the New York Public Library. It has also profited from the counsel of Morris Fine, Director of the Library of Jewish Information; Joseph Gordon, Joseph Ofman, and Bernard D. Weinryb. The author also acknowledges the fine cooperation he received from the staff of the Library of Jewish Information. To these persons I wish to express my gratitude. Needless to say, however, responsibility for the work and all opinions expressed therein is completely the author's.

I cannot mention here all the persons with whom I have discussed the questions considered in this book. I must however express my appreciation to Jacob D. Lestschinsky for his invaluable critical and bibliographical suggestions, and for his having placed at my disposal his rare collection of Soviet publications on the Jewish question.

The author owes a particular dept of gratitude to Martin Greenberg and A.R.L. Gurland for their excellent and painstaking editorial assistance; and to the latter also for many suggestions about the use of supplementary materials.

S.M.S

New York
April 1951

ix

Contents

PART ONE

Soviet Minority Policy and the Jews

CHAPTER XI–Jewish Administrative Autonomy

CHAPTER XII–Agrarianization and Industrialization

CHAPTER XIII–Birobidzhan

CHAPTER XIV–The War and After

APPENDIX–Evacuation and Re-Evacuation of the Jews in the War

PART TWO
Antisemitism in the U.S.S.R.

List of Tables

PART ONE

Soviet Minority Policy and the Jews

PART TWO

Antisemitism in the U.S.S.R.

Part One

SOVIET MINORITY POLICY
AND THE JEWS

CHAPTER I

The Historical Legacy

The Peoples of the Soviet Union

The population of the Soviet Union, like that of Tsarist Russia before
it, is made up of a Russian ("Great-Russian") majority and many minorities of different ethnic origin, political histories, languages, and cultures.
The Jewish problem is but one of many with which any government of
this multinational country, regardless of its politics, would have to deal.
No government ruling a multinational state can do without a long-range
and coherent policy on the problems of the coexistence of its nationalities.
Once evolved, such a policy necessarily exerts a determining influence on
the treatment accorded any particular minority.

Soviet terminology distinguishes between nations and nationalities,
the less developed of the latter being denominated as ethnic groups
(*narodnosti*). While usage is flexible and the terms are often interchanged
(the word "people" frequently taking the place of all three), Soviet
political philosophy insists on statehood as the determining attribute of
a *nation*. Thus, the citizenry of the USSR is called the Soviet nation (or
the Soviet people); it comprises many ethno-cultural groups called nationalities: the Great-Russians, Ukrainians, White Russians, Armenians, Jews,
Georgians, etc. In theory, any nationality may claim the right of self-
determination, including that of forming an independent national state,
and thus attain the status of a nation; but if it has no territory of its own,
which is the prerequisite of statehood, its claim to recognition as a self-
determining nationality is questionable.[1]

The ethnic map of the Soviet Union is a bizarre patchwork of many and
different national or ethnic groups. How many there are, of course,
depends upon the criteria one uses. Soviet sources usually cite impressive
figures—about 180, more than 175, etc. A classification prepared for the
census of 1926 listed 186; but of 7 of these the censustakers could find no
trace. Of the remaining 179 groups, 28 had less than 100 members, and
18 less than 1,000.[2] The census of January 1939 recorded 169 national or
ethnic groups, that is, 10 less than in 1926. Fourteen of the 169 numbered more than 1,000,000 members each, together accounting for 94.3
percent of the total population of the Soviet Union. Of these, the Russians
alone numbered roughly 99,000,000, or 58.4 percent of the total popula-

tion, the remaining 13 nationalities, 60,700,000, or 35.9 percent. Except for the Jews, some 3,000,000 people scattered over the country and accounting for only 1.8 percent of the Soviet population, each of these nationalities was concentrated in an area where it constituted the majority of the inhabitants, predominating numerically either in a Union Republic or in an Autonomous Republic (a separate administrative unit within a Union Republic).

In addition to the larger groups, the census of 1939 recorded a total of 155 nationalities or ethnic groups with an aggregate membership of less than 10,000,000, amounting to 5.7 percent of the total population. Among these lesser groups, 21 had more than 100,000 but less than 1,000,000 members each, and 14 had 20,000 to 100,000 each: these 35 groups accounted for 5.2 percent of the total population, while the remaining 120, all together numbering 807,279 people, comprised less than one-half of one percent of the total population.[3] Though it is not merely size that makes a nationality, it would seem warranted to say that a considerable number of the groups listed separately in Soviet statistics lack the characteristics of genuine nationality and do not constitute a problem which the government must take into account. A dialect or common tribal ancestry does not necessarily prove the existence of a separate nationality. How many nationalities would the United States possess if every Indian tribe with barely distinguishable traces of ethno-cultural individuality were to be counted as a distinct national group?

Nevertheless, when allowance is made for all statistical exaggeration, there are enough distinctly differentiated national groupings in the Soviet Union to raise serious political, administrative, and cultural issues; these issues, moreover, are complicated by the Tsarist heritage. The essence of Tsarist policy had been the more or less consistent oppression of almost all nationalities save the Great Russian. There was, especially after the beginning of the nineteenth century, a wide range of variation in this, from mere suppression of the minority nationality's cultural individuality (i.e., stubborn and narrow-minded Russification), as in the case of the Ukrainians; to brutal persecution of all national aspirations, as in the case of the Poles; to a policy of destruction verging on economic and cultural annihilation, as in the case of the Jews. This varied policy of oppression, accentuated by the preferential treatment granted a number of privileged nationalities (e.g., the German), not only aggravated the individual problems of each minority, but also increased friction and discord among them. The divide-and-rule strategy followed by the Tsars also deliberately kindled national, racial, and religious rivalries and antagonisms.

The Tsarist Empire, as it stood at the end of the nineteenth century, was the product of centuries of conquest and colonization. Some of the conquered peoples had been simply arrested and held at a primitive tribal stage; others, far more advanced, were halted in their progress; others again were narrowly confined to certain economic pursuits and their development markedly crippled and distorted. The coexistence of the various national and ethnic groups, with their different cultures and social structures, bred genuine problems, in addition to the conflicts deliberately provoked by Tsarist policy. As the rapid rise of industry and trade in the late nineteenth and early twentieth centuries shattered customary social forms, dissension deepened and centrifugal tendencies appeared. Unless a radically new solution of the national problem was devised, the revolutionary upheaval that threatened might have been expected to cause the multinational state to disintegrate. When the upheaval came, the revolutionary leaders undertook to prevent the disintegration of the Russian state by proposing new solutions to the national problem that the Tsarist government had been unable to resolve.

National Problems in a Multinational State

In the course of development of Tsarist Russia its minorities retained their distinctive national personalities which had been formed by different cultural, social, economic, and even political patterns. Quite a number of them began to demand autonomy, and to the extent that this conflicted with the established political system, national autonomy and even independent statehood became a goal that won adherents when oppression grew stronger, and lost them when it lightened. Yet a government abolishing the Tsarist system of national oppression had an opportunity to build a federation of autonomous nationalities unplagued by separatist tendencies.

In the anti-Tsarist revolutionary movement differences of opinion as to the extent of self-government to be granted minority peoples under a democratic system were overshadowed by the fight against the common enemy. It was taken for granted that all nationalities would have an equal opportunity to preserve and develop their own culture, that their languages would be given full recognition, their customs respected, and their cultural group interests safeguarded. There was no dissension when the democratic government, set up after the downfall of Tsarist rule in March 1917, proclaimed the principle of equal rights for all minority nationalities. The victorious Soviet revolution was following in its footsteps when it assured all nationalities full freedom of cultural development.

In addition to the cultural, there are the political rights of nationalities. Official Soviet doctrine for a number of years laid particular emphasis on the political right of self-determination, and one of the greatest revolutionary achievements was considered to be the broad administrative autonomy freely offered and guaranteed to all minorities. In later years greater importance was attached to promoting the cultural advancement of the non-Russian minorities under Soviet rule. A critical evaluation of what really happened in the three decades of Soviet rule will show that, while the right of self-determination and self-government supposedly enjoyed by minority nationalities in the Soviet Union is a myth, minority peoples that had been thwarted and dwarfed by Tsarist oppression did in fact rise to a higher cultural level.

This, however, is not true in the case of the Jewish minority, as it is one of the purposes of this work to show. Moreover, as the crystallizing totalitarian system subjected every sphere of life to its rigid control, free development of all minority nationalities was increasingly frustrated by the general lack of freedom.

Official policy in a state where the government is all-powerful, strongly influences every branch of life. In turn, Soviet policy is to a great degree the result of a process of interpretation of basic Communist teachings. The Communist Party's theory of nationalism in general, as well as its ideological and sociological appraisal of individual nationalities, their history, and their potentialities, have a determining influence on official policy. But Communist doctrine, both in general and as applied to specific groups, has its roots in the past and must be traced back to pre-revolutionary developments. In particular, this is true of Soviet policies with respect to the Jewish minority. Without a knowledge of the peculiar history of the Jewish minority under the Tsars, it would be impossible to understand the Soviet government's approach to the Jewish problem and the programs for resolving it which were adopted at different stages.

The Ghetto Nation of Russia

The Tsars ruled a considerable Jewish population for 145 years. When Jews in large numbers were first brought under Tsarist rule by the partitioning of Poland, they were an isolated, segregated, and closed community established for centuries on the Polish land. To the Russian administrators, a Jewish nation was as startling as it was novel. To be sure, Jews had settled on the northern coast of the Black Sea as early as the seventh or eighth century. But Southern Russia, the future Ukraine, after its liberation from Mongol invaders in 1320, came under Lithuanian and then Polish rule, and remained Polish until the end of the eighteenth century. Through all these centuries no Jews were tolerated in Muscovite Russia. True, Ukrainian provinces east of the Dnieper were ceded by Poland to the Moscow Tsar in 1667, but this was after the Jews of these provinces had been slaughtered in the Bogdan Khmelnitskyi uprising (1648–49), a "total extermination," as a historian of today has termed it,[4] which had left only a sprinkling of Jews in the ravaged land.[5] Not until the successive partitionings of Poland in 1772–1795 [6] did Russia acquire a large Jewish minority. Of the annexed population, about one-tenth was Jewish.[7]

It can be disputed whether the Jews of the West constitute a nationality; but it is a historical fact that the Jews living for centuries under the Polish kings were organized as and recognized to be a separate nationality. Not only did they differ in language [8] and religion from their surroundings; they also possessed their own civil administration, their own statute books and courts, and a separate, extensive, and emphatically Jewish educational system. Moreover, they virtually monopolized certain social and economic functions that would have otherwise gone more or less unperformed among either the Polish majority, or the Lithuanian, White-Russian, and Ukrainian minorities.

Through most of its history as an independent kingdom Poland lacked a commercial or industrial class of any importance. The cities were small, and there was neither industry nor shipping to speak of; trade and handicrafts were to a large extent the province of the Jewish community. The feudal lords, the churches, and the shaky feudal state left the marketing of agricultural produce, the supply of domestic and imported urban goods, and all transactions involving the collection of feudal and public revenues, to various agents: commission merchants, tenants, tavern- and innkeepers, farmers of taxes, excises, tolls, rentals, and other sources of fiscal, institutional, or proprietary income. The kings of backward Poland had not humbled the power of the feudal lords and established a centralized, absolutist state that could have performed these functions for itself. A special intermediary class was required to keep the feudal economy functioning. The job fell by and large to the Jewish community. But though it enabled the mass of the Jewish population to survive, it gave only a few fortunate ones an opportunity to amass capital, and it excluded Jews from holding any substantial amount of land.[9]

The moment feudal economy and state began to disintegrate, Jews were bound to lose most of their economic functions. Wars, military defeats, and the end of Poland's independence hastened the process. Instead of rotting slowly through the decades, feudal society in Poland fell apart within a few years. Fiscal functions hitherto performed by Jews were taken over by the Russian administration. Menaced by the competition of cheaper Russian grains and the prohibitive Prussian tariff, Polish landlords were driven into commerce and industry, taking over the Jewish agents' marketing and managerial functions. The abolition of serfdom in 1807 accelerated the transition from a barter to a money economy, drove the surplus rural population into the cities, and caused industry to thrive at the expense of agriculture and urban handicrafts. The bulk of the former Jewish traders and agents, for the most part without capital, found themselves barred from industry and modern commerce. Simultaneously, the Tsarist administration more or less consistently removed all Jews from rural communities. At the same time that rural commerce and artisan trades were denied the Jews, the number of those obliged to depend on them multiplied. A population of about one million was reduced to living on thin air, the later proverbial *luftmenshn*.[10]

The Russian administration's Jewish policy from the first partition of Poland to the early 1880's, was hesitant and vacillating; it either reversed itself constantly or moved in two different directions at the same time. On the one hand, efforts were made to "civilize" or "normalize" the Jewish population: that is, transform the Jewish peddlers and middle-men into farmers, skilled craftsmen, soldiers; make them attend non-Jewish schools, wear non-Jewish dress, speak non-Jewish languages (at first German or Polish, later Russian); and break up the ghetto-like concentration of Jews in the former Polish provinces. On the other hand, these attempts at "normalization" were superseded over and over again by measures designed to crush the "stubborn and recalcitrant lot" once and for all: they would be forced to choose between starvation and the abandonment of their faith, tradition, community, and way of life.[11]

The oppressive measures employed were many and different. At the very beginning the Jewish population was confined to a narrow area, the Pale of Jewish Residence, which in addition to the provinces incorporated in the 1770's and 1790's also included northeastern Ukraine, annexed in the seventeenth century, and the thinly populated Black Sea coast (Crimea, New Russia, Bessarabia), which Tsarist proconsuls colonized in the early part of the nineteenth century. Admission of Jews to Russian schools was rendered more and more difficult. Jews were generally excluded from the public service, and as a rule barred from agricultural occupations. Only the few who had accumulated considerable capital found access to real industry and commerce, as distinguished from the shadowy sub-marginal shops in the overcrowded ghetto towns—the typical *shtetl*—of the Jewish Pale. Residential restrictions held down to a minimum the number of Jewish industrial workers. The lack of educational facilities largely prevented the influx of Jews into the liberal professions. Special taxation and extortionate police practices worsened the miserable lot of the Jewish masses.[12]

In the 1880's, when the rapid advance of industrialization, following in the wake of the belated emancipation of the serfs in Russia proper (1861), threatened to smash the ghetto gates long before normalization measures had sufficiently de-Judaized the Jewish popular masses, the policy of oppression and persecution was given first place and was reinforced by statutory codification. Efforts directed at gradually "civilizing" the ghetto nation were abandoned, and it was left to suffocate in the narrowness, darkness, and economic hopelessness of its ghetto existence.

The Decay of the Jewish National Community

Throughout the history of the Jews under Tsarist rule, legislative and administrative restrictions slowed down or stopped completely the integration of the Jewish masses in the economy. Scarcely any of the conditions of Jewish life even remotely approached normality. Yet the tiniest successes in normalization, however limited by the steady intensification of oppression, gave odd groups a chance to escape, through Russification often accompanied by gradual withdrawal from the Jewish community, the misery and drudgery of ghetto life. Small as the number of these Jews was, it was enough to make assimilation seem to many the only possible solution to the Jewish problem. The more ruthlessly life was stifled in the Pale, and the higher mounted the wall of legal restrictions, the more powerful grew the desire to pull the ghetto down. Emancipation was as vigorously demanded and fought for by Zionism and nationalist Judaism as it was by assimilationist groups and militant Jewish socialists. Only minor sections of religious orthodoxy remained aloof.

The Tsarist policies proved markedly successful in destroying Jewish national organization. Although the *kahal*—the self-governing body permitted the Jews under Polish rule—was not abolished by the Tsarist administration until 1844, it was used chiefly to collect special meat and candle taxes, for which the Jewish community as a whole was held responsible, and to impress Jewish youths into the military service, from which only the children of the well-to-do were exempt. The abolition of the *kahal* left the community without an institutional framework, but did not relieve it of its collective responsibility for the collection of taxes and for military recruitment; special taxes levied on Jews, supposedly for the care of the poor, sick, and infirm, were henceforth collected by the government either directly or through Jewish tax farmers or special Jewish tax collectors, assisted by official Jewish assessors, while communal expenditures and all administrative decisions had to be approved by the Tsarist provincial governors or municipal officials. The official community,[13] with its "crown rabbi" (whose chief function was to register vital statistics), came to be regarded as an auxiliary of the Tsarist administration, or at best as an instrument of negotiation between the rich and privileged Jews, on the one hand, and the Tsarist bureaucracy and police, on the other.[14]

With the transformation of the communal organizations into Tsarist instruments, all communal self-government ceased to exist. The Jewish population was in fact no longer publicly represented. Private groups—charitable, cultural, etc.—had perforce to speak for Jewish interests before the authorities and public opinion. At the turn of the century, various political organizations more or less opposed to the Tsarist regime emerged;

but their activities were often semilegal. Outwardly, the Jewish community was united in its protest against oppression and persecution and in the struggle for emancipation, i.e., for the abolition of all restrictive laws and regulations. Within the community, however, dissension was rife. Social and economic conflicts had their parallels in politics and ideology.

Zionist and nationalist Jewish movements, which spread far and wide in the 1890's and after, opposed assimilationist tendencies and militantly emphasized Jewish national consciousness and individuality, Jewish separateness, and the national struggle for Jewish rights. Liberal Judaism, on the other hand, shunned this nationalist emphasis and concentrated its energies on the fight against restrictive and discriminatory legislation. It did not look with disfavor on the anticipated reduction of Judaism to a matter of religious preference. Finally, the socialist labor movement, which developed promisingly in the early 1900's, was hostile to Jewish traditions, anti-religious, and though encouraging the growth of a national Jewish culture, vehemently opposed, in its majority, to Jewish nationalism.

These internal conflicts could not be resolved so long as all strata of the Jewish population and all currents of Jewish opinion struggled in the Tsarist-imposed strait-jacket of ghetto life. It was the common goal of every rival tendency and group to burst the Tsarist bonds, and all that Russian liberal and revolutionary opinion knew of Jewish politics and Jewish communal developments was this common desire for emancipation. Emancipation from Tsarist oppression would also break the hold of religious superstition on the Jewish masses. Anti-Tsarist forces did not doubt that the downfall of Tsarist despotism would cause all specifically Jewish problems to disappear; indeed, in liberal and revolutionary circles it was widely thought that the Jews themselves would disappear as a collectivity. Jewry was deemed to be an anachronistic vestige of a tragic past kept alive only by an oppressive policy preventing its absorption into the community at large. As in nineteenth-century Western Europe, so in Russia, liberalism and socialism by and large equated emancipation and assimilation. The bulk of Russia's liberals, progressives, and revolutionary socialists thus looked forward to a speedy normalization of the Jewish condition after the downfall of Tsarism.

On the Threshold of the Twentieth Century

From the annexation of the Polish territories to the census of 1897, the Jewish population of the Tsarist Empire increased approximately five times, from about one million to over five million. This increase took place in spite of emigration, which was on a minor scale throughout most of the nineteenth century, but became a veritable mass exodus in the 1880's.

The overwhelming majority of the Jewish population resided within the Jewish Pale, as may be seen from Table I.

TABLE I

REGIONAL DISTRIBUTION OF THE JEWISH POPULATION IN THE RUSSIAN EMPIRE, 1897 [15]

Region	Jewish Population		Jewish Percent of Total Population
	Thousands	Percent	
IN THE PALE			
Poland (10 provinces)	1,321.1	25.3	14.5
North West (3 Lithuanian and 3 White-Russian provinces)	1,422.4	27.3	14.1
South West (Ukraine west of the Dnieper—4 provinces—and Bessarabia)	1,768.6	33.9	12.4
South East (Ukraine east of the Dnieper—3 provinces—and Crimea)	387.2	7.4	4.5
Total, 25 provinces	4,899.3	93.9	11.6
OUTSIDE OF THE PALE	316.5	6.1	.4
Grand Total	5,215.8	100.0	4.1

Within the Pale, which had a population of 42.2 million, Jews accounted for 11.6 percent of the total population; in other parts of the Tsarist Empire, with 85.1 million inhabitants, Jews represented less than one-half of one percent of the total population.[16] Internal migrations indeed had taken place, and about 25 percent of all Jews under Russian rule in 1897 lived in provinces which had not made part of the Polish Kingdom on the eve of its partition; but most of these new residents (some 945,000 out of 1,260,000), though no longer suffocating in the old Polish ghetto, were crowded together in the new, no less congested ghetto of the southern provinces,[17] which had been added to the annexed Polish territory to form the Jewish Pale. Within the entire Jewish Pale, more than four-fifths of the Jewish population lived in urban communities, and Jews accounted for nearly 40 percent of the urban population. The distribution is shown in Table II.

Of the 4.9 million Jews concentrated in the Jewish Pale, one-third lived in so-called "market towns," which were small semiurban communities to which the Jewish population had flocked when driven out of the villages by the Tsarist administrators. This was the legendary *shtetl*, of which Jews were often virtually the sole inhabitants. The concentration of the Jewish population in market towns was particularly pronounced in White-Russian and Lithuanian provinces, where Jews accounted for over 58 percent of the total small-town population, and was quite considerable in Poland proper, Volhynia and Podolia, where 40 to 45 percent of all small-town inhabitants were Jews. Only in the southeastern part of the

Pale (the Ukraine east of the Dnieper and the Crimea), where Jews did not strike roots until the nineteenth century, was the *shtetl* less conspicuous; there only one-tenth of the Jewish population lived in market towns, and Jews accounted for about one-fifteenth of the total number of their inhabitants.

Almost one-half, and in some regions nearly two-thirds, of the Jewish population lived in larger urban communities, where, however, their proportion within the total population was somewhat less than in market towns. Over 60 percent of the Jews of Lithuania, White Russia, and the

TABLE II

URBAN AND RURAL POPULATION IN THE JEWISH PALE, 1897 [18]

Region	Cities	Market Towns	All Urban Communities	Rural Communities	Total
	Percent Distribution of the Jewish Population				
Poland	43.8	37.5	81.3	18.7	100.0
North West	61.6	25.1	86.7	13.3	100.0
South West	40.6	40.3	80.8	19.2	100.0
South East	61.8	10.9	72.6	27.4	100.0
Jewish Pale	48.8	33.1	81.9	18.1	100.0
	Percent Ratio of Jewish to Total Population				
Poland	37.7	45.3	39.6	2.7	14.5
North West	52.6	58.2	56.8	3.3	14.1
South West	36.9	40.2	38.5	3.2	12.4
South East	23.6	6.6	17.0	1.5	4.5
Jewish Pale	37.6	39.8	38.5	2.8	11.6

Eastern Ukraine lived in the larger cities. But while they constituted the majority of the entire urban population (market towns and cities) in the Lithuanian and White-Russian provinces, their share dropped to 17 percent in the southeastern region, where Jews accounted for only 4.5 percent of the region's total population, as against 14.1 percent in the formerly Polish Lithuania and White Russia. By contrast, the southeastern area of the Pale, with its Jewish farm colonies, showed the highest percentage of villagers among the area's Jewish residents, 27.4 percent as against 13.3 percent in the northwestern area. Within the total rural population, Jews were a tiny minority, less than 3 percent on the average for the entire Jewish Pale.

The culture of the great majority of the Jewish population of the Tsarist Empire remained Jewish, and the mother tongue of nearly 97 percent still was Yiddish. The language distribution is shown in Table III.

Even outside the Jewish Pale the proportion of Jews who could read Russian was by no means high, as shown in Table IV.

No population statistics are available for the period between the census of 1897 and the Soviet revolution. These two decades affected the Jewish population in different ways. Industrial development slightly improved the submarginal living standards of the Jewish masses. But the improve-

TABLE III

JEWISH POPULATION OF THE RUSSIAN EMPIRE, BY MOTHER TONGUE, 1897 [19]

Language	Jewish Population of the Empire		Thereof: (Percent)				
			Jewish Pale				Outside the Pale
	Thousands	Percent	Poland	North West	South West	South East	
Yiddish	5,054.3	96.9	95.8	99.3	98.6	97.6	80.0
Russian, Ukrainian, White-Russian	67.1	1.3	.5	.6	1.4	1.5	7.2
Polish	47.1	.9	3.5	.0	—	.0	.1
German	22.8	.4	.2	.0	—	.0	5.8
Other Indo-European (Iranian)	12.0	.2	—	—	—	—	3.8
Kartveli (Georgian, Mingrelian)	6.0	.1	—	—	—	—	1.9
Turki	4.7	.1	—	—	—	.9	.4
Lithuanian, Latvian	1.1	.0	—	.0	—	—	.2
Others	.7	.1	.0	.1	.0	.0	.6
Total	5,215.8	100.0	100.0	100.0	100.0	100.0	100.0

ment was limited; legislative restrictions and administrative chicanery continued and in many fields increased. The barrier of the Jewish Pale remained immovable until the First World War, when considerable num-

TABLE IV

PERCENT JEWS WITH READING KNOWLEDGE OF RUSSIAN [20]

Region	Males	Females
Jewish Pale	30.5%	15.9%
Outside the Pale	43.0	31.5
Total, Russian Empire	31.2%	16.5%

bers of refugees and Jews expelled from their homes in the front areas by the Russian government reached the prohibited regions of Russia proper, especially the larger cities of what in the Soviet Union was to become the Russian Soviet Federated Socialist Republic (RSFSR). In the later stages of the war, an influx of Jews from provinces threatened by the German and Austrian forces was noticeable also in the large urban centers of the Eastern Ukraine. In addition, a rather steady migratory

movement took many Jews in the eastern and southern sections of the
Pale from the small market towns to larger cities. Large-scale migration,
however, did not begin until the overthrow of Tsarism in March 1917
had removed all residential restrictions along with the rest of the anti-
Jewish legislation.

While the World War, and the Civil War with its accompanying
massacres, took a heavy toll of Jewish lives, constant emigration to foreign
countries was a more important factor in the decline of the Jewish population in Russia; lastly, the territorial losses Russia suffered at the close
of the war removed a large part of the Tsar's Jewish subjects from the
sphere of Soviet rule. Of the Jewish population recorded by the census
of 1897, less than one-half, 2,504,000, lived in areas which later formed
the Soviet Union.[21] Major parts of the Jewish Pale—Poland, Lithuania,
Bessarabia, and considerable portions of White Russia, Volhynia, and
Podolia—passed from Russian to Polish, Lithuanian, or Rumanian sovereignty. How many Jews remained in these regions when they were
severed from the disintegrating Empire, and how many war refugees
trekked home to the lost provinces in the years of revolution and civil
war, have never been ascertained. It has been estimated that the Jewish
population living, in 1897, within what were to be the limits of the Soviet
Union, should, by 1926, have increased by about 820,000, taking account
of increased mortality and a reduced birth-rate, so that roughly 3.3 million
Jews should have been found on Soviet territory in 1926. Yet the first
comprehensive Soviet population census which took place in December
1926 counted only 2.7 million Jews; the difference between the expected
increase and the increase actually recorded should be attributed, according to Soviet statisticians, to emigration—some 600,000—and to losses
caused by the Civil War and pogroms—estimated roughly at 100,000.[22]

Dispersion and Assimilation

Such was the condition of the Jewish minority on the threshold of the
Soviet era. It will help in understanding Soviet policies, both as originally
conceived and as subsequently evolved, if the chief facts concerning the
size and distribution of the Jewish population throughout the Soviet period
are given in advance of the chronological order. The statistics are not
abundant. As has been said, the first comprehensive census of the Soviet
population was taken in December 1926. Though a second census followed in 1937, its results were discarded and withheld from publication.
Of the results of the third population census carried out in January 1939,
only the most general data have been disclosed. So far as the data permit
comparison, and after recalculating the figures for 1897 to allow for
territorial changes, Table V gives the developments in the Soviet Jewish
population to January 1939.

In 1897, within what were to be the pre-Second World War boundaries of the Soviet Union,[24] only 268,000 Jews lived outside the area of the Jewish Pale. By the end of 1926, the Jewish population outside of what had been the old Pale had risen to 699,000, and by January 1939 it had gone up

TABLE V

JEWISH POPULATION IN SOVIET TERRITORY, 1897–1939 [23]

Union Republics	Total Jewish Population						Percent Ratio of Jewish to total Population		
	Thousands			Percent					
	1897	1926	1939	1897	1926	1939	1897	1926	1939
Ukraine	1,674	1,574	1,533	66.8	58.7	50.8	7.8	5.4	4.9
White Russia	472	407	375	18.8	15.2	12.4	14.4	8.2	6.7
Russian SFSR			948			31.4			.9
Kazakh SSR	209	603	19	11.9	22.6	.6	.4	.5	.3
Kirghiz SSR			2			.1			.1
Azerbaidzhan			41			1.4			1.3
Georgia		51	42		1.9	1.4		.7	1.2
Armenia	59		1	2.5		.0	.5		.05
Turkmen SSR		2	3		.1	.1		.2	.2
Uzbek SSR		43	51		1.5	1.7		.5	.8
Tadzhik SSR			5			.2			.3
Total, Soviet Territory	2,504	2,680	3,020	100.0	100.0	100.0	2.4	1.82	1.78

to 1,112,000.[25] During the same period, the Jewish population in the Ukraine and White Russia, the area of the Pale, decreased from 2,146,000 in 1897 to 1,981,000 in 1926, to 1,908,000 in 1939.

The entire net forty-two-year increase of the Jewish population on Soviet territory, which was slightly over 500,000, plus the almost 240,000 Jews lost to the Ukraine and White Russia, were absorbed by the other member republics of the Soviet Union, especially by the Russian SFSR. Correspondingly, the proportion of Jews within the total population of the Russian SFSR went up from .4 to .9 percent, while it dropped from 14.4 to 6.7 percent in White Russia, and from 7.8 to 4.9 percent in the Ukraine.

How far the urbanization of the Jewish population had advanced in the last two decades of Tsarism, and in the first decade of Soviet rule, is difficult to gauge, because the category, "market towns," has been eliminated from Soviet statistics, and communities classed as market towns in the census of 1897 were divided up, according to size, between urban and rural communities in the census of 1926 as well as of 1939. In 1897, 81.9 percent of the Jewish population of the Pale (including areas subsequently ceded to Poland, Lithuania, and Rumania) lived in cities and market towns, and 18.1 percent in villages. In 1926, 82.4 percent of the Jewish population of the Soviet Union lived in urban, and 17.6 percent in rural, communities. In 1939, the proportion of city-dwellers in the

Jewish population rose to 87.0 percent, whereas the proportion of villagers dropped to 13.0 percent. The decline of the Jewish rural population may be seen more clearly in the fact that in 1897 Jews accounted for 2.8 percent of all villagers in the Jewish Pale, as against 1.5 percent in 1926 in the Ukraine, and 1.6 percent in White Russia; by 1939, the ratio had fallen to 1.1 percent in both the Ukraine and White Russia. The decline was all the more striking in that a number of predominantly Jewish market towns listed separately in 1897, were counted among the rural communities in 1926 and 1939.

The overall trend, and the regional differences manifesting themselves during the Soviet era, are shown in greater detail in Tables VI and VII.[26]

TABLE VI

JEWISH URBAN AND RURAL POPULATION IN THE SOVIET UNION (A)

Union Republics	Percent Distribution of the Jewish Population			
	Urban Population		Rural Population	
	1926	1939	1926	1939
Ukrainian SSR	77.4	85.5	22.6	14.5
White-Russian SSR	83.6	87.8	16.4	12.2
RSFSR, Kazakh and Kirghiz SSR's	94.2	88.9	5.8	11.1
Azerbaidzhan, Georgian and Armenian SSR's	96.7	87.3	3.3	12.7
Turkmen SSR	100.0	87.1	—	12.9
Uzbek and Tadzhik SSR's	98.5	88.9	1.5	11.1
USSR Average	82.4	87.0	17.6	13.0

TABLE VII

JEWISH URBAN AND RURAL POPULATION IN THE SOVIET UNION (B)

	Percent Ratio of Jewish to Total Population			
	Urban Communities		Rural Communities	
	1926	1939	1926	1939
Ukraine	22.7	11.7	1.5	1.1
White Russia	40.2	23.9	1.6	1.1
RSFSR, Kazakh and Kirghiz SSR's	3.1	2.2	.0	.1
Azerbaidzhan, Georgia, Armenia	2.1	2.8	.0	.2
Turkmen SSR	1.3	.7	—	.05
Uzbek and Tadzhik SSR's	1.8	2.9	.0	.1
USSR Average	8.2	4.7	.3	.3

The tremendous growth of the Soviet cities during the period of accelerated industrialization fully explains the spectacular decline in the percentage of Jews among city-dwellers at a time when the Jewish urban population increased from about 2,190,000 [27] to 2,628,000, and its proportion in the total Jewish population rose from 82.4 to 87.0 percent. At the same time, Jewish rural population dropped from roughly 490,000 [28] to 392,500, while the proportion of Jews within the total rural population remained practically unchanged. The decline was particularly noticeable in the Ukraine, where the Jewish rural population decreased from 355,800 to 222,500, i.e., 37.4 percent, and in White Russia, where it fell from 67,000 to 45,700, or 31.8 percent. This substantial loss was in no way compensated for by the much publicized agricultural settlement of Jews in the Crimea and Birobidzhan, which caused the Jewish rural population in the Russian SFSR and the Kazakh and Kirghiz areas to go up from about 50,000 [29] to 107,000; on the other hand, the considerable increase in the proportion of villagers within the Jewish population of Transcaucasia, Turkmenistan, Uzbekistan and Tadzhikistan, where the Jewish rural population in 1939 did not total more than 17,200, seems to have been purely fictitious, inasmuch as the figures for 1939 included, while those for 1926 excluded, the Oriental Jews, who made up almost the entire Jewish village population in these republics.[30]

The impact of urbanization is not easily measurable for the period 1897–1926; but in the period 1926–1939, when industrialization advanced at an exceptional pace, Jews passed into the cities in great numbers. What occurred in these momentous years is the subject of later chapters of this study. Meanwhile, in order to make more complete the picture of the Jewish community in the early years of the Soviet Revolution, and the better to understand the condition in which it faced the radical transformations brought about by the Five-Year Plans, another earlier change should be noted here. As stated in the preceding section, Yiddish in 1897 was the mother tongue of 96.9 percent of all Jews in the Tsarist Empire; of between 95.8 and 99.3 percent in the Jewish Pale; and of 80.0 percent outside the Pale. By 1926, Yiddish had fallen off as shown in Table VIII.

TABLE VIII

SPREAD OF YIDDISH IN THE SOVIET UNION, 1926 [31]

Union Republics	Jewish Population (Thousands)	Thereof: Indicating Yiddish as Mother Tongue	
		Thousands	Percent
Ukraine	1,574	1,198	76.1
White Russia	407	369	90.7
Russian SFSR (incl. Kazakh and Kirghiz areas)	603	285	47.3
Azerbaidzhan, Georgia, Armenia	51	12	23.5
Others	45	24	53.3
All USSR	2,680	1,888	70.4

Even in the Ukraine and White Russia, which in 1926 still contained 73.9 percent of the Jewish population of the Soviet Union, Yiddish was rapidly losing ground. Of the Jewish population of the Ukraine, 70.0 percent was counted as literate, but those who could read Yiddish numbered only 42.5 percent of all Ukrainian Jews (as against 76.1 percent indicating Yiddish as their mother tongue); in White Russia, 69.0 percent of the Jewish population was literate, but those who could read Yiddish accounted for only 56.4 percent of the total (as against 90.7 percent indicating Yiddish as their mother tongue).[32]

Obviously, even with many of those who still regarded Yiddish as their mother tongue, only a Yiddish vernacular survived; to many, Yiddish no longer was a medium of education and written or printed communication, and the scale on which it was transmitted to the younger generation grew ever smaller. So far as the long-term trend was concerned, the advance of assimilation was undeniable. Yet when one views the specific situation prevailing in the early and middle 1920's, the fact cannot be overlooked, and certainly should not be minimized, that as late as 1926 almost half the Jewish population of the Ukraine and White Russia not only still spoke but also read Yiddish; the long-term trend had not yet come to dominate everyday life.

The Economic Impasse

A large-scale field investigation conducted by the Jewish Colonization Association in 1898 revealed, against the background of the census of 1897, that the socio-economic pattern of the Jewish group still bore the imprint of the economic catastrophe which had befallen feudal Poland's Jewish community at the time of the Polish collapse and in the early stages of Russian rule.[33] The great majority of Jewish breadwinners led the submarginal existence of small traders, peddlers, middlemen, artisans, and "persons without permanent or definite occupation" living on the meager proceeds of sporadic strokes of business. According to JCA data, 54.4 percent of the Jews engaged in economic occupations in 1897 was made up of traders, merchants, and commercial middlemen of all kinds, commercial and industrial employers, and persons without definite or permanent occupation; and an additional 18.4 percent was accounted for by "artisans."[34] The starvation level at which the Jewish population subsisted within the framework of this economic pattern is tellingly illustrated by the fact that the number of Jews depending for their existence on relief provided by Jewish welfare institutions was estimated to be about 30 to 35 percent of the total Jewish population.[35]

Commercial occupations in the cities and market towns of the Jewish Pale were flooded with Jewish "businessmen" who more often than not lacked capital and business equipment, frequently had no place of business, and in most instances, having to rely on short-term credit at high interest rates, were driven to cut-throat competition. The condition of the Jewish artisans was not essentially different. As a rule Jewish artisans were deprived of capital, equipment, stocks of raw materials, and cheap credit facilities, and quite often worked for the account of middlemen supplying materials and accessories or acted as commission agents or subsidiary suppliers for manufacturers and wholesalers; or simply were exploited homeworkers as well as sweatshop subcontractors for somewhat bigger jobbers. Even those who operated independently often were engaged in repair work rather than in manufacture. The Jewish artisan seldom possessed particular skills or technical knowledge, and usually had a few hired hands and apprentices to assist him; but their inadequate training did not lift them out of the *luftmensh* misery any more than it did the artisan employer. Working conditions were abominable and wages pathetically low. The only escape was into trade, which supported the larger but hardly more prosperous section of the *luftmensh* community; industry and the well-established commercial world were barred to the great mass of Jews locked up in the Pale.

Considerable efforts were made in the late nineteenth and early twentieth centuries, especially by organizations such as ORT and JCA, to improve the work skills of Jewish artisans by setting up vocational training schools, and to provide credit facilities for small-scale commercial and artisan establishments. As a result, and also because of the general rise of industry, the condition of certain sections of the Jewish masses, above all in the southern and southeastern provinces of the Pale, showed a slow, irregular, but marked improvement during the last decade before the outbreak of the First World War; this modest improvement was noted in the press and in the reports of Jewish relief and welfare organizations.

In the First World War, large sections of the Jewish Pale became the theater of military operations, and in many places economic life came to a standstill. But the war made major breaches in the walls of the ghetto. Waves of Jews swept beyond the frontiers of the Jewish Pale. Disruption of normal supply channels and shortages created loopholes through which daring Jewish enterpreneurs and middlemen began to infiltrate into hitherto inaccessible spheres of economic activity. This, of course, was a mere trickle so long as the Tsarist regime remained in power. But many such rivulets combined into a powerful current when a democratic government was established in March 1917 and all anti-Jewish restrictions were removed. Thereafter, the tremendous economic dislocations of the Civil War opened new areas to Jewish commercial enterprise, though these were all of an unstable and very short-lived kind; in addition, a small number of Jewish intellectuals, commercial employees, and jobless youths entered into the government organizations of the new state.

But again, all this benefited only a fraction of the Jewish community, while the fundamental pattern remained largely intact; the crucial problem of how to integrate the Jewish population with the country's economy continued unsolved. How little this problem had been solved in three decades of farreaching social change, of which the latest was the decade of war, civil war, and economic upheaval, may be seen from a comparison of the occupational distribution of economically active Jews according to the censuses of 1897 and 1926 as shown in Table IX.

TABLE IX

OCCUPATIONAL DISTRIBUTION OF JEWS, 1897–1926 [36]

Occupation	Percent Distribution of the Economically Active Jewish Pop.	
	1897	1926
Wage earners:		
Industry and building	4.0	6.9
Commerce, service trades, transportation, etc.		4.0
Agriculture		.2
Artisan shops	11.0	3.6
All wage earners	15.0	14.7
Salary earners (non-manual workers)	10.0	23.2
Self-employed professionals	.0	1.6
Farmers	2.2	9.1
Artisans	18.4	19.0
Traders, storekeepers, peddlers, etc.	31.0	11.8
Other employers and self-employed; persons without permanent or definite occupation; and unspecified	23.4	20.6
Total Labor Force	100.0	100.0

What is most striking about the changes which occurred in the occupational distribution of Jewish breadwinners (39.9 percent of the total Jewish population in 1926) between 1897 and 1926 is that, despite the overall trend towards proletarianization, the proportion of wage labor (manual workers) among Jews gainfully employed dropped slightly, from 15.0 to 14.7 percent, while the proportion of salary earners (non-manual workers) greatly increased, from 10.0 to 23.2 percent. It may be assumed that considerable numbers of those who in 1926 were no longer listed as self-employed in commercial occupations (traders, etc.), had become salary earners, i.e., commercial, administrative, and office employees, mostly in government agencies and government-operated enterprises. Another fraction of the commercial self-employed, the percentage of whom spectacularly declined from 31.0 to 11.8, was probably to be found in 1926 among farmers and artisans.

Added together, the artisan, commercial, enterpreneurial, and indefinite occupations, which in 1897 had accounted for 72.8 percent of the Jewish gainfully employed, still accounted, in 1926, for more than one-half (51.4 percent). True, a number of those included in these categories in 1926 (e.g., part of those listed as unemployed, a group accounting for 9.7 percent) were neither former traders nor former middlemen but simply young people without special training and tangible employment opportunities. But it was characteristic of virtually all who were in these categories, whether tainted by a "non-productive" past or not, that they had found no place in the economy and lived from hand to mouth on the brink of starvation. The socio-economic core of the Jewish problem was still unchanged for at least half the Jewish population, and the problem's solution depended on the policies and attitudes of the government.

NOTES

1. Only recently a terminological change has crept into the official literature. Since the war the Soviet press has off and on been referring to the Union Republics—the sixteen constituent parts of the Soviet Union—as nations. In this usage, all citizens of the Russian Soviet Federated Socialist Republic (RSFSR), regardless of their nationality, make up the Russian nation or people, all citizens of the Ukrainian Soviet Socialist Republic make up the Ukrainian nation, etc. This terminological innovation, however, has not affected the traditional theoretical criteria for determining what is and what is not a nationality

2. USSR Central Statistical Office (*Tcentral'noye Statisticheskoye Upravleniye SSSR*), *Vsesoyuznaya perepis' naseleniya 17 dekabrya 1926 goda. Kratkiye svodki* [*All-Union Population Census of December 17, 1926. Brief Abstracts*] Issue I, Moscow, 1926, pp. 2–22.

3. All figures for 1939 are from a preliminary release of census results issued by the Central Statistical Office of the USSR—*Tsentral'noye Upravleniye Narodno-Khozyaistvennogo Ucheta* (TsUNKhU)—and published in *Izvestiya*, April 29, 1940 No further data were released in the ten years that have elapsed

4. J. S. Hertz, *Di Idn in Ukrayne fun di Eltste Tsaytn biz nokh TaKh v'TatT*, New York, 1949, pp. 187ff.

5. Yulii Gessen [Julius Hessen], *Istoriya yevreiskogo naroda v Rossii* [*History of the Jewish People in Russia*], vol. I, 2d ed., Leningrad, 1925, pp. 10ff. Cf. also Volodimir Rybynskyi, "Do istorii zhydiv na livoberezhnii Ukraini v polovyni XVIII storichchya" ["A Contribution to the History of Jews on the Left Bank of the Ukraine in the First Half of the Nineteenth Century"], in *Zbirnyk Prats' Zhydivskoi Istorychno-Arkheografichnoi Komisii* (I. V. Gallant, ed.), All-Ukrainian Academy of Sciences, vol. I, Kiev, 1928, pp. 1–97.

6. The major part of White Russia fell to Russia in 1772, followed by the rest of White Russia and all the Ukraine west of the Dnieper in 1793, and Lithuania and the major part of Poland in 1795.

7. Cf. S. B. [Bernard D.] Weinryb, *Neueste Wirtschaftsgeschichte der Juden in Russland und Polen*, vol. I, Breslau, 1934, pp. 3f.

8. In the few cities settled by the Teutonic Order, "Judaeo-German" (Yiddish) may have seemed merely a variation of the High German spoken by part of the local merchants, officials, and artisans; to the great majority of the urban and to the entire rural population of Poland proper, as well as of Lithuania, White Russia, and the Ukraine, Yiddish undoubtedly was a foreign tongue solely identified with Jews.

9. For a discussion of the various interpretations of the economic functions of Jews in feudal Poland, see Tevye Haylikman [T. B. Geilikman], *Geshikhte fun der Gezelshaftlekher Bavegung fun di Idn in Poyln un Rusland*, vol. I, Moscow, 1926;

Russian edition: *Istoriya obshchestvennogo dvizheniya yevreyev v Pol'she i Rossii,* Moscow—Leningrad, 1930.

10. Cf. Weinryb, *op. cit.,* esp. pp. 3–10, 24–40, 93–109, 128–146.

11. The effect on the Jewish community of this vacillating early policy has been analyzed by Isaac Levitats, *The Jewish Community in Russia, 1772–1844,* New York, 1943.

12. Cf. Y. Sosis, *Di Geshikhte fun di Idishe Gezelshaftlekhe Shtremungen in Rusland in XIX Yorhundert,* White-Russian Government Publishing House, Minsk, 1929. A preface by the publishers lists objections, from the official point of view of the Communist Party, to Sosis' analysis of nineteenth-century developments. A thoroughly documented presentation, to which no official exception was taken, will be found in O. Margolis, *Geshikhte fun Idn in Rusland (Etyudn un Dokumentn),* vol. I, Moscow—Kharkov—Minsk, 1930.

13. Private congregations gathered around individual synagogues retained a large measure of independence. They were unconnected with the Tsarist administration, and their prestige in religious matters was high. But they depended solely on private contributions and their activities were confined to the religious sphere.

14. The debasement of the official community in consequence of Tsarist administrative policies has been emphasized by all competent historians, *e.g.,* Gessen, *op. cit.,* vol. II, pp. 94–177. It is important to remember that the official community had no control over education. The candle tax, the proceeds of which under the terms of the laws of 1844 were earmarked for secular Jewish schools, was administered by the Ministry of Education, and the few schools which came into being under the latter's auspices were largely ignored by the Jewish population. Schooling far and wide remained the domain of privately-financed and privately-operated institutions of religious instruction committed to orthodox Judaism and not providing any secular education. Parents who wanted their children to learn more than Hebrew and the Talmud had to send them to Russian schools, or hire private tutors, or place their youngsters in boarding schools abroad. Secular study thus in most instances necessarily entailed radical assimilation.

15. A detailed analysis of the results of the census of 1897 will be found in *Statistiko-ekonomicheskiye ocherki i issledovaniya* [*Statistical and Economic Outlines and Inquiries*], prepared by the Jewish Colonization Association [*Yevreiskoye Kolonizatsionnoye Obshchestvo*]. The data summarized in the table are taken from Boris D. Brutskus, *Statistika yevreiskogo naseleniya* [*Statistic of the Jewish Population*], vol. III, St. Petersburg, 1909, Appendix, Table 1.

16. All data of the census of 1897 include the "Oriental Jews" of the Crimea, the Caucasus, and Central Asia, who inhabited these regions prior to the Russian conquest and most of whom speak Iranian, Caucasian or Turki dialects. The census counted some 23,000 Jews who indicated these languages as their mother tongue. The total number of Oriental Jews was probably twice this amount.

17. Since administrative divisions changed repeatedly, the figures given cannot claim more than an illustrative value. The provinces of Bessarabia, Tauris (Crimea), and Kherson (New Russia), as well as the Ukraine east of the Dnieper, have been counted here as not under Polish rule at the time of the Polish partitions.

18. Brutskus, *op. cit.,* pp. 3 and 8.

19. *Ibid,* Appendix, Table 5.

20. *Ibid,* pp. 52, 54.

21. Recomputation of 1897 census data in accordance with territorial changes has been done by the Joint Statistical and Economic Committee of the ORT administration in Moscow. See L. G. Zinger, *Yevreiskoye naseleniye SSSR* [*Jewish Population of the USSR*], publications of the Central Committee of ORT (*Materialy i issledovaniya,* Issue I), Moscow, 1927, p. 8.

22. L. G. Zinger, *Dos Banayte Folk (Tsifern un Faktn vegn di Idn in FSSR),* Emes publishers, Moscow, 1941, pp. 34ff.

23. For 1897, based on data from Brutskus, *op. cit.,* Appendix, Table I, and Zinger, *Yevreiskoye Naseleniye SSSR,* p. 8; for 1926 and 1939, based on data from Zinger

and B. Engel, *Idishe Bafelkerung fun FSSR in Tables un Diagrames* (Statistical and Economic Committee, ORT Administration, *Materialn un Oysforshungen*, Issue V), Tables I-1 and I-2, and Zinger, *Dos Banayte Folk*, p. 36 and Appendix II.

24. This, of course, does not include some 2 million Jews in areas annexed by the Soviet Union in 1939–40.

25. All data based on the table above include the Oriental Jews, some 70,000 to 80,000 according to the census of 1926. (No data are available for 1897 or 1939.)

26. Data on urban and rural population in the text above and in the tables were taken, for 1926, from Zinger and Engel, *op. cit.*, Table I-2; for 1939, from Zinger, *Dos Banayte Folk*, pp. 40f. Percentages for 1926 are based on figures not including the Oriental Jews.

27. Estimate includes the Oriental Jews. Without them, there were 2,144,000 Jewish city-dwellers in 1926.

28. Estimate includes the Oriental Jews. Without them, the Jewish rural population in 1926 numbered 457,100.

29. Exclusive of the Oriental Jews, the Jewish population in the rural communities of the Russian SFSR, which at that time included the territory of the future Kazakh and Kirghiz Soviet Socialist Republics, numbered in 1926 only 33,000. The estimate of 50,000 is based on the assumption that at least half the Oriental Jewish population of the RSFSR (which totaled 33,600 and was concentrated in the Crimea and the Asiatic provinces) consisted of inhabitants of communities classed as rural. In actual fact, the proportion of villagers among RSFSR Oriental Jews may have been in excess of 50 percent.

30. For sources, see n. 26 above.

31. Based on data from Zinger and Engel, *op. cit.*, Table IX-22, and Zinger, *Dos Banayte Folk*, pp. 40f. The Oriental Jews have been included so as to facilitate comparison with 1897 data; this, however, does not affect the figures indicated for the Ukraine and White Russia, which coincide approximately with the Soviet-ruled area of the old Pale.

32. Percentages based on data in Zinger and Engel, *op. cit.*, Table IX-23.

33. The results of the JCA investigation were issued in two richly documented volumes, which also contained elaborate summaries of the census materials of 1897. See Yevreiskoye Kolonizatsionneye Obshchestvo [JCA], *Sbornik materialov ob ekonomicheskom polozhenii yevreyev v Rossii* [*Collection of Materials on the Economic Condition of Jews in Russia*], vol. I and II, St. Petersburg, 1904. French edition: *Recueil de Matériaux sur la Situation Economique des Israélites de Russie d'après l'enquête de la Jewish Colonization Association*, Tome I, Paris, 1906; Tome II, Paris, 1908.

34. JCA data, as recomputed, to allow for territorial changes, by Zinger, *Dos Banayte Folk*, p. 8.

35. Cf. "Nuzhda i blagotvoritel'nost'" ["Poverty and Philanthropy"] in the JCA's *Sbornik materialov*, vol. II.

36. Percentages for 1897 are based on JCA data as recomputed by Zinger, *Dos Banayte Folk*, p. 8; percentages for 1926 have been computed from census data supplied by Zinger and Engel, *op. cit.*, Tables II-7, III-8, IV-9, V-11 and VI-13. They differ only insignificantly from inexactly rounded-out percentage figures in Zinger, *Yevreiskoye naseleniye v SSSR*, but are very much at variance with the inexplicable revised figures which the same author included in his *Dos Banayte Folk*, pp. 46ff., although the basic 1926 data, repeatedly referred to in the last-mentioned publication as corresponding to the revised percentages, invariably coincide with the unrevised figures of earlier publications. Only in one instance has it been possible to trace the discrepancy: having added up the percentages of wage earners in industry and building, commerce, service trades, transportation, etc., and agriculture, the author chose to refer to the combined percentage as the ratio of "manual workers in large-scale industry and building." What changes in category underlay the other new figures introduced by Zinger into his study in 1941, are hard to guess.

CHAPTER II

Communist Doctrine on the National Problem

The Centralist Tradition

The official ideology is a highly important factor in the development of modern dictatorships; most of these, indeed, could well be called ideocratic governments. The crude and naked use of force is not enough to impose for any length of time the all-embracing rule of the few upon a modern society; dictatorship today could not endure without the ideological integration and manipulation of the people by the ruling "elite." Also, a uniform and all-pervasive ideology brooking neither competition nor deviation is required to unite the elite itself. The official ideology may undergo substantial change in the course of time and events; but whatever the "general line" at any given moment, it influences and often determines the policies and daily practice of the regime. This is no less true of Soviet policies on the national question than it is of any other sphere of Communist activity.

Bolshevism, as a separate and distinct tendency in Russian socialism, made its first appearance in 1903, at the Second Convention of the Russian Social Democratic Workers Party; in the course of this convention, the RSDWP split into two factions, Bolshevik and Menshevik. It was at this convention that the party's stand on the national question was worked out after extensive discussion, during which there were a series of hot and passionate disputes as to whether or not the Bund, the General Jewish Workers Alliance, should be granted an autonomous position in the Social Democratic organization. The party led an underground existence, for all revolutionary organizations had been proscribed by the Tsarist government. The exigencies of the underground struggle encouraged a centralist attitude in the party leadership; and this, together with the general aversion of Russian liberals and revolutionaries to any kind of "chauvinism," led radicals and moderates alike violently to oppose the Bund's demands for a separate organization of Jewish workers.

This dislike for the Bund's alleged separatism was part of a general underestimation of the national problem, an underestimation that prevailed so long as common oppression made for a common front on all questions of equal rights and cultural freedom—that is, until March 1917, when revolutionary developments caused a farreaching clash of the differing national interests to take place. True, among the intelligentsia of minority groups—Poles, Ukrainians, and to some extent Jews—intergroup frictions had led to the recognition of the necessity of finding a satisfactory solution of the national problem. But Russian and Russified minority intellectuals (among whom there were quite a number of Jews) were widely inclined to believe that the problem would be solved automatically as it were by the establishment of a democratic system of government, which would straightway abolish all the legal restrictions and limitations imposed upon national and ethnic minorities.

Hardly any objections were raised at the Second Convention when the resolution affirming "the right of self-determination for all nations in the state" was passed. Yet when Vladimir Medem,[1] the representative of the Jewish Bund, moved an amendment "to establish institutions guaranteeing full freedom of cultural development" to national minority groups, the convention was overwhelmingly against it.[2] Levin,[3] a spokesman for the anti-Bundist majority, a moderate, and a member of the committee on the party program as well as of that on by-laws, sharply answered the Bund:

> So far as the national question is concerned, our demands can only be negative ones, that is to say, we are against all restrictions imposed on nationalities. But whether this or that nationality will be able to develop as such, is none of our business as Social Democrats. That will be decided by an elemental and spontaneous process.

And although many a Bundist in those days would have readily assented to leaving the question of the survival of a Jewish nation to history, another majority spokesman, Kol'tsov,[4] also a Menshevik, who sat on the convention's credentials committee, branded Medem's amendment as "purely nationalistic," and accused the Bund of encouraging the convention actively "to support even those nationalities on the point of dying out"—a barely veiled reference to the Jews. A second Bund amendment, less unequivocally phrased than Medem's, to the effect that minority nationalities, in addition to the right of self-determination, should be guaranteed "freedom of cultural development," was also overwhelmingly defeated.[5]

Considerable opposition had to be overcome to induce the convention to adopt at least a few guiding principles for a constructive solution of the national problem. The committee on the party program proposed amending the original draft to include the demand for "broad local and regional self-government." To the budding Bolshevik faction, even this cautious limitation of the powers of the future republic's central government was too much. Lenin, already its acknowledged leader, immediately moved to strike out the words "and regional." His motion, however, was defeated, and the convention voted a substitute amendment, offered by the future

Menshevik leader Martov,[6] advocating "regional self-government for those border areas in which the way of life and composition of the population differ from those in genuinely Russian areas."[7] The convention hesitantly broached the issue of autonomous administration for regions inhabited by minority nationalities; even thus, however, the term autonomy was repugnant to the majority.

Immediately after this debate opinions clashed again over that passage in the program which dealt with "full equality of rights for all citizens regardless of sex, religion, race, nationality, and language." Here, too, "nationality and language," absent from the original draft, had been inserted by the committee on the party program, and again a tumultuous discussion ensued. The delegates of the Bund insisted that the program should endorse "the right of every citizen to use his language everywhere —in government institutions and schools." Eighteen (!) votes were taken, when the convention decided at long last to refer the question back to the committee for further study.[8] And it was not until after further acrimonious debate that the convention voted a new formula devised by the committee. As finally formulated, the party program demanded a democratic constitution "which would guarantee" the following rights of national minorities:

> The right of a people to acquire an education in its mother tongue, which right is to be guaranteed by the establishment of such schools as are necessary herefor, at the expense of the state and the organs of self-government [i.e., municipalities and regional administrative agencies]; the right of every citizen to use his mother tongue in public meetings; the use of the mother tongue in all local public and governmental agencies together with the official language of the state.[9]

The notion that autonomous institutions should administer the special spheres of interest of minority groups, remained rejected.[10] So long as the Social Democrats dealt with the problem of nationalities, they were still united in their advocacy of a centralized state unweakened by the delegation of part of its authority to a multitude of autonomous substates. Centralistic bias was fortified by tactical considerations. But the party split in two on the rock of centralization within its organization and the closely related issue of party discipline. As a consequence of the split, less rigid, more federalistic views began to develop among the Mensheviks, whose subsequent history lies outside the scope of the present study. With the Bolsheviks, the principle of centralization, enthusiastically upheld by Lenin, acquired the sanctity of an early tradition, became an essential element of the party teachings on democratic centralism, and determined in advance what the party views would be on national problems and the governmental structure of a multinational state.

The Social Democratic program adopted by the 1903 convention in no way advocated a federal structure for the democratic government it demanded. This was no oversight. Shortly before, Lenin had categorically rejected the very idea of a federal republic. Criticizing the program of the Armenian Social Democratic Union, he wrote: "The Union must strike the demand for a federated republic out of its program; let it confine itself to a general demand for a democratic republic."[11] For a long time this remained the *leitmotiv* of Lenin's and his disciples' statements on the national problem. Ten years later this position was made even more explicit at a conference of the Bolshevik party held near Kraków (then in Austria) in 1913, where the party's Central Committee met with leading underground organizers. The conference still defended the right of national self-determination; but to avoid any federalistic misinterpretation it pointedly stated in a lengthy resolution that it meant solely each individual nationality's right "to separate and form an independent state."[12]

How violently Lenin opposed the very notion of a federated state may be gathered from a letter not intended for publication and not appearing in print until 1922. In this letter, written in 1913 to one of the outstanding leaders of the Caucasian Bolsheviks, Suren G. Shaumyan, who had vaguely discussed the idea of a federation of states as the future system of government, Lenin caustically remarked:

> You say, "The right of self-determination does not mean only the right to secede. It also means the right to federate, the right of autonomy." I absolutely disagree. It does *not* mean the right to *federate*. A federation is a union of equals, a union which requires the *common* consent. How can *one* party claim a *right* to the *consent* of another party? That is absurd. We are in principle against federation—federalism weakens economic ties, it is an impossible arrangement for a state. You want to secede? To hell with you, I say, if you can succeed in breaking the economic ties—or, to be precise, if the injustices and frictions of "cohabitation" are such as to *spoil* and ruin economic relationships. You don't want to secede? Pardon me, then; don't make up my mind *for* me, don't think you have a "right" to a federal union. . . .
>
> The right of self-determination is an *exception* to our general thesis, which is centralism. This exception is absolutely necessary in face of the Black-Hundred type of Great-Russian nationalism. . . . But a broad interpretation may not be made of an exception. There is *nothing*, absolutely nothing here, and there must be nothing here, but the *right* to secede.[13]

National self-determination was a matter of expediency rather than of principle, an "exception to our general thesis," as Lenin put it in 1913. Left-wing socialists who disliked such "exceptions," who viewed every deviation from the path of internationalism as a dangerous concession to

nationalist ideology, bitterly accused Lenin of opportunism and incon-
sistency. Particularly in the early stages of the First World War, he was
severely criticized on this score by such intransigent internationalists as
Yurii (Georgii) L. Pyatakov in his own party, and Rosa Luxemburg and
Karl Radek in the ranks of the Polish Social Democrats; in later years
the slogan of self-determination was attacked again and again by dissident
groups, whom the Bolsheviks termed "ultra-leftists," "Luxemburgists,"
"Trotskiites," etc. The writings of Rosa Luxemburg were in particular
influential; she denounced self-determination as merely another tool of
imperialist propaganda and sought to reveal its implicitly anti-socialist
nature by exposing the reactionary aims of the nationalist groups which
made it their battle-cry. In refuting this sharp criticism from the "left,"
Lenin grew more and more explicit in interpreting his idea of national
self-determination.[14]

Socialists, Lenin argued, wanted the union, the merger, of all nations
into one. But a strong and stable union could be achieved only if all nations
were first free to go their different ways, to secede. National movements
of liberation, and especially national uprisings, deserved the socialists'
support, who should strive to assume the leadership of such movements.
But to espouse every nation's *right* of self-determination, "up to and
including secession," did not mean losing sight of the ultimate goal of
unity. While defending the right to secede, the revolutionary socialists
were, within the ranks of the oppressed nations, to argue against *exercising*
this right. A certain "division of labor" was thus entailed. To the ruling
nation, the revolutionary party would insist on the right of an oppressed
nationality to determine its own future; to the oppressed nation, the same
revolutionary party would stress the benefits of voluntary union, the advantages of belonging to a large state, and advocate the "economically
progressive" merger of the smaller nations with the larger. Once the revolutionary class had seized power, multinational states would grow into
homogeneous and uniform communities; in the future socialist order, the
right of self-determination would lose all meaning. But it was a meaning-
ful revolutionary slogan in the present, harassing and dividing the enemy.

Though he flatly rejected the idea of a federal union, Lenin nonethe-
less went a step farther in 1913 than he had been willing to go in 1903 and
advocated an autonomous status for regions "with more or less essential
economic or cultural peculiarities, with a population of a specific national
composition, etc." But the autonomy envisaged was a thoroughly limited
one; when Lenin considered leaving certain decisions to the jurisdiction
of regional self-government, he was not concerned with what such regions
wanted or needed in the way of autonomy. His main, if not sole, concern
was to strengthen the central government. In fact, he wrote:

The principle of centralism, which is essential in the interest of the development of capitalism, is not only unimpaired by [the granting of] such (local and regional) autonomy; quite the contrary, this is to carry it out in practice—only in a *democratic*, not a bureaucratic way. The large-scale, free, and rapid development of capitalism would be impossible, or at least extremely difficult, *without* [the granting of] such autonomy, which facilitates, all at the same time, the concentration of capital, the development of the productive forces, and the consolidation of both bourgeoisie and proletariat on a *state-wide scale*. . . .[15]

Regional autonomy, then, fostered the growth of a centralized state with a highly integrated economy. Centralism, however, bluntly rejected the encouragement of the various national cultures. Lenin (still in 1913) declared:

From the point of view of Social Democracy, it is inadmissible to put forward the slogan, "national culture." This slogan is false, for already under capitalism mankind's entire economic, political, and intellectual life is more and more international in character. Socialism will internationalize it altogether. . . .[16]

Or more specifically, and in cruder terms:

Advanced workers have realized that the slogan, "national culture," is a clerical or bourgeois fraud—regardless of whether the Great-Russian, the Ukrainian, the Jewish, the Polish, the Georgian, or any other culture is meant. . . . In general, it is only the clericals or the bourgeois who speak of national culture. The toiling classes can speak only of the international culture of the world-wide labor movement. Only such a culture implies a complete, real, sincere equality of nations, the absence of national oppression, and the fulfilment of democracy. . . .[17]

Yet the labor movements of minority nationalities could not ignore the only realm of culture open to their adherents, namely that of their national group. Since the laboring classes were barred by their ignorance of any language save their own from exercising any choice in the matter, it was the labor movement that was obliged to insist on legal and institutional guarantees for the development of each nationality's culture. The idea of some kind of cultural autonomy for minority nationalities, on a non-territorial and optional basis, was bound to gain ground in multinational Russia. Such an idea was not easy to dismiss, and became the subject of heated debates in the Russian socialist press.

Originally, the question had been raised by the Jewish Bund. The Bundists, developing the position defended in the late 1890's by the Austrian socialist Karl Renner (President of Austria after the Second World War), and anticipating the elaborate theory of Otto Bauer, argued that in a modern multinational state, where various nationalities live promiscuously intermingled, the vital interests of minority groups could not be safe-guarded by any type of regional autonomy.[18] Special non-territorial insti-tutions had to be established to care for the cultural and educational needs of minorities. This was particularly true, the Bundists argued, of the Jewish people, who in no region constituted the majority of the population. The Bundist contention, however, was at first unanimously opposed within the ranks of the Russian Social Democratic Party. Later, around 1912, after the position of the Mensheviks had changed considerably and national-cultural autonomy had come to be regarded with favor, only the Bolsheviks maintained an adamant and increasingly hostile attitude to anything resembling minority self-government in cultural matters.

Lenin, in an article on "The Nationalities Program of the Russian Social Democratic Workers Party," declared (late in 1913):

> "National-cultural autonomy" implies the most refined and therefore the most pernicious kind of nationalism; it means that the workers are corrupted by the slogan, "national culture," and by propaganda for a thoroughly harmful and even anti-democratic division of the educa-tional system according to nationalities. In a word, this program, which satisfies the ideals only of the nationalistic petty bourgeois, is in abso-lute contradiction with the internationalism of the proletariat.[19]

This thesis was developed more fully and with still greater emphasis in "Critical Notes on the National Problem" (also late in 1913). Once more attacking the demand for cultural autonomy, Lenin argued that it merely served "to establish in practice the most refined and absolute kind of nationalism." But nationalism, even in its most justified and innocuous form, was "incompatible with Marxism." It was to be opposed by inter-nationalism, which Lenin described as "the fusion of all nations in a higher unity, which grows before our eyes with every new mile of railroad, every new international trust, every new labor union (internationalist in its economic actions, and then subsequently in its ideas and goals)."

> What is progressive is the waking of the masses from feudal sleep, their struggle against national oppression of any kind and for the sov-ereignty of the people, of the nation. Hence the *absolute* duty of a Marxist to fight for the most determined and consistent democratic philosophy in every sphere of the national problem. In the main this is a negative task. Farther than this the proletariat cannot go in its sup-port of nationalism, for beyond this point we have those "positive" (affirmative) efforts of the *bourgeoisie*, which is out to *strengthen* nationalism. . . .
>
> Struggle *against* any kind of national oppression—a decided yes. Struggle *for* any kind of national development, *for* "national culture"

in general—a decided no. . . . The proletariat not only does not undertake to fight for the national development of every nation, but, on the
contrary, warns the masses against such illusions, fights for the com-
pletest freedom of capitalist traffic and trade, and welcomes every type
of assimilation of peoples save that based on coercion or founded on
privilege.

To establish nationalism securely in a definite, "justly" delimited
sphere . . . solidly to fence all nations off from one another by means
of special governmental institutions—such is the philosophical basis, the
content of national-cultural autonomy. The idea is bourgeois through
and through. The proletariat cannot support any attempt to entrench
nationalism; quite the contrary, it supports everything that helps to
erase national distinctions and break down the barriers between nationalities, everything that helps to tighten the bonds uniting nationalities,
everything that is conducive to the fusion of nations. To do otherwise
is to take the side of the reactionary nationalistic petty-bourgeoisie.[20]

The position was rather complicated and not easy to observe in practice. Where did one draw the line between the "absolute" support of
national struggles against domination and discrimination, and the "definite"
refusal "to fight for the national development of every nation"? Was not
a certain degree of national development necessary to "awaken" the
masses to the "struggle against national oppression of any kind"? Did not
the "sovereignty of the nation" imply the "fencing off of nations from
one another"? His attention focused on the "reactionary" aspects of cultural autonomy, Lenin supplied no answer to such questions. Neither, for
that matter, did Stalin, whose only theoretical contribution prior to his
assumption of omnipotence and omniscience, "Marxism and the National
Question" (1913), merely reiterated and supported Lenin's strictures
against cultural autonomy. Stalin, however, made it quite clear that a
common territory was to be regarded as an essential characteristic of a
nation,[21] and that where there was no common territory only the concept
of a "tribe," "an ethnographical category," applied.[22] Consequently,
the problems of full-fledged nations could be solved only on a strictly
territorial basis:

The only real solution is *regional* autonomy, autonomy for such
crystallized units as Poland, Lithuania, the Ukraine, the Caucasus, etc.

The advantage of regional autonomy consists firstly in the fact that
it does not deal with a fiction deprived of territory, but with a definite
population inhabiting a definite territory.

Secondly, it does not divide people according to nations, it does not
strengthen national partitions; on the contrary, it only serves to break
down these partitions and unites the population in such manner as to
open the way for division of a different kind, division according to class.

Finally, it provides the opportunity of utilizing the natural wealth of the region and of developing its productive forces in the best possible way. . . .[23]

Revolution and the Discarding of the Right of Self-Determination

The Bolshevik party, with the collapse of Tsarism early in 1917, passed from theoretical discussion and factional wrangling to the consideration of vital issues of practical politics. At four convocations, party policy on the national question was discussed and voted upon. A party conference that met in April 1917 merely repeated, with insignificant changes, the resolution adopted in 1913. A much more animated discussion took place at the Eighth Party Convention in March 1919, in connection with deliberations on the new party program. Practical requirements had to be met at the Tenth Convention in March 1921, which adopted a resolution "on the impending tasks of the party in dealing with the national problem," and at the Twelfth Convention in April 1923, which issued a document on "multinational factors in the building of the party and the state."[24]

In all these discussions two antagonistic tendencies were clearly visible. On the one hand, the Bolshevik party, although paying lip service to rights of nationalities, increasingly tended to deny to minorities the freedom to determine their own fate. On the other hand, party leaders began to show an appreciation of the possibilities of the national cultural development of Soviet minorities.

Already at the 1917 conference an attempt was made to circumvent the right of self-determination. In contrast to the 1913 resolution, which equated this right with the right to secede, the resolution of 1917 avoided the phrase, "self-determination," which had the status of a slogan in current usage, and merely said: "All nations composing Russia must be conceded the right freely to secede and to form independent states."[25] True, at the end of the year there was some more talk of the right of self-determination,[26] and even a solemn proclamation of the right of all nations to "free self-determination."[27] But the meaning of the term was progressively narrowed. Stalin's speech at the Third Soviet Congress, convened in January 1918, is a case in point. Addressing the Congress as the People's Commissar for National Affairs, Stalin declared that the right of self-determination was not a "right of the bourgeoisie, but of the toiling masses of the nation in question."[28] Speaking for the Menshevik opposition, Martov reminded the delegates that the new interpretation conflicted with the position of the Soviet delegation at the peace parley with the Germans; the Bolshevik negotiators then had insisted that the future of Poland and the Baltic areas should be decided by a plebiscite. The answer, given by Yevgenii A. Preobrazhenskii, alternate member of the Bolshevik Central Committee, was, if not exactly pertinent, a harbinger of future developments. The Mensheviks' protest against the denial of the right of the Ukrainians, Georgians, Armenians, etc. to exercise self-determination through the medium of democratic institutions was met with the statement that "bourgeois parliamentarianism in the Ukraine, the Caucasus, etc., already is outdated, a stage that developments have gone beyond"; yet it was entirely proper to insist on a plebiscite for the German-occupied Polish and Baltic areas, because the popular masses there still had "to fight for the establishment of the democratic order."[29] In his concluding remarks Stalin wholeheartedly endorsed Preobrazhenskii's sophistic reasoning.[30]

In a draft of the party program submitted to the Eighth Party Convention (March 1919), the right of self-determination disappeared, in its stead recognition being given to "the right of colonies and nations not enjoying legal equality to secede as states."[31] Now, however, it was specified in the text of the program as to who was authorized to exercise this narrowly limited "right to secede":

> On the question as to who represents the nation in its will to secede, the Russian Communist Party adopts the historical class point of view and takes into account the stage which the nation in question has reached in its historical development—whether it is on the road from medievalism to bourgeois democracy or from bourgeois democracy to Soviet or proletarian democracy, etc.[32]

A subtle substitution had been made. The right of the "nation" was replaced by the right of the "toiling masses," it soon being taken for granted that it was the prerogative of the Communist Party to decide what the "toiling masses" wanted. And in a few years time the Politburo in turn arrogated this prerogative to itself. Thus the right of self-determination came to mean the Kremlin's right to determine what was to be.

The formula adopted in 1919, which merely elaborated what Stalin and Preobrazhenskii had told the Third Soviet Congress fourteen months earlier, provoked heated debates at the party convention. Not that anyone had opposed the distortion of the principle of self-determination—on the contrary, a number of the members of the "left opposition" attacked the draft for giving way before nationalism, reaction, and imperialism. Nikolai I. Bukharin, leading Communist theoretician after Lenin, after referring explicitly to Stalin's speech at the Third Congress, demanded that the party program state without equivocation that only the "laboring classes of each nationality" were entitled to decide questions of secession; that raising the slogan of self-determination was proper only in countries "where the proletariat does not set itself the task of establishing its own workers' government, the proletarian dictatorship"—as, for instance, among "Hottentots, Bushmen, Negroes, Hindus, etc. [sic]."[33] Another outstanding Bolshevik, Yurii Pyatakov, chief of the Communist Party in the recently Sovietized Ukraine, went even farther; he demanded that all "Second-International leftovers" be got rid of, and wished to deny the right even of the "laboring classes of each nation" to decide on questions of national sovereignty or allegiance. This decision, according to him, only the proletarian International was competent to make: "This is precisely our purpose in creating an international union of the proletariat, namely, to be able in every important instance to determine, from the point of view of the revolutionary movement as a whole, what the decision should be."[34]

How little remained of the program of national rights was strikingly demonstrated by speakers who argued against Bukharin and Pyatakov. These "rightists," failing to notice that the draft program contemplated merely a restricted right of secession rather than the right of national self-determination, continued to defend the latter. But in what terms! Said David B. Ryazanov, expert on nineteenth-century international affairs:

> You cannot with impunity shout that you want to abandon the battle-cry of . . . self-determination under the Soviet system of government just at a time when, to save this system, you have to set as many and different oppressed nations as you can upon the imperialist wolves.[35]

Mikhail P. Tomskii, for many years boss of the Soviet labor unions, cautiously observed:

> I don't think there is a man in this room who would say that the self-determination of nations, or even a national movement, is something normal or desirable. We regard such things as unavoidable evils. And though perhaps risky from the international point of view, still, it must be said that we shall have to reckon to a certain extent with national self-determination for some time to come.[36]

Valerian V. Osinskii, alternate delegate of the Russian Communist Party to the founding congress of the Communist International and chief spokesman at the convention for the group against Bukharin, was most eloquent. The party ought not to give up the slogan of self-determination, he said. Nevertheless, the slogan was merely a "conditional" one, useful in the "unmasking of imperialism" so long as the proletariat had not won its struggle for power. So long as the proletariat had not seized the reins of government, a nation must be free to secede if it so willed. But what, exactly, was the will of a nation? Osinskii said:

> When we speak of the will of a nation, do we by any chance mean the opinions of that nation? Not at all. Will expresses itself not merely in the spoken word, but in deeds, in action. And it does not do this only

through the vote, it is sometimes carried out by force of arms. It is a long, long way from simply voting to [the exercising of] the will of the nation. It is not without reason that our program points out that completely different institutions serve to express the national will at different stages of a nation's development. . . .

We are for the proletarian class dictatorship. Thus it is very clear from this whom we mean when we refer to the will of the nation. . . . The will of the nation finds its supreme expression in the Soviet organization. Hence, claims based on universal suffrage mean nothing and prove nothing to us.[37]

Thus clarified, the matter was referred back to the committee on the party program, which reported out the section on nationalities without a single change, and so it was passed by the convention. Stalin was right when, two years later, at the Tenth Party Convention (1921), he said that national self-determination "has become an empty slogan," and it was no longer acceptable to the Communist Party:

It has been two years now that we have bidden farewell to this slogan. It is no longer in the text of our program. Our program makes no mention of national self-determination—a completely hazy slogan; it refers to a more precisely formulated and defined slogan, the right of nations to secede as states. . . . But for us at the present moment, when the movement of liberation is blazing up in the colonies, this slogan is a revolutionary one. Insofar as Soviet states join in a federation on a voluntary basis, the right to secede is not invoked, because the peoples making up the RSFSR have themselves so willed. Insofar, however, as we are dealing with colonies in the clutches of England, France, America, Japan, . . . with such subject countries as Arabia, Mesopotamia, Turkey, Hindustan, i.e., countries which are colonies or semi-colonies, the slogan of the right of peoples to secede is a revolutionary one, and to abandon it would be to play into the hands of imperialists.[38]

The conditional character of the rights of nationalities in Communist doctrine was thus clearly exposed. The right to secede (occasionally still called the right of self-determination) was to be used henceforth solely as propaganda against the imperialists. Its ideological value was solely for export; domestically, the right of national self-determination, having been "voluntarily" abandoned by the member nations of the Soviet state, was no longer recognized as a revolutionary slogan and was discarded.

At the 1921 convention, some democratic pretense was still maintained; the Soviet nationalities themselves, Stalin claimed, by joining together in the Russian Soviet Federated Socialist Republic, precursor of the USSR, renounced their right to secede. On other occasions—both before and after the Tenth Party Convention—this pretense was dropped. "Of course," Stalin wrote in Pravda on October 10, 1920, drawing the lesson of three years of practical experience in Soviet nationality policies, "the border regions of Russia, the nations and tribes which inhabit these regions . . . possess the inalienable right to secede from Russia"; but "the demand for the secession of the border regions" had become, "at the present stage of the revolution, a profoundly counterrevolutionary one."[39] The right was "inalienable," but to insist on exercising it was "counterrevolutionary"— the threat was obvious.

In greater detail, though not quite so "bluntly," the same idea was expounded in Stalin's report to the Twelfth Party Convention (April 1923). He said:

> It should be borne in mind that besides the right of nations to self-determination there is also the right of the working class to consolidate its power, and to this latter right the right of self-determination is subordinate. There are occasions when the right to self-determination conflicts with the other, the higher right—the right of a working class that has assumed power to consolidate its power. In such cases—this must be said bluntly—the right to self-determination cannot and must not serve as an obstacle to the exercise by the working class of its right to dictatorship. The former must give way to the latter. That, for instance, was the case in 1920, when in order to defend the power of the working class we were obliged to march on Warsaw.[40]

The "higher right" of the Soviet state was not to be questioned. What once had been a beacon of liberation summoning oppressed peoples to the making of their own destiny, was now the very opposite, a weapon of foreign aggression.

National Culture Vindicated

While the right of self-determination was gradually denied, the party attitude to the cultural aspirations of minority nationalities underwent a slow change in the opposite direction. Officially, there was for a number of years a tendency to go on denying the very existence of "national cultures." The belief that any manifestation of national consciousness was intrinsically evil predominated in Communist ranks. National movements, as Tomskii had put it at the 1919 party convention, were deemed neither "normal" nor "desirable."[41] And yet practical exigencies required some modification of this intransigent attitude, at least with respect to backward ethnic groups.

It was impossible to draw these oppressed peoples and tribes into a Soviet economy based on modern industrial technology, so long as they continued to live under medieval or primitive tribal conditions. Prodigious efforts had to be made so that these minorities might catch up with the rest of the country. The Soviet bureaucracy, in regions inhabited by minorities lacking an intelligentsia of their own, was predominantly

Russian, and not always proof against the influence of Tsarist tradition. It frequently displayed a callous indifference to the interests of "backward natives," and their cultural needs were often scorned and neglected. This greatly damaged the Soviet cause, and the Communist leadership, early confronted with the danger, launched a determined battle against the Russifiers and supported the economic and cultural improvement of minority nationalities, especially of the more backward ones. As early as 1921 the Tenth Party Convention emphatically stated:

The task of the party is to assist the toiling masses of the non-Great-Russian peoples in catching up with Central Russia, which has far outstripped them, and to help them:

(a) To develop and consolidate their own Soviet state system in forms consistent with these people's national way of life;

(b) To develop and consolidate their own courts, administrative agencies, economic bodies, and government organs, using the native tongue and staffed by local people familiar with the customs and psychological characteristics of the local population;

(c) To set up a press, schools, theaters, community centers, and cultural and educational institutions generally, using the native tongue;

(d) To organize and develop a comprehensive system of instruction and schools (with first attention to the Kirghiz, Bashkirs, Turkmen, Uzbeks, Tadzhiks, Azerbaidzhanians, Tatars, and Daghestanians), for the purposes both of general education and vocational and technical training, and conducted in the native tongue, in order more speedily to train indigenous personnel as skilled workers and as Soviet and party staff members in all spheres of administration, and above all in the sphere of education.[42]

The resolution further stressed that "existing national inequalities" had not yet been eliminated, and that their elimination would be "a long-drawn-out process requiring stubborn and unremitting struggle against all vestiges of national oppression and colonial slavery." It said that the "systematic extirpation of national inequalities in all spheres of social and economic life" was "the first and foremost task" of the proletarian revolution, and urged "the planned introduction of industry in border regions by moving factories close to the sources of raw materials."[43] In a subsequent passage the resolution referred to "the right of national minorities to free national development," which was "guaranteed by the very nature of the Soviet system."[44] An obvious change had taken place—at least in the phrasing—that markedly contrasted with Lenin's formula of 1913. What then had been termed an illusion—"The proletariat not only does not undertake to fight for the national development of every nation, but . . . warns the masses against such illusions"[45]—was now guaranteed as a right.

In rejecting at the same convention of 1921 an amendment that spoke of national-cultural self-determination, Stalin sneered: "I must say that I cannot accept this amendment because it smacks of Bundism. National-cultural self-determination—this is a Bundist formulation. We bade fare-well long ago to the nebulous slogans of self-determination, and there is no need to revive them now." But in the same breath he added:

I have here a note [from the floor] to the effect that we Communists artificially cultivate a White-Russian nationality. This is not true, for a White-Russian nationality does exist that has a language of its own distinct from the Russian, and for this reason the cultural level of the White-Russian people can be raised only in its native tongue. Some five years ago the same speeches were made about the Ukraine and the Ukrainian nationality. And only recently it was said that the Ukrainian republic and the Ukrainian nationality are an invention of the Germans. It is obvious, however, that the Ukrainian nationality exists, and to develop its culture is a duty of the Communists.[46]

A new theory had not yet been developed, but the categorical denial of the very existence of national cultures had ceased. The naive cosmopoli-tanism of Lenin's early pronouncements on national culture was being superseded in the daily practice of the Soviet government by a more differentiated treatment of individual nationalities. In its day-to-day adap-tation to the requirements of the changing situation, the Communist Party thus was ahead of its own theory—until Stalin set about revising the theory in 1925. The revised position, summed up in a now famous formula, was set forth by Stalin in an address delivered at the Communist University of the Toilers of the East, on May 18, 1925:

How are we to make the building of a national culture, the develop-ment of schools and courses in the native tongue, and the training of personnel from among the ranks of local people, compatible with the building of socialism, with the building of a proletarian culture? Is this not an unresolvable contradiction? Of course not! We are build-ing a proletarian culture. That is absolutely true. But it is also true that proletarian culture, which is socialist in content, assumes different forms and modes of expression among the various peoples that have been drawn into the work of socialist construction, depending on differences of language, way of life, and so forth. Proletarian in content and national in form—such is the universal human culture towards which socialism is marching. Proletarian culture does not eliminate national culture, but lends it content. Conversely, national culture does not eliminate proletarian culture, but lends it form. "National culture" was a bourgeois slogan so long as the bourgeoisie held power and the consolidation of nations took place under a proletarian slogan with the assumption of power by the proletariat and the carrying-forward of national consolidation under the aegis of the Soviet government. Whoever has not grasped the difference in principle between these two different situations will never understand either Leninism or the essence of the national question from the standpoint of Leninism.[47]

This interpretation of the "essence of the national question" was an attempt to reconcile the practical necessities of the multinational Soviet reality with Lenin's plainly stated opposition to all forms of national culture. At the Sixteenth Party Convention in June 1930, Stalin argued that "Lenin had actually described the slogan, national culture, as reactionary under the rule of the bourgeoisie;"[48] but "Lenin never said that the slogan calling for the development of national culture was reactionary under the conditions of proletarian dictatorship."[49] Actually, however, Lenin had not qualified his disdain of national culture; he had not limited his opposition to the national cultures of capitalism alone. And Stalin himself, in the speech just quoted, sought to preserve the traditional Leninist conception for the future:

> It may seem strange that we, who are in favor of the future *fusion* of national cultures into one common culture (both in form and content), with a single common language, at the same time favor the *burgeoning* of national cultures today, in the period of the dictatorship of the proletariat. Yet there is nothing strange in this. National cultures must be given an opportunity to develop, expand, and reveal all their potentialities, in order to establish the conditions for their fusion into a single common culture with a single common language. The burgeoning of cultures that are national in form and socialist in content, under the conditions of the dictatorship of the proletariat in one country, *so that* they may, at a time when the proletariat will have triumphed throughout the world and socialism become a part of the universal way of life, fuse into a single common culture, socialist both in form and content, and employing a common language—such is the dialectical nature of the Leninist approach to the problem of national culture.[50]

The striking difference between Lenin's old and Stalin's new formula was reduced to a question of time. This was not too adroitly done, and an essential contradiction remained.

National Patrimony Restricted to "Form"

Stalin's revision of the Leninist doctrine on national culture gave a host of Communist officials broad authority to initiate and promote the cultural improvement of undeveloped, downtrodden minority nationalities. This has won the Soviet government universal acclaim; and, indeed, a great deal was done to raise the cultural level of many ethnic groups and tribes that had led a pathetic pariah existence in the shadow of the Tsarist Empire.[51] But these improvements—the overcoming of illiteracy, the establishment of schools, the fostering of art, and similar achievements—called in Soviet jargon "cultural construction" or "the building of culture"—must not be mistaken for a genuine national development based on the growth of national consciousness and creativeness. The Soviet conception of "national culture," defined as the "form" of cultural expression, is narrowly limited; it should not be confused with Western conceptions, with which it shares nothing but the name. It is inseparable from Stalin's definition of the nation as developed in 1913, and can be understood only in its light.

Language, territory, common economic development, and "a common mental constitution, which manifests itself in a common culture," are the components which, according to Stalin, make up a nation. "Nations differ not only in their conditions of life, but also in their mental complexion, which finds expression in the specific features of national culture. If England, America and Ireland, speaking one language, nevertheless figure as three distinct nations, it is in no small measure due to that specific mental constitution which they have developed from generation to generation as a result of different conditions of existence." But this "national character" in turn "is not a thing fixed once and for all, but changes with the changing conditions of life."[52]

What national differences then remain in the Soviet Union, where the various nationalities of earlier times are all engaged in the common economic life of "socialist construction," are few. Their conditions of existence are identical, and except for minor differences in geographical location ("territory"), there are only, as Stalin put it in 1925, "differences in language, way of life [byt], and so forth."[53] The scarcely translatable byt, which comprises the folkways, customs, and other manifestations of the specific character of the daily life of a group, plus the indefinite "and so forth," are the only vestiges of that specific "mental constitution" which underlies "specific features of national culture." These, then, are the only national—actually sectional—forms in which the proletarian class content of the socialist culture common to all nationalities of the Soviet Union is enclosed. In his recent statement on "Marxist linguistics" Stalin has dispelled all doubts as to the meaning of the formula, "national in form," by simply equating "form" and language: "Can it be that our comrades are not aware of the well-known Marxist formula that . . . cultures are socialist in content and national in form, that is, in language?"[54]

Whenever Soviet pronouncements refer to "the building of national culture" or "national development of minority nationalities," what is meant are solely these "national forms", i.e., language and perhaps sectional custom. No nationality is ever encouraged to develop a culture of its own that would differ "in content" from the Soviet culture. The development of national cultures is paradoxically—or "dialectically"—their extinction; for, as Stalin said in 1925, it means the proletarianization of their content.[55]

But the "proletarian culture" of the Soviet state was, owing to the historical circumstances of its inception, the culture of the majority nationality, of the Russians. It is this predominantly Russian culture which the national minorities were to be allowed to partake of. Every attempt on the part of minority nationalities "to isolate themselves and retreat within the national shell . . . to ignore what . . . unites the toiling masses of the nationalities of the USSR and to see only what tends to estrange them," was "bourgeois nationalism," and aided and abetted the foreign enemies of the Soviet Union.[56]

There was no reason, from the point of view of official doctrine, why the national "form" of the majority nationality's culture should not predominate, once the participation of minority nationalities in "socialist construction" was secured and there was no longer a danger of their falling prey to "reactionary nationalism." Any "deviation in the direction of local nationalism" was to be condemned no less severely than that "towards Great-Russian chauvinism."[57] There was no necessity for *all* existing nationalities to develop and survive, nor was it the duty of the Communist Party to oppose "the assimilation of individual nationalities in the process of the building of a proletarian culture for all mankind." Replying to questions as to how "the assimilation of peculiarities of individual national cultures (language, etc.)" should proceed, Stalin said in 1925:

> Undoubtedly, some nationalities may, and even certainly will, undergo a process of assimilation. Such things have happened before. But the point is, that the process of assimilation of some nationalities does not preclude, but rather presupposes, the opposite process of the strengthening and developing of a number of powerful nationalities; for a partial process of assimilation is the result of the general process of development of nationalities. This is why the possible assimilation of some individual nationalities does not weaken, but rather supports, the entirely correct statement that universal proletarian culture does not preclude, but rather presupposes and fosters, national culture, just as national culture does not eliminate, but rather supplements and enriches universal proletarian culture.[58]

It was, of course, the Communist Party's prerogative to determine which nationalities were condemned by history to "undergo the process of assimilation," and which were destined to become "powerful" and to absorb those doomed to disappear. What treatment was reserved in this connection for Jews, and how it was modified at different stages in the development of Communist policy, will be discussed in subsequent chapters.

During the Second World War and in the early postwar years it has been possible to detect a new inflection in Soviet pronouncements on the national question. There is an inclination to lay particular stress upon the superior qualities (political and cultural) of the Russian people as compared with other Soviet nationalities, and to treat some of the minority nationalities as no longer deserving of a free national development. With growing insistence, specifically Russian virtues and accomplishments are being contrasted with "cosmopolitan" weaknesses and depravities. Whether this is a prelude to consigning an increasing number of nationalities to "the partial process of assimilation," remains to be seen. Both Lenin's teachings on the benefits of centralization and Stalin's advocacy of cultures "national in form," are sufficiently flexible to justify a gradual return to Russification policies on grounds of "historical necessity" and "the dialectical nature of the Leninist approach to the problem of national culture."[59] Thus, Stalin had always insisted that if a single language was to replace—in the remote future—the Babel of existing tongues, it would be a new language rather than that of any predominant nationality;[60] but in the recent discussion of linguistics in *Pravda* he has stated that there can be no revolutionary fusion of two existing languages into an entirely different new one, and that "in the process of hybridization, one of the languages usually emerges victorious." "This is," he added, "what happened, for example, with Russian, with which the languages of a number of other peoples blended in the course of historical development, and which always emerged victorious."[61]

NOTES

1. Vladimir Medem (listed in the convention's proceedings as "Goldblat," and at other conferences under his pen name, "Michael Vinnitskii"), was the youngest son of a high-ranking military surgeon in the Tsarist army. At birth he had been baptized in the Greek Orthodox faith and was reared in the bosom of a completely Russified family. In his middle twenties he was the outstanding interpreter—or rather creator—of the Bundist doctrine on the national problem. During the decade preceding the First World War, Medem was one of the leaders of the All-Russian Bund. In 1915-1920 he transformed the Bund into a mass party and influential force within the nascent Polish state. Although he learned Yiddish as a grown man, and never wrote a line of it until well in his thirties, Medem in those years became a fine Yiddish essayist and political writer, and a great Yiddish orator. The cultural renaissance of the Jewish popular masses in Poland, and the creation of a powerful Jewish school movement and a network of Jewish child-welfare institutions, were largely the result of his inspiring initiative. Through some of his disciples, among whom B. Charney Vladeck was perhaps the closest, he exerted a great intellectual influence on the Jewish labor movement in the United States. Medem, a sick man, came to this country early in 1921 and devoted his last years to encouraging a Jewish popular culture outside of, and in opposition to, Zionist ideas, and to criticizing indefatigably the dictatorial trend of Soviet rule in Russia. He was not yet 44 when he died in New York in 1923, leaving behind him a unique monument in his memoirs, *Fun Mayn Lebn*, New York, 1923.

2. The general atmosphere of the convention was anti-Bundist. The Bundist delegation, another Bund representative at the convention, Vladimir Kossovskii (listed in the proceedings as "Gofman"), wrote 25 years later, "was isolated in and encircled by a host of enemies." See V. Kossovskii, "V. Medem un di Natsionale Frage," in

Vladimir Medem tsum Tsvantsikstn Yortsayt, issued by the American Representation of the General Jewish Workers' Union in Poland, New York, 1943, p. 133.

3. Yefrem Yakovlevich Levin ("Yegorov" in the convention transcript) later became a well-known Menshevik.

4. D. Kol'tsov (Boris Abramovich Ginzburg) wrote on labor problems; subsequently he was prominent in formulating the Menshevik position on industrial relations, labor legislation, etc.

5. For all facts and quotations above, see *Protokoly 2-go syezda Rossiiskoi Sotsial-Demokraticheskoi Rabochei Partii (1903 g.)* [*Proceedings of the 2d Convention of the Russian Social Democratic Workers Party, 1903*] Party History Department, Central Committee, Communist Party of the Soviet Union, Leningrad, 1924, pp 162ff. Original edition: *Vtoroi ocherednoi syezd Ross. Sots.-Dem. Rabochei Partii,* Central Committee, RSDWP, Geneva, n.d., pp. 176ff.

6. L. Martov (Yulii Osipovich Tsederbaum), one of the first to propagandize Social Democratic ideas among the Yiddish-speaking Jewish workers in Lithuania, though thus actually a forerunner of the Bund, was no less uncompromisingly opposed to Bundist "nationalism" and "separatism" than were other leading Social Democrats.

7. *Protokoly* . . . , pp. 157f.; original ed., pp. 170f.

8. *Ibid.,* pp. 159ff.; original ed., pp. 171–175.

9. *Ibid.,* pp. 215f.; original ed., pp. 4 and 232f.

10. See Chap. VI below.

11. "O manifeste armyanskikh sotsial-demokratov" ["On the Manifesto of the Armenian Social Democrats"], in *Iskra,* the party publication printed abroad, February 1, 1903; reprinted in N. Lenin (V. I. Ul'yanov), *Sochineniya* [*Works*], 2d ed., vol. V, p. 242.

12. Lenin, *Sochineniya,* vol. XVII, p. 13.

13. *Op. cit.,* pp. 90f. Emphasis Lenin's.

14. See *Sochineniya,* vol. XVIII and XIX, for Lenin's writings on the subject.

15. "Kriticheskiye zametki po natsional'nomu voprosu" ["Critical Notes on the National Problem"], in *Sochineniya,* vol. XVII, pp. 155f

16. "Tezisy po natsional'nomu voprosu" ["Theses on the National Problem"], in *Ibid.,* vol. XVI, p. 512.

17. "Kak yepiskop Nikon zashchishchayet ukraintsev" ["How Bishop Nikon Defends the Ukrainians"], in *Sochineniya,* vol. XVI, p. 618

18. "Territorial autonomy," wrote Medem, "at best frees the dominant nation of a province from oppression. It does not solve the problem of the other nationalities living there. And it may be added that even the members of the ruling nation are free only so long as they remain inside the boundaries of 'their' province." ("Di Sotsial-Demokratie un di Natsionale Frage" [1904], reprinted in *Vladimir Medem tsum Tsvantsikstn Yortsayt,* p. 218.)

19. "O natsional'noi programme RSDRP," in *Sochineniya,* vol. XVII, p. 118.

20. "Kriticheskiye zametki . . . ," in *Sochineniya,* vol. XVI, pp. 144f. Emphasis Lenin's.

21. "A nation is formed only as a result of lengthy and systematic intercourse, as a result of the fact that people live together from generation to generation. But people cannot live together for lengthy periods unless they have a common territory. . . . Thus community of territory is one of the characteristic features of a nation." (Joseph Stalin, *Marxism and the National and Colonial Question. A Collection of Articles and Speeches* [Marxist Library, vol. XXXVIII], New York, n.d., p. 6.)

22. *Ibid.,* p. 12.

23. *Ibid.,* pp. 57f. Emphasis Stalin's.

24. At the 1917 conference and the 1921 and 1923 conventions, reports on national problems were presented by Stalin (the 1917 resolution, however, was drafted by Lenin; cf. J. V. Stalin, *Sochineniya* [*Works*], vol. 5, p. 418, n. 68). In 1919 Stalin

did not take part in the debates on the section on nationalities of the party program, although he attended the convention.

25. Reprinted in Appendix I to Stalin, *Marxism and the National Question*, p. 269, though in a translation that gives the wording of the resolution a more affirmative sound.

26. See, e.g., Stalin, "Otvet tovarishcham ukraintsam v tylu i na fronte" ["Reply to Ukrainian Comrades at the Front and Behind the Lines"] (December 1917), in *Sochineniya*, vol. 4, p. 8.

27. Appeal of the Second Soviet Congress "to workers, soldiers, and peasants" announcing the transfer of power to the Soviets, October 25 (November 7), 1917, reprinted in Lenin, *Sochineniya*, vol. XXII, p. 11.

28. *Tretii Vserossiiskii Syezd Sovetov Rabochikh, Krest'yanskikh i Soldatskikh Deputatov* [*Third All-Russian Congress of Soviets of Workers', Peasants' and Soldiers' Delegates*], St. Petersburg, 1918, p. 73. Reprinted in Stalin, *Sochineniya*, vol. 4, pp. 31f.

29. *Ibid.*, p. 77.

30. *Ibid.*, p. 80; Stalin, *Sochineniya*, vol. 4, p. 36.

31. The draft was first published in *Pravda*, February 26, 1919; cf. the official translation in Appendix I to Stalin, *Marxism and the National Question*, p. 288.

32. Translated from the original *Pravda* text. The official translation in the appendix to Stalin's work on the national question obscures the meaning of the Russian text.

33. *Vos'moi Syezd Rossiiskoi Kommunisticheskoi Partii, Moskva, 18–23 marta 1919 goda. Stenograficheskii otchet* [*Eighth Convention of the Russian Communist Party, Moscow, March 18 to 23, 1919. Stenographic Record of Proceedings*], Moscow, 1919, p. 41.

34. *Ibid.*, pp. 67f.

35. *Ibid.*, p. 59.

36. *Ibid.*, p. 71.

37. *Ibid.*, pp. 79f.

38. Translated from the revised text in Stalin, *Sochineniya*, vol. 5, pp. 42f. The original text of the convention proceedings speaks, *e.g.*, of the "Entente" where the revised version has "imperialists," etc.

39. "The Policy of the Soviet Government on the National Question in Russia," in *Marxism and the National Question*, pp. 79f.

40. *Marxism and the National Question*, p. 168.

41. *Vos'moi Syezd* . . . , p. 71.

42. Stalin, *Marksizm i natsional'no-kolonial'nyi vopros. Sbornik izbrannykh statei i rechei* [*Marxism and the National and Colonial Question. Collection of Selected Articles and Speeches*], Moscow, 1937, pp. 207f. The official American translation is marred by inaccuracies.

43. *Ibid.* (American ed., p. 276).

44. *Ibid.*, p. 209 (American ed., p. 278).

45. See n. 20 above.

46. *Op. cit.*, p. 81 (American ed., p. 110).

47. Stalin, "O politicheskikh zadachakh Universiteta Narodov Vostoka" ["The Political Tasks of the University of the Peoples of the East"], in *Marksizm* . . . , p. 158 (American ed., pp. 209f.).

48. *Op. cit.*, p. 194 (American ed., p. 260).

49. *Ibid.*, p. 193 (American ed., p. 259).

50. *Ibid.*, pp. 194f. (American ed., p. 261). Emphasis Stalin's.

51. See "Cultural Awakening" in Chap. V.

52. Stalin, "Marksizm i natsional'nyi vopros" [1913], in *Marksizm* . . . , p. 6 (American ed., pp. 7f.).

53. See n. 47 above.

54. "O marksizme v yazykovedenii" ["On Marxism in Linguistics"], in *Pravda*, June 20, 1950.

55. Stalin characterized the development of national cultures as "the accession of

various nationalities to proletarian culture," which "will take its course in forms corresponding to the languages and the way of life of these nationalities." (*Marksizm* . . . , p. 158 [American ed., p. 211]).

56. *Ibid.*, p. 196 (American ed., p. 263).
57. *Ibid.*, pp. 126ff., 160f., 195f. (American ed., pp. 168ff., 213f., 262f.).
58. *Ibid.*, p. 159 (American ed., p. 211).
59. See n. 55 above.
60. *E.g.*, Stalin, *Marksizm* . . . , p. 197 (American ed., p. 264).
61. See n. 54 above.

Chapter III

The Jewish People in Leninist Perspective

Cosmopolitan Disdain of Historical Jewry

The Leninist theory of the Jewish problem was shaped, in its main points, by the essentially cosmopolitan thought of nineteenth-century European socialism. But its specific views and particular conclusions were the result of Lenin's approach to the struggles of oppressed nationalities for emancipation, on the one hand, and of considerations of organizational tactics, on the other.

To nineteenth-century socialism, nationalism seemed obsolete and destined for oblivion. Industrial civilization day in, day out was breaking down national boundaries, peculiarities, and traditions. To be sure, "the struggle of the proletariat with the bourgeoisie," Marx and Engels said in the *Communist Manifesto* in 1847, had been "at first a national struggle," but "in form only," "not in substance." Only insofar as "the proletariat must first of all acquire political supremacy, must rise to be the leading class of the nation, must constitute itself the nation, it is . . . itself national, though not in the bourgeois sense of the word." Was it not a self-evident truth that "national differences and antagonisms between the peoples are vanishing, owing to the development of the bourgeoisie, to freedom of commerce, to the world market, to uniformity in the mode of production and in the conditions of life corresponding thereto," and that "the supremacy of the proletariat will cause them to vanish still faster"? The inescapable conclusion was: "In proportion as the exploitation of one individual by another is put an end to, the exploitation of one nation by another will also be put an end to. In proportion as the antagonism between the classes within the nation vanishes, the hostility of one nation to another will come to an end."

But in the last decades of the nineteenth-century socialist movements in Europe's two leading multinational states, Russia and Austria-Hungary, emerged, and their problems gradually began to attract attention. It then appeared that even within the supposedly homogeneous socialist world "national differences and antagonisms between peoples" had not vanished. The working masses, contrary to optimistic predictions, were indeed "nationalistic," even "in the bourgeois sense of the word."

In Russia the dispute between the Russian Social Democrats and the

46

Jewish Bundists over the latter's claim to recognition as an extra-territorial organization for Jewish workers on a national rather than regional or local basis, resulted in the Bund's withdrawal from the Social Democratic Party at its 1903 convention. This had an important consequence, for the withdrawal of the Bundist delegates gave the majority of the votes to Lenin's group, thereafter called Bolsheviks (from *bol'shinstvo*, majority). This permitted the Leninists to seize the central party organization, and precipitated the split that gave birth to Bolshevism as a distinct political movement.

In principle, European socialism from its early beginnings had sided with those movements of national liberation which were deemed "historically progressive." Now, when the interests and aspirations of different national sections of the socialist movement clashed, the question as to which national movements were to be supported, assumed immediate political importance. How was the socialist movement to reconcile its basic internationalism with the support it wished to give movements of national emancipation? And if all nations had the right to an independent national life, what about those nations, like the Jews, which had no territory of their own and lived scattered among other peoples? Were they a nation, too, and if not, what were they?

Liberal and, even more, socialist thought in nineteenth-century Europe was largely synonymous with anticlericalism, and frequently even with militant atheism. The Jewish collectivity, identified as a religious community, appeared as backwardness incarnate. Karl Marx expressed a view held by many when he argued that the emancipation of Europe's Jews could be truly accomplished only through their and society's "emancipation from Judaism."[1] It was taken for granted that the progress of liberalism, bringing with it the emancipation of the Jews and the abolition of the legal, social, and economic restrictions to which they had been subjected since early medieval times, would cause the Jews to disappear into the surrounding peoples.

Matters, however, took a different turn. Strong antisemitic movements made their appearance in the last third of the century in France and Germany. Devastating pogroms swept Russia and had their echo in the southeast of Europe. This renascent antisemitism, however, was regarded as a temporary episode. Although there was skepticism in the new national minority movements, socialist opinion by and large continued to feel confident of the rapid disappearance of nationalism. To assist the development of nationalities doomed by the laws of economic development was to balk historical progress; it would delay the maturing of capitalism and postpone the advent of socialism. From the point of view of international socialism, those who advocated such reactionary policies were nationalists serving other interests than those of the socialist working class. Those in particular who set up for spokesmen of a "Jewish nation" were suspected of wishing to drag society back into medieval times.[2]

Jews an Anachronism

Continental socialists, whose thinking was directed to the economic roots of social and political phenomena, saw the outstanding characteristics of the Jewish minority in territorial dispersal and the absence of essential productive classes, i.e., farmers and industrial workers. The bulk of the Jewish population was made up of various middle-class groups, particularly lower-middle-class, that were steadily and ineluctably disintegrating. It seemed logical to conclude that the Jewish masses must either vanish altogether as a significant social group, or be subjected to proletarianization and assimilation.

The idea of a Jewish nationality deserving at least of cultural autonomy was rejected even by the Austrian Marxist, Otto Bauer, who of all socialist theoreticians did most to make intransigent internationalists accept the claims of oppressed nationalities to independence. "To contend that the Jews are not a nation," Bauer said, "is perhaps to go too far today, even in Western and Central Europe. But one may well contend that they are ceasing to be a nation."[3]

It seemed obvious that Jews in Western Europe no longer constituted a national group. The Jewish population was far advanced along the road of assimilation. Such was not the case in Eastern Europe, where only small propertied and intellectual classes could break out of the ghetto and merge with the non-Jewish population. Was this ethno-cultural community, which had enjoyed a large measure of self-government under the most abject conditions of medieval oppression, not a national minority group? Was it not entitled to enjoy the rights of self-determination and an autonomous status, like any other national group? Or would emancipation and the development of capitalism abolish the ghetto and cause all Jews to be assimilated wholesale?

The latter view prevailed in Russian socialist and liberal circles. The economic decay of Jewry was plainly evident, and so was the miserable condition of the Jewish masses. These basic economic facts counted heavily with the anti-Tsarist movement in the 1890's and 1900's, which was strongly influenced by Marxism. However, the young Marx's notion of the Jews as a money-making and huckstering fraternity[4] had barely penetrated Russian socialist thinking, and was too strikingly refuted by the conspicuous plight of Russia's Jews to have any influence.

Social Democracy and the Bund

Though moribund in theory, Jews were very much alive in fact. They continued to exist as a community *sui generis,* which even under the conditions of Tsarist oppression had enough strength to develop Jewish cultural institutions, Jewish schools, and a Jewish labor movement. The most striking proof of the vitality of the Jewish group was its first large-scale labor organization, the General Jewish Workers Alliance [Bund] in Russia and Poland. The Bund was little inclined to depart from the traditional internationalism of its orthodox Marxism; and yet it became a dominating factor in Jewish national rebirth. It inspired an ambitious cultural renaissance and exerted a great influence on all political and ideological movements within the Jewish community in Eastern Europe.[5]

In their everyday activities among Jewish workers the Bundists had come to accept the fact that Eastern Europe's Jews were a separate minority, not only as a target of discriminatory legislation and social and economic restrictions, but also, and primarily, because they constituted an ethno-cultural community based on a common language, cultural heritage, mores, communal tradition, and a specific social stratification. Not that the Bundists wanted to preserve this community; they were as suspicious of the "reactionary and obscurantist ghetto culture" as were the most "antichauvinist" of their opponents in the ranks of the Russian socialist movement. But the Bundists believed that, owing to historical circumstances not of their own making, the Jewish masses were bound to remain Jewish for quite some time to come, and would retain their language and way of life; and that in consequence they were forced to insist on the fulfilment of specifically Jewish demands, legal, educational, economic, social, etc.

The Bundists fought tooth and nail for a separate Jewish socialist organization, and for such methods and tactics as were appropriate to the conduct of the class struggle "in the Jewish street." They were conspicuously successful. At an early date they established a close-knit central organization. They made spectacular advances in organizing Jewish labor unions (e.g., in the tobacco and brush industries, printing shops, textile and leather trades). They conducted labor disputes and political demonstrations, issued publications, and initiated educational activities.

In 1901, the national convention of the Bund passed a resolution saying that the concept, nation, was applicable to the Jewish people; the convention also subscribed to the principle of national autonomy, to be formulated more concretely at a later date.[6] And in 1905 the Bund went so far as officially to espouse the demand for "national-cultural autonomy" for the Jewish minority.[7] Thereafter the Bund was to advocate extra-territorial self-government for all minorities, above all for Jews, and to demand that this be endorsed by the entire socialist movement. Even before this, the Bund had strongly insisted that its organizational autonomy be recognized by the nationwide Social Democratic organization, and that its authority as sole spokesman for the Jewish working class be respected.

Lenin on the Jewish Nationality

Lenin, after the Bund's withdrawal from the Social Democratic party in 1903, gave a more detailed statement of his views on Jewish nationality in an article entitled "The Bund's Position within the Party," appearing on October 22, 1903 in *Iskra*, the Social Democratic periodical of which he had assumed virtually the sole editorship. Having dismissed as unessential two technical considerations advanced by the Bund, he went on to say:

> The Bund's third argument, which consists of invoking the idea of a Jewish nation, indubitably raises a question of principle. Unfortunately, however, this Zionist idea is entirely false and reactionary in its essence. "The Jews ceased to be a nation, for a nation is inconceivable without a territory," says one of the most outstanding Marxist theoreticians, Karl Kautsky. . . . Also, more recently, in his analysis of the problem of nationalities in Austria, the same writer, attempting to furnish a scientific definition of nationality, lays down two fundamental criteria for this concept: language and territory. . . . The only thing perhaps remaining to the Bundists is to elaborate the idea of a separate Russian Jewish nationality, having Yiddish for its language and the Jewish Pale for its territory.
>
> The idea of a separate Jewish people, which is utterly untenable scientifically, is reactionary in its political implications. The incontrovertible empirical proof is furnished by the well-known facts of history and of the political reality of today. Everywhere in Europe the downfall of medievalism and the development of political freedom went hand in hand with the political emancipation of the Jews, their substituting for Yiddish the language of the people among whom they lived, and in general their indubitably progressive assimilation by the surrounding population. . . .
>
> The Jewish question is this exactly: assimilation or separateness? And the idea of a Jewish "nationality" is manifestly reactionary, not only when put forward by its consistent partisans (the Zionists), but also when put forward by those who try to make it agree with the ideas of Social Democracy (the Bundists). The idea of a Jewish nationality is in conflict with the interests of the Jewish proletariat, for, directly or indirectly, it engenders in its ranks a mood hostile to assimilation, a "ghetto" mood.[8]

This thesis subsequently came very near to being Bolshevik gospel; when discussing Jewish issues, the Bolshevik press rarely failed to quote Lenin's pronouncement, which had the additional advantage of seeming to be supported by the authority of Karl Kautsky. Actually, Lenin modified Kautsky's views by stating, dogmatically and out of context, what had been only one step in a tentative sociological and historical analysis of the roots of antisemitism, especially as manifested in the South-Russian pogroms. Kautsky had not sought to give an abstract answer to the question as to whether or not the Jews were a nation, but had merely discussed what the socialist movement should do in order to cope with antisemitism. With this purpose in mind, he traced antisemitism back to the exilic segregation of the Jews among the alien peoples in whose midst they had been compelled to settle. To refute early racist arguments, he briefly surveyed the history of the Jewish people, which had been "exterminated in its mother country" and "lived on only in numerous emigrant colonies in alien lands." "For this reason," Kautsky said, the Jews had "ceased to be a nation, for a nation is inconceivable without a territory." His reference is unmistakably to an event that occurred more than two thousand years ago, and not to the present.

After having lost nationhood, the Jews, according to Kautsky, "became a tribe unique of its kind, namely, the only one . . . to live on as an alien among aliens, with strong emotional ties to its home country, but without that home country."[9] This fatal position of Jews as "aliens" was one of the deepest roots of antisemitism. Antisemitism would be "most radically" eliminated, he contended, if the alien group ceased to be so, if it "merged with the mass of the population." "This, after all," he concluded, "is the only possible solution of the Jewish problem, and everything helping to break down Jewish seclusion should be supported."[10]

Nor did Kautsky undertake to lay down "fundamental criteria" for a "scientific definition" of the "concept of nationality." He traced the growth of peoples beyond the merely tribal stage, and the successive common features marking the establishment of more or less stable societies. While "the first firm bond uniting human society" was common descent, in later stages it was community of language that signified the separate, national existence of a given society; still later, when this society had come to have a common, continuous territory, an awareness of national identity arose. In the article on national problems in Austria-Hungary to which Lenin referred, Kautsky pointed out that national groups might well lose this or that historical criterion which had determined their nationality at a formative stage, and still remain distinct nationalities. Language appeared to him to be "the most outstanding feature of nationality," "one of the most important constituent elements" of national existence; but one also had to take into account other elements, "which may acquire such importance that by themselves they will suffice to preserve a nationality, even though unfavorable circumstances should cause it to lose its language, as for example, in the case of the Irish."

This, however, Kautsky viewed as "an exception." In general, the formation of a nation depended on the development of a national language; "as a rule," a nation without a language of its own could not continue to exist. Moreover, Kautsky believed that economic developments encouraged linguistic unification within modern societies: "The more bourgeois society expands, and the closer the relationships within it, the stronger the tendency for people inhabiting one territory to speak the same language."[11] National distinctions, however, were still preponderant in a multinational state like Austria-Hungary. Kautsky was fully aware of the persistence of national differences and was not naive enough to contend that the Jewish group had already vanished as a nationality. He foresaw its disappearance as a result of a long-drawn-out process of assimilation, yet this process, in his view, was far from having reached the point where it would be absurd to refer to Jews as a national group. The balanced reasoning of the historian is in sharp contrast with Lenin's sarcastic gibe at a Yiddish-speaking nation of the Pale.

Lenin's one-sided view of "Jewish nationalism" was unaffected by new facts and changing conditions. In 1912 and 1913 the notion of a "Jewish nation" aroused Lenin's indignation no less than it had in 1903. In an article published late in 1913, he wrote:

> Out of ten and a half million Jews throughout the world, *about one-half* live in a civilized world, under conditions favoring *maximum* "assimilationism," whereas only the wretched and oppressed Jews of Russia and Galicia, deprived of legal rights and downtrodden by (Russian and Polish) Purishkeviches, live under conditions favoring *minimum* "assimilationism" and maximum segregation, which includes the "Pale of Residence," the *numerus clausus,* and similar Purishkevich delights.
>
> In the civilized world, the Jews are not a nation; there they have achieved the highest degree of assimilation, say Kautsky and O. Bauer. In Galicia and Russia the Jews are not a nation; there they are unfortunately (not through any fault of theirs, but through that of the Purishkeviches) still a *caste.* Such is the indisputable opinion of men who indisputably know the history of the Jews. . . .[12]

The repeated reference to the "indisputable" authority of Kautsky and Bauer was only partly justified. Kautsky did not share Lenin's rejection of the Jewish "caste" outside of the "civilized world"; Bauer did. Bauer, whose concept of nationality Lenin vehemently opposed on theoretical grounds, also was in agreement with Lenin as to the evils of a program of cultural autonomy for the Jewish minority. He refrained, however, from sweeping denunciations of "Jewish national culture." And it was precisely on this point that Lenin was implacable:

> Anyone defending the slogan of national culture belongs among the nationalistic petty bourgeois and not among Marxists. . . .

This is also true of the most oppressed and persecuted nation, the Jews. Jewish national culture is the slogan of rabbis and bourgeois, the slogan of our enemies. . . . Anyone directly or indirectly putting forward the slogan of Jewish "national culture" is (whatever his good intentions) an enemy of the proletariat, a partisan of the *old* and the *caste-like* in the Jewish group, an accomplice of the rabbis and bourgeois. Contrariwise, those Jewish Marxists who merge with Russian, Lithuanian, Ukrainian, and other workers in international Marxist organizations, contributing their share (in both Russian and Yiddish) to the creation of an international culture of the labor movement— those Jews carry on (in defiance of the separatism of the Bund) the best Jewish tradition when they combat the slogan of "national culture."[13]

Lenin's position is easy to summarize: The Jewish group is neither a nation nor a nationality,[14] but a caste; and, in the interests of social progress, all castes must be inexorably destroyed. Insofar as the Jewish question is one of oppression and discrimination, the establishment of racial and national equality will solve that problem. Beyond this, the Jewish problem shall not be considered. "National culture" in general is a fraudulent ideology; "Jewish national culture" is doubly fraudulent, and implicitly reactionary, for there is no Jewish nation, and so-called Jewish culture can only serve the turn of those eager to preserve an obsolete, harmful and disintegrating caste of "rabbis and bourgeois." It is not enough to ignore or disregard Jewish national aspirations; they must be actively opposed as assisting "the enemies of the proletariat." Cultural autonomy in general is "refined nationalism"; in the case of the Jewish group it is doubly "reactionary," "bourgeois through and through," etc., for it would give "our enemies" an institutional support.

Such is the gist of the theory that became the official Bolshevik doctrine. It is true that the Bolshevik Party in Lenin's day was not yet a totalitarian organization, and differences of opinion were not prohibited; even Lenin's views were debated, and his writings on the national question were a subject of controversy. Yet the Leninist position on the Jewish problem was never questioned at any time. From the very first, it found official acceptance and no one thought to criticize it. It remained unassailable after Lenin's death, having been sanctified by Stalin's article on "Marxism and the National Question" (1913).

Stalin on the Jewish Problem

Stalin's uninspired polemic, crudely echoing Lenin's views, harshly criticized the Bundist program of cultural autonomy for two reasons: first, because extra-territorial autonomy was "a refined species of nationalism," a "nationalism masked and unrecognizable behind its mask";[15] and secondly, because—an expression of Bundist "separatism" and "nationalism"—it was claiming autonomy for "a nation whose future is denied and whose present existence remains to be proven."[16] The almost literal following of Lenin's reasoning was striking. Indeed, Stalin's article contained scarcely a single original idea.[17] But it dotted the *i*'s and crossed the *t*'s in places where Lenin had chosen to be less explicit.

Stalin based his argument chiefly on quotations. He followed Lenin in offering an abstract definition of the concept nation as "a historically evolved, stable community of language, territory, economic life, and mental constitution expressed in a community of culture." Moreover, he insisted emphatically: "It is only when all these characteristics are present that we have a nation."[18] By definition, the Jews were excluded. Stalin did not fail to stress the point. "It is possible," he explained, "to imagine people who have a common 'national character,' but who nevertheless cannot be said to constitute a nation when they are economically disunited, inhabit different territories, speak different languages, etc. Such, for instance, are the Russian, Galician, American, Georgian, and Caucasian Mountain Jews, who do not, in our opinion, constitute a single nation."[19] And again more explicitly:

> These Jews undoubtedly take part in a common economic and political life with the Georgians, Daghestanians, Russians, and Americans . . . living with them in a common cultural atmosphere; this cannot but leave an imprint on their national character; if they have anything left in common, it is religion, common descent, and certain vestiges of a national character. All this is beyond question. But how then can it be seriously maintained that ossified religious rites and fading psychological residues have a greater influence on the "fate" of these Jews than the living socio-economic and cultural environment which surrounds them? But only when this assumption is made, is it possible to speak of Jews in general as a single nation."[20]

Not only were all Jews together not to be regarded as a single nation, but they lacked nationality in their separate groups as well. One of the reasons for this, to be sure, was the Jews' lack of a continuous territory of their own. This, however, failed to "express the whole truth":

> The point is, first of all, that the Jews have no large and stable stratum established on the soil, which would hold the nation together in a natural way, serving not only as its framework but also as a "national" market. Out of five or six million Russian Jews, only three to four percent are connected with agriculture in any way. The remaining 96 percent are engaged in commerce, industry, municipal service, and generally live in cities; moreover, scattered over Russia as they are, they do not constitute a majority in a single province.

Thus, interspersed as national minorities in areas inhabited by other nationalities, the Jews chiefly serve "foreign" nations as manufacturers and traders, and as members of the liberal professions, naturally adapting themselves to the "foreign nations" in respect to language, etc. All this, together with the increasing mobility of nationalities characteristic of higher forms of capitalism, leads to the assimilation of Jews. The destruction of the "Pale of Settlement" will merely serve to hasten assimilation.[21]

It was its socio-economic structure which deprived the Jewish group of a present and future as a nation, rendering assimilation inevitable. But the very absence of another way out evoked an antiassimilatory reaction on the part of the Jews and caused them to demand "a guarantee against assimilation," i.e., the protection of their minority rights and an autonomous status.[22] Autonomy, harmful in general, was particularly so when "foisted upon a 'nation' whose present and future are open to doubt," for its partisans were forced "to guard and preserve all specific traits of the 'nation,' not only the useful but also the harmful ones, just for the sake of 'salvaging' it."[23] Attempts to provide Jews with "guarantees against assimilation" must necessarily, Stalin insisted, disorganize and demoralize the labor movement,[24] and foster "national narrowmindedness and the spread of prejudice." With respect to such tendencies there could be no "middle course," "no reconciliation."[25]

Since the late 1920's when Stalin took over the leadership of the Communist Party, his version of the Leninist doctrine has been as mandatory for the Communist Party and the Soviet government as the original.

The Answer—Equality Before the Law and Cultural Assimilation

The Leninist answer to the Jewish question, then, as can be seen from the foregoing, consisted in the abrogation of all legal restrictions imposed upon the Jews in Russia, and in the establishment of the equality of all citizens before the law, regardless of nationality. Lenin advocated this program with untiring vigor and perseverance. The bill he drafted early in 1914 for "the repeal of all restrictions upon the rights of Jews, and in general of all restrictions based on a person's descent or nationality," was exemplary in its clarity. The principal clauses of the bill read:

The citizens of all the nationalities of Russia are equal before the law.

No citizen of Russia, regardless of his sex or religious faith, shall be restricted in his political or other rights by reason of his descent or nationality.

All statutes of any kind, all provisional regulations, annotative clauses, etc., which impose restrictions upon Jews in any sphere of social or public life, are herewith repealed. . . . All restrictions imposed on Jews as to their rights of residence and freedom of movement, educational rights, rights in governmental and public service, suffrage, military service, the right to acquire or lease real property in cities, rural communities, etc., are herewith repealed; all provisions restricting the entry of Jews into the liberal professions are herewith repealed. . . .[26]

Politically, Lenin conceived the solution of the Jewish problem as simply the annulment of all statutory and administrative restrictions; sociologically, assimilation was its solution. In those days a clear distinction was made between "assimilation" as an objective social and historical process, and an "assimilationist" policy aimed at furthering and accelerating this process. When the Bundist press indignantly accused him of being an "assimilationist," Lenin did not shrink from acknowledging it. In "Critical Notes on the National Problem," he declared:

> The issue of assimilationism . . . gives one an opportunity to show clearly what must be the outcome of the nationalistic vagaries of the Bundists and like-minded people. . . .
> Whoever does not espouse and defend the equal rights of nations and languages, and does not combat every kind of national oppression and discrimination, is neither a Marxist nor even a democrat. This is unquestionable. But it is equally unquestionable that the would-be Marxist who berates a Marxist of another nation on the ground of his "assimilationism" is in fact nothing but a *nationalistic petty bourgeois*. . . .
> "Assimilationism" can be cried down only by reactionary Jewish petty bourgeois who want to turn the wheel of history back and force it to run not from Russia and Galicia to Paris and New York, but the other way round.[27]

To oppose assimilation was petty-bourgeois reaction; actively to further it was to be in step with history. Since the development of capitalism was thought to be obliterating all national boundaries and distinctions, any kind of assimilation, except coercive, was cheerfully "welcomed."[28] This applied *a fortiori* to "the wretched and oppressed Jews of Russia and Galicia," who were not even a national group.

NOTES

1. This was the basic idea of the young Marx's famous and often misinterpreted article, "Zur Judenfrage." Marx's "antisemitism" was essentially a hostility to religion both in its institutionalized form and as a way of life or a system of thought.

2. Karl Kautsky, the most authoritative interpreter of Marxist doctrine among European socialists, and a scholar not only interested in the Jewish problem but also acquainted with the Jewish developments of his time, *viz.*, the rise of a Jewish popular culture and a Jewish labor movement in Eastern Europe, wrote as late as 1914: "It seems to me that Jewry's mode of life, the ghetto, is not of such a nature as to evoke nostalgic memories among the Jews themselves. And for the friends of human progress there is even less reason than for conservative Jews to shed tears over the death of Jewry. . . . The Jews are an appreciable revolutionary factor, whereas Jewry is a reactionary one. Jewry is a leaden weight which hampers the stride of those Jews who want to push on towards progress; it is one of the last remnants of the feudal Middle Ages, a social ghetto which still has a hold on the

mind after the tangible ghetto has disappeared. We are not entirely free of the ghetto so long as Jewry still exists in our midst. The sooner it disappears, the better for society and for the Jews themselves." Kautsky identified this nefarious "Jewry" as "those Jews who are united in a separate corporate body and segregated as such from the rest of mankind." ("Rasse und Judentum," in *Die Neue Zeit, Ergänzungshefte*, no. 20 [October 1914], pp. 93f. In the book version of the study [Stuttgart, 1921], the so-called 2d edition, of which the American edition [*Are the Jews a Race?*, New York, 1926] is a translation, the entire passage is missing.)

3. Otto Bauer, *Die Nationalitätenfrage und die Sozialdemokratie*, Vienna, 1907, p. 370.

4. For the genesis of Marx's sweeping condemnation of "the Jews," see Solomon F. Bloom, "Karl Marx and the Jews," in *Jewish Social Studies*, vol. IV, pp. 3–16.

5. For the historical role of the Bund, see Medem, *Fun Mayn Lebn;* the memorial volume *Vladimir Medem tsum Tsvantsikstn Yortsayt;* and Raphael Abramovitch, *In Tsvay Revolutsies. Di Geshikhte fun a Dor*, vol. I and II, New York, 1944. See also N. A. Bukhbinder, *Istoriya yevreiskogo rabochego dvizheniya v Rossii* [*History of the Jewish Labor Movement in Russia*], Leningrad, 1923, and Yephim H. Jeshurin, ed., *Vilne*, New York, 1935. A concise survey in English will be found in Raphael R. Abramovitch, "The Jewish Socialist Movement in Russia and Poland (1897–1919)," in *The Jewish People; Past and Present*, Central Yiddish Cultural Organization (CYCO), New York, 1948, vol. II, pp. 369–398.

6. The resolution adopted by the Fourth Convention of the Bund in 1901 said: "The convention holds that a state such as Russia, which is made up of a great number of nationalities, must be transformed in the future into a federation of nationalities with complete national autonomy for each, without consideration of the territory they inhabit.

"The convention holds that the concept 'nation' must also be applied to the Jewish people.

"Considering, however, that under the present circumstances the demand for national autonomy for Jews would be premature, the convention declares that it is only necessary meanwhile to fight against all discriminatory legislation directed against Jews, to make known and protest against all oppression of the Jewish nationality, taking care not to fan national passions, which would merely obfuscate the class-consciousness of the proletariat and lead to chauvinism." (Quoted from Vladimir Medem, "Natsionale Bavegung un Natsionale Sotsialistishe Partayen in Rusland" [1908], in *Vladimir Medem tsum . . .*, p. 249).

7. Resolution of the Sixth Convention of the Bund. (Medem, *op. cit.*, pp. 250 and 253f., nn. 13 and 14.)

8. Lenin, *Sochineniya*, vol. VI, pp. 83ff.

9. All quotations from Karl Kautsky, "Das Massaker von Kischineff und die Judenfrage," in *Die Neue Zeit*, vol. XXI, 2, pp. 304f. [June 3, 1903].

10. *Ibid.*, p. 306.

11. "Die Krisis in Osterreich," in *Die Neue Zeit*, vol. XXII, 2, pp. 39ff. [September 9, 1903].

12. "Kriticheskiye zametki po natsional'nomu voprosu" ["Critical Notes on the National Problem"], in *Sochineniya*, vol. XVII, p. 141. Emphasis Lenin's. The name of Vladimir M. Purishkevich, leading political exponent of extreme antisemitism in pre-revolutionary Russia, stands in Lenin's writings for government-promoted persecution and oppression of Jews as well as rabble-rousing antisemitic action.

13. *Ibid.*, pp. 138f. Emphasis Lenin's.

14. Occasionally attempts were made by Communist writers outside the Soviet Union—never, however, by authorized party interpreters of Leninist theory—to reinterpret Lenin's teachings on the Jewish problem. It has been said that Lenin refused to regard Jews as a nation but considered them a "nationality" entitled to full development as such (Otto Heller, *Der Untergang des Judentums*, Berlin and Vienna, 1931, pp. 204 and 208.) This was a gross falsification. Lenin used the terms nation

and nationality interchangeably, and here and there, obviously for brevity's sake, he spoke of a Jewish nation, Jewish nationality, a Jewish people. Yet he never failed to add that, properly speaking, Jews in modern times were not a national group at all. This attitude also was at all times maintained by the Communist Party. Even when individual Soviet dignitaries in the late 1920's discussed the possibility of Jewish national consolidation on Soviet soil, it was always stressed that the Jewish group was *not* as yet a national group.

15. *Marksizm* . . . , p. 25 (American ed., p. 33f.)

16. *Ibid.*, p. 27 (American ed., p. 36).

17. Lenin himself, who guided Stalin's pen (cf. Bertram D. Wolfe, *Three Who Made a Revolution*, New York, 1948, pp. 581ff.), did not like the result, as may be gathered from the following: Stalin's article appeared in the March–May issue of the St. Petersburg Bolshevik periodical *Prosveshcheniye* [*Enlightenment*]. It was followed by two lengthy articles by Lenin, which dealt with the same topic: "Critical Notes on the National Problem" (October–December 1913) and "Concerning the Right of Nations to Self-Determination" (February–May 1914). Stalin's piece was neither quoted from nor mentioned; Lenin, however, quoted in "Critical Notes . . ." the Russian translation of the 1899 program on nationalities of the Austrian Social Democratic Party, which had been included in Stalin's paper, and gave as his source *Prosveshcheniye*, citing issue and page, but neither the name of the author nor the title of the article. The absence of any desire on Lenin's part to be associated with Stalin's contribution was evident. This now has been "corrected" in the latest edition of Lenin's Works. The editors have added a footnote, which reads: "Lenin is referring to the article by J. V. Stalin, 'Marxism and the National Question,' where . . . etc." See Lenin, *Sochineniya*, 4th ed., vol. XX, 1948, p. 530.

18. *Op. cit.*, pp. 6f. (American ed., pp. 8f.).

19. *Ibid.*, pp. 6f. (American ed., p. 8).

20. *Ibid.*, p. 8 (American ed., p. 10).

21. *Ibid.*, p. 27 (American ed., p. 36).

22. *Ibid.*, p. 28 (American ed., p. 37).

23. *Ibid.*, p. 30 (American ed., p. 41).

24. *Ibid.*, p. 34 (American ed., p. 46).

25. *Ibid.*, p. 45 (American ed., pp. 6of.).

26. Lenin, "Zakonoproyekt ob otmene vsekh organichenii prav yevreyev i vsekh voobshche ogranichenii, svyazannykh s proiskhozhdeniyem ili prinadlezhnost'yu k kakoi by to ni bylo natsional'nosti," in *Sochineniya*, 2d ed., vol. XVII, p. 292. It was intended that Bolshevik members introduce the bill in the State Duma; it was never, however, introduced, probably because the Bolsheviks were among the twenty-four left-wing parliamentarians barred from attendance at fifteen consecutive Duma meetings.

27. "Critical Notes . . . ," in *Sochineniya*, vol. XVII, pp. 139ff. Emphasis Lenin's.

28. *Ibid.*, p. 144.

CHAPTER IV

Self-Determination and Self-Government in Soviet Practice

The Structure of the Soviet State

Bolshevik thinking, as we have seen, was strongly opposed to federalism, and to any form of true regional autonomy. But after its advent to power the Bolshevik Party faced the necessity of preserving the unity of the huge multinational country, among many of whose nationalities strong autonomist, not to speak of secessionist tendencies, were in evidence. The party's task, since largely realized, consisted in the setting-up of a form of government strictly centralized in fact, but making large concessions to federalism and autonomy in form.

The formal structure of the Soviet state merits attention. Under the terms of the constitution now in force, the Soviet Union is a federation of sixteen Union Republics. In each of these, one nationality constitutes the bulk of the population.[1] But in addition to an ethnically homogeneous majority, most Union Republics contain a multitude of national and ethnic minority groups, each of which in turn is entitled to demand an autonomous administration in the area where it comprises the majority of the population. There are three kinds of autonomous national units, in descending order of size: the Autonomous Socialist Soviet Republic; the National Autonomous Province (*oblast'*); and the National Area (*okrug*). An Autonomous Republic is considered a state; the executive branch of its government is the Council of Ministers, the legislative, the Supreme Soviet—as with the government of the Soviet Union and of the sixteen Union Republics. The Autonomous Province, on the other hand, is merely an administrative unit like any other province, and enjoys little more autonomy than the latter. National Areas have been set up only in remote, thinly peopled regions with a seminomadic population and a low cultural level; in practice, these "areas" are parts of the regular administrative divisions—the provinces or regions (*kraya*)—and are hardly autonomous in any sense.

There are at present in the Soviet Union sixteen Autonomous Republics, nine Autonomous Provinces (the Jewish Autonomous Province of Birobidzhan is one of these), and ten National Areas. Added to the sixteen Union Republics, these make fifty-one national units possessed of varying degrees of autonomy. All are separately represented in the Council of Nationalities, the so-called second chamber of the Supreme Soviet of the USSR, each of the Union Republics having 25 representatives, the Autonomous Republics 11, the Autonomous Provinces 5, and the National Areas one. In each of these divisions the language of the dominant nationality enjoys preferential status in administrative agencies, courts, and schools. In addition to the fifty-one units mentioned, some Union Republics also have organized a number of minor administrative subdivisions of districts (*raiony*) for individual, locally predominant minorities.

Such is the structure designed to combine the maximum efficiency of a centralized government with the federalistic requirements of a multinational state. These institutions constitute, in law, the political and administrative setting in which the nationalities of the Soviet Union live. In fact, however, effective control lies elsewhere, and the life and development of national minorities have been shaped by forces that conflict with the seemingly liberal, pluralistic character of Soviet government and law.

Self-Determination from Above

In its appeal to the workers, soldiers, and peasants announcing the seizure of power (November 7, 1917), the new Soviet government undertook to guarantee to all nations inhabiting Russia the unrestricted right of self-determination.[2] A week later, on November 15, the Council of People's Commissars promulgated a Declaration of the Rights of the Peoples of Russia, in which it solemnly promised that its "activity regarding Russia's nationalities" would be based on the following principles:

(1) The equality and sovereignty of the peoples of Russia.
(2) The right of the peoples of Russia to free self-determination, including the right to separate and form independent states.
(3) The abolition of all national and national-religious restrictions.
(4) The free development of national minorities and ethnic groups inhabiting the territory of Russia.

It was no accident that the Declaration failed to mention a federal union, for the Bolshevik leadership was still strongly opposed to any kind of federalism. But individual national groups were already insistently raising the question. The Ukrainians in particular championed federalism. As early as the summer of 1917 the Ukrainians had set up a provisional parliament of their own in Kiev, the Ukrainian Central Rada (Diet), which vigorously defended Ukrainian national rights against the Russian Provisional Government, and later against the Council of People's Commissars. In the fall of 1917 the Rada demanded the creation of a federated republic of Russian states, of which the Ukrainian republic would make one. The pertinacity of the Ukrainians made the Soviet government give way, though reluctantly, to the idea of a federal union. In an interview with Sergei Bakinskii on December 6, 1917, Stalin, then the People's Commissar for National Affairs, was asked pointblank about the Soviet government's attitude to the Central Rada's demand for a federal union. Stalin replied: "Should the will of the nation express itself in favor of a federal republic, the Council of People's Commissars could have no objection. Such is the right of every nation, and the government will respect it." Moreover, he emphasized, "The will of the nation is to be expressed through a direct referendum or through a national constituent assembly."[3] This, to be sure, was no bar to Stalin's insisting in the same interview that the Ukraine accept and establish the Soviet system: "All power to the Soviets, from the base to the top—this is the revolutionary commandment that we must not disobey, an axiom that we do not see how the Rada can contest."

In its dealings with the Ukrainians the Soviet government employed a strategy which it used on an international scale after the Second World War. The advance of the Red Army, reinforced by Russian-trained cadres of the "national" pro-Soviet armies to be levied in the future, was coordinated with the political activity of (often very small) Bolshevik groups. The Soviet leaders were not troubled by the number of Russian nationalists and chauvinists suddenly emerging as Bolsheviks in non-Russian areas destined for speedy Sovietization.[4] The "spontaneous" pro-Russian demonstrations of the local population obviously betrayed their inspiration. "It is not we, the lowly people, who strive for Little Russia's separation from Russia. . . . We affirm our allegiance as Russian subjects," Ukrainian peasants from one of the districts of the province of Kiev were supposed to have written. The very words—"Little Russia" for the Ukraine, and "subjects" for citizens—made known the identity of these "Ukrainians." In another letter the peasants of the province of Chernigov voiced their "protest against encroachments by the Ukrainian government," and declared their "desire to affiliate with Great Russia."[5] Such letters were conspicuously displayed as genuinely expressing the aspirations of the tillers of the soil in typically Ukrainian provinces. Under Moscow's direct guidance, a Soviet government was set up to overthrow the Rada and seize power in the Ukraine.

What was represented as self-determination in reality was but the carrying-out of directives issued in Moscow. How this was done is even plainer in the case of White Russia (Belorussiya) than of the Ukraine. While an independent White-Russian democratic republic was in the making, Moscow hastily produced a ready-made White-Russian Soviet republic of its own. The affair is frankly described in the most recent official textbook of Soviet law:

In December 1918, the Central Committee of the Russian Communist Party (Bolsheviks) decided to create the White-Russian Socialist Soviet Republic. On December 29, 1918, Comrade Stalin telegraphed the chairman of the Northwestern Regional Committee of the RCP(B) that White Russians on their way [from Moscow] to Smolensk had with them a manifesto on the formation of the White-Russian SSR, and that the Central Committee of the RCP(B), and Comrade Lenin personally requested that they be received as younger brothers who, though perhaps inexperienced, were willing to devote their lives to party and Soviet work.

The following day, the Sixth Northwestern Regional Conference of Bolsheviks began its proceedings; it constituted itself as the First Convention of the Communist Party (Bolsheviks) of White Russia, and voted to establish the White-Russian SSR. On January 1, 1919, White Russia's Provisional Workers' and Peasants' Government adopted a manifesto, edited by Comrade Stalin, on the establishment of the Soviet system in the new republic.[6]

According to Soviet legal theory, only a Soviet Congress was empowered to make such a decision. But the First White-Russian Soviet Congress, which of course confirmed the Bolshevik creation of the White-Russian SSR, did not meet until a month later, on February 2, 1919. By that time the legally non-existent White-Russian SSR already had been officially recognized (on January 31) by the Central Executive Committee of the Russian Socialist Federated Soviet Republic. The Communist Central Committee, we see, did not wait for the White-Russian Soviet Congress to exercise the White-Russian people's right of self-determination—it took it upon itself to exercise that right for them.

Constitutional Safeguards Abolished

The Declaration of the Rights of the Toiling and Exploited Peoples, promulgated by the Third Soviet Congress in January 1918 and subsequently made Part I of Soviet Russia's first constitution, said: "The Russian Soviet Republic is founded on a free union of free nations in the federation of Soviet national republics" (Sec. 2). Section 8 reserved to the "workers and peasants of every nation" the right "independently to decide, in their duly constituted regional Soviet Congresses," whether or not they wanted to remain part of the Russian federation, and if so, "on what conditions." In July 1918, the first constitution of the Russian Soviet Republic (not yet the Soviet Union) introduced an additional guarantee. Regions with "a particular way of life and national composition" were forthwith entitled to constitute themselves as "autonomous" national units (Sec. 11) within the Russian Republic. To the right of separation thus was added the right of "self-segregation" (*vydeleniye*).

The right of self-determination, including the right to secede, to this day is guaranteed by the Soviet Constitution, but its force has been considerably weakened. The right to secede had already been curtailed in the first constitution of the USSR (promulgated on July 6, 1923); only Union Republics could "freely disaffiliate from the Union" (Sec. 4), whereas nationalities not so organized could not. Nor was any such right specified in the constitutions of the individual Union Republics, drawn up after the promulgation of the USSR constitution of 1923. The "Stalin Constitution" now in force (promulgated on December 5, 1936), the second constitution of the USSR, is modeled upon the first as regards the right to secede (Sec. 15), though not without a characteristic modification. The Constitution of 1923 explicitly stated that "modification, restriction, or abrogation of Section 4," guaranteeing the right of "disaffiliation," required "the consent of all the republics of the USSR" (Sec. 6). The Constitution of 1936 did not retain this safeguard. It permits the right of secession to be nullified by constitutional amendment, that is, by a two-thirds vote of both chambers of the Supreme Soviet of the USSR.

The right of autonomy ("self-segregation") was likewise modified. The constitution of the Russian SFSR, the largest Union Republic, promulgated on May 11, 1925, reiterated the provision of 1918 guaranteeing the right of all nationalities to establish "autonomous socialist Soviet republics or provinces"; but this right was made contingent upon the approval of the All-Russian Central Executive Committee and the All-Russian Soviet Congress, the highest governmental bodies of the RSFSR (Sec. 17,b). The restrictive character of this provision was stressed by the People's Commissar for Justice of the RSFSR, Kurskii, when the All-Russian Central Executive Committee discussed the draft of the new constitution. The nationalities making part of the RSFSR, said Kurskii, were granted "the basic right to constitute themselves as autonomous republics by decision of their respective congresses, with one limitation, namely, that this must be sanctioned by the supreme bodies of the RSFSR, as is clearly implied by the sovereign power of the latter."[7] Similar provisions were embodied in the constitutions of Georgia and Azerbaidzhan, drafted at about the same time. The Ukrainian and White-Russian constitutions also limited the right of autonomy while the constitutions of the Armenian, Uzbek, and Turkmenian republics failed to mention it at all.[8] No mention was made of the right of nationalities to constitute themselves as autonomous republics or provinces in any of the constitutions of the Union Republics drawn up after the promulgation of the "Stalin Constitution" of 1936. The creation of new autonomous republics or provinces, as determined by the latter constitution, does not even fall within the jurisdiction of the Union Republics. The Soviet Union alone is competent in such matters; but even on the Union level such decisions must take the form of constitutional amendments, for the subdivisions of the Union Republics are all listed in the Constitution (Sec. 22–29).

Public opinion in the Soviet Union has scarcely heeded the progressive limitation and ultimate elimination of the statutory guarantees of self-determination; all such guarantees had not been taken very seriously. Several nationalities, indeed, seceded during the first years of Soviet rule. These states, however, gained their independence not by Soviet constitutional right, but by simply breaking away.[9] Within the Soviet Republic, and later the Soviet Union, freedom of national self-determination and secession, whatever the constitutional guarantees, did not in fact exist. The right of self-determination had never been more than a slogan, a tactical device, to help the party through the difficult first years of the revolution; it never has been implemented in practice.

The Rule of the Party

In consenting to the establishment of a federal union, the Communist Party would seem to have abandoned its traditional opposition to federalism. However, no change in the party's centralist policy was intended, nor did any such change take place. "The creation of a Soviet federation and the building of Soviet autonomy in no way implied the proclamation of the principle of decentralization, or abandonment of the intention to create a centralized proletarian state."[10] The federal organization of the Soviet state was merely a façade. At an early stage the Communist Party devised an efficient means to make the seemingly federal union into a strictly unitary and highly centralized state. From the very first, all government (Soviet) agencies were subordinated to the party, whose original centralized organization became even more so as the years went by.

How the Soviet state became a one-party state is too well known to warrant discussion here. But the absolute rule which the party's Central Committee exercises over all divisions and subdivisions of the party merits attention as showing the illusory nature of that "self-government" which Soviet nationalities are officially said to enjoy.

At the first public convention of the Communist Party of the Ukraine, held in Kharkov early in March 1919, the subordination of all branches of the party to the Central Committee in Moscow was unequivocally upheld by one of Moscow's most authoritative spokesmen, Yakov M. Sverdlov, chairman of the Central Executive Committee of the Russian Soviet Republic and member of the Central Committee of the Russian Communist Party. With ardor, Sverdlov stressed "the inseparability, the wholeness, the unity of our party in its entirety, regardless of how our old unitary Russia is going to be subdivided, regardless of whether, depending on this or that political or international situation, we shall have to divide what was Russia into separate republics—Latvia, Lithuania, White Russia, Estonia, the Ukraine." More specifically, he said:

> We shall remain the united Russian Communist Party, with various branches in this or that republic, yet one single party electing one single Central Committee for all Communist organizations.
>
> I do not doubt that the line carried out by the Central Committee of our party through the corresponding central organizations in different places is a common line for all of us. I do not doubt that your resolutions will underscore the fact that our Russian Communist Party, which in the course of many years forged homogeneous tactics, has succeeded in ruling everywhere, in all places, through the force of its unity, through its . . . organization and discipline. I believe that at the present moment our party will more than ever strengthen that unity which it always was so necessary for us to have.[11]

In less than a fortnight the same principle was proclaimed by the Eighth Party Convention, meeting in Moscow during the third week of March 1919:

> At the present time the Ukraine, Lithuania, Latvia, and White Russia exist as separate Soviet republics. Such at the moment is the solution of the problem of the form in which the State has to exist.
>
> This in no way implies that the Russian Communist Party in turn must organize itself as a federation of independent Communist parties.
>
> RESOLVED by the Eighth Convention of the Russian Communist Party: There must be *one* centralized Communist Party with a single Central Committte. . . . All decisions of the Russian Communist Party and of its directing agencies are unconditionally binding upon all divisions of the party, regardless of the divisions' national composition. The Central Committees of the Ukrainian, Latvian, and Lithuanian Communist Parties enjoy the legal status of regional committees of the party, and are wholly subordinate to the Central Committee of the Russian Communist Party.[12]

Thus even the Communist parties of the Ukraine, Latvia, and Lithuania, countries not even a part of the federated Soviet state at that time, were subjected to the control of the Central Committee in Moscow. Three months later federal ties were established between the RSFSR and the other Soviet republics. The party by-laws voted by the Eighth Party Conference in December 1919 once more emphasized that the Communist parties in the individual national republics were "wholly subordinate to the Central Committee of the Russian Communist Party." The party constitution was revised in 1922 and 1926, but the clause stipulating the national units' complete subjection to the Central Committee in Moscow (since 1926 the Central Committee of the Communist Party of the Soviet Union [CPSU]) was retained in all its rigor. The revision of 1926 introduced a still harsher innovation: the executive boards of the national Communist parties, the so-called presidiums or bureaus of their Central Committees, could no longer take office without the confirmation of the Central Committee of the CPSU. The party by-laws were seemingly liberalized in 1934 and 1936. But the revision did not restore any degree of independence to the national branches of the CPSU; the party's organizational policy stood unchanged. The changes merely indicated that the need no longer existed to have a written stipulation of Moscow's prerogative.

The Central Committee of the CPSU thus controlled the leadership of the national Communist parties, and through the latter it controlled the governments of the national republics.

NOTES

1. There is one exception—the Karelian-Finnish Republic, where the number of Russians (Great Russians) is slightly higher than that of Karelians and Finns.

2. Reprinted in Lenin, *Sochineniya*, vol. XXII, p. 11.

3. The interview was carried by both *Izvestiya* and *Pravda* on December 7 (November 24), 1917. It is not, however, included in vol. IV of Stalin, *Sochineniya*, which contains the author's utterances from November 1917 through 1920. Apparently it was considered unwise to recall such things as "national constituent assembly" and "direct referendum." The Russian collection of Stalin's writings on the national problem (*Marksizm i natsional'no-kolonial'nyi vopros*, Moscow, 1938) still mentioned the interview in n. 31 (p. 223). The major part of this note has been retained—as n. 30—in the later official American edition, *Marxism and the National and Colonial Question*, p. 296, but without any reference to the Bakinskii—Stalin interview.

4. The indulgence of Great-Russian anti-minority chauvinism was particularly flagrant in Turkestan. This was described in great detail by a leading Bolshevik, Grigorii I. Safarov (later a victim of Stalin's purges), in a revealing book, *Kolonial'naya revolyutsiya. Opyt Turkestana* [*Colonial Revolution. The Turkestan Experience*], Moscow, 1921.

5. S. I. Dunayevskaya, *Obyedinitel'noye dvizheniye za obrazovaniye SSSR* [*The Unification Movement for the Formation of the USSR*], Moscow, 1947, p. 37f.

6. A. I. Denisov, *Sovetskoye gosudarstvennoye pravo* [*Soviet Constitutional Law*], Moscow, 1947, p. 211.

7. *Izvestiya*, May 7, 1925.

8. The author had no access to the constitution of the Tadzhik Republic.

9. Most of the territories which seceded from the Russian state in the revolutionary period were later reincorporated in the Soviet Union; needless to say, this did not come about by their peoples' choice.

10. E. B. Genkina, *Obrazovaniye SSSR* [*The Formation of the USSR*], 2d ed., Moscow, 1947, p. 40.

11. Ya. M. Sverdlov, *Izbrannyye stat'yi i rechi, 1917–1919* [*Selected Articles and Speeches, 1917–1919*], Leningrad, 1939, pp. 162f.

12. *Vos'moi Syezd Rossiiskoi Kommunisticheskoi Partii, Moskva, 18–23 marta 1919 goda. Stenograficheskii otchet* [*Eighth Convention of the Russian Communist Party, Moscow, March 18–23, 1919. Stenographic Record of Proceedings*], Moscow, 1919, p. 367. Original emphasis.

CHAPTER V

The Awakening of the Non-Russian Nationalities

The revolution infused new life in the numerous non-Russian nationalities of old Russia. The Soviet government from the first realized that the satisfaction of their national aspirations was a prerequisite for the consolidation of its power. This, however, was scarcely possible without the establishment of real national self-government and Russia's transformation into a democratic and truly federal union. Nevertheless, the Communist Party embarked upon a series of cultural, and later also economic, reforms that met some of the demands of the non-Russian nationalities. The Declaration of the Rights of the Peoples of Russia made on November 15, 1917, proclaimed a purely negative goal: the abolition of all legal and other restrictions that had hampered the progress of the minority nationalities. More active measures were needed. The Tenth Convention of the Communist Party (March 1921) indicated a series of steps to ensure administrative adaptation to national differences: the inclusion of "native" representatives in the administration, the introduction of minority languages in administrative, judiciary, and educational practice, the fostering of local intelligentsia, etc.[1]

Economic Advance

With particular insistence the Communist leadership pointed out that the backwardness of many of Russia's peoples (particularly of the Turki peoples of Central Asia) was largely owing to an archaic, pre-capitalist, seminomadic economy, and that cultural improvements were contingent upon economic. The resolution on the national problem passed by the Tenth Party Convention advocated the "transition of the native toiling masses from backward economic forms to higher forms—from a nomadic life to agriculture, from guild handicrafts working for the open market to *artels* [producer cooperatives] working for the Soviet state (the semi-proletarian artisans to be drawn into trade unions), from artel handicraft production to factory production, from small-scale farming to the planned collective cultivation of the soil." It was recognized that "any mechanical transplantation to the eastern border regions of the economic measures of Central Russia, which are suitable only for a higher stage of economic development, must be rejected. Only by organizing the broad masses of

67

the native poor on the basis of their vital economic interests will the Soviets of the toilers succeed in arousing the peoples of the East to join, shoulder to shoulder, in the common struggle with the proletariat of the advanced countries."[2]

At the end of the 1920's, when the Five-Year Plans were inaugurated, the modernization of regions with a primitive economy, and the accelerated industrialization of remote areas with a predominantly non-Russian population, were proclaimed the primary objectives of the nationalities program. More, however, than the "national problem" was at stake here. The general trend towards intensified industrialization, the strategy of economic reconstruction, as well as military considerations dictating a shift of the industrial frontier from west to east—all these things played their part.

A number of national and ethnic groups, including some seminomadic and nomadic tribes completely ignorant of modern technology and factory labor, were thrust, almost at one stroke, into modern industrial conditions. The life of millions of people was on the way to being revolutionized. This called for tremendous exertions to raise their cultural level.

Cultural Awakening

Whatever its motives, the Communist Party encouraged and developed cultural activities and was successful in raising the cultural level of backward national groups. Minority languages were recognized and used in the local administration, courts, elementary schools, and secondary schools and universities wherever possible. The study of Russian, however, was required in all schools. The indigenous population was employed in governmental and public institutions, and strenuous efforts were exerted to draw it into the Communist Party and especially into the Communist Youth organization. Much was done to foster the development of native literature and art.

As a result, the minority languages of national republics with a cultural level approaching the Soviet Union's have become solidly established. In less developed regions, where the native personnel was insufficient to carry on all governmental business and the administration of justice in the native language, Russian remains the chief official language, wide scope being given to the native language. Such is the case, for example, in the Kazakh, Tadzhik, and Kirghiz Socialist Soviet Republics. The great number of schools giving instruction in the native language has resulted in a rapid increase of literacy.[3]

If the cultural progress of minority nationalities has, nevertheless, been retarded, it is not owing to interference from above. The shortage of trained and educated people in the ranks of the minorities has been the major obstacle. Judging from Soviet press reports, this lack apparently increased considerably during the war; there were many complaints about the scarcity of native teachers and the precarious condition of minority schools.[4]

In this connection it should be mentioned that prior to the Soviet reforms, many minorities not only had no educational institutions, but even lacked a written language or an adequate alphabet; in other cases, the traditional alphabet was so complicated that many years of study were required to learn to read and write and literacy was the monopoly of the upper class, generally of the clergy. During the last thirty years these peoples have been provided with a modern and simple alphabet.[5] A strong movement in favor of reforming the alphabet originated in Azerbaidzhan during its short-lived period of independence,[6] but the plans were not put into effect until 1924–25. By then, Azerbaidzhan was part of the Soviet Union, and the movement rapidly caught on among other nationalities.

The introduction of a modernized ("Latinized") alphabet for all "peoples of Arabic letters" was decreed by the Soviet Government in 1929 (after a similar reform had been carried out in Turkey). The alphabets of other peoples, too, were Latinized: the peoples of the Russian North (some of whom had no alphabet at all), the Kalmucks, Buryats, Caucasian Jews, Chinese, etc. The Soviet government, which pressed such reforms in order to undermine the influence of the native clergy, did not avoid all pitfalls. The Latin script was forced upon the Oirats and Shortsy (dwelling in the lower Altai ranges), who had previously used an alphabet akin to the Russian. Then, in the late 1930's, in an about-face, all Latinized alphabets were thoroughly de-Latinized. Now the new alphabets were based on Russian (Cyrillic) characters. Extravagant experiments of this kind, affecting the cultural life of millions, frequently provoked resentment. Still, the modernization of traditional alphabets has greatly encouraged the spread of literacy.

The last prewar decade saw further improvements. In many republics there was a notable development of the national theater. Scientific research forged ahead, and important scholarly institutions were founded, including national branches of the USSR Academy of Sciences and national academies of sciences.

Rise and Fall of Minority Leaderships

The progress made by national cultures was not an altogether painless one. It encountered grave difficulties and engendered farreaching internal contradictions and conflict. The growth of national consciousness, stimulated by literacy, education, and cultural advancement, encouraged new leaders to develop, who began to aspire towards national self-government and the establishment of democratic institutions—something the Soviet government would not permit.

Relations were particularly tense between the Soviet government and those nationalities which had experienced a national awakening already under the Tsarist regime. The Kremlin's drive against Ukrainian nationalism repeatedly shook the Ukrainian Communist Party. Ukrainian hostility to the Soviet government caused widespread disaffection during the recent war with Germany, and smolders to this day. Another center of unrest was Georgia, Stalin's native country, whose independence was destroyed by force in 1921. After its incorporation in the Soviet state, this restive land time and again rose in rebellion, and Moscow-directed purges were frequent. In the early years of Soviet rule, the government also repeatedly clashed with the larger peoples of Central Asia; but this unrest subsided later on. Relations have been more peaceful between the government in Moscow and smaller nationalities whose first experience of national life has been under Soviet patronage.

Most minority nationalities saw their national cultures flower during the tranquil period extending to the mid-1930's. The new political and intellectual leaders of the minority nationalities were intimately linked with the Communist Party, under whose tutelage they had developed. And yet they retained specific national features, and to a certain degree were imbued with the cultural and spiritual traditions of an earlier, pre-revolutionary intelligentsia, some of whose members they had absorbed. This was the climax of the development of the non-Russian nationalities of the Soviet Union. But the very success of this development invited the destruction of minorities' leaders.

In the mid-1930's the Communist Party underwent its gravest crisis. If the dictatorship was to be preserved in face of increasing social conflicts, political and administrative control had to be tightened. The social position of the ruling group, its traditions and ideology, and the natural tendencies of dictatorial rule, made it impossible to democratize the government gradually, or even to lift a little the party's omnipresent heavy hand. Nevertheless, there was a momentary vacillation in the party leadership, a faint and imperfect willingness to consider some degree of democratization as a way out of the difficulties besetting party and country. But this moment was shortlived and there followed the Great Purge. The triumph, in the late 1930's, of the totalitarian regime was consummated in the social and political exclusion, and in large part physical annihilation, of the overwhelming majority of those who had been more or less prominent in the early years of Soviet rule, and who stood for the revolution's larger aspirations and democratic promise. A new elite came to power that had been trained up under the dictatorship and was indifferent to the old heroic tradition. The replacement of the former leadership by new career officials is the true meaning of the notorious Moscow Trials.

The Great Purge struck the leaderships of the minority nationalities with particular fury. The national resurgence in which they had participated inevitably bred anticentralist and antitotalitarian tendencies among them. In the eyes of the totalitarian rulers, they were unreliable, subversive, a menace to the unity of the country. They were struck down remorselessly.[7]

One example will illustrate the extent of the ravages suffered by the minority leaderships. In 1935 preparations were made for drafting the new Soviet constitution. Under Stalin's chairmanship, a drafting committee of thirty was formed, on which were to serve the most outstanding and influential Communist leaders. Among these founding fathers of the new Soviet Constitution were ten eminent representatives of the minority nationalities. The Soviet Union then comprised seven Union Republics, and the chairmen of their Central Executive Committees were the joint "presidents" of the USSR as co-chairmen of its Central Executive Committee; while Mikhail I. Kalinin represented the Russian SFSR, six co-chairmen headed the governments of minority nationalities. Along with four representatives of smaller nationalities, these six were selected as spokesmen of the minorities on the drafting committee. The list thus read:

Petrovskii	Chairman, CEC, Ukraine
Chervyakov	Chairman, CEC, White Russia
Aitakov	Chairman, CEC, Turkmen SSR
Musabekov	Chairman, Transcaucasian Federation
Rakhimbayev	Chairman, CEC, Tadzhik SSR
Khodzhayev	Chairman, CEC, Uzbek SSR
Goloded,	Chairman, Council of People's Commissars, White Russia
Lyubchenko	Chairman, Council of People's Commissars, Ukraine
Ikramov	First Secretary, Central Committee Communist Party, Uzbekistan
Yerbanov	First Secretary, Communist Party, Buryat-Mongolia

On December 5, 1936, the day the Stalin Constitution was adopted, the ten were at the height of their glory. In 1937, all save Petrovskii, who disappeared from politics somewhat later, were branded "enemies" and "spies," and either "vanished," or were driven to suicide (Chervyakov, Goloded, Lyubchenko), or were shot. These were the most prominent non-Russians among the thousands of victims of the purge. With the extirpation of the old leadership, which had risen to prominence in the first two decades of Soviet rule and had been inspired with the emancipatory spirit of the revolution, a new leadership, raised up under the dictatorship and wholly subservient to the Politburo, was thrust upon the minority peoples.

Impact of the War

The effects of the purges' frustrating of the aspirations of minority nationalities were strongly felt during the Second World War. The Soviet press constantly repeated that the government's policy had borne fruit: all the peoples of the Soviet Union were one in their determination to repel the enemy. Yet this was only partly true. The multinational front betrayed appalling weak spots. None other than Stalin exposed the disaffection that prevailed among some national minorities when he ostentatiously praised the Russians as the best of all Soviet peoples. At a Kremlin banquet for Red Army commanders on May 24, 1945, this was the astonishing toast the Generalissimo proposed:

> I should like to propose a toast to the health of our Soviet people, and above all of our Russian people. I drink in particular to the health of the Russian people because it is the most outstanding of all the nations of the Soviet Union. . . . Our government committed more than a few mistakes, and we had some bad moments in 1941 and 1942. Another people might have told the government: "Get out, we'll put some other government in charge." . . . But the Russian people chose not to do so, for it believed in the adequacy of its government's policy, and it accepted sacrifices as necessary to help smash Germany. And this confidence on the part of the Russian people in the Soviet government proved to be the decisive force ensuring our historic victory over mankind's foe, fascism. Let us thank them, the Russian people, for this confidence![8]

This strong intimation of disloyalty among the non-Russian peoples was all the more ominous for its lack of specificity. It soon appeared that the government's mind was made up as to who were the major culprits. In June 1945 the Supreme Soviet of the Russian SFSR met for the first time after the outbreak of the war. A budget was submitted. In this budget are included appropriations for all the Autonomous Republics within the RSFSR; but now several of these republics were not listed. The absence of the Volga-German Autonomous SSR was no surprise, for the German population had been deported early in the war and the dissolution of the republic had been occasionally referred to. In addition, however, the Kalmuck and Chechen-Ingush republics were missing, while the binational republic of the Kabards and Balkars had apparently been dismembered, leaving only a rump Kabard republic to figure in the budget.[9]

No explanations were either asked for or given. The disappearance of several Autonomous Republics, whose existence is guaranteed by the Soviet Constitution, was never mentioned during the sessions of the Supreme Soviet. Not until a year later—June 1946—did the Supreme Soviet pass a law confirming the action of its Presidium (without mention of any dates or details) and dissolving the Chechen-Ingush Autonomous SSR and demoting the Crimean Autonomous SSR (still listed as such in the 1945 budget) to the rank of a province without autonomous status. The reasons for this were stated in a single paragraph:

> Many Chechen and Crimean Tatars, at the behest of German agents, joined volunteer detachments organized by the Germans that fought in cooperation with the German troops against Red Army formations; likewise, under German orders they organized diversionist bands to fight the Soviet government behind the lines, and the bulk of the population of the Chechen-Ingush and Crimean Autonomous Socialist Soviet Republics failed to oppose the actions of these traitors to the homeland.[10]

No mention was made, then or since, of the abolition of the Kalmuck Autonomous SSR; nor was anything said about the transformation of the Autonomous SSR of the Kabards and Balkars into the Kabardinian ASSR.

Stalin's pro-Russian toast has been followed in postwar years by campaigns against "cosmopolitanism," in which a certain tendency to disparage everything non-Russian is noticeable. This need not mean that the prewar program for the cultural and technological advancement of the least developed minority nationalities has been discarded. But the fact still remains that the cultural progress of minorities is bound to generate specifically national trends opposed to the totalitarian Soviet system. The antagonisms so nakedly revealed in 1937, which had such grave consequences during the war, are likely to appear again. No government policy on the national question, however well-considered, is likely to cause them to subside, for they spring, not so much from the clashing interests of the minority nationalities with the majority, but from the basic contradictions of the totalitarian system imposed on all the nationalities of the Soviet Union.

NOTES

1. Stalin, *Marksizm* . . . , p. 207f. (American ed., p. 275).
2. *Ibid*, pp. 208 f. (American ed., p. 276f.)
3. Detailed material on the legal status of minority languages during the first decade of Soviet rule may be found in V. N. Durdinevskii, *Ravnopraviye yazykov v sovetskom stroye* [*Legal Equality of Languages in the Soviet System*], Moscow, 1927.
4. See, *e.g.*, reports from the Tadzhik SSR in *Izvestiya*, October 6, 1944; from the Kirghiz SSR in *Pravda*, September 18, 1944; from the Mordvin Autonomous Republic in *Uchitel'skaya Gazeta* [*Teachers' Journal*], May 16, 1945.
5. Cf. "Latinizatsiya pis'mennosti" ["Latinization of Letters"] in *Bol'shaya Sovetskaya Entsiklopediya* [*Great Soviet Encyclopedia*], vol. 36, Moscow, 1938, pp. 88–90.
6. A. Kamchik-Bek, *Novyi Tyurkskii alfavit v Sovetskom Soyuze* [*The New Turki Alphabet in the Soviet Union*], Moscow and Baku, 1930, p. 12. The idea of modernizing the alphabet of Arabic letters dates back to the second half of the nineteenth century. Cf. N. Tyuryakulov, "K voprosu o latinizatsii tyurkskikh

alfavitov" ["Contribution to the Problem of Latinizing Turki Alphabets"], in *Novyi Vostok* [*New East*], 1925, no. 10–11, pp. 218–222.

7. For additional details on the annihilation of national leaderships, see Solomon M. Schwarz, in *Sotsialisticheskii Vestnik*, Paris, 1937, nos. 17–18 and 19.

8. *Izvestiya*, May 25, 1945.

9. *Ibid.*, June 10, 1945.

10. *Pravda*, June 28, 1946.

CHAPTER VI

Protection of Minority Rights

The Meaning of Equality

The extent of the autonomous powers to be granted by the central government to governments of territories with non-Russian majorities was a central issue with Bolshevik policy on the national question. Within the boundaries of such territories (Union or Autonomous Republics), the same problem arose with respect to groups other than the majority group of the territory in question who inhabited a continuous area suitable for the establishment of a separate autonomous administration (Moldavia in the Ukrainian SSR, Adzharistan and Abkhasia in the Georgian SSR, etc.). Moreover, a majority in one place may be a minority in another; even the Great-Russian majority of the USSR is a minority in all Union Republics save the Russian SFSR. The predominance of this or that group in an area called for statutory guarantees of the rights of other groups living within its territory. In all Union Republics, and in a number of national Autonomous Republics, autonomous provinces, and autonomous districts, majority nationals live side by side with minority; were the minority nationalities entitled to special schools, the use of their own language in public life, and public protection of their special cultural requirements?

In pre-revolutionary days the Bolsheviks had generously promised full equality to all minority nationalities. Every nationality was to possess all the rights and privileges of the majority nationality. In "Critical Notes on the National Problem," Lenin, for instance, considered this situation: a census of the elementary schools in St. Petersburg, taken on January 18, 1911, recorded a total of 48,076 students, of whom 396 were Jews, 2 Rumanians, 3 Armenians, 1 Georgian, etc. How was the equal status of the Jewish, Rumanian, Armenian, Georgian students to be enforced?

> If the state constitution included a basic law rendering invalid all measures that violate the rights of a minority, any citizen could demand the rescinding of a ruling that, for example, rejected the hiring at government expense of special teachers of the Jewish language, of Jewish history, etc., or that declined to provide public classrooms for the Jewish, Armenian, and Rumanian children, or even for the one Georgian child.[1]

Was it actually Lenin's idea to guarantee full equality to each and every member of a minority nationality in such a way that "a Georgian child" in St. Petersburg could insist on its being provided with a public classroom? This was stated explicitly in a bill "concerning the equal rights of nations and the protection of the rights of minority nationalities," drawn up by Lenin a few months earlier for submission to the State Duma. The bill's principal provisions were:

> All nations within the state shall enjoy equal rights without reservation; and special privileges of any kind for any nation or language shall be inadmissible and unconstitutional.
> Local institutions of self-government and autonomous diets shall determine in which languages the affairs of all governmental and public institutions of the respective localities or areas shall be conducted, and any minority belonging to another nationality shall be entitled to demand absolute safeguards for the rights of its language . . . such as the right to receive replies from governmental and public institutions in the language in which the request was made, and so forth. Acts of provincial, city, and other governments infringing upon the equal rights of the languages of minority nationalities, be it in the financial, administrative, judicial, or any other field, shall be invalid and shall be annulled upon the filing of an objection by any citizen of the land regardless of his place of residence.[2]

The bill expressly stipulated the right of every citizen to dispute, and demand the annulment of, any act of government considered to be in violation of the principle of equal rights. The bill encouraged endless administrative disputes and judicial litigation wherever the government refused to comply with such absurd demands as the provision of special classes "for one Georgian child," or the hiring of innumerable employees to answer inquiries and requests in dozens of languages. Lenin was certainly not so simple as to believe that his bill provided a practicable solution of minority problems. In a letter to Suren G. Shaumyan, leading Armenian Bolshevik, he plainly stated what he had had in mind when drafting the bill. With complete candor he declared that "in this way it would be possible to demonstrate, in popular terms, the foolishness of national-cultural autonomy, and to *kill* for good the advocates of this foolishness."[3] The problem, then, was not one of assuring equal treatment to all minority nationalities, but of ridiculing and "killing" the idea of autonomous institutions ministering to the minorities' cultural needs. The same bill explicitly denied the claims of minorities to autonomous representation as corporate bodies:

> Every self-governing unit of the state, whether rural or urban, shall elect school councils by universal, equal, and direct suffrage, on a proportional basis and by a secret ballot, which councils shall exclusively

and autonomously administer disbursements for all the cultural and educational needs of the population, subject only to supervision and guidance by municipal and provincial governments.[4]

What Lenin envisaged, he said in his letter to Shaumyan, was a "common school council" for the entire population of a given territorial unit (with proportional representation of the groups participating in the elections); there was to be no special corporate body for any one minority group. If necessary, minority schools would be granted separate premises, and there might be established special minority departments in public museums and libraries, even special minority theaters, etc. But all these institutions would be administered by "common councils," not by autonomous minority bodies. This conception was directed against any autonomist ambitions on the part of minority nationalities; it was no accident that these ideas were elaborated by Lenin in a fight against the autonomist aspirations of that most inveterate of minorities, the Jews.

Lenin's hostility to any kind of minority self-government was clearly expressed in December 1912 in his criticism of a statement, made by the Social Democratic group in the Duma, asking for "the establishment of institutions necessary for the free development of each and every nationality." This happened prior to the split in the Social Democratic group, which then included seven Menshevik and six Bolshevik deputies. The statement was read from the floor by Roman V. Malinovskii, the leader of the Bolshevik caucus and, as later transpired, an agent of the Tsarist police, who, "acting under instructions of the Director of the Police Department [in the Ministry of the Interior], Beletskii, omitted in reading a number of pages."[5] The passage dealing with the "establishment of institutions" was among those skipped; it was subsequently restored by another Social Democratic speaker, Akakii I. Chkhenkeli, a Menshevik, who did not fail to note that "this point was included in the statement of the Social Democratic group which Malinovskii has not succeeded in making public in full."[6] This association of the Bolsheviks with a demand for autonomous national institutions aroused Lenin's ire. He took his representatives in St. Petersburg, Malinovskii and Stalin, to task in a vituperative letter signed by his wife, Nadezhda K. Krupskaya, permanent secretary of the Bolshevik headquarters in exile:[7]

Today we received your news to the effect that the majority of the Cooperative [Social Democratic group] enthroned cultural-national autonomy again to please the Jewish nationalists and others in that gang. What is this—a deliberate affront to the Six [Bolshevik members of the Duma]? . . . This is a public shame. We do not know what the Six tried to do in this matter. But how one can silently submit to this, how No. 3 [Malinovskii] can agree to utter such disgusting filth in public (and thus assume responsibility), how the Six (or at least No. 3 alone) could neglect immediately to make a statement in *Den'* [*Pravda?*] saying that these [Menshevik] gentlemen scorn the [party] program and are working for a split—this we absolutely fail to understand. Because if we are to keep silent, the Jewish Marxists [i.e., the Bundists] will be riding astride us tomorrow. After all, there is a limit. And if these gentlemen think that the minority [8] is duty-bound to submit even when they tear the program to pieces, they are grossly mistaken. . . . Since they are ready for steps of this kind, we shall have to wage war. . . .[9]

Subsequently, a conference of the Bolshevik Central Committee in Kraków in January 1913 branded the Duma group's demand for "the establishment of institutions necessary for the free development of each and every nationality" a disguised endorsement of national-cultural autonomy, "a direct violation of the party program," and "a concession to nationalist leanings inadmissible in a proletarian party."[10]

For a number of years after the Bolsheviks took power, the issue of minority rights, in its general and theoretical form, was, strange to say, not even discussed. But in practice government agencies very early faced the problem and had to find makeshift solutions. The Declaration of the Rights of Peoples (November 15, 1917) did not even mention the language rights of minority nationalities.

The Soviet government's indecision in this matter in the early revolutionary years has been well described in an outstanding study by Vladimir N. Durdinevskii, a Soviet scholar of high reputation:

In evolving a new policy on languages Soviet legislation proceeded very cautiously during the first years, feeling out the ground, as it were. There is, characteristically, no mention of the language question in the first decree creating a politically autonomous national unit—the Tatar-Bashkir Republic—which was issued on March 22, 1918; nor is any such mention made in the enactments of the years 1919–1920 establishing the separate Bashkir and Tatar Republics, the Kirghiz Republic, the Chuvash, Mari, Kalmuck and Votyak provinces and the Karelian Labor Commune, although the People's Commissar for Nationalities [Stalin], in a statement on the establishment of local autonomy in April 1918, pointed out that it was necessary to provide guarantees for "the local language which is the native language of the laboring masses."

To the extent that the legislator touches upon the language question during this period . . . , he cleaves to vague formulae. . . .

By the end of 1921 and in 1922 the necessity arose to face the language question in a more determined manner.

On the one hand, the fight with nationalist bourgeois groupings and "Green" movements of different appellations in White Russia, the Ukraine, Fergana, and the Crimea had made the Soviet government realize at last how acute the national problem was and how important it was to have administrative staffs that were familiar with the local languages, were able to understand the Ukrainian, Crimean, or Fergana peasant, and would not strike him as strange and foreign.

On the other hand, the great famine in the Volga region drove huge masses of people into the cities, particularly women and orphaned children, who knew no other language but that of their native village and found themselves in dire straits when face to face with imported government employees who did not understand them.[11]

The first Soviet constitution, that of the Russian Socialist Federated Soviet Republic of July 10, 1918, declared that "any oppression of minority nationalities or restriction of their legal equality" was "in contradiction to the basic laws of the Republic"—it did not go beyond this negative statement. A lengthy resolution on "the immediate tasks of the party as regards the national question," adopted by the Tenth Convention of the Communist Party in 1921, for the first time raised the question of guarantees for national minorities; it said, in the most general terms:

Now that national privileges have been abolished, the equality of nationalities established, and the right of national minorities to free national development stands guaranteed by the very nature of the Soviet system, it is the duty of the party to help the laboring masses of such national groups to make the fullest possible use of this guaranteed right of free development.[12]

How little prepared, however, the Communist Party was at that time for an earnest consideration of minorities' problems is clearly shown by the casual nature of the list of nationalities mentioned in the resolution: "Letts, Estonians, Poles, Jews, and others"—all but the Jews tiny fractions of peoples the greatest part of whom lived outside the Soviet Union.

The Twelfth Convention in 1923 was more specific. It recommended special legislation providing for the use of minority languages "in all government agencies and in all institutions serving the local population of a different nationality and of national minorities."[13] No action, however, either legislative or administrative, was taken. Two drafts of a far-reaching statute on languages were prepared, but neither was enacted.[14]

Not until the mid-1920's did Soviet policy-makers adopt a broader and more concrete policy on the problem of minority rights. In a resolution passed by the Third Soviet Congress in 1925 after a report on Soviet construction by Mikhail I. Kalinin, it was said:

. . . the activity of the Soviets in the national republics and provinces must be developed still further to the end of fully securing the rights of minority nationalities everywhere; [the Congress] instructs the Central Executive Committee of the Soviets of the USSR to assure fully the carrying out of appropriate measures, such as: inclusion of representatives of minority nationalities in all elective Soviet organs; establishment of separate Soviets wherever minority nationalities exist in substantial numbers, the languages of these nationalities to be introduced into [official] use; establishment of schools and courts conducted in the native tongues, etc.[15]

Before voting on this resolution, the Congress heard Kalinin denounce the "inconsiderate treatment of minority nationalities" that he said was the rule in all republics of the Soviet Union, "from the RSFSR down to the smallest"; Kalinin urged the Congress to put an end to a situation that caused minority nationalities to feel like "stepdaughters."[16] The Congress also heard the following comment by Yurii M. Larin on Kalinin's report:

> It is about time that we took the second step in carrying out our policy on nationalities. The first step was the securing of the national rights of the toiling population of the peoples of Russia, through the establishment of national republics and provinces. The second step must be the complete carrying out, within these republics and provinces, of measures guaranteeing the absence of any national inequality, oppression, or depreciation. . . .[17]

Such equality depended to a large extent on the cultural advancement of the minority nationalities, and this in turn was determined by the degree to which their languages were recognized and admitted in education and in public life. The problem was complex; it "must not be simplified and reduced to one of merely transferring the administrative business of our national republics and provinces to the local language," remarked Avel S. Yenukidze in 1926, for many years secretary of the Central Executive Committee (first of the RSFSR, later of the USSR). "This might be considered as a solution if the population of our newly formed republics and provinces were uniform and made up of a homogeneous mass of inhabitants, if it had reached an adequate level of economic and cultural development, and if there were no USSR. . . . But the complexity of the problem is rooted precisely in the fact that in all our republics and provinces we find newly emerged minorities as well as newly organized national majorities. Furthermore, we find in them a Great-Russian population which prior to [the establishment of] the Soviet regime occupied a dominant position and which could not now be regarded simply as another minority nationality. Finally, there is a varying numerical relationship between the principal nationality and the minority nationalities both in the towns and in the countryside."[18]

It seemed impossible under the circumstances to single out a local language as the official one of a republic or province, and to forget about the rest. A compromise had to be found, but it was difficult, particularly in the non-Russian republics, to hit on one, precisely because of national differences between the populations of city and country.

The urban-rural cleavage was, and to some extent still is, particularly deep in the Ukraine and White Russia. There the urban population was chiefly Russian and Jewish, whereas their respective rural populations were made up almost entirely of Ukrainians and White-Russians; this complicated the problem much more than was the case in the Russian SFSR,[19] where the overwhelming majority of both the urban and the rural population was Russian. The small and backward minority nationalities of the RSFSR lived more or less isolated in separate areas, where there were very few Russians. Under Soviet rule they were granted autonomous status as national republics or provinces, and this largely solved the problem in the RSFSR.

In the Ukraine and White Russia, however, the principal minority nationalities, Russians and Jews, were ahead of the Ukrainian and White Russian majorities both economically and culturally. But since the Russians and Jews were concentrated in the cities, territorial autonomy was out of the question; no autonomous national republic or province, with one exception, was ever established in either the Ukrainian or the White Russian SSR.[20] Here, in these two republics, lay the real problem of minority rights.

Minority Languages in the Russian SFSR

Though the minority problem was not nearly so complicated in the Russian SFSR, a large number of statutes and regulations were enacted, especially as regards the use of languages in schools, courts and, notably, local administrative bodies. But these were chiefly for the protection of those nationalities which constituted the majority in individual autonomous republics and provinces. The minority problem proper, i.e., the protection of local minority groups, failed to attract particular attention, and effective safeguards were established only for the Russian minority in non-Russian areas. So far as the other minorities were concerned, even their right to schools conducted in their own languages frequently remained on paper; the Ukrainians and White Russians, who were sizable minorities in the RSFSR, had scarcely any schools with Ukrainian or White Russian as the language of instruction.[21]

In most instances, local minority groups had none but Russian schools to send their children to, or schools conducted in the language of the non-Russian local majority; the younger generation was increasingly "de-nationalized" by exposure to the language and culture of the local majorities. Lack of interest on the part of the local administration was not the only reason for this neglect of the educational needs of minorities. The ban on non-territorial national or communal institutions atomized the minorities and paralyzed their initiative. The administrative chiefs of the Soviet educational system of course realized that adequate schools for minority nationalities could not possibly be established without the active participation of minority representatives; but all they did was to appoint a number of such minority nationals, selected by the general party or Soviet organization, to the local staffs of the school administration.

Greater latitude was granted in those places, especially in the country, where minority nationalities were geographically more concentrated and constituted the majority of the population either of individual villages or townships, or of entire districts (*raiony*), the next higher administrative subdivision. In such cases, the village Soviet became a national village Soviet, or the entire district was made a "national" district, the locally predominant national group acquiring a preferential status, i.e., a semblance of local autonomy. A general reorganization of the local administration along these lines began in the mid-1920's and was completed in the early 1930's. National administrative units were first established in the non-Russian republics, particularly in the Ukraine, but their numbers also mounted in the Russian SFSR, especially in Siberia, with its small population and diversity of minor ethnic groups and seminomadic tribes, in the Volga region, the Crimea,[22] and in the Western and Leningrad[23] provinces. In 1931, out of a total of some 3,000 administrative districts in the Soviet Union, 242 were national districts; and of over 60,000 village (and township) Soviets, 5,266 were national Soviets.[24]

It is questionable to what extent such administrative units really assured minorities the enjoyment of their rights. Often, the transformation of an administrative unit changed nothing but the official designation; as late as 1928, an authoritative Soviet source stated that "a uniform concept of the national village Soviet has not yet crystallized." There was widespread confusion in practice as to what a national village Soviet was supposed to be: "Some call a national Soviet that village Soviet which has started conducting its affairs in the mother tongue, whereas others so designate any village Soviet in places where the predominant population is non-Russian."[25] The "nationalization" of the local administration apparently did not amount to much; but it did permit the local minorities, whenever there was a stirring of national endeavor, to adapt the local administrative bodies to certain of their cultural needs.

For minorities proper, the establishment of national administrative units on the local level offered no real advantages; these institutions were meant to represent the locally predominant nationality; a different arrangement would have clashed with the basic territorial principle of Soviet policy. As late as 1934 a Soviet authority on minority affairs complained that in the RSFSR "there is no unified law which would regulate the rights of minority nationalities."[26] Nor was any such law enacted in later years.

The Ukraine

Traditionally, in the Ukraine, Russian was the language of the cities and was used exclusively in the administration, schools, courts, etc. With the upsurge of Ukrainian national feeling during the revolution, the eventual Ukrainization of the government machinery, due respect being paid to minority rights,[27] came to be regarded as a matter of course. As early as July 1917, when the new Ukrainian regime was still in the process of formation, the Central Ukrainian Rada, the self-constituted provisional government, provided for the publication of all official enactments and regulations not only in Ukrainian, but also in Russian, Yiddish, and Polish.[28] Currency issued by the Rada was inscribed in these four languages.[29] The Ukrainian Soviet government that succeeded the Rada maintained the principle of Ukrainization combined with the protection of minority rights. In actual Soviet practice, however, majority and minority claims were not so easily reconciled.

The Ukrainian language only gradually took precedence over Russian. In the early period the Soviet Ukraine was officially bilingual. The first Ukrainian Soviet constitution (March 14, 1919) provided for a legend "in Russian and Ukrainian" on the republic's crest.[30] The Code of Criminal Procedure (September 13, 1922) prescribed court proceedings "in one of the two languages of the state (Ukrainian and Russian), or in the language of the majority of the population of the locality concerned."[31] An early act on "measures for the Ukrainization of educational and cultural institutions" (July 27, 1923) contemplated an extensive program for the Ukrainization of schools; it stipulated, however, that the teaching of Russian was to be mandatory in all Ukrainian schools. Non-Ukrainian schools, conducted in minority languages, were required to teach either Russian or Ukrainian, as the particular minority chose.[32]

The more general and systematic decree of August 1, 1923, "concerning measures to ensure the legal equality of languages and to foster the development of the Ukrainian language," aimed at promoting Ukrainization while protecting the rights of the minority nationalities. All officials were directed to use both Russian and Ukrainian in their dealings with the population. Ukrainian was proclaimed the language "having precedence in official intercourse"—"in accordance with the numerical predominance of the Ukrainian-speaking population"; but Russian, because of its "political and cultural importance" and "its widespread use in the Ukraine," was recognized officially as one of the two "most widespread languages." As for urban and rural localities where one of the minority nationalities was in the majority, the law required the authorities to use the language of the local majority, but also to protect the rights of other nationalities residing in the district.[33] This later was the legal basis for the establishment of "national" units of local administration.

Ukrainization and the diminution of the Russian influence in administration and education made swift progress in the mid-1920's. As de-Russification advanced, the favored position of Russian was somewhat modified; at the same time the Ukrainian leadership gradually grew less militant in its defense of the rights of other minorities. By 1927 the pre-eminence of Ukrainian was firmly established. New comprehensive regulations supplanting those of 1923 were promulgated on July 6, 1927, in an act "concerning guarantees for the legal equality of languages and the furtherance of the development of Ukrainian culture."[34] Russian was no longer considered, with Ukrainian, as the "most widespread language"; the act also dispensed with the required publication in both Ukrainian and Russian of laws and official announcements. While the clauses dealing with the protection of minority rights were retained, the establishment of national units of local administration was henceforth permitted only in rural communities; it was explicitly prohibited in "cities and urban-type communities." In Ukrainian schools, the teaching of Russian continued to be mandatory. In minority schools, the choice between Russian and Ukrainian as the second language was eliminated; instead, both languages were required to be taught, in addition to the students' native tongue, so that children in elementary school faced the difficult task of learning three languages.

Nevertheless, minorities in the Ukraine continued through the 1920's to enjoy broad legal rights in the fields of education, local government, and the administration of justice; and everyday practice largely conformed to the spirit of the law. An adverse trend, however, began to manifest itself in the early 1930's, gradually resulting in a noticeable weakening of the minorities' position, especially that of the Jews, who represented the biggest minority problem in the Ukrainian SSR—of which more hereafter.

White Russia

The first solution envisaged in White Russia for the problem of language was a very generous, pluralistic one. A decree of March 21, 1919 recognized five official languages: Lithuanian, Polish, Yiddish, Russian, and White Russian.[35] This, to be sure, was during the attempted creation of a Lithuanian-White Russian state; when the attempt failed and the White-Russian Soviet Republic was established, "the full legal equality of the languages (White Russian, Russian, Polish, and Yiddish) in relations with government agencies and in organizations and institutions of public education and socialist culture" was proclaimed in the White-

Russian Declaration of Independence of August 1, 1920.[36] The principle of equal rights for the four languages was reiterated in an act "concerning local languages" issued by the Central Executive Committee of the White-Russian SSR on February 4, 1921,[37] and in a number of later legislative acts and administrative orders.

A decree of July 15, 1924, "concerning practical measures to implement the policy on nationalities,"[38] summed up previous legislation and laid down general rules, as did the decree of August 1, 1923 for the Ukraine. In principle, equal rights were guaranteed to the four "languages of the nationalities inhabiting the territory of the White-Russian SSR," but in its more specific provisions there was a certain amount of discrimination. In view of the "considerable preponderance" of the White-Russian population, White Russian was given "precedence in relations between governmental, trade-union, and social institutions and organizations," while Russian was proclaimed "the language of communication between the organs of the White-Russian SSR and those of the USSR and other Union Republics." Only the "basic laws of the republic" were to be made public in four languages; for all other enactments and announcements, publication in White Russian and Russian became the general rule, publication in Yiddish and Polish being required only "if necessary." A knowledge of White Russian and Russian was required for the personnel of the administration, public services, trade unions, and all public organizations; both languages were required subjects in all schools: White Russian "as the language of the majority of the population," and Russian "as being generally current in the Soviet Union." Every citizen, whatever his nationality, was guaranteed "the right and the actual possibility of using his mother tongue in dealing with any kind of organ and institution of the republic"; every nationality was to have schools of its own (with mandatory teaching of White Russian and Russian), and every public agency or organization was required to have "the necessary number" of Yiddish- and Polish-speaking employees.

In White Russia, too, "national" Soviets were established in villages or townships inhabited by minority nationals. This, however, was done on a much more limited scale than in the Ukraine or even in the Russian SFSR. It was officially explained that White Russia's endeavor was centered "on adapting the *entire* governmental, cooperative, and social machinery to serving all the principal nationalities on an equal basis," rather than on organizing special "national" units.[39] This end was far from being reached. On the one hand, it took more time than had been anticipated to ensure White-Russian preponderance in administration, public life, and cultural pursuits; on the other hand, minority nationalities often did not enjoy in actual practice the extensive rights and privileges they had been promised on paper.[40]

The subsequent retrogression, however, did not affect minority rights in White Russia as early as it did in the Ukraine. The Constitution of the White-Russian SSR of April 11, 1927 still required the publication of "the most important legislative acts" in four languages, and still provided for a legend in the four languages on the crest of the republic.[41] A less favorable attitude towards minorities developed in the early 1930's. The establishment of national units within the local administration was halted, minority schools began to decline, and the new constitution of February 19, 1937—which is still in force—failed to mention several essential minority rights provided for in 1927. Where the constitution of 1927 proclaimed "the full equality of the White-Russian, Russian, Yiddish, and Polish languages," the present constitution says nothing, merely echoing the Stalin Constitution's general affirmation of the "equal rights of citizens regardless of nationality or race." Important legislative acts are no longer published in the four languages, and the crest of the republic now bears a legend only in White Russian and Russian.

After the promulgation of the constitution of 1937, Polish and Yiddish ceased in many essential particulars to enjoy "equal rights"; and in the atmosphere that prevailed after the Second World War, the status of minority groups could not but deteriorate. In White Russia as in other places, the tightening of dictatorial rule has stifled the democratic achievements of the early revolutionary period.

NOTES

1. In *Sochineniya*, vol. XVII, p. 153.

2. Lenin, "Proyekt zakona o ravnopravii natsii i o zashchite prav natsional'nykh men'shinstv," in *Sochineniya*, (4th ed. 1948), vol. XX, pp. 258ff. The bill was drafted by Lenin alone, although he originally had asked the Armenian Bolshevik Suren G. Shaumyan to take a hand in it (cf. n. 3 below). The text of the bill, not included in the first three editions of Lenin's works, was first printed in *Leninskii Sbornik* (*Lenin Collectanea*), vol. XXX (Moscow, 1937). Why the bill was not introduced in the State Duma has not so far been ascertained.

3. May 19, 1913, in *Sochineniya*, vol. XXIX, pp. 107f. Emphasis Lenin's.

4. Lenin, "Proyekt zakona . . ."

5. Cf. Lenin, *Sochineniya*, vol. XVI, Editors' Notes, pp. 720f.

6. *Ibid.*, p. 729.

7. Much of Lenin's party correspondence was handled by Krupskaya. The abusive tone of the letter points to Lenin's authorship rather than his wife's.

8. The six Bolsheviks were, as already noted, the minority in the 13-man Social Democratic group.

9. *Sochineniya*, vol. XVI, Editors' Notes, p. 730.

10. Lenin, *Sochineniya*, vol. XVI, p. 231.

11. *Ravnopraviye yazykov v sovetskom stroye* [*Legal Equality of Languages in the Soviet System*], Institute of Soviet Law, Moscow, 1927, pp. 55f.

12. J. V. Stalin, *Marksizm . . .*, p. 209. The American edition (p. 278) is not quite accurate.

13. *Ibid.*, p. 215. The American edition is incorrect. It has "*non-native* population" (p. 285) where the original speaks of the "*local* population of a *different* nationality," meaning *native non-Russians*.

14. Cf. Durdinevskii, *op. cit.*, pp. 59 and 237ff.

15. *Izvestiya*, May 24, 1925.

16. *Ibid.*, May 19, 1925.

17. *Ibid.* One year later Larin again brought the matter up in the second session of the third Central Executive Committee—see *Izvestiya*, April 17, 1926—and discussed in greater detail encroachments upon the rights of the Russian minority in the Ukraine.

18. A. S. Yenukidze, "K voprosu o natsional'nykh yazykakh" ["In Re National Languages"], in *Sovetskoye Stroitel'stvo*, monthly publication of the Central Executive Committee of the USSR, 1926, no. 1 (August), p. 39.

19. This, of course, refers to the Russian Union Republic within the USSR, which retained the original appellation of the Soviet state—RSFSR—when the latter was renamed the Union of Soviet Socialist Republics.

20. The exception was the Moldavian Autonomous SSR, which after the annexation of Bessarabia was merged with the latter into a separate Union Republic, and thus no longer is part of the Ukrainian SSR. No autonomous republics ever existed in White Russia, and neither the Ukraine nor White Russia ever had autonomous national provinces.

21. In the elementary schools of the RSFSR, the percentage of Ukrainian and White-Russian children attending schools with Ukrainian or White Russian, respectively, as the language of instruction was "catastrophically low," namely, 9.0 to 9.5 percent, according to a report submitted to the Collegium of the People's Commissariat for Education of the RSFRS by its Committee on Education for Minority Nationalities, on July 15, 1930. Cf. A. R. Rakhimbayev, ed., *Sostoyaniye i ocherednyye zadachi prosvetitel'noi raboty natsmen'shinstv v RSFSR* [*Present Conditions and Impending Tasks in the Education of Minority Nationalities in the RSFSR*], RSFSR People's Commissariat for Education, Moscow, 1930, p. 29.

22. When the reorganization of the administration was started in the Crimea, it had 143 national village Soviets; the reorganization was to be completed with the establishment of 522 such Soviets, thereof 200 Russian, 184 Tatar, 45 German, 8 Bulgarian, 7 Greek, 2 Estonian, 1 Jewish, 1 Czech, 1 Armenian, and 73 mixed. Subsequently, the number of Jewish national village Soviets in the Crimea increased considerably (cf. Chap. XI below). (Data from G. Volkov, "Natsional'nosti v sovetskom stroitel'stve Kryma" ["The Nationalities in Soviet Construction in the Crimea"], in *Vlast' Sovetov*, weekly publication of the Central Executive Committee of the Russian SFSR, 1927, no. 33–34, p. 10.)

23. After its administrative reorganization had been completed, the Leningrad province had 2 national (Finnish) districts and 118 national village Soviets. Of the latter, 67 were Finnish representing a population of about 75,000, i.e., some 65 percent of the total Finnish rural population of the province. Only one minority group fared better, with a complete representation of the rural population in a national administrative unit, *viz.*, the Norwegians: there was just one Norwegian village in the province, with 120 inhabitants. Of other rural minority groups, a smaller proportion lived in villages administered by corresponding national Soviets. There were 6 such Lopari villages (52 percent of the rural Lopari population), 2 German villages (28 percent of the rural German population), 5 Lett villages (16 percent), 8 Estonian villages (10 percent), etc. The percentage of minority nationals represented by national village Soviets varied considerably in accordance with the degree of local concentration of the minority population. See P. Yanson, "Sovetskoye stroitel'stvo sredi natsional'nykh men'shinstv Leningradskoi oblasti" ["Soviet Construction Among Minority Nationalities in the Leningrad Province"], in *Vlast' Sovetov*, 1929, no. 25, p. 20.

24. I. Trainin, "Sovetskaya federatsiya i natsional'nyi vopros" ("Soviet Federation and the National Problem"), in Ye. Pashukanis, ed., *Pyatnadtsat' let sovetskogo stroitel'stva* [*Fifteen Years of Soviet Construction*], Communist Academy, Institute of Soviet Construction and Law, Moscow, 1932, p. 80.

25. Ye. Mostovaya, "Natsmen'shinstva i ozhivleniye sovetov" ["Minority Nationalities and the Stimulation of Soviet Activity"], in *Vlast' Sovetov*, 1928, no. 7, p. 9.

26. Ya. Kantor, *Natsional'noye stroitel'stvo sredi yevreyev SSSR* [*National Construction among USSR Jews*], ed. by Z. Ostrovskii, *Vlast' Sovetov* publications of the Presidium of the Central Executive Committee of the Russian SFSR, Moscow, 1934, p. 28.

27. The Ukraine was the first country of the world to introduce extra-territorial cultural autonomy for minority nationalities.

28. See the text of the act in S. Dimanshtein, ed., *Revolyutsiya i natsional'nyi vopros. Dokumenty i materialy po istorii natsional'nogo voprosa v Rossii i SSSR v XX veke* [*Revolution and the National Problem. Documents and Materials on the History of the National Problem in Russia and the USSR in the Twentieth Century*], Communist Academy, Moscow, 1930, vol. III, pp. 174f.

29. N. Gergel, *Di Lage fun Idn in Rusland*, Warsaw, 1929, p. 185.

30. According to Durdinevskii, Russian was mentioned first in order to emphasize the absence of "Ukrainian chauvinism" on the part of the constitution-makers (*op. cit.*, p. 76).

31. The Code is included in the official collection of statutes and government regulations: *Sobraniye Uzakonenii i Rasporyazhenii Rabochego i Krest'yanskogo Pravitel'stva Ukrainskoi SSR*, 1922, no. 41, item 598.

32. *Ibid.*, 1923, no. 29, item 430.

33. *Ibid.*, item 435.

34. *Ibid.*, 1927, no. 34, item 157; reprinted also in Durdenevskii, *op. cit.*, pp. 145–154.

35. Durdinevskii, *op. cit.*, p. 76. As in the first Ukrainian constitution, the majority nationality's language was mentioned last.

36. The text of the Declaration is in *Praktischeskoye resheniye natsional'nogo voprosa v Belorusskoi SSR* [*The Practical Solution of the National Problem in the White-Russian SSR*], publications of the Central Executive Committee of the White-Russian SSR, Central Commission on Nationalities, Part I, Minsk, 1927, pp. 120ff.

37. *Ibid.*, pp. 128ff.

38. Official collection of statutes and ordinances: *Sobraniye Zakonov i Rasporyazhenii Raboche-Krest'yanskogo Pravitel'stva BSSR*, 1924, no. 11, item 108; also included in *Prakticheskoye resheniye . . .*, pp. 133–139, and Durdenevskii, *op. cit.*, pp. 163–168.

39. Kantor, *op. cit.*, p. 27.

40. The central authorities from time to time reprimanded the local administration for repeated violations of minority rights. Thus, a circular letter from White Russia's People's Commissariat for the Interior, dated June 9, 1926, stated that a number of provincial, district, and local authorities ("including district executive committees and village and township Soviets") were failing to carry out the government's policy. Certain discriminatory practices were cited, as for instance:

"(1) [These local authorities] do not accept, and if they do, fail to act upon, written applications made in Yiddish or Polish . . . and suggest that the applications be written in White Russian or Russian;

"(2) [They] fail to staff their organizations with people able to speak and write one or several of the languages which enjoy equal rights in the White-Russian SSR;

"(3) In the national Soviets [they] neglect to hold meetings, conferences, plenary sessions, etc., in the language of the respective nationality;

"(4) [They] fail to produce books and forms and to supply them to the national Soviets, and neglect to make provision for transferring the conduct of affairs in these Soviets to the language of the nationality concerned." (Reprinted in *Prakticheskoye resheniye . . .*, Part II, Minsk, 1928, pp. 127ff.)

According to Kantor, such official remonstrances were often repeated, and it can be assumed that certain improvements were effected (*op. cit.*, p. 32). But the mere fact that the local authorities had to be reminded of the existence of minority rights—in White Russia as in the Ukraine the chief minority affected was the Jewish—and that it was necessary to reprimand them time and again, indicate that administrative neglect of the constitutional rights of minority nationalities was a frequent occurrence.

41. See sections 23 and 24 of the White-Russian constitution of April 11, 1927 in Durdinevskii, *op. cit.*, p. 163.

CHAPTER VII

The Communist Party and the Jewish Masses
in the Revolutionary Period

1917: The Beginning of Jewish Autonomy

The revolution of March 1917, which laid the groundwork for a democratic Russian government, was a tremendous stimulus to the aspirations of minority nationalities rid at last of the ancient yoke of Tsarism. The heavier the oppression had been, the more stirring was the experience of freedom and the greater the eagerness to develop a culture and erect a democratic institutional framework in which the social and communal life of the different nationalities could grow. Among Russia's Jews, to whom the First World War had brought suffering unheard-of even in the Tsarist Empire (monster trials, charges of espionage leveled against the entire group, mass deportations, seizure of hostages, suppression of the press, etc.), the collapse of the old regime aroused radiant hopes. Constructive and creative energies were released that made 1917 a year of communal growth and intensive political and organizational activity.

In its first manifesto of March 15, 1917, the Provisional Government of the revolution proclaimed the elimination of all restrictions imposed upon the various "estates" and national and religious groups as one of its immediate objectives.[1] Soon after, on April 2, 1917, an act "concerning the repeal of all restrictions imposed on members of estates, religions, and nationalities" was promulgated. "Unalterably convinced that in a free country all citizens must be equal before the law, and that the conscience of the people cannot countenance any restrictions imposed upon individual citizens because of their religion or descent," the Provisional Government decreed that "all restrictions imposed upon the rights of Russian citizens by legislative acts now in force and based upon their adherence to a particular religious faith, religious sect, or nationality, are herewith repealed." A long list of restrictions thus abrogated and of statutes and individual clauses affected by the repeal was attached.[2]

The act of April 1917 merely got rid of the Tsarist obstacles in the way of the free development of Russia's nationalities. The Provisional Government at the time was reluctant to deal positively with the complex issues of the national question, thinking it best to leave such matters to the Constituent Assembly to be convened in the near future. A number of national groups, however, tried to go ahead on their own; some of their arrangements were temporary, pending a definitive constitutional decision, and some aimed at a *fait accompli* with which to confront the Constituent Assembly. The Provisional Government avoided announcing any thoroughgoing plan. Even in its last statement of policy in September 1917, it set forth its aims only in general terms:

> Recognition of the right of self-determination for all nationalities, under such conditions as shall be determined by the Constituent Assembly.
>
> Drafting and promulgation of laws that shall guarantee to national minorities in the places of their permanent establishment the free use of their native tongues in schools, courts, and organs of local self-government, and in their relations with the local organs of the [central] government.
>
> Establishment of a Council for National Affairs attached to the Provisional Government, in which all the nationalities of Russia shall be represented and which shall prepare materials on the national question for the Constituent Assembly.[3]

On the eve of the revolution, the official Jewish community, as we have seen, was hardly more than an auxiliary of the Tsarist bureaucracy. Whatever communal institutions—religious schools, hospitals, homes for the aged, etc.—had managed to survive were, as a rule, managed by more or less private groups; some were semilegal and existed on sufferance. The abolition of all legal restrictions by the revolution uncapped long pent-up energies and overnight Jewish communal life burgeoned astonishingly. The communal administration passed into the hands of elected officials; everywhere the Jewish communities began to organize themselves democratically.

The newly constituted communal authorities advanced by leaps and bounds in organizing Jewish welfare activities, establishing Jewish public schools, promoting adult education, etc. Preparations were made for an All-Russian Jewish Convention, which was to coordinate Jewish communal activities and to lay the foundation for a national organization of the Jewish minority within the future democratic state.

With the repeal of all legal restrictions binding all non-converted descendants of Jewish families to the Jewish community, participation in Jewish life became optional, and the community was freed from administrative and narrowly religious limitations. Since the government did not interfere with the activities of the new communities, they were in effect autonomous national-cultural bodies. With few exceptions, all Jewish opinion and political parties were agreed in endorsing extra-territorial national-cultural autonomy on the basis of optional affiliation, although there was some disagreement on the specific functions and legal limitations of the autonomous community. In the Ukraine, which was about to constitute itself as an autonomous division within the Russian republic, the national-cultural autonomy of the Jewish minority found early recognition in law, and only the events that soon engulfed the first Ukrainian government prevented the Jewish minority from reaping the benefits of its legally recognized autonomous status.[4]

The idea of national-cultural autonomy found increasing acceptance outside of the Jewish group as well, and was soon endorsed by all the principal political parties except the Bolsheviks. As early as May 1917, the principle was adopted by the Socialist-Revolutionary Party,[5] which won an overwhelming majority of the popular vote in the elections for the Constituent Assembly in November 1917; the Menshevik Social Democrats followed suit in August.[6] Autonomy was less favorably regarded by the middle-class parties; but after animated discussion the Constitutional Democrats (Cadets), most influential of the non-socialist parties, also endorsed national-cultural autonomy at their July convention.[7] The principle of extra-territorial autonomy would certainly have been upheld by the Constituent Assembly, had it had the opportunity to write a constitution. When the Assembly convened in January 1918, Viktor M. Chernov, the elected chairman, said: "The Jewish people, which has no continuous territory of its own, shall be entitled, equally with the other peoples, to fashion on the territory of the Russian Republic organs of national self-government, and to express in these the will of its active elements."[8] But the Constituent Assembly enjoyed only a few hours' existence and was forcibly dissolved by the Soviet dictatorship. The developments that had been taking place in the direction of Jewish national autonomy were stopped.

Communist Party without Influence among Russia's Jews

The Jewish political scene in 1917 was dominated by three main tendencies: (1) several middle-class groups, of a Zionist, non-Zionist, or orthodox character, more or less closely allied with the Russian Constitutional Democrats; (2) the Social Democratic (Menshevik) Bundists; and (3) a number of socialist-Zionist, socialist-territorialist, and kindred groups, which in general politics espoused a moderate Russian or Ukrainian socialism. Of the latter, only the Poale-Zion had any considerable number of sympathizers with the extremist revolutionary groups who after the Bolshevik seizure of power sided with the Soviet government. In addition, there were a few leaders of the pro-Soviet left wing of the Russian Socialist-Revolutionary Party who were active in Jewish affairs. The Bolshevik Party (called the Communist Party after March 1918) as such did not figure at all upon the Jewish scene, nor did it have among its leaders any men familiar with or active in Jewish life.

To be sure, a large number of Bolshevik leaders and active party members were of Jewish parentage; but they had been completely assimilated, had no ties with the Jewish masses, neither read nor wrote Yiddish, and in many cases understood scarcely a word of it. But the Bolsheviks, having become the rulers of a multinational state, were perforce obliged to find some way to bridge the gulf that separated them from the mass of Jewish working people.

A Commissariat for Jewish National Affairs was established in January 1918, as a special section of the People's Commissariat for National Affairs under Stalin. No Bolsheviks, however, were available to staff the Jewish Commissariat. The Jewish Commissar, Semen M. Dimanshtein, was indeed an old Bolshevik; but he had never been active in the Jewish field, and his sole qualification was his experience in the early Bolshevik campaigns against the "Jewish separatism" of the Bund. His chief lieutenant, Samuil Agurskii, a member of the Commissariat's Board, was a Bolshevik of recent vintage; in the years between the revolutions of 1905 and 1917 he was supposed to have been active in the Jewish labor movement in the United States, and had just returned from exile. The other leading officials of the Commissariat, recruited from the ranks of the Left Poale-Zion or the Russian Left Socialist-Revolutionary Party, were neither Bolsheviks nor experienced in Jewish affairs. The outlook for the Bolshevik invasion of "the Jewish street" was not propitious. In later years, Dimanshtein confessed:

> A handful of Jewish Communists, we had to wage a hard struggle for the Jewish working masses against parties heretofore exercising exclusive influence over them, having at their disposal complete teams of experienced party workers and an extensive press, and enjoying the benefits of a rich past, a "hallowed" national tradition. Yet our situation at that time was such that we had to place a comrade who did not understand a bit of Yiddish in the post of executive secretary of the Commissariat for Jewish National Affairs.[9]

It was virtually impossible to find an editorial staff for a Yiddish newspaper not even Communist but merely pro-Soviet in outlook. For the first time in the history of the Jewish socialist movement, Agurskii later related, enough money was available to start a daily paper, and still the plan did not work "because the Jewish socialist intelligentsia opposed the October Revolution, shunned participation in its activities, and sabotaged the efforts of those who were willing to be active." It took time and effort to recruit two editors, A. Shapiro, a well-known London anarchist, and A. Kantor, formerly secretary of the London Jewish Workmen's Fund and secretary of the London Board of Jewish Trade Unions,[10] both of whom had just returned from exile in England. Presently the plans for a newspaper were laid aside pending the establishment of the Jewish Commissariat, which it was thought would be in a better position to handle the matter.[11] But matters hardly improved with the establishment of the Commissariat. Dimanshtein bluntly said at the First Conference of Jewish Sections in October 1918:

> When we Jewish Communists working in the general party organi-
> zation saw how isolated the Jewish masses were from the Russian
> workers, when we saw that all the Jewish socialist parties held the
> Jewish workers back and prevented them from taking an active part
> in the proletarian revolution, we decided that something had to be
> done about it. But, I have to say this unequivocally, those who under-
> took this work were not familiar with the Jewish workers' life, and
> some could not even speak Yiddish.[12]

The Communist Party's apostles to the Jews had undertaken a task that required "the establishment of a Jewish press and the supplying of Communist literature to the Jewish masses." To quote Agurskii:

> The fulfilment of this task was beset with the greatest difficulties.
> Bolshevik literature in Yiddish that could have been reprinted immedi-
> ately, did not exist. . . . Among the few Jewish Communists who had
> gathered round the Jewish Commissariat, there was none who could
> have written [in Yiddish] a pamphlet for publication. Consequently,
> translations had to be made from the Russian. But even translators were
> hard to come by. Everybody had so much work to do that you did not
> know where to start. We had to look for Jewish writers willing to do
> the job for a substantial fee. But no money on earth could produce a
> Jewish writer willing to translate Bolshevik literature.[13]

When the Commissariat began to plan a Yiddish newspaper, it encoun-
tered the same difficulties that the Bolsheviks had encountered a few months earlier. "We had," says Dimanshtein, "to take on two exiles who just had returned from abroad, one of whom knew no Russian and the other no Yiddish; we handed them dictionaries and put them to work translating articles."[14] Even of the three members of the original editorial board of the paper, Dimanshtein, Torchinskii, and Bukhbinder, the two latter wrote no Yiddish.[15] The newspaper, called *Di Varhayt*,[16] nonethe-
less appeared on March 8, 1918, and irregularly thereafter.[17] Neither in content nor in presentation did it prove satisfactory.

The Communist leadership looked to the Commissariat to win the Jewish destitute over to Communism. According to Agurskii, "the first task confronting the Jewish Commissariat was to spread the ideas of the October Revolution among the Jewish masses and to combat the social-
patriotic and conciliatory elements at the head of the Bund and other Jewish petty-bourgeois 'socialist groupings.' "[18] To establish "the dictator-
ship of the proletariat in the Jewish street"[19] became the guiding idea of

Communist activity among Jews. The Bolsheviks did not think of the Jewish Commissariat as an agency with which to deal with specific social, economic, or cultural matters, but regarded it simply as a means for the Communist indoctrination of the Jewish masses.

The Jewish Commissariats and Sections

The Soviet government created two types of organization for Jewish affairs: the central and local (provincial) Jewish Commissariats [20] and the Jewish Sections. While the Commissariats were thought of as administrative agencies, the Sections were thought of as organizations in which to enlist the Jewish masses. In actual practice, this division of function was less clear-cut. Commissariats were often established locally where the lack of a following did not warrant setting up a Section; to prepare the ground for the setting-up of local Sections was one of the principal duties of the Commissariats. Where the launching of a Section was possible, the Commissariat was frequently dispensed with.

At first, huge difficulties stood in the way of all such plans, and the Communists were forced to compromise some of their most cherished principles. The plans of the Jewish Commissariat in 1918 spoke of the Jewish Sections as "national" divisions of the Soviets, as organs of government and administration. In its very first issue, *Di Varhayt*—in an article entitled "Our Program"—announced that "within the Soviets of Workers', Soldiers', and Peasants' Delegates everywhere, Jewish sections shall be organized, to join with the corresponding Soviet sections of other nationalities, thus forming local Soviets. . . ." There were also to be "provincial and all-Russian federations of [national] sections of the Soviets."[21] The notion that the Soviets should be composed of various national sections, obviously a slip on the part of the writer, was never mentioned again; but the plans of the Jewish Commissariat did call for the setting-up of Jewish Soviet sections and announced regional and national conferences of such bodies for the purpose of settling Jewish problems on the largest scale. A manifesto addressed by the Commissariat "To the Jewish Working Masses" said:

> Within the framework of the existing Soviets of Workers' and Peasants' Delegates, the Jewish workers in every city must establish a section of their own, which shall constitute the Soviet of Jewish Workers. Such Soviets shall function in all regions and shall hold regional conventions, where all issues relative to internal national life shall be decided.
>
> An All-Russian Congress of Jewish Soviets shall determine policy with respect to all issues concerning Jewish public life, and also shall designate the Commissar for Jewish National Affairs.[22]

This plan implied the establishment of extra-territorial organs for the administration of Jewish affairs, thus virtually subscribing to that principle of national-cultural autonomy which the Bolsheviks abhorred; the Jewish Commissariat itself was to become the executive agency of a nationwide Jewish Soviet Congress. The Commissariat in Moscow issued "instructions to agents going to the provinces and to the commissars of [its] local agencies" directing the latter—in June 1918—"to prepare for the convening of an All-Russian Congress of Jewish Soviets," adding that the Congress "shall elect the Central Jewish Commissariat," and that "regional conferences shall be called to decide upon more important issues and questions of principle affecting particular regions."[23]

Such departures from the traditional party line were, of course, short-lived. That they occurred at all was due to the pressure of events. Something had to be done without delay to overcome the reluctance and reservations of the Jewish masses; concessions were made in order to enlist the support of smaller non-Communist groups which, though cooperating with the Bolsheviks, still held to the idea of extra-territorial national autonomy. These—the Left Socialist-Revolutionary Party and a left Poale-Zion group—were represented on the Board of the Jewish Commissariat and had to be placated. This uneasy coalition did not last long. In July 1918 the Bolsheviks and the Left Socialist-Revolutionaries quarrelled hotly over general political matters, and the latter resigned from the Soviet government; Left Socialist-Revolutionaries in individual Commissariats and other government agencies either stepped or were forced out of their jobs. In the Jewish Commissariat the situation was no different; after the Left Socialist-Revolutionaries had been eliminated, the Bolsheviks sent the Poale-Zion member of the Commissariat's Board packing:

> Early in July 1918 the Jewish Commissariat got rid of its partners. The Left SR's were eliminated from the Commissariat, and from the government in general, because of their attempted uprising against the Soviet government on July 5, 1918. And the Poale-Zionists were eliminated—because the Poale-Zionist Rabinovich, a member of the Board of the Jewish Commissariat, took part as a delegate in the convention of Jewish communities [kehiles] that met in Moscow in July 1918. At this convention Rabinovich stated that the Poale-Zion participated in the work of the Commissariat in order to make it possible to prepare for a convention of communities. . . . Put differently, this means: the Poale-Zionists, according to Rabinovich, had joined the Jewish Commissariat to protect the interests of the clerical communities upon which the Jewish Commissariat had declared merciless war. This is why the Poale-Zionists were promptly removed from the Commissariat.
>
> After [this], the work at once took a different direction. Instead of non-party Jewish Workers' Soviets, Jewish Sections of the Communist Party began to be established at once.[24]

Thus ended all hope of autonomous or semi-autonomous Jewish institutions. The June manifesto of the Commissariat remained merely a historical document, for no Jewish sections were created within the Soviets.[25] Having abandoned without regret the notion of representative minority bodies functioning as part of the government, the Communist Party proceeded to organize its own Jewish Sections (*Yevsektsii*). The party saw to it that no "autonomistic" leanings developed in the Jewish "apparatus." At the First Conference of Jewish Sections and Jewish Commissariats in October 1918,[26] discussing the organization of Jewish Sections at the caucus of Communist delegates, Commissar Dimanshtein said:

> The general [organization of the] Russian Communist Party is not in a position to conduct its activities in different languages. Jewish Communist Sections have to be set up. The Sections will face a dual task: on the one hand, the purely technical assignment of propagandizing among Jewish workers; on the other hand, we must make the dictatorship of the proletariat prevail in the Jewish street. . . .
>
> Our main task is to carry out everything the Communist Party undertakes to do. We are not a separate party existing by itself; we are merely a part of the Communist Party, the part made up of Jewish workers.
>
> Since we are internationalists, we do not set ourselves any special national tasks, but only class tasks as proletarians. Since we speak our own language, we have to see to it that the Jewish masses have a chance to satisfy all their intellectual needs in that language. . . .
>
> As for organizational matters, our Jewish Communist Sections in every city must function inside the [party] organization under the common [city-wide party] committee, as do all other members of the Communist Party.[27]

Not only was there no provision made for representing the Jewish minority in public life and institutions outside the Communist Party, but even inside the party it was not intended that the Jewish Sections represent minority Jewish interests as distinguished from general party interests. Nor were the Sections to elect their own officers; Section officials were appointed by the party and were answerable solely to the general party in the persons of the local party officials (the city committee). The Commissar for Jewish Affairs deemed it necessary to point out that even the party's membership cards for the Jewish Sections were to be issued by the general party organization, rather than by the Sections.[28] In short, the Jewish Sections were not a national organization within the party, but appointed agencies for the more effective control by the party of the Jewish minority.

Destruction of the Jewish Parties

It took time, however, for the Communist leadership to make its organizational scheme effective. Following the collapse of the Central Powers in

October and November 1918, the German and Austrian armies evacuated the vast territories that they had occupied after the Treaty of Brest-Litovsk; the Ukraine and White Russia were virtually surrendered to Soviet sovereignty. The Jewish population under Soviet rule thus was tripled. This only added to the already formidable difficulties that the Communists encountered in their attempts to impose their organizations and control on the Jewish community.

But the withdrawal of German and Austrian troops caused the Russian Civil War, hitherto raging mainly in the Volga region and the northern provinces, to be extended to the entire south and southwest. Waves of pogroms swept the Ukraine in 1918–1920, following after every change in the fortunes of war.

In the first year of Soviet rule, the Jewish masses had been unmistakably anti-Soviet, for Communist interference threatened the newly acquired independence of the Jewish community. From late 1918 on, the outlook changed. Almost everywhere the victories of the anti-Soviet armies and guerrillas meant the death of Jews and the looting of Jewish property; nor was the news from across the Polish border encouraging. By contrast, where the rule of the Soviets had been established, anti-Jewish discrimination, persecution and violence disappeared. Communist antagonism to religion, the middle class, and Jewish autonomy paled beside the fact that Soviet rule had come to mean protection from Jew-baiting and pogroms.

Could anything, many asked themselves, be worse than the "White" and "Green" orgies of lawlessness and murder? A willingness to tolerate the Soviet regime as the lesser evil made itself increasingly felt in socialist and democratic groups, both Jewish and non-Jewish. This feeling weighed most heavily on the Jewish socialist parties, whose following was concentrated in the areas of the pogroms.

In this atmosphere the Communists were strongly tempted once more to seek a quasi-alliance with non-Bolshevik Jewish groups. This policy had failed in Russia proper in 1918, but a different climate prevailed in 1919–20 in the Jewish towns of the Ukraine and White Russia. The Communist Party used this opportunity to involve the Jewish socialist parties with their large followings in the task of Sovietizing the Jewish community; once a part of the Soviet system, it would be easy to absorb and liquidate them. Such in fact happened in 1919–1921. Jewish socialists, soon subjected to the heavy pressure of agitation for "unity," were gradually maneuvered into fusing with the Communists in the belief that a certain degree of autonomy would be preserved in Jewish affairs. Thus, in the Ukraine the majority of the Bund, renamed the Kombund, headed by Moses Rafes and Aleksandr Chemeriskii, and the majority of the United Jewish Socialist Workers Party (Socialist-Zionists and socialist territorialists and autonomists), renamed the United Jewish Communist Party, together formed a Communist League (Komfarband) as early as May 1919; in August 1919 the League was permitted to join the Communist Party of the Ukraine in a body. The liquidation of the organized socialist opposition was completed early in 1921, when even what remained of the Bund, led by Rakhmiel (Aaron Vainshtein) and Ester (Maria Ya. Frumkina), decided to dissolve; only a minority group of unreconstructed opponents of the dictatorship was left, who suffered imprisonment, exile, internment in concentration camps, and worse. The Communist Party had become the sole organized political force "in the Jewish street."

All this took skilful maneuvering on the part of the Communist Party. Time and again the party made concessions to the idea of Jewish autonomy, only to take them back when they had served their purpose. In White Russia, for example, a separate Jewish Communist Party was organized, in defiance of all Bolshevik tradition, in January 1919, by decision of the Central Bureau of the Communist Party of White Russia. Its functions were described in a statement issued by the Steering Committee of the new organization on January 27, 1919:

> In addition to the common political tasks that unite it with the Russian and world proletariat, the Jewish proletariat also has its special tasks in the Jewish street, which it can best fulfil when organized in a Jewish Communist Party of its own closely united with the Russian Communist Party. . . .
> Dictatorship of the Jewish proletariat in the Jewish street—this is our slogan. . . .
> Let us take into our hands all creative work in all spheres of Jewish national-cultural life, establishing, as we do so, special institutions formed on the basis of the Soviet constitution! Let us destroy the old, outmoded forms of national activity and create new ones in the spirit of the new world, a world which has arisen from the social revolution![29]

The Jewish Communist Party of White Russia, which so glowingly endorsed "special institutions" for the development of "Jewish national-cultural life"—evidence of contamination by "Kombundists" (Communist ex-Bundists) and other recent recruits from the ranks of the Jewish socialist parties—took less than two months to exhaust its usefulness. At its first and only convention in Minsk (February 28, 1919), the new Communists insisted on the preservation of an autonomous Jewish Communist organization, colliding head on with more orthodox members, mostly men from Russia proper, who insisted upon the introduction of the type of Jewish Section that had been established in the Russian provinces during the previous year. The Jewish Communist Party was dissolved and, as a compromise, set up as the Jewish Communist League (Komfarband) of

White Russia and Lithuania.[30] As in the Ukraine, the League served merely as a temporary vessel for containing the former socialists, for the members of the Komfarband of White Russia were soon herded into the Communist Party.

Yevsektsiya

The Second All-Russian Conference of Jewish Communist Sections in Moscow in May 1919 decreed the end of any separate Jewish organization: all Komfarbands were to be disbanded and their members transferred to the Jewish Sections.[31] The rapporteur on problems of organization, M. Al'skii, a member of the Sections' Central Board, said:

> The idea of creating a united Farband embracing all Jewish Sections, with their central boards attached to the central committees of the Communists of Lithuania, White Russia, the Ukraine, Latvia, and Great Russia, though it had a certain Bundist overtone, was in a way justified so long as separate party centers were maintained in these regions. But the existence of Jewish Farbands can no longer be justified in any way now that the Eighth Convention of the Russian Communist Party has authoritatively decided that it is essential to create a unitary, centralized Communist party with a single central committee, to which the central committees of Lithuania, White Russia, the Ukraine, and Latvia shall be entirely subordinate, retaining only the rights of regional organizations.[32]

Only regional units completely subordinated to a central command were to be permitted. But this alone was not enough to swallow up the Jewish mass organizations, which had grown up outside the realm of rigid Bolshevik discipline. The structure of the Jewish organization under the Communist Party was again discussed at the Third All-Russian Conference of Jewish Sections, in July 1920, and the following resolution was passed:

> The Conference firmly rejects the proposals, dictated by nationalist and separatist tendencies, to combine the Sections into an autonomous Jewish organization inside the party. . . . Like all other national sections within the party, the Jewish Section is merely a ramified technical apparatus of the party that carries out among the Jewish masses the party directives on all issues raised by the revolution. . . . Nor is the Jewish Section an autonomous organization with respect to issues arising out of the specific conditions of Jewish life; its job is confined to preparing and elaborating pertinent proposals and projects for submission through the appropriate party channels to the party as a whole.[33]

There was no further pretense that the Jewish Sections represented special Jewish interests. The Sections had only one function: to see to the execution of party orders, and this remained their function so long as the party leadership thought a special Jewish "apparatus" necessary. The point was made over and over again in official statements and documents. A few years later, the subsidiary role of the Sections was frankly described by Aleksandr Chemeriskii, leading official of the Sections' Central Board, an agency attached to the renowned "Agitprop," the propaganda department of the Communist Central Committee. Addressing a conference of Section delegates from White Russia on October 15, 1925, Chemeriskii said:

> What are the Sections? They are not a separate organization with a separate membership, as was once demanded by the Bund in urging that the party as a whole be set up as a federation of national organizations. Our Section is not an organization, but only an apparatus, part of the apparatus; it may change its form, its place, its jurisdiction, according to the operational necessities of any given moment. Whoever wants to work in a Section must be a party member or a candidate for membership, and must have been assigned by the party to work in the Section.
>
> Like every part of the party apparatus, the Sections are *directed* by the governing party bodies and are answerable to them alone. It goes without saying that in meetings and conferences called by the Sections, Jewish Communists may make decisions and nominate candidates for Section membership; but all this requires the approval of the competent leading party committee, which alone is responsible to party conferences or conventions and to the supreme party bodies for all activities in the Jewish as in any other field. The latter rule must be strongly emphasized: the party committee as a whole is responsible for Jewish work, regardless of what particular apparatus carries it out. . . .
>
> The Section cannot be regarded as monopolizing the Jewish field, as the sole representative of the Jewish masses, as demanded by the Bundist Torah. The party committee can also cause other apparatuses, in addition to the Jewish Section, to take up and solve Jewish issues; the committee does not have to agree to the Section's proposals; *it is not the Section but the committee that meets the masses face to face.* It is plain to everybody that only the committee . . . is in a position correctly to appraise the relative importance of the specific phenomena of Jewish life. Certainly, so far as Jewish work is concerned, the Section is the most sensitive apparatus, and therefore virtually all of this work is done *through* the Section, but this is not a *must* for the committee.[34]

It was the province of the Communist Party to decide the kind of "Jewish work" to be carried on and how and when, and no Jewish organization, Communist or non-Communist, might interfere. A Jewish "apparatus" had been necessary for the *Gleichschaltung* of all Jewish mass organizations. Once this objective was attained, the usefulness of the apparatus became questionable.

Downfall of the Jewish "Apparatus"

At first, as we have remarked, the functions of the local Jewish Commissariats often did not go beyond the setting-up of Jewish Sections. Later, after the Jewish communities had been abolished in 1919, the local Commissariats for a while managed the communities' secular affairs: health, education, social welfare, etc. But this contradicted Soviet policy, which permitted minority nationalities to handle their own affairs only on a territorial basis. By and by the administration of Jewish hospitals, schools, and welfare institutions was transferred to the competent local Soviet authorities, leaving the local Jewish Commissariats virtually without function.

Now Jewish affairs lost their urgency for the government, and the Jewish Commissariat was easily dispensed with. As early as 1920, in the reorganization of the People's Commissariat for National Affairs, the Jewish Commissariat was demoted to a Jewish Department in the People's Commissariat. After the liquidation of Jewish political parties had been completed in 1921, even this small department was superfluous; at the beginning of 1923 its staff was reduced to five, which by the end of the year shrank to a single official.[35]

Large minority nationalities now had their own Union Republics, Autonomous Republics, or Autonomous Provinces and their problems were no longer considered to have a Union-wide significance. The People's Commissariat for National Affairs (together with its Jewish Department) was dissolved in April 1924, its duties devolving upon the Department of Nationalities under the Presidium of the Central Executive Committee of the Russian SFSR [36]—a republic with a number of minority groups that only recently had been granted autonomous status, or that were not yet considered economically full-grown and capable of self-government. The Department of Nationalities had no special office for Jewish Affairs, and although the Fifth All-Russian Conference of Jewish Sections (April 1924) emphatically requested it, none was established.[37]

The Jewish minority was to be dealt with entirely as a local one, within the jurisdiction of provincial, district, and municipal Soviet authorities. One matter only was considered to transcend local boundaries and to require attention on an extra-territorial scale—the agricultural resettlement of large groups of Jewish "déclassé petty bourgeois" from areas of the old Jewish Pale. A central agency was established at the highest level: the Commission for the Rural Placement of Jewish Toilers (the KOMZET in Russian abbreviation, and the KOMERD in Yiddish), under Petr G. Smidovich, a non-Jewish old Bolshevik, and attached to the Presidium of the Soviet of Nationalities of the Central Executive Committee of the

Soviet Union. KOMZET, sponsored by Mikhail I. Kalinin, chairman of the CEC of the USSR,[38] was the Soviet government's last nationwide Jewish agency.

The Jewish Sections of the Communist Party outlived the Commissariats by several years. But after the triumph over the Jewish mass organizations, the consummation of which had been the final elimination of the Bund in 1921, the fanatical zeal of the Sections declined into bureaucratic routine. In Communist eyes, the Sections had lost their *raison d'être*. The Fourth All-Russian Conference of Jewish Sections in September 1921, in which erstwhile leaders of the Bund took part in their new capacity as Communist officials, marked the end of an era. Organized opposition "in the Jewish street" was now a thing of the past; the final liquidation of those Jewish institutions which had managed to preserve a semblance of independence was in full career. After 1921, all-Russian Conferences of Jewish Sections were held only in April 1924 and December 1926; thereafter they were discontinued for good. But even the moribund Jewish Sections were suspected by party leaders of perhaps developing into a sounding-board for "Jewish nationalism." In 1930 the Jewish Sections without further ado were ordered dissolved. The official explanation of this, in the *Great Soviet Encyclopedia*, reads: "In order to overcome once and for all the nationalist tendencies still observable in the activity of the Jewish Sections, the latter had been reorganized into a Jewish Bureau according to a decision of the Central Committee of the Communist Party of the Soviet Union. In January 1930, the Jewish Sections were liquidated at the center as well as locally."[39]

No political, administrative, or cultural organization representing the Jewish minority as a distinct national or ethnic group has existed in the Soviet Union since the dissolution of the Jewish Sections. Local administrative bodies, in districts with a predominantly Jewish population, at times gave the appearance of Jewish national units; and the Far Eastern settlement in Birobidzhan was granted the status of a Jewish autonomous province. But these "national" privileges were on a severely limited regional basis and were never enjoyed by more than a tiny minority of the Jewish population.

By destroying all Jewish political parties and independent organizations and by taking over all Jewish social institutions, the "apparatus" eliminated every articulate element of opposition within the Jewish community; thereafter it was easy for the Communist Party to do away with all organized Jewish communal life in general, and subsequently, casting aside a tool it no longer required, to destroy the "apparatus" itself. But a whole cluster of specific problems affecting the very existence of the Jewish population remained; and since the Jewish group was not permitted to solve them by organized efforts of its own, the Soviet government—perhaps to its own surprise—found itself charged with that onerous task.

NOTES

1. Cf. the official collection of the Provisional Government's enactments: *Sbornik ukazov i postanovlenii Vremennogo Pravitel'stva*, Issue I, March 12–May 18, 1917, Petrograd, p. 8.

2. *Ibid.*, pp. 46f.

3. S. Dimanshtein, ed., *Revolyutsiya i natsional'nyi vopros. Dokumenty i materialy po istorii natsional'nogo voprosa v Rossii i SSSR v XX veke* [*Revolution and the National Problem. Documents and Materials on the History of the National Problem in Russia and the USSR in the Twentieth Century*], Communist Academy, Moscow, 1930, vol. III, p. 56.

4. Regime followed regime in rapid succession until the final establishment of Soviet rule. The Ukrainian experience, though brief, merits attention. It was summarized by the then Minister for Jewish Affairs, Dr. Moisei Zilberfarb, *Dos Idishe Ministerium un di Idishe Avtonomie in Ukrayne*, Kiev, 1918, and in a later Soviet publication, *Di Idishe Avtonomie un der Natsionaler Sekretariat in Ukrayne. Materialn un Dokumentn*, Kiev, 1920. See also Oscar I. Janowsky, *The Jews and Minority Rights* (Studies in History, Economics and Public Law edited by the Faculty of Political Sciences, Columbia University, no. 384), New York, 1933, pp. 230–240.

5. The resolution on the national question adopted at its Third Convention said that "both nations without territory and national minorities in regions with a mixed population, in order to administer their cultural and national affairs, may unite into extra-territorial autonomous bodies based on optional affiliation. . . ." Cf. Dimanshtein, *op. cit.*, p. 89.

6. At its Eighth Convention the Mensheviks declared themselves for the protection of rights of minority nationalities "on the basis of the principle of national-cultural autonomy." *Ibid.*, p. 96.

7. The Ninth Convention of the Constitutional Democrats declared: "The government may delegate to nationalities constituted as non-territorial public bodies the fulfilment of certain tasks of cultural administration (cultural, religious, public assistance, economic, etc.), as determined by law and for all persons who declare themselves as belonging to such nationalities." *Ibid.*, p. 56.

8. *Uchreditel'noye Sobraniye. Stenograficheskii otchet* [*Constituent Assembly. Stenographic Transcript of Proceedings*], Petrograd, 1918, p. 13.

9. S. Dimanshtein, Preface to S. Agurskii, *Yevreiskii rabochii v kommunisticheskom dvizhenii (1917–1921 gg.)* [*The Jewish Worker in the Communist Movement 1917–1921*], Minsk, 1926, p. 6; quoted from the Russian rather than from the earlier Yiddish version (see following note), as it can be assumed that Dimanshtein's original contribution was in Russian.

10. S. Agurskii, *Der Idisher Arbeter in der Komunistisher Bavegung, 1917–1921*, Minsk, 1925, pp. 5f.

11. *Ibid.*, p. 6.

12. Quoted from S. Agurskii, ed., *Di Idishe Komisariatn un di Idishe Komunistishe Sektsiyes (Protokoln, Rezolutsiyes un Dokumentn, 1918–1921)*, Party History Department, Central Committee of the Communist Party of White Russia, Minsk, 1928, p. 32.

13. Agurskii, *Der Idisher Arbeter . . .*, p. 9.

14. Agurskii, ed., *Di Idishe Komisariatn . . .*, p. 6. The two translators soon left for Poland.

15. Agurskii, *Der Idisher Arbeter . . .*, p. 15.

16. The title echoed the Russian Communist *Pravda* [*Truth*]. Why *Varhayt* was chosen rather than *Emes*, later the title of the leading Yiddish-language Communist daily, is a matter of conjecture. Either the editors knew German better than Yiddish,

or they believed, as Communist "experts" every now and again insisted, that it was necessary to liberate Yiddish from the "reactionary" influence of Hebrew.

17. In five months a total of 12 issues were printed. See A. Kirzhnits, *Di Idishe Prese in Ratnfarband (1917–1927)*, White-Russian Book Chamber, Minsk, 1928, p. 13.

18. Agurskii, *Der Idisher Arbeter . . .* , p. 9.

19. *Ibid.*, p. 157.

20. The Central Jewish Commissariat was habitually called the Jewish Commissariat, whereas local Commissariats were sometimes referred to as "local agencies of the Jewish Commissariat."

21. *Di Varhayt*, March 8, 1918, quoted from Agurskii, *Der Idisher Arbeter . . .* , p. 14.

22. *Di Varhayt*, no. 8–9 (June 1918), quoted from Agurskii, *Yevreiskii Rabochii . . .* , p. 56. The Yiddish text of the manifesto, because of inept translating, is in part unintelligible.

23. The instructions were first printed in S. Agurskii, ed., *Di Oktyabr-Revolutsie in Vaysrusland*, Party History Department, Central Committee of the Communist Party of White Russia, Minsk, 1927, pp. 292ff. Agurskii, in his *Yevreiskii Rabochii . . .* , pp. 183ff., briefly lists the directives to the Jewish Commissariat's provincial agencies (without date), but does not print the matter quoted above. The earlier, Yiddish version of the book (see n. 10 *supra*) makes no mention of these matters at all.

24. Agurskii, *Der Idisher Arbeter . . .* , pp. 23f.; in the Russian edition, the removal of the Poale-Zionist member is described with less candor.

25. *Ibid.*, p. 23.

26. At the conference there were, in addition to delegates from Jewish Sections and Commissariats, persons active in Jewish cultural life, particularly teachers, who had been invited as individuals. Several meetings of the Communist caucus were officially held apart from the plenary sessions.

27. Agurskii, ed., *Di Idishe Komisariatn . . .* , pp. 21f.; *Der Idisher Arbeter . . .* , pp. 44f.

28. Agurskii, *Der Idisher Arbeter . . .* , p. 45.

29. *Ibid.*, pp. 155ff.

30. *Ibid.*, pp. 70ff.

31. *Bol'shaya Sovetskaya Entsiklopediya* [*Great Soviet Encyclopedia*], vol. 24 (1932), pp. 337f.

32. Agurskii, ed., *Di Idishe Komisariatn . . .* , p. 205; *Der Idisher Arbeter . . .* , p. 92.

33. *Di Idishe Komisariatn . . .* , p. 342; *Der Idisher Arbeter . . .* , pp. 98f.

34. Chemeriskii, *Di Alfarbandishe Komunistishe Partay (Bolshevikes) un di Idishe Masn*, Publications Shul un Bukh, Moscow, 1926, pp. 27f. Emphasis Chemeriskii's.

35. *A Yor Arbet fun der RKP in der Idisher Svive*, Central Board of Jewish Sections of the Russian Communist Party, Moscow, 1924, p. 61.

36. Act of the All-Russian Central Executive Committee and the Council of People's Commissars of the RSFSR, April 9, 1924, in *Sobraniye Uzakonenii i Rasporyazhenii Pravitel'stva RSFSR*, the official collection of statutes, 1924, no. 39.

37. *A Yor Arbet . . .* , p. 62.

38. Cf. Mikhail I. Kalinin and Petr G. Smidovich, *O zemel'nom ustroistve trudyashchikhsya yevreyev v SSR* [*On the Rural Placement of Toiling Jews in the USSR*], ed. KOMZET, Moscow, 1927. A supposedly non-governmental Association for the Rural Placement of Jewish Toilers—OZET (in Yiddish, GEZERD)—established at the same time, won, in the Soviet Union as well as abroad, the reputation of being a representative body entitled to speak for the USSR's Jews. Actually, OZET was government-controlled, and the majority of its executive board was made up of KOMZET members.

39. *Bol'shaya Sovetskaya Entsiklopediya*, vol. 24 (1932), p. 338.

CHAPTER VIII

Destruction of the Jewish Community

Regimentation of Social Work

When the Commissariat for Jewish National Affairs was established in January 1918, the Soviet government had neither inclination nor opportunity to ponder the meaning of the phrase, "Jewish national affairs," or to define the agency's functions with respect to the national aspirations of any Jewish collectivity. What urgently required attention was the anti-Bolshevik attitude of the Jewish population, which it was the Commissariat's task to rectify in one way or another. The Commissariat was a purely political creation and behaved as such from the very first. Samuil Agurskii, a member of the Commissariat's original Board, in later years described the first public meeting arranged by the Commissariat in Petrograd a few days after it had begun to function, at which Ilya G. Dobkovskii, Deputy Commissar for Jewish National Affairs, informed the Jewish public of its purpose and program:

> Leningrad's entire Jewish intelligentsia came to the meeting. It was opened by Dobkovskii. In his introductory address he said nothing of the tasks of the Jewish Commissariat, for neither he nor the rest of us knew yet what kind of work the Commissariat would have to do. Only one thing was clear to everybody: the Jewish masses had been lagging far behind the revolution, they had not grasped its meaning, and it was necessary to acquaint them with the idea of Soviet rule and to foster a friendly attitude in them to the revolution. This was more or less the gist of Dobkovskii's introductory address.[1]

The Deputy Commissar had conveyed exactly what the Commissariat wanted known about its position, and the tumultuous reaction of the audience troubled it not a whit. What the Commissariat thought, said, and did accorded perfectly with the official position of the Communist Party. The Communists, as Commissar Dimanshtein put it in October 1918, had only two tasks: the "technical" one of assuring a flow of party propaganda in Yiddish; and the political one of making "the dictatorship of the proletariat" prevail "in the Yiddish Street." "Special national tasks" simply did not exist for Jewish Communist "internationalists."[2]

But a Jewish community most certainly did exist, with an extensive network of hospitals, orphanages, homes for the aged, schools, kindergartens, libraries, and other educational, welfare, and religious institutions.

Revolutionary propaganda neither eliminated the need for such institutions nor provided the funds and administrative services to keep them functioning. What then did "dictatorship of the proletariat in the Jewish street" mean in the case of these indispensable communal functions? Were they to be abolished? Would the government provide the same services, perform the same functions, grant the same benefits to the community at large? Under the chaotic revolutionary circumstances of 1918, it was inevitable that the Jewish communal institutions should continue to function. The dictatorship of the proletariat by necessity was reduced to the more or less effective supervision of existing institutions by Jewish Sections and Commissariats.

This involved the Communist organizations in matters of a specifically national nature more or less in conflict with their anti-national political tasks and propaganda, for the Jewish communal institutions were of course tightly interwoven with the special conditions of Jewish life. Ideology clashed with practical requirements. As a consequence, the statements of policy and instructions issued by the Jewish Communist organizations abounded in contradictions and inconsistencies, and their implementation led to frequent conflicts among different governmental and party authorities. Their involvement with "Jewish national affairs" left its imprint on official pronouncements and influenced day-to-day decisions.

This was particularly noticeable during the early period of the Jewish Commissariat's operations, when non-Bolsheviks took part in the policy-making. The Jewish Commissariat's manifesto of June 1918, as we have seen, recommended the establishment of local Jewish Soviets "in every city," which would then unite into regional bodies and a nationwide federation; but it also outlined the communal functions to be undertaken by the Jewish Soviets or the Jewish sections of local Soviets. The entire program betrayed an unmistakable concern for Jewish national life and achievements. The manifesto said:

We, the Jewish working masses, now have an opportunity to shape our internal national life according to our own desires and interests. . . .

Our community, our schools, all our communal institutions, [now] serve every interest but that of the broad popular masses.

Many among the Jewish masses still trail along behind the bourgeois Zionists, who confuse the minds of the poverty-stricken strata of the people in the interest of an "all-Israel policy." Others among our Jewish workers still cling to the Bund, not realizing that the former workers' organizations of the Bund, because of their leaders' treachery, are now being turned into petty-bourgeois organizations that, together with the Russian bourgeoisie, wage a shameful struggle against all the achievements of the revolution, against full national and social emancipation. . . .

We call upon the Jewish workers to support with all their strength the Soviet system and its socialist and national achievements. . . .

The Jewish Commissariat's task is to rebuild Jewish national life on proletarian-socialist foundations. The Jewish masses now have full freedom to control all existing Jewish public institutions, to steer our public schools in a socialist direction, to open up the farming of socialized land to Jews, to settle the problems of the refugees, to see to it that the needy receive such social assistance from the government as they require, to combat antisemitism and pogroms, etc.[3]

Although still primarily concerned with combating Zionist, Bundist, and other non-Communist influences, the Commissariat in the nature of things was obliged to consider the concrete problems of the community; and in so doing, it occasionally sounded a suspiciously "national" note. The manifesto was soon followed by detailed instructions to representatives-at-large and provincial agencies of the Commissariat, in which the latter were expressly directed to "take under control all Jewish public institutions." All such institutions were to be registered with the Commissariat's provincial agencies; "their entire activity, including the financial administration of all [Jewish] institutions," was to be subjected to supervision by the Commissariats, which were asked to recommend institutions for subsidizing by the government. Impatient for results, yet fearful at the same time, the Commissariat demanded the near-impossible in a special "annotation" of the instructions: "Wherever possible, the Commissariats shall take under their administration individual institutions, without thereby disrupting the proper functioning of the work."[4]

The Commissariat's local agencies were in addition told to keep a watchful eye on the schools; to consider the question of providing social assistance "for the laboring masses and the needy"; to assume the administration of private hospitals and homes for the aged, reorganizing them into a kind of system of social security; to supervise the assistance given to refugees, to organize the fight against antisemitism and pogroms; and to arm members of pro-Soviet workers organizations. Finally, the Commissariat said of the democratically organized Jewish communities (*kehiles*): "One's attitude to the activities of the *kehiles* and their electoral system must be negative; without disrupting their activities or impairing the work, efforts must be made to reorganize them on the basis of the dictatorship of the workers and the poor."[5]

The Administrators' Dilemma

The elimination of all non-Communists from the Commissariat in July 1918 allowed it to take a sharper tone in its announcements and orders. But the concrete tasks of the Soviet Jewish organs remained basically the same. Indeed, so long as local Jewish Soviet organs were of mixed character and strongly influenced by the Left Poale-Zionists (the Left-Social-Revolutionaries played no role in Jewish provincial life), they were inclined to take their tasks seriously and not subordinate them completely to the task of "conquering" the Jewish working masses. For the Communists, however, the latter duty was a primary and basic one. Their social work "in the Jewish street" has thus the character of a maneuver, but a "maneuver" that drew the "maneuverers" themselves into positive constructive work. "Deviations" were inevitable and the Communist leadership took pains to rectify them.

The conflicting demands of Soviet politics and the daily necessities of Jewish life enmeshed the Communist administrators of Jewish affairs in a tangle of disputes and bureaucratic rivalries. This has been vividly described by Agurskii in the story of his experiences as a representative-at-large of the Jewish Commissariat in 1918–19. Agurskii was commissioned to survey the operations of local Jewish agencies and left Moscow on July 10, 1918, just after the expulsion of the non-Communist officials from the Commissariat. He first proceeded to Smolensk, where a local Jewish Commissariat had been established on the initiative of Left Poale-Zionists. By the time he reached Smolensk, the local Commissariat had ceased to exist. "The Poale-Zionists, instead of conducting matters in such a way as to make the first and foremost task of the Jewish Commissariat the rallying of the Jewish workers to the Soviet regime, had turned the Commissariat into a nationalist outfit which the Smolensk Soviet was forced to close." But Agurskii was eager to carry out the "constructive" policy of the Central Commissariat, and undertook to reconstitute and revive the defunct Smolensk office. It then developed that "there was no Jewish labor in Smolensk among whom one would have needed to work, and on whom such an agency must have been based"—so the Commissariat "was not raised from the dead."[6] This missing Jewish proletariat was a constant source of irritation to Jewish Communists.

From Smolensk Agurskii turned to Orsha, crowded at the time by Jewish refugees from areas still occupied by German and Austrian troops. In Orsha, too, Agurskii's efforts to create a Jewish Commissariat were frustrated. Nothing daunted, our Commissar betook himself to Vitebsk, a city of over 100,000 and with a sizable Jewish community, at that time the largest in non-occupied Soviet Russia.[7] In Vitebsk Agurskii assumed the position of provincial Commissar for Jewish Affairs and applied himself to carrying out some of the June instructions of the Central Commissariat.

In the course of Agurskii's work a state of war developed between the Jewish agency and the local Soviet authorities, which he later, in an understatement, termed a "very interesting dispute." The affair started late in 1918 as a by-product of the central authorities' efforts to "denationalize" the local administration by merging the special agencies of minority nationalities with the corresponding agencies of the general administration. By a decree of the People's Commissariat for Education, all activities hitherto directed by the educational departments of national minorities were transferred to agencies of the provincial and local Soviets. And so the Department of Education of the Jewish Commissariat in Vitebsk was supplanted by Jewish desks in the departments of education of the provincial and city Soviets. In the same way the Commissariat of Social Security assumed the functions of the corresponding offices of the local Jewish Commissariat. "The Jewish Commissariat was left as a mere agency for governmental supervision of special Jewish institutions."

The Jewish old-age homes thus became the object of the local Communists' solicitude:

> When the Vitebsk Commissariat of Social Security took over from the Jewish Commissariat the supervision of the homes for the aged and infirm, it introduced the same regulations as governed all such homes, and all were supplied with the same food. It so happened that the meat allotted to the Jewish institutions was almost exclusively pork. Of course, it is no great calamity for people to eat pork. But the old Jewish people not only stopped eating meat, they stopped eating altogether; they refused to eat non-ritual food and simply had to starve.
>
> The Jewish Commissariat brought this matter up, stressed the impropriety of experimenting with the aged in this way, and asked the Commissariat of Social Security to issue such meat to the elderly people as they could eat. But the Commissar [of Social Security], himself a Jewish comrade by the way and a former Zionist to boot, was adamant. So the old people simply died of starvation. The Jewish Commissariat protested the situation in the Vitebsk *Izvestiya*, in an article entitled "Social Security or Social Murder?" The article pointed out that this kind of thing was intolerable, but nothing was done.[8]

The Jewish Commissariat protested and protested, but the local Soviet people were inflexible; and so the matter rested until June 1919, when the Jewish Commissar succeeded in gaining the ear of Mikhail I. Kalinin, who happened to stop at Vitebsk during a campaign tour. Kalinin, famous among Soviet dignitaries for the often embarrassingly paternalistic interest he took in all things Jewish, studied the Vitebsk affair and subsequently sent a special representative to the city to investigate. The result was a victory for the Jewish Commissariat. On June 17, 1919 the Vitebsk Committee of the Communist Party was ordered by higher party authorities "to prosecute the former chief of the Provincial Department of Social Security before the party tribunal, for having permitted elderly people to be starved and subjected to medieval treatment, and for thus having undermined the confidence of the masses in the Communist principle of social security," and to have all his assistants tried before the Revolutionary Tribunal.[9]

This affair is an example of the imbroglios that Communist intervention in the actual administration of the Jewish community produced. The Communist officialdom of Jewish departments, because of its compromising with national or even religious tendencies, was looked askance at by other sections of the Communist bureaucracy. But in the long run there was only one way to prevent this kind of "nationalist deviation," and that was to break up the Jewish communities and to "socialize" their institutions.

Dissolution of the Jewish Communities

Communist hostility to the Jewish community was based on two things: a political rejection of its "formal democracy," and a denial of Jewish claims to national self-government. Yet the Jewish community was not destroyed at one stroke. Though the reorganization of Jewish communities was already envisaged in the Jewish Commissariat's instructions of June 1918, it took care to warn against any "disrupting" or "impairing" of communal activities. These instructions, however, were not made public.[10] In a short time the attitude of the officials of the Jewish Sections hardened, and the First Conference of Jewish Commissariats and Jewish Sections, which met in October 1918, demanded in no uncertain terms that the Jewish communities be abolished. The resolution adopted by the Conference said:

> The First Conference of Jewish Commissariats and Jewish Sections declares that there is no longer a place in our life for the various institutions which thus far have been running things in the Jewish street, or for a Jewish community elected on the basis of the famous "four-tail" ballot [universal, equal, and direct suffrage, and the secret ballot].
>
> At a time of perilous struggle, there can be no compromise of any kind with the bourgeoisie; all such agencies and institutions injure the interests of the broad Jewish working masses by lulling them with sugary songs about alleged democratic principles.
>
> Made strong by the victory of the proletariat and the October revolution, the Jewish worker takes power into his own hands, proclaiming the dictatorship of the proletariat in the Jewish street and calling upon all Jewish workers to rally round the Jewish Commissariat to safeguard this dictatorship.
>
> The First All-Russian Conference of Jewish Commissariats and Jewish Sections empowers the Board of the Central Commissariat for Jewish Affairs to take such steps as are necessary to liquidate all bourgeois institutions in a systematic fashion.[11]

The decree abolishing the Jewish communities was not drafted by the Jewish Commissariat until April 1919, and its promulgation was delayed for another two months. The Commissariat procrastinated for a simple reason—it simply did not possess the qualified personnel to administer communal institutions. Where technical difficulties were less formidable, the local Jewish Sections and Commissariats had begun to dissolve communal organizations long before the decree's promulgation; instances of the complete dissolution of Jewish communities were reported as early as the end of 1918.[12] The Central Commissariat's decree was held back pending the Second All-Russian Conference of Jewish Sections and Jewish Commissariats; only after the latter had approved it in June 1919 was it finally promulgated as follows:

The Central Commissariat for Jewish National Affairs, having examined the activities of the Jewish communities and their Central Board, finds:

(1) That the Jewish communities and their Central Board serve as rallying points for undisguised enemies of the interests of the working class and the achievements of the October Revolution;

(2) That the said communities and the said Board pursue an injurious policy directed at dimming the class-consciousness of the Jewish working masses;

(3) That the communities, in the performance of governmental functions in such spheres as culture, education, and social security, trained up the growing Jewish generation in an anti-proletarian spirit.

Therefore be it resolved by the Central Commissariat for Jewish National Affairs:

That the Central Board of Jewish Communities and all Jewish Communities and their branches located on the territory of the Russian Socialist Federated Soviet Republic shall be dissolved forever;

That such funds and property as exist shall be transferred to the local Jewish Commissariats;

That the present enactment shall take effect at the time of its publication in one of the official organs of the Soviet government.[13]

Following the promulgation of the act, all Jewish communities were suppressed without further ado, and all their assets, facilities, and institutions passed into the hands of the government. Their rights to the use of real estate and buildings, which had become public property, were voided. The Jewish community, since the collapse of its Tsarist-controlled predecessor, had administered religious institutions and their property; this property also went to the state. Religious observance was permitted, but disapproved of. A very complicated situation resulted from all this, with important consequences for the Soviet Jewish life of the future.

Religious and Communal Life

All pre-Soviet churches had been suppressed by Soviet legislation, but any group of 50 citizens or more could constitute itself a private religious association and was authorized to levy contributions from its membership. The Soviet government subjected the lawfully established religious associations to various types of close surveillance and persecution: (1) Religious associations were required to register with the authorities and to submit their lists of members and officials. (2) Premises for worship or for any kind of religious activity had to be leased from municipal housing departments. (3) All priests, ministers, and rabbis and all persons professionally engaged in religious functions (which in the interpretation of some local authorities also meant the *shokhet* [ritual slaughterer]) were deprived of the vote and of all political rights,[14] and their children incurred all the occupational and educational disabilities borne by persons of "non-labor descent." (4) Religious instruction, and especially the instruction of children under 18 years of age, was—and still is—punishable by law. (5) Since all religious activity was suspect, any persons so engaged were especially liable to prosecution for "counterrevolutionary" or "anti-Soviet" acts or leanings.

Schools such as the kheder or yeshivah became illegal and were driven into hiding, although for a number of years there were no public schools to take their place,[15] especially in the *shtetl*, where these had been the only schools available to the overwhelming majority of Jewish children. To be an open "servant of religion" in any capacity meant one's virtual exclusion from non-religious employment; either religious functions had to be performed underground so as not to make persons holding religious office or performing religious functions ineligible for other employment, or else all such persons had to be supported by the congregation. But it was just that section of the Jewish community which practised its religion whose economic lot was the wretchedest. There were two related reasons for this: orthodoxy lived on mainly in that ghetto-like sector of the Jewish community doomed to economic annihilation; and strict adherence to rabbinical law made life extremely difficult in a modern industrial society.

Understandably, under these circumstances the memberships of congregations declined.[16] Clandestine religious observance, worship, and instruction persisted only among those groups living on the margins of Soviet society. But these margins progressively shrank after the 1920's and largely disappeared on the eve of the Second World War.[17]

A number of organizations not directly a part of the community continued to exist: ORT, OZE, the Jewish Colonization Association, the Society for Promoting Education among Jews, etc. But they were no longer free associations based on the voluntary and active participation of their members. Only the institutional machinery was preserved, to be operated under government orders, even though former executives of the old organizations quite often were retained as members of the new boards and directorates approved by the Soviet authorities.

This was particularly the case with organizations well known abroad or affiliated internationally, and therefore in a position to enlist financial and technical aid from foreign Jewish communities.[18] For a considerable period of time, the Soviet government strongly supported skeleton organizations able to bring foreign Jewish capital into the Soviet Union, and in a number of instances representatives of Jewish organizations abroad were permitted to serve on staffs functioning in the Soviet Union. In the mid-1920's, when the Soviet government approved plans for the agricultural resettlement of Jews, special committees were established to assist the government and to enlist foreign financial support. These, too, included "representatives of the Jewish public," i.e., non-Communist officials of the old Jewish organizations. All, of course, had been hand-picked by the government and enjoyed not a semblance of independence.

The democratic Jewish community was destroyed in 1919–20 and nothing of it has since been revived, not even during the Second World War, in spite of all the publicity that Soviet propaganda gave to the "antifascist" committee created after the commencement of Nazi-Soviet hostilities. The committee was simply another government-appointed and government-directed propaganda agency to enlist foreign Jewish assistance.[19]

NOTES

1. S. Agurskii, *Der Idisher Arbeter . . .* , p. 7.
2. S. Agurskii, ed., *Di Idishe Komisariatn . . .* , pp. 21f.
3. Agurskii, *Der Idisher Arbeter . . .* , pp. 21f.
4. S. Agurskii, ed., *Di Oktyabr-Revolutsie in Vaysrusland*, pp. 292ff.
5. *Ibid.*, p. 294.
6. *Ibid.*
7. Vitebsk at that time had close to 60,000 Jewish inhabitants, of whom 9,000 were workers, according to Agurskii, *Der Idisher Arbeter . . .* , p. 34
8. Agurskii, ed., *Di Oktyabr-Revolutsie in Vaysrusland*, pp. 306f.
9. *Ibid.*
10. Cf. Chap. VII above, n. 23.
11. Agurskii, *Der Idisher Arbeter . . .* , pp. 48f.
12. *Ibid.*, p. 89.
13. *Izvestiya*, June 19, 1919.
14. Such restrictions remained in force until the promulgation of the Stalin Constitution in 1936.
15. In the first decade of Soviet rule the number of public schools was utterly insufficient, and compulsory primary education was not introduced until 1930–31.
16. Statistics on the number and membership of registered religious associations are not as a rule released for publication by Soviet authorities. On September 1, 1926, at a time when organized Jewish activities were less hampered by the administration and a number of international Jewish organizations were operating in the Soviet Union, and when substantial contributions from the United States supported communal religious activities, a total of 1,003 Jewish congregations was recorded in the Ukraine, with a membership of 137,437, or roughly 8 percent of the Jewish population, that is, perhaps 12 or 13 percent of all Jewish adults. Cf. *Alfarbandishe Baratung fun di Idishe Sektsies fun der A1KP/B (Dekabr 1926)*, publications Shul un Bukh, Moscow, 1927, p. 79.

17. The Jewish Communists' fanatical hatred of "clericalism" may have led them to overstate the number and influence of the clandestine centers of religious instruction, and particularly of the Hassidim, who were exposed, pilloried, and denounced to the police in *Emes* and other Yiddish-language newspapers, especially in the late 1930's. Underground groups of orthodox Jews apparently existed in various places at the close of the Second World War, according to testimony of Polish and Soviet Jews who left the Soviet Union in 1944-45 and later. (Cf. the recorded interviews on file in the Library of Jewish Information, American Jewish Committee.) Jewish cooperatives of small producers seem to have served as screens for tiny religious congregations.

18. It was originally intended that the Jewish Colonization Association (JCA— in Russian YEKO) discontinue its activities in Russia. But then it was granted permission to resume work in 1923, under a supervisory board made up of three government members and two leading people of the Association.

19. See Chap. XIV below.

CHAPTER IX

A "National" Policy for Jews?

A Jewish Way to Socialism

To the extent that the Jewish minority ceased to exist as an organized group, the responsibility for the fate of the Jewish population devolved upon the Communist Party, and, more specifically, upon its Jewish Sections. This responsibility was considerable. War and revolution had destroyed the economic basis of the existence of most Jews under Soviet rule. The ghetto economy was disintegrating. The government took the wholesale and retail trade more and more into its own hands. A general scarcity of raw materials, as well as administrative and inflationary pressures, gradually squeezed out the small manufacturing and repair businesses in which the bulk of the Jewish artisans were engaged. Innumerable tradesmen, middlemen, and semiskilled workers joined the army of starving *luftmenshn*.

The economic impasse of the Jewish minority may not have seemed so patent so long as economic conditions in general were chaotic. And later, in the early 1920's, the New Economic Policy (NEP) provided a breathing spell. The peasant economy was revived; market controls of consumer goods were relaxed; private persons could trade between city and country; and even a measure of urban industry was given over to private enterprise. In the years of the NEP, the program of the Jewish Sections was a relatively simple one. They sponsored the organization of Jewish artisans into producers' cooperatives, the establishment of credit facilities, the transfer of the dispossessed and needy to farm colonies, and the placement of Jewish youths in industry. A certain "non-assimilationist" aura was given things by the establishment of Yiddish-language public schools and the official use of Yiddish in the administration of districts with a large Jewish population.

But as the Soviet government succeeded in reviving the Russian economy and in extending the scope of the "socialized sector," the "Jewish problem" grew more acute. The NEP period came to an end in the late 1920's. Planning, accelerated industrialization, and government operation of the entire economic process, were made the immediate objectives of Soviet policy. This threatened the very existence of the non-integrated and non-assimilated majority of the Jewish population.

And on the other hand it was unlikely that the "productivization" of millions of Jews could be accomplished overnight by turning them into industrial workers.

The Jewish masses were concentrated in specific regions, lacked industrial skills, and were untrained, culturally and otherwise, for work in heavy industry. Language barriers, differences in customs, and the Utopian attempt to shorten the process of acculturation into a few months resulted in a marked increase of anti-Jewish feeling. There was obviously a special Jewish problem, not to be solved by the advance of "socialist construction"; it called for a special solution and a specifically Jewish program over the years.

The actual masters of the Jewish community, the Jewish Sections, found themselves in a difficult position. Orthodox Bolshevism neither envisaged nor countenanced a special, "national way [for Jews] to Socialism," a way different from that of other Soviet peoples. No Jewish program existed. But something like one kept sporadically emerging. As early as October 1918 Commissar Dimanshtein declared at the First All-Russian Conference of Jewish Commissariats and Jewish Sections:

> Under Tsarist rule the Jewish masses were crowded together in the ghetto and barred from tilling the soil, so that they were forced to become traders. This has begotten a class of people among us who have a bourgeois mentality, but a proletarian pocketbook.
>
> The economic changes now taking place in our midst cause these traders to lose their livelihood. Many of them now dangle in thin air, developing anti-Soviet attitudes as a result. We have to reckon with this fact. We must take such steps as will enable these people to become useful citizens and serve our socialist Soviet Republic. We must organize Jewish farm labor communes and call Jewish farmers into existence; we must build a Palestine in Moscow. We must wipe out the bourgeois mentality of these people who have a proletarian pocketbook.[1]

Why dream of tilling the land in far-off Palestine when you can have "a Palestine in Moscow"? Why remember Zion, the vassal of British imperialism, when Jewish farm labor communes can be set up right here in socialist Russia, to the immediate advantage of the destitute and unemployed? The plan did not fail to make a favorable impression on many of the followers of socialist-Zionist and socialist-territorialist groups.

The Jewish Sections' support of agricultural resettlement was at first simply a means of political agitation, and was not thought of as having any immediate bearing on the fate of the Jewish masses. The organized placement of Jews on farms, with the aid of government loans and equipment, took place scarcely at all before 1924. Then, in 1924, the Soviet government, with the establishment of KOMZET, began seriously to promote the settlement on the land of the destitute town Jews. And in

1926 it was decided to give 100,000 Jewish families, or roughly half a million individuals, an opportunity to settle as farmers in Jewish rural communities.

The government's interest in the expansion of Jewish agriculture was apparently prompted by a number of different factors: growing misery in the *shtetl*, resulting in unorganized migrations that swelled the already considerable number of unemployed in the cities; an alarming growth of pro-Zionist sentiment in the Jewish population; a desire to bring new land under cultivation; and the prospect of enlisting the aid of foreign Jewish capital [2] to this end; etc. Whatever reason finally proved decisive for the government, its approval of agrarianization as a principal means of solving the Jewish problem certainly gave a new orientation to the doctrinal position of the Jewish Sections. It implied official recognition of the existence of a specifically Jewish problem, and official approval of once heretical discussions of national solutions. Government endorsement of Jewish colonization plans coincided in time with the program of "national culture" put forward by Stalin in his address before the Communist University of the Peoples of the East in May 1925.[3] The Jewish Communists now began to consider the possibilities of a Jewish nation on Soviet soil, a Jewish culture "proletarian in content and national in form."

The Prospect of National Autonomy

In 1913, Stalin wrote that the absence of a stable agricultural class was the main reason why the Jews did not constitute a nation.[4] Now that the Soviet government was about to create a Jewish farm population of perhaps half a million, it seemed logical to think that a paranational Jewish collectivity was about to be reborn under Soviet conditions. And if the bulk of the newly settled Jewish farmers were to inhabit a specific area in which they would constitute the majority of the inhabitants, there was even the possibility of the Jews attaining full-fledged nationhood and being granted territorial autonomy as a recognized minority nationality. It is along these lines, then, that the first attempts were made to evolve an admittedly "national" program for the "normalization" of the Jewish group. Once large-scale agricultural settlement of Jews had been announced as a Soviet objective, age-old dreams of a "Jewish state," heretofore condemned as an expression of reactionary Zionism, began to be openly discussed. Suddenly Jewish nationhood and even statehood became a legitimate topic of official Communist debate.

The first to acknowledge the legitimacy of a Jewish claim to nationhood in the form of an autonomous Jewish republic in the USSR, was Aleksandr Chemeriskii, for many years First Secretary of the Central Board of Jewish Sections. Speaking at a White-Russian Conference of Jewish Sections in Minsk on October 15, 1925, he not only discussed "the question of statehood, of a republic," but went so far as to declare that "in principle" the idea of a Jewish Soviet state "had never been denied." Once large numbers of Jews had been settled as farmers in some one territory where they constituted a majority, there was no reason why they should not be granted national autonomy. In a book on the Communist Party and the Jewish masses issued early in 1926, Chemeriskii not only included his speech of October 1925 *in toto*, but also commented more extensively and in greater detail on autonomy:

> In large measure the national problem in the USSR is solved by means of national territorial autonomy, by the establishment of autonomous national provinces, national republics, etc. The question is whether the possibility of national territorial autonomy is closed to the Jewish masses of the USSR. *By no means!* Politically, it is possible in our Soviet country to establish Jewish territorial autonomy whenever . . . *a considerable Jewish majority is established in some continuous territory*
>
> The question then is whether such an opportunity *can materialize*, whether such a territory with a Jewish majority can emerge in our country. *Most certainly yes!* The rural placement of Jewish masses now under way *can provide this opportunity*, for if we succeed in settling on continuous territory not even all of the 100,000 families but only half that number, it would already mark the beginning of a Jewish autonomous province.[5]

Territorial autonomy, Chemeriskii cautioned his readers, was not an immediate objective; it was only a "perspective," yet it seemed "desirable and useful" and was "possible politically and practically." He was, Chemeriskii said, only sketching the matter in outline, not naming time or place for the experiment, since both would depend on the speed of agricultural colonization and the financial resources available. But merely to envisage the prospect of autonomy would "give an entirely different coloring to our work." Though writing boldly in this way, Chemeriskii was anxious to keep within the bounds of orthodoxy. He emphasized that any kind of extra-territorial autonomy, in contradistinction to territorial self-government, was not only unnecessary but harmful:

> We are strongly opposed to all forms of personal [i.e., corporate, extra-territorial] autonomy. It is the duty of the workers' state to use all its facilities, all its machinery, and all its resources to serve the Jewish population to the fullest extent, as it serves all other sections of the population. Any self-segregation, any vestige of autonomy harms the Jewish masses, since *it is the duty of the government as a whole to conduct activities in the Jewish field.* . . .
>
> We also combat autonomism in the field of culture and education. In language only, not in content, are there differences in these activities

among the different nations of our country. And it is not the configuration of forces within *each nation*, but the configuration of forces *in the country as a whole* that determines the content of our work. We have the dictatorship of the proletariat in the country. It is the proletarian state itself which looks for ways to adapt the culture of proletarian dictatorship to the different national languages and environments. All activities are conducted by the centralized government apparatus, which sets up special agencies to work among the [minority] nations. . . .[6]

The political implication was unmistakable to anyone familiar with Communist terminology. In general, only two types of culture were at hand: the bourgeois culture of capitalism, which tended to hide its capitalist essence behind various national masks, the better to disguise the common bourgeois content; and the socialist culture of the proletarian dictatorship, which knew no national differences and merely expressed the uniform proletarian class content in different national media, that is, in different languages. Once the proletarian dictatorship was established and capitalism done away with, it was impossible for different cultures to exist even in a multinational country. The culture of the victorious proletariat was by definition identical for all nationalities; another culture was not even conceivable so long as the cultural content was determined by the "configuration of forces in the country as a whole," i.e., by the economic and political predominance of the proletariat.

Whoever insisted on cultural autonomy for the Jews thus spoke for an ethnic group made up of chiefly non-proletarian ("bourgeois," "petty-bourgeois," etc.) classes opposed to the dictatorship. For a Jewish people of this kind there was no place in Soviet society. If, however, the Jewish people should build a socio-economic structure like that of the Soviet system, that is, if its "normalization" should result in the preponderance, among the Jewish population concentrated in a specific region, of industrial wage earners and small farmers, then this "healthy" Jewish group might even be considered a nationality deserving of territorial autonomy and entitled to express in its own "national form" the common "socialist" culture of all Soviet peoples.

Chemeriskii's quasi-Leninist version of a Jewish "national program" presented obvious advantages from the point of view of the Communist party. It not only enabled the government to divert certain national currents in the Jewish community into approved colonization projects, so checking the spread of Zionist feelings; it also benefited the Soviet government internationally. The prospect of the rebirth of a Jewish nation on Soviet soil was bound to arouse the sympathies of Jews in Eastern Europe and the United States, and might induce international Jewish organizations (the JCA, JDC, ORT, etc.) to contribute funds. Moreover, the Soviet government could continue to support and promote Arab nationalist movements in the Middle East and to expose Zionism as an agent of British imperialism in Palestine without noticeably antagonizing Jewish opinion in Europe and America, or making enemies of those influential political and intellectual groups in many capitalist countries which had given lukewarm support to Zionism in Palestine because "something had to be done about the Jewish problem." All this was well served by a theory that envisaged the possibility that Jews *might* become a nation under Soviet rule, but did not commit the Soviet government to recognizing any existing Jewish group as such either in or outside the Soviet Union.

Considerations of this kind were more or less obvious in the stand taken in 1926 by the Central Board of Jewish Sections of the Communist Party of the Soviet Union. In endorsing the idea of "Jewish territorial autonomy" in a resolution adopted on September 4, 1926, the Central Board pointed to the economic advantages inherent in the establishment of an autonomous territory, but dissociated itself from any nationalistic interpretation of autonomy:

> The desirability of establishing an autonomous Jewish territory follows from the consideration that in an autonomous territory, full use could be made of all opportunities resulting from the concentration of large Jewish masses in order to improve their condition by a series of economic measures and intensified cultural activities, and that it would strengthen the USSR's influence on the Jewish masses in capitalist countries. Yet we must take into account the likelihood of nationalistic overestimation of Jewish territorial autonomy, and we must make provision for the struggle against this in our preparatory activities and reports.[7]

No doubt was left as to where, exactly, "nationalistic overestimation" would be most dangerous: "To proclaim territorial autonomy openly in the USSR, as distinguished from abroad, is untimely, for its realization depends on the progress of agricultural resettlement, which is attended by colossal difficulties. . . ."[8] The resolution culminated in an attack on the "purely bourgeois and moreover Utopian" objectives of Zionists and territorialists. As against these, the Soviet course was praised as the best way "to help make the Jewish needy part of the universal cause of building socialism."[9]

Conditional Recognition of Jewish Nationhood

Having accepted the idea of autonomy, the leadership of the Jewish Sections had to plan its further moves with the utmost caution. Lenin's and Stalin's old thesis denying the existence of a Jewish nation had not been officially abandoned. Stalin's vindication of national cultures in

1925, while naming a number of nationalities awakened to new life by the Soviet revolution, had made no specific reference to Jews; it had, indeed, stated that even under socialism "Undoubtedly some nationalities may, and even certainly will, undergo a process of assimilation."[10] Did this refer to Jews or did it not? To be on the safe side, the Jewish Sections had occasionally to insist upon the possibility of the ultimate triumph of assimilation. On the other hand, the mere announcement of plans for autonomy had an electrifying effect on Jewish opinion and strengthened the nationalistic sentiments of the Jewish masses. It was no longer easy to declare that the establishment of Jewish territorial autonomy had no bearing on the survival of the Jews as a people.

Difficulties cropped up immediately at the Sixth All-Union Conference of the Jewish Sections of the Communist Party, which met in Moscow in December 1926. The proceedings of the conference betrayed a pervasive "deviationist" spirit, and although the Central Board stalwartly opposed all nationalist sentiment in the delegates, it was plainly considered too lenient by the party, and no further conferences of the Jewish Sections were held. The Sixth Conference was, in effect, the swan song of the Sections, whose disbanding, as we have mentioned, followed in a few years.

What the opposition said has not been preserved for posterity. Only an expurgated report of the proceedings was published (*Alfarbandishe Baratung fun di Idishe Sektsies fun der A1KP/B [Dekabr 1926]*) that omits the discussion on the floor entirely; it contains only the resolutions adopted, the reports read, and the concluding speeches of the leading officials who presented the reports. From these concluding speeches, however, in which spokesmen for the Central Board, especially Chemeriskii, Moisei Litvakov, and Ester (Maria Ya. Frumkina), rebutted the critics, it is apparent that the Central Board, made up as it was of former Bundists and territorialists, was sharply attacked by less "Bolshevized" former Bundists (Rafes and Kiper) and territorialists (Novakovskii). Both oppositions pointed out that if it was sincere in anticipating a rapid advance of assimilation, the special Jewish program made no sense and ought to be abandoned forthwith; but if it was really looking forward to the establishment of an autonomous Jewish national division, then the Jewish people would and indeed must be preserved outside of the autonomous territory as well, and this in turn required a firm stand *against* assimilation.

Attacking both, Ester, the chief theorist of the official position, said:

> In this question there is no clarity even among Jewish Communists. Some of them, mostly Russified apparatus people . . . conclude that the Soviet government's policy on nationalities does not apply to the

Jews because the Jews are not a nation. They hold that Jews must be Russified, Ukrainized, White-Russianized, etc., that no activity should be conducted among them in their mother tongue. . . . On the other hand, we have comrades who slip from the class into a national point of view. They put forward an all-Israel goal: to preserve the Jewish nation. . . . They thus fall under the influence of Jewish National Bolshevism, which . . . regards the nation and its preservation as the end, and everything else as a means to that end.[11]

Ester denounced "petty-bourgeois nationalism" and dismissed the "demand for Jewish Soviets" and all "idle talk about the dictatorship of the Jewish proletariat in the Jewish street." Dictatorship, she said, was a "territorial concept," and the Jewish proletariat had no special call to dictate to the Jewish bourgeoisie, or to impose its leadership upon the Jewish petty-bourgeois toilers; both these things were the province of the proletariat of the Soviet Union as a whole. Nation, too, was a "territorial concept," and only a "territorial solution" was proper in the case of the problems of nationalities:

The proletarian revolution awakens forgotten peoples and tribes. It opens up a road for them to national development and consolidation, the road to national statehood. And among these peoples and tribes, for whom new opportunities have been disclosed by the October revolution, there is the extra-territorial Jewish people. It is not yet a nation in the strictly scientific sense of the word, since it has neither territory nor a common economic basis. But all nations, peoples, and tribes are, of course [sic], treated in practice by the policy on nationalities of the party and Soviet government as separate national units possessing equal rights to national development. . . .

The consequences of the national policy of our party and the Soviet government with respect to the Jewish masses are enormous in every sphere of life. . . . But this is not the end of it. New processes have started in Jewish life. Under the dictatorship of the proletariat, the opportunity arises for the Jewish people to consolidate itself as a nation. . . .

The agricultural settlement of large Jewish masses in a continuous territory makes it possible to achieve autonomous Jewish statehood, a national territory (perhaps not just one, perhaps two or three—this makes no difference in principle). . . . It must be kept in mind that difficulties are very great, and they must not be concealed from the Jewish masses; but the establishment of such a territory, and with it the national consolidation, are quite conceivable, possible, and desirable—as much in harmony with the interests of the proletarian revolution and the building of socialism as are national consolidation and . . . national statehood among all the other peoples of the Soviet Union. We must apply all our energies towards making this possibility a reality.[12]

In accordance with this, a lengthy resolution adopted by the conference stated:

It is absolutely clear and definite that this [national] consolidation is a positive phenomenon in accord with the direction of socialist construction; it will organize in a normal way the active efforts of the Jewish masses, help channel the national tendencies of the toilers into the revolutionary mainstream, and may exert a revolutionizing influence on the Jewish masses in capitalist countries. This consolidation thus coincides with the interests of the dictatorship of the proletariat. . . .[13]

This future Jewish nation, however, was under no circumstances to be thought of as a continuation of the Jewish national remnant of the past. "The struggle for the preservation of the Jewish nation through the establishment of a Jewish state," said Chemeriskii, "is the very form in which nationalism disguises itself in Soviet or even Communist colors in order to gain a greater influence." Things had gone so far, he apprehensively exclaimed, that in the absence of other parties a clamor was being raised to make the Jewish Sections "the representatives of the people." This was a dangerous "nationalist ideology." It was essential to produce a "Communist antitoxin" to combat such tendencies.[14]

Assimilation Foreseen

The "nationalists" found an unexpected ally in Mikhail I. Kalinin, who in negotiating the unfamiliar theoretical ground of the historical significance of the rural settlement of Jews, came rather a dangerous cropper. The head of the Soviet state, speaking at the first convention of the Association for the Rural Placement of Jewish Toilers (OZET in its Russian abbreviation, GEZERD in Yiddish) on November 17, 1926, had not only deplored the "losses to the Jewish nation" caused by Jewish migration to the large industrial cities and the ensuing rise of mixed marriages, but also solemnly declared: "The Jewish people face a great task, that of preserving its nationality. . . ."[15] The opposition's references to Kalinin caused Chemeriskii to remark maliciously:

The way Comrade Kalinin may talk and needs to talk as the representative of the government and of the former ruling nation is one thing, and the way we must talk is another. And even Comrade Kalinin's speech contained no slogan directly calling for the establishment of a [Jewish] state. Why do we have to agree with his view about the preservation of the nation? The party has issued no such directive. Why do I have to agree with the rabbi and share his grief about the consequences of the mixed marriages that the Jewish girls who come to Moscow make? So far as I know, not a single party decision exists touching on the national question in matters of alimony.[16]

That there were two ways along which Soviet Jews could advance towards Socialism—through the creation of an autonomous region *and* through participating in the constructive efforts of other nations—was emphasized by Ester in her main address to the conference:

In the Jewish autonomous province as we conceived it, the task of building socialism will be a national one within its own territory. But under no circumstances can national autonomy be pieced together out of the Jewish *shtetl*, on the one hand, and the [agricultural] areas of the Crimea and Siberia, on the other. The Jewish masses will help to build socialism in two ways: as a nation presumably gathered together in its own territory, and as participants, in other territories, in the inter-national work of construction.

Now that we are calling Jewish metal workers and Jewish miners into existence in those areas where Jews are numerically weak, we have every reason to expect that in those places the Jewish worker of the coming generations will assimilate with the proletariat of the other nationalities around him. . . . From a national point of view this is an unwelcome phenomenon. From the class point of view industrialization is a tremendous victory regardless of whatever assimilation may take place. . . .

It is very likely that the process of assimilation will embrace those national minorities which are scattered in the cities. . . . We must consider the probability of the assimilation of such minorities, and we must, by our approach, accustom Jewish workers and Jewish public figures not to judge this or that activity from the point of view of national self-preservation, but from the point of view of its usefulness to socialist construction.[17]

Replying in her concluding remarks to a number of opponents, Ester vigorously insisted on the inevitability of large-scale assimilation as a consequence of economic developments:

This happens not only to Jews but also to Poles, Latvians, and Germans; this may even happen to minor sections of the Russian people. . . . We must not pass over in silence the prospect of partial assimilation. We must implant the notion that industrialization is an enormous achievement, even if it does not proceed along the road of national consolidation, even if in the last result it means assimilation. If we don't do this we align ourselves with the Zionists.[18]

The resolution voted by the conference referred to Stalin's statement about the probable assimilation of some national groups, and strongly emphasized that the prospect of assimilation might in particular confront "extra-territorial minority nationalities scattered through the cities, especially the Jews." The employment of Jews in the mines of the Donets Basin and in the metallurgical industries of the Ural, which in all likelihood meant their assimilation, might be deplorable from the point of view of "national self-preservation," but from that of the Jewish Sections was no less important than the placement of Jews in agriculture. The main objective was "to create a Jewish industrial proletariat, a Jewish peasantry, and a proletarian Jewish intelligentsia." Those "national nihilists" who no longer wanted to keep the Yiddish language in official use were to be opposed; but those "national Bolsheviks" who wished "to preserve the Jewish people" and who thus "strengthened nationalist leanings" in the Jewish masses, were to be opposed with even "greater energy."[19]

"A People of Proletarians"

Both the report presented by Ester and the Conference's resolution pointed out that the establishment of an autonomous Jewish territory would also have "great importance" for the Jewish masses outside the national territory; and for so doing Ester was charged with "Akhad-Haam-ism."[20] But the superficial employment of Akhad-Haam's chief argument—that the establishment of a Jewish state, by putting an end to the pariah existence of Jews among the nations, would fortify and raise their self-respect and prestige—certainly did not imply a reversal of the fundamentally anti-national position of the Jewish Sections. Ester said:

> Of course, we do not want to repel, we want to attract the national-minded intelligentsia. And although we have never said that extra-territorial Jewish minorities will survive nationally, although as early as 1922 . . . we emphasized the [existence of] assimilationist processes, [and] although we never took an oath to promise eternal life to the Jewish people, still, the national-minded intelligentsia is increasingly drawn to us as it sees us working sincerely and enthusiastically at the creation of a new Jewish culture, and as it sees us raising the Jewish masses to a higher level. We do not demand that petty-bourgeois nationalists become revolutionary Marxists. Let the source of their inspiration continue to be the nation. . . . If only by nation they mean the great toiling mass, they are obliged to go along with and help us in any case. But the source of *our* inspiration and *our* enthusiasm must not be the preservation of the nation, but the victory of the proletarian revolution, the building of socialism.[21]

For a short while the building of socialism had seemed to require first of all the speedy establishment of Jewish farm colonies. Less than a year earlier, Chemeriskii had praised agricultural colonization as the Jewish masses' "highway" to socialism. But the situation in the mid-1920's changed rapidly. For the most part, the Central Board's activities report, presented to the conference by the same Chemeriskii, described the advances made by industrialization, not agrarianization, amongst Jews,

Chemeriskii confessed a number of times to having erred in placing the greater emphasis on agricultural settlement. He said flatly: "The main road to socialism is the industrialization of the Jewish population, the reinforcement of the army of wage earners." Only because the slow pace of economic development did "not permit a more speedy absorption of all the masses into [industrial] production" was recourse to be had to a "detour"—the creation of a Jewish farm population. The problem, then, of an autonomous status for a territory settled by newly-created Jewish farmers arose only as part of a secondary matter. It was a possibility, "but there is a long way from possibility to realization, to the proclamation of such a slogan, and we are against proclaiming it."[22] The chief purpose of the Soviet experiments in rural settlement of Jews was to win over to the Soviet government "the Jewish petty-bourgeois masses in the USSR and abroad," and to deal "a deadly blow to Zionism and to the ideology of the petty-bourgeois masses."[23] Decidedly, national autonomy could play only a subordinate role:

An autonomous territory, a republic, etc. for Jews has a place within the entire complex of activities carried out among the Jewish masses only in relation to the greatest task ever undertaken and now on the point of being accomplished . . . the task of transforming the Jewish population of the USSR into a people principally composed of wage earners, with a predominance of manual laborers and a declining proportion of officials, and with a peasant and artisan stratum. A people with a tiny proletariat and a large stratum of small producers and artisans is being transformed by the Communist Party and the Soviet government into a people of proletarians with its share of farmers and artisan craftsmen, and the autonomous province that we envisage shall be one of the ways of linking together the proletariat and the peasantry.[24]

Even the rehabilitation of the destitute *luftmenshn* through the creation of farm settlements, originally planned on a large scale, was losing its importance. Urban unemployment was about to be succeeded by a scarcity of industrial manpower. Intensive industrialization was about to be proclaimed the primary objective of government policy; the era of the Five-Year Plans was about to begin. At a time when all the resources of the country were devoted to industrial construction, the only acceptable "national" policy for Jews was the concentration of all their efforts on transforming themselves into a "people of proletarians"—"regardless of whatever assimilation may take place." The leadership of the Jewish Sections realized that industrialization was bound to have "elemental assimilatory effects."[25] No matter. Industrialization was to be regarded as "an enormous achievement, . . . even if in the last result it means assimilation." Summing up the results of the Sixth Conference almost a year later, Chemeriskii stated:

> Any attempt to treat the Jewish masses in the USSR as a nation with a separate economy of its own must result in nationalist Utopianism, and the most pernicious kind of nationalist Utopianism . . . so long as the Jewish population, led by the Communist Party of the Soviet Union, has not established a separate national territory as the basis for a possible national consolidation of a part of the Jewish population. . . . In our *socialist* work among the Jewish masses, we can undertake various and far reaching *concrete, practical* tasks insofar as they contribute to the building of socialism. The same tasks are out of the question and pernicious when they contribute to the fulfilment of the "national ideal." Socialism is incompatible with any "national ideal"; it alone in its onward march solves the *practical problems* of the national masses. Our work among the Jewish masses has such concrete objectives as the radical alteration of the social composition of the Jewish population, the creation of a Jewish peasantry, and the establishment of a proletarian preponderance in the Jewish population; from village Soviets we advance to [national] districts; and we look forward to the necessity of setting up an autonomous territorial unit. But all this [we envisage] as *steps along the international proletariat's path to socialism, and certainly not along the path to the . . . preservation of the nation. . . .*
>
> We consider the industrialization of the Jewish masses the shortest and soundest way to socialism, regardless of the fact that assimilatory influences are more powerful in this direction. . . . Along the road to socialism, the creation of a Jewish republic is to be desired. . . . It may happen that in spite of all our efforts we shall not succeed in establishing it . . . ; this might make the productivization of the Jewish masses more difficult and complicated, and yet they shall not halt in their march towards socialism. . . . The "Jewish Republic" is not only a harmful but a Utopian slogan. We decide all practical questions of our work among the Jewish masses not according as they contribute to the preservation of the Jewish nation or any other national ideal, but according only as *they assist the Jewish masses to take part in the building of socialism.*[26]

The dispersal and assimilation of the Jewish masses, and the ultimate annihilation of their national or cultural identity, were viewed with equanimity by the leaders of the Jewish Sections (Ester, Chemeriskii, Litvakov, etc.), whose attacks on Jewish nationalism nevertheless did not save them in the great purges of 1936–38 from liquidation as "unreconstructed Bundists" or "counterrevolutionary nationalists." What began as the reconstruction of the Jewish people again ended in national destruction.

NOTES

1. Agurskii, *Der Idisher Arbeter* . . . , p. 43.

2. This financial motive was frankly admitted in official statements. President Mikhail I. Kalinin said: ". . . You can't just put the settlers on the land; to put them there you have to invest [large sums]; neither the Soviet government nor the population . . . has that much money. But such amounts may be raised abroad, and the Jews do raise them." (*Izvestiya*, July 11, 1926.)

3. Cf. p. 38.

4. Cf. p. 54.

5. *Op. cit.*, pp. 74f. Emphasis Chemeriskii's.

6. *Ibid.*, p. 77. Emphasis Chemeriskii's.

7. *Alfarbandishe Baratung fun di Idishe Sektsies*, p. 97.

8. *Ibid.*

9. *Ibid.*, p. 98.

10. See p. 41.

11. *Alfarbandishe Baratung fun die Idishe Sektsies*, p. 123.

12. *Ibid.*, pp. 127f. Emphasis Ester's.

13. *Ibid.*, p 211.

14. *Ibid.*, p. 91.

15. *Pervyi Vsesoyuznyi Syezd OZET*, Moscow, 1927, pp. 65f.

16. *Alfarbandishe Baratung fun di Idishe Sektsies*, pp. 105f.

17. *Ibid.*, pp. 130f.

18. *Ibid.*, pp. 141f.

19. *Ibid.*, pp. 212f.

20. *Ibid.*, pp. 129, 135, 211.

21. *Ibid.*, p. 137.

22. *Ibid.*, p. 105.

23. *Ibid.*, p. 49.

24. *Ibid.*, pp. 49f.

25. *Ibid.*, p. 141.

26. "Orientirung in der Idisher Arbet," introduction to *Alfarbandishe Baratung fun di Idishe Sektsies*, pp. 6f. Emphasis Chemeriskii's.

CHAPTER X

Cultural Activities and Institutions

Schools for the Jewish Minority

The Tsarist Empire stubbornly resisted the establishment of schools providing instruction in the native languages of the different minorities. It was not until the revolution of 1905 that some, though not all, minority nationalities—the Poles, Lithuanians, Estonians, Germans, and several Turki and Caucasian peoples—were permitted a number of such schools. The Ukrainians, White Russians, and Jews, however, were still forbidden them. In the years of reaction following the revolution, much of what had been won in 1905–1907 was partly or wholly lost again.[1] Before 1917, regular primary and secondary private schools for Jewish children existed only in a few places. Jewish public schools were non-existent. The *kheder*, a private institution principally giving instruction in religion, was the primary school for most of the Jewish population. After the democratic revolution of March 1917, all the major parties upheld the principle of public schools for minority nationalities conducted in the native tongue. The Bolsheviks, when they came to power, likewise accepted the principle without reservation.

The use of its own language, though a major desideratum in a minority's schools,[2] does not by itself make them institutions of national culture; the schools must teach such things as the minority's literature and national history as well. Given cultural autonomy, this is a relatively easy thing to do. But the Communist leadership was uncompromising in its opposition not only to any kind of Jewish cultural autonomy, but also to any liberalization of the curriculum so that it might include specifically Jewish subjects. The cultural and educational activities of the different nationalities in the Soviet Union, Aleksandr Chemeriskii stated, must differ "in language only, not in content."[3]

Of course, it was impossible to exclude all Jewish subjects from the curriculum of Jewish schools. Thus, the study of contemporary Yiddish literature was required in all Jewish educational institutions. In principle, however, both the Jewish Commissariat in the early years and the Jewish Sections subsequently strove to reduce the "national" element to the barest minimum, and made concessions only when compelled to do so. In the early years of Soviet rule public Jewish schools had to compete with the kheder, especially the so-called "reformed kheder" of the democratic Jewish community, which gave some instruction in secular subjects and approached the standards of regular primary schools. To meet this competition, "recognized" (i.e., government-subsidized) Jewish schools were permitted to teach Hebrew from the second grade on.[4] But this was short-lived, and soon the teaching not only of Hebrew,[5] but of Jewish history as well, was banned. Everything was proscribed in any way reminiscent of the traditional life of the Jewish community, including the Saturday Sabbath. This was closely joined with the government's war on religion, which in the first decade of Soviet rule played a prominent part in Communist propaganda. Years later, a Soviet author proudly recalled what Soviet opinion considered the first outstanding achievements of the Jewish school:

> The employment of all means at the disposal of the Soviet government helped the school achieve one victory after the other. First, the Sabbath day of rest was done away with. Secondly, all books tinctured with nationalism were removed from the schools. This enabled the school to raise its level and to include anti-religious and internationalist material in its program. School work is conducted in accordance with the general program of the People's Commissariat for Education. The very concept, "Jewish history," has no place in the school. The general course in the history of the class struggle has sections dealing with the struggle of Jewish craftsmen against the boss, of Jewish workers against the Jewish and every bourgeoisie; all subjects are taught in the mother tongue and a special course in Yiddish literature is included.[6]

The Soviet school quickly triumphed in the field of Jewish primary education, for the simple reason that it was the only one to give general instruction in Yiddish. Yiddish was the language of the great majority of Soviet Jews. According to the census of 1897, 97 percent of the Jewish population of the Tsarist Empire gave Yiddish as their mother tongue. Assimilation, of course, had made considerable inroads in the following decades, and Poland and Lithuania, homeland of the least assimilated Jewish groups, were no longer a part of the Soviet state; yet Yiddish was still the Jewish tongue. Of the total population recorded as "of Jewish nationality" in the census of 1926, 72.6 percent gave Yiddish as their mother tongue, and in the major Union Republics the percentage was: White Russia, 90.7; Ukraine, 76.1; Russian SFSR, 50.3.[7] It is obvious that schools in Yiddish were indispensable. Despite the new Jewish schools' active hostility to Jewish tradition and religion, the majority of the Jewish parents—at least in White Russia and the Ukraine—preferred Jewish to non-Jewish schools because of the language of instruction.

Extension of the Jewish Educational System

The need for Jewish schools was greatest in White Russia, where Yiddish was the native language of more than nine-tenths of the Jewish population. The beginnings were modest. In August 1922, White Russia had a total of 109 Soviet Jewish schools, with only 10,745 students.[8] But a rapid increase took place in the following five years, continuing, though at a diminished pace, through the later years—until the early 1930's, when a standstill was reached; then a marked decline occurred. This decline, which set in about 1934-35, was, as so often happens in the Soviet Union, accompanied by the discontinuance of the publication of statistical data. Only scattered statistics pieced together from occasional references in the press are available to show the decay of the Jewish school system on the eve of the Second World War. The increase in the number of Jewish primary and secondary schools in White Russia to 1933, after which no statistics were regularly released, is shown in Table X:

TABLE X

SOVIET JEWISH SCHOOLS IN WHITE RUSSIA [9]

Year (Ending in August)	Number of Primary and Secondary Schools	Number of Students
1922	106	10,745
1923	98	12,241
1924	—	—
1925	140	19,085
1926	175	22,535
1927	184	24,073
1928	190	26,020
1929	—	—
1930	209	28,310
1931	262	31,340
1932	334	33,398
1933	339	36,501

Thereafter the statistics are fragmentary. On June 24, 1937, for example, *Emes* mentioned in passing that the number of students in White Russia's Jewish schools approximated 30,000,[10] that is to say, 18 percent less than what it had been four years before. Scattered information from sources outside of the Soviet Union indicates that the decline was speedier in the years that followed, and that when the Soviet Union entered the war the Jewish school system in White Russia was in a state of disintegration.

In the Ukraine the development was not unlike that in White Russia— rapid advance in the 1920's, followed by a marked decline in the 1930's. On January 1, 1923 the entire Ukrainian SSR had only 128 schools teaching in Yiddish, i.e., less than 1 percent of the total number of schools in the Ukraine at a time when Jews accounted for an estimated 6 or 7 percent of the total population. The inadequacy of the Jewish school system may be seen from Table XI.

TABLE XI

SOVIET JEWISH SCHOOLS IN THE UKRAINE,
January 1, 1923 [11]

Province	Total Number of Schools (All Nationalities)	Number of Jewish Schools
Kharkov	1,083	1
Yekaterinoslav	2,119	1
Kiev	2,070	32
Volhynia	897	22
Podolia	1,961	43
Donets	1,687	5
Poltava ⎱	2,048	5
Odessa ⎰	2,111	12
Chernigov	1,007	7
Ukrainian SSR	14,983	128

By January 1, 1924 the number of Jewish schools had risen to 189, and by January 1, 1925 to 249, accounting for 1.3 and 1.7 percent, respectively, of the total number of schools in the Ukrainian SSR.[12] Detailed data, including the number of students, were regularly released from 1925 through 1928. The statistical picture is somewhat complicated, because, apart from the national schools, until the late 1920's a limited number of mixed, multilingual schools existed—Ukrainian-Jewish, Russian-Jewish, Ukrainian-Russian-Jewish, and Ukrainian-Jewish-Polish—in which instruction in all subjects was given to students of different national groups in their respective languages. Ukrainian statistics on Jewish schools sometimes included the number of Jewish students in the mixed schools and sometimes did not, nor did they always state which was the case. Table XII is a summary of such figures as we possess.

TABLE XII

SOVIET JEWISH SCHOOLS IN THE UKRAINE, 1925–1928 [13]

Year	Jewish Schools		Students with Yiddish as Language of Instruction					
			Jewish Schools		Mixed Schools		Total	
	Number	Percent of all schools, Ukraine	Number	Percent all students, Ukraine	Number	Percent all students, Ukraine	Number	Percent all students, Ukraine
1925	249	1.7	39,474	2.3				
1926	295	1.7	46,309	2.3	12,075	.6	58,384	2.9
1927	393	2.1	61,352	2.8	8,517	.4	69,869	3.2
1928	475		68,836					

Reliable statistics are not available for later years, although the increase in the Jewish schools and student body must have continued for some years, more than compensating for the decline in the number of multi-lingual schools. Rather high figures were given for 1930 and 1931 by Yakov Kantor, a leading Soviet writer on Jewish minority problems, who mentioned 786 Jewish schools with 82,414 students in 1930, and 831 Jewish schools with 94,872 students in 1931.[14] These, however, are obvious exaggerations; the number of schools was apparently much smaller, and the enrollment somewhat lower.[15] According to all available indications, the number of students in Jewish schools in the Ukraine never went beyond 90,000. An apparent decline set in in 1934, when the number of students dropped to 85,489.[16] In 1935, only 73,413 students were recorded.[17] As far as can be ascertained, comprehensive data were no longer published in subsequent years. The absence of data may in itself be taken to indicate that the Jewish school system rapidly deteriorated in the late 1930's. This is borne out by information on particular aspects of educational developments, which require a more detailed discussion.

Assimilation Stifles the Soviet Jewish School

The Jewish school throve triumphantly in the crumbling *shtetl* of the 1920's. To a certain extent its success was the result of pressure exerted by local Jewish officials inflexibly carrying out what was later termed "the compulsory Yiddishizing of the school," prompted by the consideration that the "counterrevolutionary" influences of "clericalism," "Jewish nationalism," "reactionary Zionist Hebraizing," etc., would be frustrated more thoroughly if all Jewish children could be made to attend the anti-religious and anti-national Yiddish-language Soviet school. "In 1924–1928," Kantor wrote in 1934, "no consideration was given in many places to the wishes of the children and their parents. . . . It was enough to establish that the child's mother tongue was Yiddish to *force* him—in many instances—to attend a Yiddish-language school against his wishes."[18] This happened often enough in White Russia, but was a flagrant practice in the Ukraine. Another Soviet author wrote: "In order to force Jewish children to attend the Jewish school, they were denied admission to general schools; a situation arose in which non-Jewish schools were closed to Jewish children."[19] For a number of years the practice was not objected to by the higher authorities.

In the late 1920's, when the Jewish school system was at its height, the Yiddishizers' avid expansionism began to collide with the wishes of the government. Political considerations required that greater stress be laid on "Ukrainization" (or "White-Russification"). The Ukrainian school was given precedence not only in rural communities, where the population was almost exclusively Ukrainian, but also in the cities, where Ukrainians were often a minority. When necessary, this was done at the expense of the Jewish school. But while promoting Ukrainization, the government took great care to preserve and expand Russian cultural influences, and to maintain, if possible even to extend, the province of the Russian school. Moscow's ever present inclination to "Russify" the non-Ukrainian minorities concentrated in the cities, was given free rein. The party proper, in contrast to the Jewish Sections, had probably never been disturbed by the fact that Jewish parents here and there preferred to send their children to Russian schools; but it had not interfered with the Sections' "Yiddishizing" zeal. Now, however, it actively intervened.

"Compulsory Yiddishizing" was harshly censured. It was denounced, on the one hand, as an anti-Jewish attitude that brought the government into disrepute with the Jewish popular masses,[20] and on the other, as a Jewish nationalist deviation.[21] Such contradictory censure merely expressed the Soviet and Communist loss of interest in the Jewish school. The Jewish masses were moving away from the old ghetto locales. The Soviet government had no reason to oppose the dispersal of the Jewish population in industrial districts, a development that accelerated assimilation and made the Jewish school seem a hindrance rather than a help to progress.

Even without administrative pressure, large sections of the Jewish community had had to send their children to the Soviet Yiddish-language school, especially in the small towns, where virtually all Jewish children spoke no other language but Yiddish. Two examples will illustrate the situation. In Shpola, a small, predominantly Jewish semirural town in the Ukraine, with a Jewish population of about 8,000, there were some 1,600 Jewish school-age children in 1925–26; of these, only 372—less than 25 percent—attended school in 1926, 360 at the Jewish school, and 12 at the non-Jewish school. At the beginning of the new school year in August 1926, 200 new Jewish students were enrolled in the first grade, all of them in the Jewish school. In Cherkasy, a Ukrainian city of about 35,000, where a Jewish community of 12,000 accounted for 35 percent of the total population, the number of Jewish school-age children in 1925–26 was near to 2,400; of these, 1,150—some 48 percent—attended school in 1926; of the 1,150 Jewish students, 810 were in the Jewish school and 340 in the non-Jewish school. Fall enrollment in 1926 added 134 Jewish children to the first grade; of these, only 5 were enrolled in the non-Jewish school while 129 went to the Jewish school.[22]

Not only were school facilities more abundant in larger cities; the Jewish community was smaller relative to the general population, Yiddish was less frequently in use, and there was a more widespread desire on the part of Jewish parents to send their children to non-Jewish schools.

The larger the city, the less the importance of the Yiddish-language school; in large urban centers in the Ukraine it virtually did not exist. At the height of the development of the Jewish school system, the school census of December 15, 1927 showed that of all students in the six largest cities of the Ukraine, only 5.5 percent had Yiddish as their language of instruction in the school year 1927–28. Yet Jews accounted for 26.2 percent of the population of these cities. Assuming that the percentage of Jews in the student body was about the same as that in the total population, this would mean that only 21 percent of all Jewish students attended schools taught in Yiddish. Table XIII gives a breakdown by cities in percentages.

TABLE XIII

JEWISH STUDENTS ATTENDING YIDDISH SCHOOLS

City	Percent Jews within Total Population	Students Attending Classes Taught in Yiddish, as Percentage of Total Enrollment, Jewish and Non-Jewish
Odessa	36.4	9.0
Kiev	27.3	8.0
Dnepropetrovsk (Yekaterinoslav)	26.6	2.9
Nikolayev	20.8	2.3
Kharkov	19.4	2.9
Stalino (Yuzovka, Donets Basin)	10.7	None

In smaller Ukrainian cities, Jews accounted for 29.4 percent of the total population, and students in schools using Yiddish as language of instruction, for 10.4 percent of the total student body. Assuming that the percentage of Jewish students approximated the percentage of Jews within the total population, this would mean that some 35 percent of the Jewish students in the smaller cities attended Jewish schools, or Jewish sections of mixed schools. In all communities classified as urban in the school census (but apparently not including the semirural *shtetl*), the Jewish population amounted to 27.4 percent of the total population, and the number of students in Jewish schools and Jewish sections of mixed schools, to 7.6 percent of the total enrollment—or, on the same assumption, about 28 percent of the total number of Jewish students.[23]

The situation in the *shtetl* was obviously much different. This may be seen not only in individual cases, where the number of students in Jewish schools accounted for over 90 percent of all Jewish students, but also in the percentage statistics for all schools in the Ukrainian SSR. On December 15, 1927, some 49.6 percent of all Jewish students attended Yiddish-language schools,[24] and on July 1, 1932, it was 53 percent (probably the highest point ever reached).[25] The proportion of Jewish children attending schools with Yiddish as the language of instruction must have been considerably larger in communities not classed as urban in the school census. The decline of the *shtetl*, clearly discernible in the late 1920's, reduced the demand for schools in Yiddish and radically changed the climate in which they had thrived.

The gradual disintegration of the Jewish school system, more apparent in the Ukraine than in White Russia, was reflected in the Soviet Yiddish-language press, which printed numerous reports from all over plainly indicating a state of decay; such news items were particularly frequent in the mid-1930's.[26] Most striking was the decline in yearly enrollment. Again and again the Jewish newspapers' local correspondents complained that it was difficult, even impossible to "fill" the first grade on the scale provided for. This was reported from the largest cities, such as Kiev,[27] Odessa, Dnepropetrovsk; from medium-sized and smaller cities, such as Belaya Tserkov', Fastov, Uman';[28] and from a number of small "market towns," such as Monastyrishche and Luplov, with populations of some 7,500, of whom two-thirds were recorded as Jewish.

The development of Jewish schools in the Russian SFSR and the Asiatic republics does not require special attention. Outside the Ukraine and White Russia, Jewish schools were practically nonexistent, except in the new agricultural settlements in the Crimea and Birobidzhan, and there only a few schools were needed. Everywhere in the Soviet Union, the condition of Jewish schools in the late 1930's was precarious. Jacob Lestschinsky summarized the results of prewar developments as follows:

> From all available material the conclusion may be drawn that at present—the end of 1940—some 85,000 to 90,000 Jewish children throughout the Soviet Union attend schools with Yiddish as the language of instruction. This amounts to about 20 percent of all Jewish children attending school. The total of about 90,000 is distributed as follows: Ukraine, some 50,000; White Russia, some 25,000; Birobidzhan, 3,000; Crimea, 3,000; Western province (Russian SFSR), 5,000; all other parts of the Soviet Union, 2,000 to 3,000.[29]

These estimates may have erred on the optimistic side. In the early 1940's the situation became hopeless. The war completely annihilated Soviet Jewish schools in the Ukraine and White Russia. No Jewish schools were reopened subsequently; the timid attempts of a few Jewish educators to win government approval for the reconstruction of Jewish schools were of no avail. And so it has remained.

Science in Fetters

The Jewish school, as has been shown, prospered for a short period only, and only within a narrow range. What above has been termed the Yiddish-language school chiefly encompassed primary and secondary education. Other types of educational institutions—kindergartens, vocational schools, institutions of higher learning—lagged far behind; and the decline of Jewish institutions in general that began in the early 1930's hit them harder than it did the public school. The non-educational branches of Jewish culture—scientific thought, creative art, the Yiddish press—lacked that solid basis which only a flourishing communal life can provide. Their growth in the 1920's was less spectacular, and the blight that struck them in later years was not even noticed by many.

At the very outset the atmosphere was hostile to scientific endeavor, and in particular to the "science of Judaism"—the study, that is, of Jewish history, sociology, philosophy, religion, literature, etc. Even linguistic studies, because of the ties of Yiddish with Hebrew and religious literature, were looked at with a jaundiced eye. Independent scholarship in Jewish subjects was still possible on a small scale in the 1920's, when the totalitarian character of the Soviet regime had not yet fully manifested itself and rigid conformity was not enforced in spheres divorced from politics. But even this limited freedom came to an end in the 1930's.

What were the accomplishments of Jewish science in the Soviet Union from the official point of view? In reviewing individual aspects of Jewish "socialist construction" Yakov Kantor [30] revealed what were already in 1934 the narrow limits of Judaica in Soviet science, which he defined as "scientific research in the field of Jewish proletarian culture: the study of history, literature, linguistics, education, socio-economic investigation, etc." Before the revolution, according to Kantor, serious work in these fields had been plainly out of the question, and the little that had been accomplished—he mentioned the names of Dubnov, Tsinberg, Lestschinsky, "and so on"—bore "the visible imprint of national narrow-mindedness, eclecticism, and the pseudo-scientific approach." Post-revolutionary developments were seen differently:

> In the past ten years very much has been done in the USSR in this field. Two leading institutions have been created: the Institute of Jewish Proletarian Culture, attached to the All-Ukrainian Academy of Sciences, and the Jewish Sector of the White-Russian Academy of Sciences. These institutions became the laboratories of scientific thought in the field of Jewish culture, i.e., the history of the revolutionary movement within the Jewish population, problems of art and literature, public education, linguistics, and [studies of the] socio-economic conditions of the Jewish population. . . . Of particular value are studies of the history of the Jewish labor movement, aimed at unmasking the fairy-tale of the supposedly unlimited influence over the Jewish working masses of the Bund, their would-be "sole representative," and also unmasking the pseudo-scientific nature of the "work" of foreign scholars grouped mainly around the notorious Yiddish Scientific Institute [YIVO] in Vilna. . . .

These praiseworthy accomplishments were unfortunately marred by certain "deviations," which here and there resulted in "breaches" in the cultural "front." "Marxist-Leninist methodology," however, triumphed in the end:

> Jewish science and research did not fail to suffer serious breaches in individual sectors. The particularly strong influence of the petty-bourgeois environment on the Jewish population; the influence of the Bundist tradition, which had taken root in the pre-revolutionary period among groups of the Jewish intelligentsia and petty bourgeoisie; the effects of cultural ties with, and the influence of, the bourgeois West— all this was bound to leave some trace on Soviet scientific studies. A number of errors and distortions were permitted to be introduced into the study of history, into Jewish criticism and literary research, into literature, and into socio-economic research. By severest criticism and self-criticism Jewish scientific and research workers and scholarly institutions succeeded, as a rule, in exposing these errors and in having them acknowledged and corrected. . . . More than ever, Jewish institutions of science and research now concentrate their attention on this task, *their work being guided chiefly by Bolshevik intransigence towards all deviations from the general line of the party and from the correct Marxist-Leninist position.*[31]

Not only was research confined to the few subjects of proletarian culture and made to "unmask" all pre-Soviet and foreign, non-Soviet scholarship, but scholars were also compelled to disavow and denounce their own work and to "correct" it in accordance with party pronouncements. Hardly a branch of Jewish science escaped exposure by "severest criticism and self-criticism." Humbled and demoralized by compulsory self-castigation, scholarship was reduced to the routine enunciation of the approved view.

It is true that the number of books and pamphlets published in Yiddish was impressive. The numbers are shown in Table XIV.

There was a marked decline in the totals, which included fiction and

TABLE XIV

YIDDISH BOOKS PUBLISHED IN THE USSR [32]

Year	Number of Titles	Number of Sheets[33]	Aggregate Circulation
1928	238	1,368	875,000
1929	319	1,963	1,224,000
1930	471	2,220	2,305,000
1931	496	. . . .	. . . . . .
1932	653	3,087	2,558,585
1933	668	. . . . .	. . . . . .
1934	348	2,424	1,551,880
1935	437	2,816	1,887,960

non-fiction as well as political propaganda, after 1933. And when such subjects as history, geography, regional studies, anthropology, and folklore are considered, the downward trend is apparent both in the number and the quality of publications in these fields.

The total number of such works was 41 in 1932, 17 in 1933, 23 in 1934, and 4 in 1935. The catalogue, issued by the Bibliographical Institute of the White-Russian SSR,[34] of all books and pamphlets in Yiddish published in the Soviet Union in 1932 listed 36 books on history. This total included 16 memoirs, chiefly by old Bolsheviks; 5 translations of articles and speeches by Stalin and Kaganovich; 6 studies on the history of the Communist International and the Communist Youth International; 6 publications on the history of the revolutionary movement, the Russian Civil War, the Communist Party of the Soviet Union, and the Hungarian Soviet Republic. Jewish topics were dealt with in 3 books on the history of the Jewish labor movement, all devoted to "rectifying" this history in the light of Communist dogma and carefully eliminating all vestiges of the non-Bolshevik past of Jewish labor. In 1933, there were 14 historical publications; none had a direct connection with Jewish history or even with the Jewish labor movement. In 1934, there was a total of 23 publications, all translations, including 12 memoirs (of which 8 commemorated Lenin on the occasion of the tenth anniversary of his death); 8 books on the history of the Communist Party; 2 books on the Communist leader Kirov assassinated that year; and one on the history of the revolutionary movement. In 1935, only 3 books in Yiddish were published on historical subjects, of which one was on a Jewish topic: a large volume on Yiddish socialist literature in the period 1875–1897.

In the field of geography and regional studies, Yiddish publications totaled 4 in 1932, 3 in 1933, and one in 1935. These publications dealt with Adzharistan in the Northern Caucasus, Northern Osetia, the Arctic regions of the Soviet Union, Magnitogorsk, and the Transcaspian Desert. Only in the sphere of folklore were there two studies of importance for Jewish research: a symposium on folklore research in 1932, and a volume of Jewish songs in 1933, both issued by the Institute of Jewish Culture of the Ukrainian Academy of Sciences.

This reduced output of a people of three million who only a decade or two before had been in the forefront of Jewish intellectual and scholarly endeavor throughout the world, was an unmistakable sign of cultural stagnation. The decline was even more marked in the late 1930's.

Rise and Fall of the Jewish Theater

A product of the twentieth century, the Jewish theater had scarcely grown beyond the experimental stage when the Soviet revolution furnished it with undreamed-of material and technical resources. The theater was a secular domain untainted by the influence of "Jewish clericalism." It was also free from any counterrevolutionary political blemish and met with full acceptance as a vehicle of pro-Soviet culture. The notable interest that the Soviet government took in and the assistance it lavished on the dramatic art greatly benefited the Jewish stage.

In its early days the Jewish stage had had to adapt itself to undeveloped and artistically uncultivated audiences, and barely ventured beyond cheap entertainment. In the last pre-revolutionary decade new, creative signs had appeared; beset by financial difficulties, however, serious drama was hard put to win public recognition.

While the Russian theater, with its well-established high standards and long pre-revolutionary history, suffered rather a setback when it was taken over by the government, nationalization proved a boon to the Jewish stage and for the first time it was not limited by its pathetically inadequate earning capacity. When Soviet authors enthusiastically recall how "in 1919 the curtain rose for the first time in the Jewish state theater,"[35] they do not have in mind the theater as an expression of Jewish national culture, but simply the—not to be minimized—fact of government financial support. The opportunity to produce plays and conduct experimental workshops at government expense enabled the Jewish theater to achieve such success as would otherwise have been denied to it for long years to come.

From the mid-1920's on the Jewish stage rapidly developed. Not only were Jewish theaters established on a permanent basis in a number of cities, but the artistic level of the Jewish stage—at least in some of the best theatrical institutions—came to equal that of the outstanding Russian theaters. For the first time, Jewish dramatic art was able to train future performers and directors in special schools: the Jewish department of the Kiev Dramatic Institute, the Jewish Theater College in Moscow, and the dramatic school of the Jewish State Theater in Minsk.[36] This upward course reached its peak in the mid-1930's, when the Soviet Union had almost a score of permanent theatrical establishments for the Jewish population (not including the so-called "activity" groups that often developed into amateur theatrical companies). The trend, however, was reversed in the era of the great purges, and one Jewish theater after another began to disappear.

Summary data on the rise and fall of the Jewish stage in the individual republics are as follows:[37] Theatrical progress was most marked in the Ukrainian SSR. In 1933 and 1934, the Ukraine mustered, in addition to the central Jewish stage in Kharkov, Jewish city theaters in Kiev, Odessa, Kremenchug, Nikolayev, and Dnepropetrovsk, a Jewish dramatic company on the Kharkov-Vinnitsa circuit, a stage for one-act plays in Kharkov, a children's theater in Kiev, and two *kolkhoz* theaters in the

Jewish national districts of Kalinindorf and Stalindorf. At the beginning
of the 1937–38 season, the Ukrainian Jewish Theater in Kharkov was
transferred to Kiev and merged with the Kiev Jewish city theater. The
Kharkov-Vinnitsa theater circuit was discontinued, as was the stage for
one-act plays, so that no Jewish stage at all was left in Kharkov. The
Jewish city theaters in Kremenchug, Nikolayev, and Dnepropetrovsk and
one of the district theaters (Kalinindorf) also had disappeared by that
time. Of the 11 Jewish theaters in operation in the Ukraine in 1933 and
1934, only 4 remained in 1937–38, while a new Jewish workers' and
farmers' theater (perhaps a remnant of the Kharkov-Vinnitsa circuit)
was opened in Tul'china, a small town in the province of Vinnitsa. One
or the other of the discontinued theaters may possibly have reopened on
the eve of the war, but even so the general picture is one of decline and
dissolution.

In White Russia the Jewish stage found fewer opportunities. In 1933
only a central Jewish theater existed in Minsk, and also a traveling troupe
with its headquarters in that city. Only the former was alive in 1937. The
Russian SFSR was in a slightly more fortunate position, with its outstanding Moscow Theater inspired and led by Mikhoels, a local stage in
Birobidzhan, and a *kolkhoz* theater in the Crimea. These three establishments continued to function in 1937, and a circuit company was added in
Smolensk. Jewish theaters existed both in 1933 and 1937–38 in Baku and
Tashkent; in 1937–38 a Jewish theater was mentioned in Bukhara, which
probably served the native Jewish population (playing, that is, not in
Yiddish but in Parsi).

Throughout the Soviet Union a total of 18 Jewish theaters were active
in 1933 and 1934, but only 12 (not counting Bukhara) remained in the
1937–38 season. A number of them succumbed to the war, and though
little information is available for the postwar years, there is no doubt
that the activities of the Jewish stage have been considerably curtailed.

Regimentation and Suppression of the Jewish Press

The possibilities that the revolution had disclosed to Jewish education
and the Jewish stage failed to materialize in fields more directly related
to politics and more rigidly regulated. The press from the very first days
of Soviet rule was the principal target of political "totalitarianization."
Since no substantial section of the Jewish public gave articulate support
to the Soviet government in print, the pressure brought to bear on the
press resulted within a short time in a great decline in the number of
Jewish newspapers and periodicals. Through three decades of Soviet
history the decline continued with only minor abatements.

Under the Tsar, the Jewish press had grown rapidly from the 1890's
on. On the threshold of the First World War, 13 daily newspapers were

published in Yiddish and 2 in Hebrew, with an aggregate circulation of several hundred thousand.[38] Wartime persecution crushed this promising development—the entire Jewish press was suppressed by the military authorities in 1915, and even the use of Hebrew type was prohibited in 1916; Moscow and the eastern provinces were exempted, but few Jews lived there and they had no local publications. An exception was made in 1916 of a Yiddish daily in Odessa (*Unzer Lebn*) and a Hebrew weekly in Moscow (*Haam*), which together constituted the entire Yiddish and Hebrew press in existence at the time of the revolution of March 1917.[39] But then the Jewish press grew by leaps and bounds. Daily and weekly newspapers and different magazines were issued in large numbers, which were increased by occasional publications serving a special purpose (e.g., pre-election campaigning for the Constituent Assembly or for the All-Russian Jewish Convention, which was never permitted to meet). The total number of Jewish newspapers and periodicals issued in Russia in 1917 and 1918 amounted to 171, of which 81 were in Yiddish, 10 in Hebrew, and 80 in Russian.[40]

Jewish pro-Communist publications began to appear in 1918, but already in 1919 their number exceeded that of the non-Communist publications, which were speedily suppressed. A Communist writer later collated the figures, given in Table XV, on regularly issued newspapers and periodicals in Yiddish and Hebrew, i.e., not including special pre-election publications or the Jewish Russian-language press.

TABLE XV

YIDDISH AND HEBREW NEWSPAPERS AND PERIODICALS [41]

Year	Total Number	Thereof Communist or Pro-Communist
1917	49	None
1918	63	9
1919	58	30
1920	96	66
1921	62	50

From 1918 to 1921 the number of pro-Communist publications rose from 9 to 50, while the number of non-Communist publications dropped from 54 to 12. No statistics were given for the following years, for the non-Communist Jewish press went out of existence altogether. Its disappearance was followed by a marked decline in the total number of Jewish newspapers and periodicals, which fell from 62 in 1921 to 27 in 1922, and to 21 in 1923–1925.[42] An increase began to take place in 1926, and the number of publications attained a new high in 1935; thereafter it declined abruptly.

This movement is clearly seen in a survey of the fate of the daily newspapers. Prior to the First World War, as mentioned before, Greater Russia (with Poland, Lithuania, etc.) had 15 Jewish dailies in Yiddish or

Hebrew. In 1918, in spite of the general suppression of non-Communist newspapers, Soviet Russia (with a substantially smaller Jewish population) still had 11 daily newspapers in Yiddish (and none in Hebrew), of which 8 were non-Communist and 3 were Communist (one, founded in August 1918, in Moscow and one each in Minsk and Vilna, which was occupied by the Red Army in December 1918 and remained for a few months under Soviet rule).[43] By 1935 only 4 or possibly 5 daily newspapers (about 300 issues a year) were left, all of them, of course, Communist: one each in Moscow, Kharkov, Minsk, and Birobidzhan, and a special newspaper for artisans (*Kustar'*) in the Ukraine, of which it is not certain if it was issued daily. In 1939 the number of daily newspapers in Yiddish was still smaller—one each in Minsk, Kiev (replacing the Kharkov paper), and Birobidzhan.[44]

A still bleaker picture emerges when the numbers of daily and non-daily newspapers are added together. Ten Yiddish newspapers were published in the Ukraine in 1935: the central daily in Kharkov (300 issues a year); local non-daily newspapers in Kiev (120 issues), Odessa (180), Berdichev (120), and Kremenchug (60); 2 non-daily newspapers in Jewish national districts (180 and 84 issues, respectively); a newspaper for artisans (300[?]); 2 newspapers issued by the Communist Youth—one for Young Communists and one for the Communist Pioneer children (120 issues each). But in 1939 only 5 Yiddish newspapers were published: the central daily (now in Kiev), a local non-daily in Kremenchug, and 3 non-dailies in the national districts.[45]

The downward trend was no less obvious in White Russia, where of the 4 Yiddish newspapers published in 1935—a central newspaper in Minsk, a local one in Liozno, and 2 newspapers of the Communist Youth —only the central paper in Minsk remained in 1939. After the Soviet occupation of Polish White Russia in August 1939, a new Yiddish paper began to appear in Bialystok.

The Jewish press suffered most conspicuously in the Russian SFSR. In 1935 the RSFSR had 4 Yiddish newspapers: *Emes* in Moscow, the leading Jewish newspaper of the RSFSR and the entire Soviet Union; a local newspaper in Birobidzhan; and 2 district newspapers in the Jewish agricultural districts in the Crimea. *Emes* was suppressed in 1938 during the purge, which vented itself with particular ferocity on the minority nationalities. Both Yiddish newspapers in the Crimea also went out of existence, and for the entire Russian SFSR only one Yiddish newspaper remained, in Birobidzhan, with a circulation officially given as 1,500. Within the Soviet Union (excluding Bialystok) only 7 Yiddish newspapers were left in 1939, as against 18 in 1935. The aggregate circulation of the remaining newspapers totaled 38,700, for a Jewish population of over 3,000,000.[46]

The dissolution of Jewish periodicals during the purges was less conspicuous, for most of them had perished as early as 1935. Of the scholarly publications, the following were issued regularly or occasionally in 1935: *Afn Shprakhfront*, in Kharkov, occasional volumes of studies; *Afn Visnshaftlekhen Front*, in Minsk, a bulletin published jointly by the Institutes for Jewish Proletarian Culture of the Ukrainian and White-Russian Academies of Sciences; and *Visnshaft un Revolutsie*, in Kiev, a monthly publication of the Ukrainian Academy of Sciences. Of these, only *Afn Shprakhfront* (transferred to Kiev) remained in 1939. *Ratnbildung*, an educational monthly published in Kiev in the earlier years, was no longer issued. However, literary reviews continued to be published in Minsk and Kiev, the Kiev review having been transferred thither from Kharkov.[47] New literary publications, however, appeared in 1939: a bimonthly in Birobidzhan, and a literary almanac (collections of short stories, novelettes, and essays) in Moscow.

The Leninist disregard of Jewish "nationhood" expressed itself in the fact that the Communist Party never published a theoretical periodical in Yiddish. At no time was there an official party journal devoted to problems of "Jewish national construction" such as were issued for other minority nationalities. For a number of years a small periodical, *Tribuna*, was issued by OZET (GEZERD), in which the socio-economic problems of Jewish reconstruction were discussed with a view to advancing the government's plans for the rural settlement of Jews; but *Tribuna* was published in Russian in Moscow and never reached the Jewish masses. It was discontinued in January 1938 and nothing took its place, either in Russian or in Yiddish.

NOTES

1. The history of minority schools in pre-revolutionary Russia is most comprehensively treated in G. G. Tumim and V. A. Zelenko, ed., *Inorodcheskaya shkola. Sbornik statei i materialov [School for Alien Peoples. Collection of Articles and Materials]*, St. Petersburg, 1916, based on materials prepared for the first nationwide convention on public education held in 1913, where a great deal of attention was paid to the use of minority languages in schools.

2. It is not unusual in multinational areas for the children of a minority nationality, though reared in the culture of their ethnic group, not to speak its language. In Russia this was particularly the case with Jewish children in the medium-sized and larger cities. With this in mind, the program of national-cultural autonomy adopted by the Bund in April 1917 demanded, as well as Yiddish-language schools for the majority of Jewish children, Jewish schools using "another, non-Jewish language." (Cf. S. Dimanshtein, ed., *Revolutsiya i natsional'nyi vopros*, vol. III, p. 278). Russian was the literary language of many Jews and had a tremendous influence on Jewish culture and even on the development of what may be termed Jewish national consciousness. The most prominent philosophers of Jewish national rebirth in Russia, Simon Dubnov and Akhad-Haam, neither wrote nor published in Yiddish. Dubnov wrote in Russian, and Akhad-Haam in Hebrew and occasionally in Russian; his Hebrew writings, however, reached the bulk of readers in Russian translation; secular Hebrew literature was read only by a small minority.

3. *Di Alfarbandishe Kommunistishe Partay (Bolshevikes) un di Idishe Masn*, p. 77.

4. Administrative order issued by the Commissariat for Jewish National Affairs in 1918, quoted by S. Agurskii, *Der Idisher Arbeter* . . . , p. 29.

5. In 1922, when the prohibitions on private enterprise were relaxed, it was possible to discuss the creation of a privately financed and operated Hebrew stage. The question was raised as to whether permission would be granted for a school to teach the actors Hebrew. The Jewish Sections held that rigid limitations should be imposed on any such schools. Moisei Litvakov, the Sections' most prominent literary man, wrote in *Emes* in June 1922: "First, the students may not be under the age of 18. The Soviet government cannot permit children to be concerned with subjects of no practical use. Moreover, only the Hebrew language should be taught. . . . There will be no room for Jewish history or for the history of Hebrew culture and literature. It goes without saying that only lawful associations of private persons will be permitted to open such schools. No fund-raising will be permitted. Since the purpose of such schools is purely instructional, the religious communities will not be permitted any connection with them." (Quoted from L. Tsintsiper, *Esher Sh'noth Rdifoth [Ten Years of Persecution]*, Tel Aviv, 1930, pp. 87f.)

6. I. Dardak, "Unzre Dergraykhungen in 15 Yor Oktyabr afn Gebit fun Folk-Bildung," in *Tsum 15 Yortog fun der Oktyabr-Revolutsie. Sotsial-Ekonomisher Zamlbukh*, White-Russian Academy of Sciences, Jewish Sector, Minsk, 1932, pp. 172f.

7. For details and source references, see "Dispersion and Assimilation" in Chapter I above.

8. Dardak, *op. cit.*, p. 156. The Soviet school year usually begins on August 15.

9. Data for 1922–1931, from Dardak, *op. cit.*, pp. 156f.; for 1932 and 1933, from S. Dimanshtein, ed., *Idn in FSSR. Zamlbukh*, published by *Mezhdunarodnaya Kniga* and *Emes*, 1935, p. 262. Figures for 1922–1927 do not include Gomel (city and district), which was part of the Russian SFSR until early 1926, but did not figure in White Russia's school statistics until 1928. Dimanshtein's yearbook issued in 1935 does not give any figures for 1934, although complete data for 1934 must have been in by that time, and also figures on the number of schools and the enrollment for 1935.

10. Quoted from Jacob Lestschinsky, *Dos Sovetishe Identum. Di Fargangenhayt un Gegnvart*, New York, 1941, p. 330.

11. Data from the official publication of the Central Statistical Office of the Ukrainian SSR, *Statistika Ukrainy*, Series VII (Education), vol. III, issue 1 (serial no. 46), pp. 9–17.

12. *Ibid.*, Series VII, vol. IV, issue 1 (serial no. 61), pp. 3, 85; vol. V, issue 1 (serial no. 71), pp. 50, 108f.

13. *Ibid.*, Series VII, vol. V, issue 1 (serial no. 71), pp. 50, 108f.; vol. VI, issue 1 (serial no. 95), pp. xxv, 10f., 15; vol. VII, issue 1 (serial no. 131), p. 20; vol. VIII, issue 1 (serial no. 138), pp. 10f., 16. Data for 1925 and 1927 are as of January 1; for 1926 and 1928, as of December 1 and December 15 of the preceding year, i.e., after enrollment for the years indicated.

14. Ya. Kantor, *Natsional'noye stroitel'stvo sredi yevreyev SSSR [National Construction among USSR Jews]*, *Vlast' Sovetov* publications of the Presidium of the Central Executive Committee of the Russian SFSR, Moscow, 1934, p. 172.

15. Kantor's figures, which show 502 Jewish schools with an enrollment of 78,000 for 1927, and 587 schools with 79,000 students for 1928, apparently refer to both Jewish and multilingual schools, and include in the enrollment not only students of Jewish sections of multilingual schools, but *all* Jewish students in such schools. This may account for the difference between his figures and the official ones of the above table. This also accords with the assumption, borne out by other evidence, that enrollment in Jewish schools in 1928–1931 increased a little more than the enrollment in Jewish sections of multilingual schools decreased.

16. Dimanshtein, ed., *Idn in FSSR*, p. 262.

17. D. Mats, "Na vysokom podyeme (O rabote sredi natsional'nykh men'shinstv Ukrainy)" ["At the Crest of the Wave (Work among National Minorities in the Ukraine)"], in *Revolyutsiya i Natsional'nosti*, June 1935, p. 60.

18. Kantor, *op. cit.*, p. 173.

19. M. Kiper, *10 Yor Oktyabr-Revolutsie. Di Oktyabr-Revolutsie un di Idishe Arbetndike fun Ukrayne*, Kiev, 1927, p. 75.

20. Administrative pressure in favor of Yiddish-language schools "gave rise to charges of antisemitism leveled at the Soviet government," according to Kiper, *op. cit.*, p. 173. While it is doubtful that the Jewish population would have accused the Soviet government of antisemitism in the mid-1920's, it is quite likely that religious parents were made indignant by the "*rishes*" of militantly atheist Jewish Communists. They may well have reasoned that if their children must be exposed to blasphemous teaching, let it be in a school where a faith other than their own was the chief target.

21. See Kantor, *op. cit.*, p. 173. Originally, "Yiddishizing" had been praised as the model application to Jewish school problems of Leninist doctrine; it was contrasted to the "nationalist," "Bundist" heresy of special Jewish schools for non-Yiddish-speaking children. Though already warning against overzealousness in "Yiddishizing" in 1926, Chemeriskii took pains to give the impression that the chief enemy was the "nationalist" non-Yiddish school for Jewish children (which did not exist and was not even seriously considered as a possibility). The Jewish school, he wrote, "does not grab the child just because the parents are Jewish; the child is enrolled in the Jewish school because it talks Yiddish. Children who speak Russian or Ukrainian or White-Russian must attend the respective [Russian, Ukrainian, or White-Russian] schools, and it is with a view to this that we fight against non-Yiddish schools for Jewish children and have, with minor exceptions, succeeded." (*Di Alfarbandishe Kommunistishe Partay [Bolshevikes] un di Idishe Masn*, p. 79.)

22. Chemeriskii, *op. cit.*, p. 80.

23. All data from *Statistika Ukrainy*, Series VII, vol. VII, issue 1 (serial no. 131), pp. 28f.

24. *Statistichnyi shchorichnyk na 1929 rik*, issued by the Central Statistical Office of the Ukrainian SSR, Kharkov, 1929, p. 83.

25. Kantor, *op. cit.*, p. 172.

26. Many such press items have been collected by Jacob Lestschinsky, *op. cit.*, pp. 332–342.

27. E.g., *Emes* reported on June 24, 1937: "Enrollment began on June 1. Jewish school officials in Kiev ought to have considered the lesson of last year's failure . . . when several schools were unable to fill the first grade. Such, regrettably, has not been the case. . . . Many Jewish schools will have no first grade this year." The same correspondent said: ."Kiev has a considerable network of Jewish kindergartens, but they are Jewish in name only. Actually, educational work there is conducted in Russian." Similar trends in White Russia (Bobruisk) had been recorded in *Emes* on May 27, 1937.

28. A dispatch referring to the Uman', Fastov, Skvirsk, and Makarov districts in Kiev province (*Emes*, February 17, 1938) mentioned the discontinuance of many Jewish schools. The Vilna writer Szmerl Kaczerginsky, who spent some time in Moscow in 1945 and had frequent meetings with Jewish writers and educators, was told by Soviet Jews that the lower grades of the Jewish schools in the Ukraine had been discontinued in the years preceding the war. This led to the schools' complete disappearance within a few years. (*Tsvishn Hamer un Serp*, Paris, 1949, pp. 82f.)

29. Lestschinsky, *op. cit.*, p. 342.

30. Kantor, *op. cit.*, pp. 184ff.

31. *Ibid.*, p. 186. Emphasis Kantor's.

32. Based on data in N. Rubinshtein, *Dos Idishe Bukh in Sovetfarband* [for 1932, 1933, 1934, and 1935], joint annual publication of the State Library and the Lenin Bibliographical Institute of the White-Russian SSR, Minsk, 1933–1936.

33. The Russian unit of measurement for printed matter is a "printed sheet" of either 36,000 or 40,000 units of print, which would correspond to about 5,000 to 6,000 words in English. As can be seen from the table, the average size of a book in Yiddish was less than 6 sheets, i.e., approximately 30,000 to 35,000 words.

34. See n. 32 above.

35. S. Mikhoels and I. Dobrushin, "Idishe Teatr-Kultur in Ratnfarband," in Dimanshtein, ed., *Idn in FSSR*, p. 151.

36. Dimanshtein, ed., *op. cit.*, p. 161.

37. Data for the individual Republics and the Soviet Union have been compiled from Kantor's book (*supra* n. 14, pp. 179ff.), Dimanshtein's *Idn in FSSR* (pp. 151–162), and the official Theater Directory: *Teatral'nyi Spravochnik SSSR, 1937/38, Iskusstvo* publishing house, Moscow, 1937, pp. 174–178, 421, 435, 440f., 443, 445, 449, 453, 460f., 468.

38. Based on data in the newspaper directory *Gazetnyi Mir, Adresnaya i spravochnaya kniga*, I. V. Volfson, ed., 2d ed., St. Petersburg, 1913.

39. I. V. Yashunskii, "Yevreiskaya periodicheskaya pechat' v 1917 i 1918 godakh" ["The Jewish Press in 1917 and 1918"], in *Vremennik Rossiiskoi Knizhnoi Palaty* [*Periodical Record of the Book Chamber of Russia*], issue III, Petrograd, 1920, pp. 3f.

40. *Ibid.*, pp. 2, 5ff.

41. A. Kirzhnits, *Di Idishe Presse in Ratnfarband (1917–1927)*, White-Russian Book Chamber, Minsk, 1928, p. 68.

42. *Ibid.*, p. 69.

43. The individual publications are listed in Kirzhnits, *op. cit.*

44. Data for 1935 and 1939 are from the yearbooks issued by the Central State Book Chamber (in 1939 renamed All-Union Book Chamber): *Letopis' Periodicheskikh Izdanii SSSR v 1935 godu* and *Yezhegodnik Periodicheskikh Izdanii, 1939 g.* In the 1935 yearbook, *Kustar'* was listed as being published in Vinnitsa, and the number of issues per year was not indicated; in the Book Chamber's yearbook for the preceding year, it had been mentioned as a daily published in Kharkov.

45. The Jewish national districts were predominantly agricultural, whereas the cities were industrial centers. That it was no longer deemed necessary to issue Yiddish publications for youngsters is particularly striking.

46. All data from Book Chamber yearbooks (see n. 44 *supra*). For most of the Yiddish newspapers listed, no figures on circulation were given in the 1935 yearbook.

47. In addition to its literary magazine, Kharkov, a city with over 100,000 Jews, within a few years lost, as has been mentioned, its daily Yiddish newspaper, a Yiddish publication for artisans, the only existing Yiddish philological publication, and three Yiddish theaters. What was not discontinued was transferred to Kiev, whose 150,- to 200,000 Jews constituted about one-third of the city's population, as against a Jewish percentage of 15 to 20 percent in Kharkov. Kiev's Jews, living for the most part in a sort of ghetto and constantly reinforced by newcomers from near-by *shtetls*, were less assimilated and preserved Yiddish to a larger extent than the Jews of Kharkov. The removal of Yiddish cultural facilities from Kharkov may be taken to indicate the government's firm resolve to eliminate everything impeding assimilation wherever strong assimilatory influences were at work.

Chapter XI

Jewish Administrative Autonomy

Local Self-Government

Official Soviet theory allows national groups constituting the majority of the population in a given area to claim a certain measure of self-government, while minority groups are entitled to the recognition of their languages in local administrative agencies, courts, schools, etc. So far as the Jewish minority was concerned, this meant two major administrative operations. In those districts and communities where Jews constituted a large minority, Yiddish was to be introduced into the administration of the government and the public services. And in those districts and communities where the majority of the population was Jewish, the local administration was to be made "Jewish."[1]

The establishment of Jewish municipal Soviets and Jewish districts did not, however, imply the existence of a specifically Jewish policy which they were intended to serve. It merely meant that the numerical preponderance of Jews within a given area was officially recognized and that Yiddish was to be the principal official language, the non-Jewish local minorities of course retaining their language rights.

The protection of Jewish local minority rights acquired importance chiefly in White Russia. In other parts of the country, the establishment of Jewish municipal Soviets or Jewish districts in places where there were Jewish majorities relegated other procedures to the background. Municipal Soviets, as a rule, were proclaimed Jewish only in rural communities, semirural market towns of the *shtetl* type, and semiurban workers' settlements around isolated industrial plants or organized as non-incorporated communities on the outskirts of larger cities. Only in a few rural areas of Jewish agricultural settlement were entire districts (usually comprising one small town—the district seat—and a number of villages) made Jewish.

Jewish administrative units were considered desirable only in areas with compact Jewish populations. They found little favor in the Russian SFSR, where large Jewish enclaves were few. Progress was made only after the establishment of two Jewish national districts in the Crimea, and then later the autonomous province of Birobidzhan. The government's sponsorship of Jewish agricultural colonization gave the impression that Jewish nationhood was officially recognized, and this apparently encouraged the setting-up of Jewish administrative units also in the RSFSR's Western (Smolensk) province. There the first Jewish village Soviet was established in 1927, and at the same time several mixed Russian-Jewish units (i.e., administrations conducted in two official languages), viz., one Russian-Jewish city Soviet and five Russian-Jewish village Soviets [2] (together with six national and mixed Soviets for other minorities). By 1930 the number of national and mixed village Soviets—there is no longer any mention of such Soviets in cities—had increased to 26, and of these 12 were Jewish (one completely Jewish and 11 mixed).[3] In 1932, 11 Jewish village Soviets were still in existence;[4] but a tabulation of all Jewish Soviets in the Soviet Union, apparently for the middle of 1933, gave only 2 Jewish village Soviets for the Western province, the other 9 obviously having been "de-nationalized" in the meantime.[5]

That Jewish Soviets should have proved short-lived in the RSFSR's Western province was not surprising. Frequently the Soviets were Jewish in name only. It was pointed out in Soviet publications that at a provincial convention of "toiling Jews" in Smolensk in 1928, "the chairmen of several Jewish village Soviets spoke against conducting official business in the national language [Yiddish], because they thought that it was impossible to do it."[6] Conditions in the Western province in 1930 were described as follows: "Practically all [national] Soviets conduct their business exclusively in Russian. . . . Thus far no energetic measures have been taken to enforce the rights of the native tongues of national minorities in government agencies."[7] The Jewish village Soviets of the Western province (in the early part of 1932) were not so much Jewish as mixed agencies of rather limited significance, "and the conduct of affairs in these [Soviets] has not been transferred everywhere to the native language of the minority nationality."[8]

The development of Jewish administrative units in the Russian SFSR —outside of the Jewish districts in the Crimea and Birobidzhan—came to a halt in the 1930's, and no such bodies are mentioned in later years. Actually, the establishment of Jewish organs of local administration had been confined for the most part to the Ukraine from the very beginning.

Jewish Soviets and Districts in the Ukraine

Because of the large size of the Russian minority in the Ukrainian SSR, the administrative rights of non-Ukrainian local majorities found early recognition; in 1925 the Ukraine already had over 250 non-Ukrainian Soviets of various kinds. In the following years the Ukrainization of the central, regional, and local governments was paralleled by the rapid growth of non-Ukrainian units at the base of the administrative pyramid.

In the spring of 1931, the total number of non-Ukrainian municipal Soviets reached 1,139, of which 1,021 were village Soviets and 118 were market-town Soviets.[9] Most of these were Russian; only about 14 percent were officially Jewish. But while only 9 percent of the non-Ukrainian village Soviets were Jewish, the proportion of the Jewish Soviets of market towns and workers' settlements was much larger (56 percent), although by no means did every Jewish *shtetl* have a Jewish administration. The increase in the number of Jewish Soviets was considerable up to 1930 as shown in Table XVI.

TABLE XVI

JEWISH MUNICIPAL SOVIETS IN THE UKRAINE [10]

Year	Village Soviets	Market-Town Soviets	Total
1925	19	19	38
1926	34	52	86
1927	56	69	125
1928	77	69	146
1930	94	66	160
1931	95	66	161
1932	113	55	168
1933	99	55	154

No statistics were published for later years. When, after 1933, Soviet authors praised the record of the Ukrainian administration in protecting the administrative rights of the Jewish minority, reference was no longer made to Jewish village or market-town Soviets; only the three Jewish national districts were ever mentioned.[11] Jewish Soviets most certainly did not disappear after 1933, but it is plain that it was no longer deemed advisable to foster their growth or to publicize their existing number. The decline in the total number of Jewish Soviets in 1933 may be assumed to have continued in subsequent years, owing mainly to the drop in the number of market-town Soviets. Of the latter, over 20 percent lost their Jewish status between 1927 and 1932.

There are two explanations for the government's dwindling interest in the Jewish town Soviets. As originally conceived, the Jewish Soviet was intended to divide the *shtetl* along class lines; the younger, more "proletarian" elements in the community were expected to be most "anti-bourgeois," "anti-clerical," and pro-Communist, and to rout "Jewish reaction."[12] But it was precisely the uprooted younger generation of the "poor," that is, the young people more or less under Communist influence, who escaped the *shtetl* in droves throughout the 1920's, especially in the latter part of the decade, leaving behind the old folks, "clericals" and inveterate "petty bourgeois." The flight of what might have been the *shtetl's* Communist elite defeated the purpose of the establishment of Jewish local Soviets.

On the other hand, the market town was the commercial and administrative center of a rural area, and the government, after a few years of
experimentation, grew wary lest Jewish Soviets seem an instrument of
"Jewish domination" in the eyes of a restive and sometimes openly hostile
peasantry. As early as 1926 the establishment of Jewish Soviets was rigor-
ously limited by party order. A resolution "concerning the adaptation of
the Soviet apparatus to the needs of the Jewish toiling population," passed
by the Sixth and last Conference of the Communist Party's Jewish Sections, warned against Jewish Soviets in urban communities. The resolution
said, in somewhat veiled phrases: "In Soviet construction among the
Jewish population in the cities, attention must not so much center on the
establishment of Jewish city Soviets as on the adaptation of all organs to
serving the Jewish population in Yiddish. As for market towns and the
activities of Jewish . . . Soviets in process of establishment in such places,
there, too, the necessity of providing services to the surrounding [rural]
population must be taken into account."[13] The resolution placed limitations on the official use of Yiddish:

> In transferring [the conduct of official business in] *shtetl* Soviets into
> the native tongue, it is essential that there be an overwhelming and
> absolute majority of the [Jewish] population; arrangements must be
> made for minority nationalities, and the language of the surrounding
> population must be taken into consideration.
> In Soviets serving villages or market towns with a heterogeneous
> national composition, information and publication services and [all
> official] intercourse with the population must be conducted in the local
> languages.[14]

This policy effectively halted the growth of Jewish market-town Soviets.
The last increase in their number was recorded in 1927; no change took
place in 1928; from then on, the decrease was visible and rapid. The increase in the number of Jewish Soviets in 1930–1932 was owing to the
new Jewish village Soviets that resulted from the growing agricultural
employment of town Jews, particularly in areas marked out for Jewish
colonization; of the 113 Jewish village Soviets listed in 1932, 33 were in
Jewish national districts.[15] After 1933, however, the number of Jewish
village Soviets also began to decline.

In practice, there was a growing tendency to limit the administrative
recognition of Jewish minority status. Even in major Jewish centers the
official use of Yiddish was occasionally restricted. Sporadic complaints
about the elimination of Yiddish from use in government agencies found
their way into the Jewish Soviet press as early as 1930; thus, the Kharkov
Shtern reported that such was the case in Berdichev, a predominantly
Jewish city.[16] Such reports became more frequent, especially in the case
of village and town Soviets. They were much alike: "In all official inter-

course with the population Ukrainian is employed," said a report about the Jewish village Soviet in Murafa, in the province of Vinnitsa;[17] and the languages in use in the Jewish town Soviet in Shpola, a typical *shtetl* in the province of Kiev, were Ukrainian and Russian.[18] As time went by, this sort of "de-nationalization" increased throughout the Ukraine.[19] In the later 1930's even the Jewish national districts were affected, indicating a new retrogressive trend in Jewish agricultural settlement.

The first Jewish national district was that of Kalinindorf, established in 1927 in the province of Kherson on the site of the old Jewish farm colonies of the nineteenth century. The district, which consisted of large estates of big landowners dispossessed by the revolution, was intended to be one of the main settlement areas for the destitute Jews of decaying market towns. In addition to the old, new Jewish villages were settled. But the success of the plan was less than expected, and soon the settlers, new and old alike, began to move away. According to I. Sudarskii, executive secretary of the Ukrainian KOMZET, the population of the old Jewish colonies dropped from 3,031 on July 1, 1930 to 2,643 on July 1, 1931, a loss of 12.8 percent; during the same period, the population of the new Jewish villages decreased 32 percent, from 8,714 to 5,929; and even the non-Jewish villages in the district of Kalinindorf saw their population fall from 2,530 to 2,273, or 10.1 percent.[20] It was not simply the attraction of the growing industrial cities that made the Jewish farmers leave the land; quite a number of them fled in desperation back to their starving hometowns. "There was not a *shtetl* in the Ukraine where we did not encounter people back from the Kalinindorf district," said Sudarskii.[21] Things went from bad to worse. From the middle of February to the end of March 1932, KOMZET brought 3,559 new settlers (913 families) to Kalinindorf, but of these, 1,855, or 52 percent, left by April 15.[22]

Kalinindorf, it is true, was in a particularly bad way. But conditions were scarcely better in the other two Jewish national districts. A survey of Novo-Zlatopol'ye, made a Jewish district in July 1929, said: "It is unfortunately a fact that the outgoing tide of new settlers is no smaller in Novo-Zlatopol'ye than in other districts. The reflux in 1932 approached 50 percent of all the families that had come to settle in the district in the course of the year."[23] A large exodus of new settlers was also reported from Stalindorf, the third Jewish national district, established in 1930.[24]

The flight of the settlers from the new Jewish agricultural centers was not confined to the Ukraine. It also took place, though on a lesser scale, in the Crimea, and at times in Birobidzhan it assumed catastrophic proportions. The Jewish character of these districts suffered from this failure of Jewish colonization to continue to expand; apparently the mere recognition of Yiddish as the districts' official language was not enough to make them organs of national self-government. But there was much to be desired even in the employment of Yiddish in the national districts. What had happened in the schools, and in Jewish village and town Soviets, happened here as well; assimilation undermined the recognized position of Yiddish. In 1937, a report from Novo-Zlatopol'ye stated: "In the course of the last two years the atmosphere has become such that the use of Yiddish and Ukrainian is avoided. All meetings, conferences, and executive sessions are conducted in Russian. Official business is transacted in Yiddish in only one village Soviet; administrative affairs are conducted in Russian in all other village Soviets, the district executive committee, the district agencies, the land department, and the finance department. All announcements, ordinances, and signs are in Russian."[25] In another Jewish district, even the district newspaper abandoned Yiddish entirely for Russian.[26]

There is no evidence at hand to indicate what point "de-nationalization" had reached in the national districts by the time of the outbreak of the Nazi-Soviet war. The silence of the Soviet Jewish press on all matters concerning the use of Yiddish—and indeed on all important "national" matters—in the Jewish districts is significant.

De-Nationalization in White Russia

The Ukraine was the only Soviet republic where the establishment of separate Jewish administrations—Jewish village and market-town Soviets and Jewish national districts—assumed large proportions in the late 1920's and early 1930's. According to the estimates of Soviet Jewish writers, who perhaps exaggerate, the Jewish population residing in areas administered by Jewish local Soviets or Jewish district executive committees in the early 1930's, accounted for some 14 percent of the total Jewish population of the Ukrainian SSR.[27] One-seventh of the Ukrainian Jews thus enjoyed the legal status of a self-governing minority nationality, however little that may mean in Soviet practice. In the White Russian Republic, which possessed the second largest Jewish population, such formal self-government was largely' nonexistent. "In White Russia efforts were centered not on setting up national districts, but on adapting the *entire* governmental, cooperative, and social machinery to serving all the principal nationalities on an equal basis."[28] Only a few Jewish village and town Soviets were established, and there were no Jewish national districts at all.

The White-Russian Soviet Republic had originally been organized as a multinational state with four official languages. This was deemed sufficient to protect the major national groups, and the government was reluctant to establish special local administrative units for them. While the Ukraine had over 250 minority village and market-town Soviets as early as the spring of 1925, and almost 1,000 in 1927, there were only 9 such units in White Russia in 1924, and 54 in 1927.[29] In 1928, at the peak, the number of all minority units, Jewish and otherwise, in White Russia did not exceed

78.[30] The number of Jewish Soviets was remarkably small, although, because there were few large cities, a large proportion of the Jews lived in tiny places where they constituted a majority. In all of White Russia there were only 7 Jewish municipal Soviets in 1924, 11 in 1925, 18 in 1926, 22 in 1927, and 27 in 1931.[31] In contrast to the Ukraine, very few of these were in rural communities; of the 27 Jewish Soviets listed in 1931, 23 were in small towns and only 4 in villages.[32] A downward trend set in immediately after 1931; as in the Ukraine, it first affected Jewish administration in the *shtetl*. Kantor lists, apparently for 1932 or 1933, only 24 Jewish Soviets—20 in small towns and 4 in villages.[33]

Under these circumstances, the degree of recognition accorded Yiddish in the general administration was important. Over nine-tenths of White Russia's Jews regarded Yiddish as their mother tongue in 1926, and in subsequent years Yiddish lost out less in White Russia than in the Ukraine. The number of Jews in White Russia was about one-quarter of that in the Ukraine, but the number of children attending Jewish schools in White Russia was almost half.[34]

One of the four official languages protected by White Russia's constitution, Yiddish was widely used in the 1920's in official announcements; many public notices, posters, street and shop signs, inscriptions on buildings, etc., were in Yiddish. For Jews and non-Jews alike, the use of Yiddish soon became a familiar part of daily life. This, of course, delayed its displacement by White Russian and Russian, even at a time when "White-Russianization" was encouraged by the Soviet government.

Nevertheless, nationwide tendencies, so strongly felt in the Ukraine, were felt in White Russia as well. Imperceptibly at first, Yiddish was forced to give way before the increasing hostility to its administrative use. In 1930 this hostility was openly displayed in several places. A report from Gorki, a small town in the province of Minsk with an overwhelming Jewish majority, told of a group of Jewish school children that went to see the chairman of the local Soviet to discuss library and school matters, who harshly rapped out: "Speak Russian, we do not understand Yiddish."[35] Seemingly isolated incidents of this kind grew more frequent from one year to the next. By 1934 the battle of languages, though little publicized, had spread so far as to cause the *Emes* to protest:

> Very disquieting news has recently come from a number of cities, market towns, and villages, pointing to a falling-off in national minority activities, and even to their thorough neglect. This newspaper has been in daily [*sic*] receipt of letters, reports, and articles from Jewish workers and toilers, bitterly and justifiably complaining about the abject state of the political and cultural services [for minorities, and] saying that enthusiasm for [their] liquidation is spreading like wildfire among officials in various districts in the province of Vinitsa [Ukraine],

the Western province [Russian SFSR], and in White Russia. They abolish special agents for national minority affairs on the staffs of executive committees and education departments. They abolish national clubs. They abolish libraries. All this is termed "raising the level of the work." In Mogilev [White Russia] Jewish schools are already being merged with White-Russian schools—that is, Jewish schools are actually being abolished.

It would be difficult to enumerate all such instances, for unfortunately there are too many where enthusiasm for such "mergers" is particularly rife.[36]

The "enthusiastic liquidation" of Jewish cultural activities and institutions, paralleled by the displacement of Yiddish in the administration, reduced to nought the effectiveness of the handful of Jewish administrative units established in earlier years. A few seemed to have been functioning on the eve of the war, but they neither influenced Jewish life nor could they stem the tide of administrative "de-nationalization."

Jewish Courts

The right of every citizen to use his native language in courts of law is guaranteed by Soviet law, and the courts are obligated to provide official interpreters whenever needed. In addition, however, the Soviet Jewish press in the 1920's and early 1930's laid great stress on the advantages for the Jewish minority of the establishment of special Jewish courts where, instead of using interpreters, all proceedings would be conducted in Yiddish. Such courts were chiefly established in those places (villages and small towns) where the local administration was made Jewish, and, of course, in Jewish national districts. Jewish courts were also set up in some of the larger cities having a large proportion of Jewish inhabitants.[37] Notwithstanding the praise lavished on Jewish courts in Soviet Jewish publications, factual information about them is scant. There is something to be got from Kantor's *National Construction among USSR Jews* (1934), the most recent Soviet publication to consider Jewish institutions of justice at length. In later years, there is hardly a reference to Jewish court divisions in the writings of Soviet authors.

Kantor gives figures, shown in Table XVII, for a few years on the number and regional distribution of Jewish courts.

Rules regulating the jurisdiction of national courts (Jewish or other) varied in the different Soviet republics. In the Ukraine, proceedings were referred to such division whenever the accused in a criminal action or the defendant in a civil suit so requested. In White Russia, the agreement of both parties was required, or the Soviet court could so rule.[39]

In Jewish districts and in villages and market towns under Jewish administration, the establishment of Jewish courts was apparently looked on as a matter of course. In larger Ukrainian or White-Russian cities, however, the fact that justice was meted out in Yiddish by a duly established court was bound to impress both the Jewish and non-Jewish population. But the example this afforded of national equality was of less moment to the authorities than the political usefulness of the courts. They

TABLE XVII

JEWISH DIVISIONS OF SOVIET COURTS [38]

Year	Ukraine	White Russia	Russian SFSR	Total
1928	36	6	1	43
1929	39	6	2	47
1931	46	10	11	67

rivaled and displaced rabbinical justice, thus undermining the authority of religion and destroying the ties that still bound large sections of the Jewish population to the religious community and rabbinate; and they served the purpose of disseminating antireligious propaganda among the Jews. Kantor writes with visible satisfaction:

The national court divisions have made an important contribution to the eradication of pernicious attitudes, superstitions, and anachronistic religious survivals within the Jewish population; they have driven out the rabbinical practice of justice so widespread in the Jewish *shtetl,* and have thus liberated large sections of the *shtetl* poor from the influence of the class enemy. In particular, the role of the national court divisions in the struggle for the Soviet work school and against the kheder deserves to be emphasized. In the trials [of people accused of giving illegal religious instruction to minors in the kheder], held in Vitebsk, Gomel and a number of other cities, the fact that the proceedings of the court were conducted in Yiddish did a great service of exposure and educational propaganda.[40]

At a time when national courts were still a novel phenomenon, a Soviet Jewish author made a point of their "Sovietizing" role in the Ukraine: "The national court divisions have played a not insignificant role in promoting the Sovietization of backward masses. In earlier days minority nationalities used to submit their disputes for adjudication to clerics, such as rabbis, Catholic priests, etc.; now the national court divisions are dislodging the clergy."[41] These "backward masses" were exclusively Jewish. Only in the Jewish community was it a practice to appeal to ecclesiastical authority in the adjudication of disputes; of all "servants of religion," only the rabbis were vested with judicial power in secular matters. Legal recourse in a regular way to the church in either civil or criminal cases was unheard of among Catholics; when the writer refers to the adjudication of disputes by Catholic priests he is only attempting to conceal the fact that these courts were primarily Jewish courts, whose special task it was to break the special judicial hold of the rabbinate on the Jewish community. This is corroborated by official statistics. Of a total of 58 national court divisions in session in the Ukraine in 1927, 36 were Jewish.[42] These 36 accounted for 62 percent of all such courts, whereas only 12 percent of all "national" Soviets in the Ukrainian SSR were Jewish.[43]

The Jewish courts lost their usefulness for the Soviet government with the defeat of organized religion. As assimilation advanced and official policy came more and more to support it, their number rapidly declined. Only a few continued to function in the late 1930's. "De-nationalization," which destroyed the Jewish schools and abolished the Jewish press, made a special Jewish judicature as unnecessary as Jewish Soviets.

NOTES

1. Self-government at higher administrative levels—the province or the republic—is tantamount in Soviet law to national autonomy. Only one autonomous Jewish province has ever been established in the Soviet Union, that of Birobidzhan.

2. Z. Shefter, "Obsledovaniye natsional'nykh sel'sovetsov" ["A Field Study of National Village Soviets"], in *Vlast' Sovetov*, 1928, no. 8, p. 14.

3. Z. Ostrovskii, "Polozheniye natsional'nykh men'shinstv v Zapadnoi oblasti" ["The Condition of National Minorities in the Western Province"], in *Sovetskoye Stroitel'stvo*, issued monthly by the Central Executive Committee of the USSR, March 1930, p. 121.

4. Ya. Kantor, *Natsional'noye stroitel'stvo sredi yevreyev SSSR* [*National Construction among USSR Jews*], p. 28.

5. *Ibid.*, Appendix, pp. 198f.

6. Shefter, *op. cit.*, p. 14.

7. Ostrovskii, *op. cit.*, p. 121.

8. Kantor, *op. cit.*, p. 28.

9. *Ibid.*, p. 22.

10. Data for 1925–1931, as of April 1; for 1932, mid-year; for 1933, end of year. For 1925–1931, from a table compiled by Kantor, *op. cit.*, p. 23; for 1932, based on a listing of Jewish Soviets, *ibid.*, pp. 194ff.; for 1933, *ibid.*, p. 22. There is no explicit indication, in the source quoted, as to the exact date to which the appended listing of Jewish Soviets applied; it may be assumed, for a number of reasons, that the list, with a certain approximation, reflected conditions prevailing in mid-1932.

11. See, e.g., D. Mats, "Na vysokom podyeme" ["At the Crest of the Wave"], in *Revolyutsiya i Natsional'nosti*, June 1935, p. 62; also D. Levin, "Dvadtsat' let sovetskogo mnogonatsional'nogo gosudarstva" ["Twenty Years as a Multinational Soviet State"], in *Sovetskoye Gosudarstvo* [*The Soviet State*], issued by the Law Institute, Academy of Sciences of the USSR, 1937, no. 5, p. 89.

12. Ya. Chemeriskii declared in 1927: ". . . We intend to smash Jewish clericalism, the new focus of counterrevolutionary concentration. The network of Jewish Soviets and the new [Jewish] districts provide a new form of governmental organization of the Jewish masses. Social differentiation and class struggle will also be stimulated by the new stratum of Jewish officeholders wielding power in the [Jewish] Soviet. The national unity [of the Jewish group] will be dealt a deathblow by the poor, who now hold power under the leadership of the proletariat." See "Orientirung in der Idisher Arbet (Araynfir)," in *Alfarbandishe Baratung fun di Idishe Sektsies fun der A1KP/B (Dekabr 1926)*, p. 15.

13. *Alfarbandishe Baratung fun di Idishe Sektsies*, p. 15.

14. *Ibid.*, pp. 247f.
15. Kantor, *op. cit.*, pp. 194ff.
16. Quoted in a Moscow dispatch to the *Jewish Daily Bulletin*, December 15, 1930. The trend did not subside in later years, as shown in a report from Berdichev in *Emes*, November 15, 1935.
17. *Ibid.*, July 22, 1934.
18. *Ibid.*, April 2, 1937.
19. See Jacob Lestschinsky, *op. cit.*, pp. 352ff.
20. I. Sudarskii, *Kalinindorfer Rayon, Emes* publishers, Moscow, 1932, p. 22.
21. *Ibid.*, p. 23.
22. Ye. Eidenman [executive secretary, OZET Central Council] in *Tribuna*, 1932, no. 13, pp. 2ff.; cf. also *Tribuna*, 1932, no. 10–11, p. 11.
23. I. Sudarskii, *Nay-Zlatopoler Rayon, Emes* pub., Moscow, 1933, p. 68.
24. I. Sudarskii, *Stalindorfer Rayon, Emes* pub., Moscow, 1933, p. 26.
25. *Emes*, July 12, 1937.
26. *Ibid.*, March 20, 1935. Only the newspaper's name (*Leninveg*) and the name of the editor continued to be printed in Yiddish.
27. According to Kantor, *op. cit.*, p. 23, early in 1932 some 14.2 percent of the Ukraine's Jewish population lived within the jurisdiction of Jewish municipal Soviets or national districts. The same figure was given in *Bol'shaya Sovetskaya Entsiklopediya*, vol. 24 (1932), p. 92. An estimated 14 to 15 percent was mentioned by Mats, *op. cit.*, p. 62.
28. Kantor, *op. cit.*, p. 27.
29. *Prakticheskoye resheniye natsional'nogo voprosa v Belorusskoi SSR* [*The Practical Solution of the National Problem in the White-Russian SSR*], publications of the Central Executive Committee of the White-Russian SSR, Central Commission on Nationalities, Part II, Minsk, 1928, p. 96.
30. Kantor, *op. cit.*, p. 27.
31. *Ibid.*
32. Dimanshtein, ed., *Idn in FSSR*, p. 253.
33. Kantor, *op. cit.*, pp. 197f.
34. Cf. p. 132.
35. Moscow dispatch to the *Jewish Daily Bulletin*. November 20, 1930.
36. *Emes*, June 30, 1934, as quoted by Lestschinsky, *op. cit.*, p. 332.
37. The first Jewish division of a Soviet court was set up in 1924 in Berdichev, in the Ukraine, a city with a population of about 60,000, most of whom were Jews.
38. *Op. cit.*, p. 33. Data as of January 1 for each year indicated.
39. *Ibid.*, p. 31.
40. *Ibid.*, p. 31.
41. Ya. Rives, "Rabota sredi natsmenov na Ukraine" ["Work Among Minority Nationalities in the Ukraine"], in *Vlast' Sovetov*, 1927, no. 21, p. 9.
42. *Ibid.*
43. Of the 22 non-Jewish national courts, 12 were German, 6 Polish, and 4 Bulgarian. At the same time Jews had 117 village and market-town Soviets; Germans, 228; Poles, 138; and Bulgarians, 44. That is to say, the Bulgarian minority had one national court to every 11 national Soviets; the German minority, one court to every 19 Soviets; the Polish (the only numerically important Catholic minority), one court to every 23 Soviets. In contrast, there was one Jewish court to every 3.25 Jewish Soviets.

CHAPTER XII

Agrarianization and Industrialization

The Shtetl Turns to the Plow

Revolution and Civil War disrupted the Russian economy and reduced the Jewish masses to abject misery. A fraction of the Jewish population found employment in the government and public services; for the great majority, however, there was nothing. The only conceivable solution was their speedy absorption into industry and agriculture. But since Russia's industry in the early years of Soviet rule was in a state of collapse, agriculture appeared as the most realistic possibility.

Industrial plants shut down, urban trade fell off to nothing, and the cities starved. The population of the cities, largely made up of former villagers with more or less close ties with the countryside, trekked back to the villages, where food continued to be grown and some prospect existed of keeping body and soul together. But this was excluded for such age-old city-dwellers as the Jews. They had to devise another expedient: the farming of small plots of ground on the outskirts of their famished market towns. As early as 1918 suburban agriculture began to attract increasing numbers from the *shtetl*. At this time the big private estates and the land holdings of the Imperial treasury and of the municipalities were being divided up in a chaotic and unorganized way, and Jews in many of the smaller townships were able to get hold of a few suburban tracts. Government authorities, especially those active in the Jewish field, for a while paid hardly any attention to this spontaneous development. Jewish Communists regarded the destitute *luftmenshn* of the ghetto as a "socially alien element," "retired speculators" whom it was best to ignore. The steady advances of this "non-planned" farming thus went unheeded for the most part. In later years Kantor said of the Ukraine:

> In the beginning, Jewish agriculture on the peripheries of the small towns was for the most part neither promoted nor regulated by the government. No assistance of any kind was given these new producers of bread. It is to be ascribed in part to the fact that in some local agencies in the Ukraine it was erroneously thought at the time that the Jewish market-town population consisted solely of speculators.

Nor, until 1927, did the authorities in charge of Jewish rural settlement pay any attention to non-planned agriculture outside the small Jewish towns, except in the Odessa district, which was under the care of KOMZET. Jewish suburban farmers not controlled by any plan were not even recorded. . . . Meanwhile suburban [Jewish] farming continued to grow and expand. When in 1928 a spotcheck census of [Jewish] farming on the peripheries of small towns was taken by the Ukrainian KOMZET, its utterly unexpected result was to show that, according to incomplete data, the number of suburban [Jewish] farms had reached 8,000.[1]

In time this Jewish interest in suburban farming made an impression on the Jewish Communist leadership, who worked out various plans for the establishment of suburban collective farms of different types. Until the late 1920's, however, government-sponsored, plan-controlled and collectivized farms on the outskirts of the *shtetl* lagged behind the private. Of the 8,000 farms unexpectedly recorded in the Ukraine in 1928, only 1,824, or about 23 percent, were part of collective establishments.[2] In White Russia a study carried out in June 1926 found a Jewish population of 32,408 engaged in suburban farming, i.e., presumably some 6,500 Jewish family farms; of these, only about 1,000, or about 15 percent, were joined together in collectives. By January 1, 1930, 9,331 Jewish families were running suburban farms in White Russia; of these farms, only 2,457, or about 26 percent, belonged to any kind of collective.[3]

However, most of the Jews in the small towns, because of the scarcity of free land, found their way barred to this kind of farming, and this was even more the case, of course, with Jews living in cities. The overwhelming majority of the Jewish population could become farmers only if they were prepared to move lock, stock, and barrel into the old nineteenth-century Jewish farm colonies in the Ukraine, or if they settled on virgin land in new agricultural districts.

The idea of an organized settlement of the Jewish masses upon the land found favor with some of the Communist Jewish officials as early as 1918. Commissar Dimanshtein endorsed it in October 1918, at the First Conference of Jewish Sections, for the reason that agricultural employment would help allay anti-Soviet feeling among the "déclassé" strata of the Jewish petty bourgeoisie.[4] In addition to this political reason, Dimanshtein, at the Second Conference of Jewish Sections in June 1919, emphasized the economic advantages of putting idle Jewish manpower to work: "We have more than political objectives in view—above all, we want to place idle hands at the service of the country in a productive way; we want to cut down the number of small speculators on the point of turning into anti-social elements, and we also want to save them from the hunger they feel more and more each day."[5] The elimination of the "Jewish speculator" was the prevailing consideration. In the debate on the report presented by Dimanshtein, another leading Communist, Samuil Agurskii, Dimanshtein's lieutenant in the Jewish Commissariat, minced no words:

> If I thought speculation could be wiped out by repression, by driving the *shtetl* to the wall, I should be the first to advocate establishing Jewish detachments of the Cheka; but since repression won't work, we must put the Jewish petty bourgeois in the way to becoming useful to society, instead of a parasite and a burden. As soon as possible we must use exceptional measures to rescue the Jewish masses from hunger and want—and from engaging in speculation—which will surely weaken antisemitism also.[6]

The resettlement program was not to be entrusted to special Jewish organizations, or even to the Jewish Commissariat. "I do not think," said Dimanshtein, "that we should do this work on our own, after the example of the JCA or ORT, which seek to create small Jewish bosses and shopkeepers. Oh no! The work must be carried out by the regular People's Commissariats, and we must act only as auxiliary agencies to help and support them."[7] The Jewish Commissariat, after the conference, submitted to the People's Commissariat for Agriculture a detailed plan "for the introduction of farm labor among the Jewish masses and the establishment of Jewish agricultural communes and cooperatives." On July 12, 1919 the plan was approved by the Commissariat for Agriculture.[8]

But the Civil War, and the occupation of White Russia and the Ukrainian provinces west of the Dnieper by Polish forces, prevented the Soviet government from acting on the plan. Jewish agriculture, until 1924, remained essentially of the impromptu kind that existed on the outskirts of the *shtetl*.

Government-Sponsored Resettlement

In 1923, the ORT proposed the large-scale resettlement of all Jews willing to become farmers. In 1924 it was taken under advisement by the governments of White Russia and the Ukraine, and then by Moscow. In July 1924, the Ukraine and White Russia issued regulations to govern the allocation of farm land to urban Jewish applicants on an equal basis with the local peasant population. And on August 29, 1924, the Presidium of the Central Executive Committee of the USSR created the Commission for the Rural Placement of Jewish Toilers,—KOMZET (KOM-ERD).[9] Official Soviet statements and the utterances of non-Jewish Soviet leaders sponsoring resettlement (Mikhail I. Kalinin, Petr G. Smidovich, etc.) chiefly stressed its humanitarian and egalitarian aspects, whereas the Communist leadership "in the Jewish street" talked of economic "normalization," the "agrarianization" of the Jewish poor, and the "liquidation of speculators." In practice it was the latter who were charged with the execution of the resettlement program, and economic and political considerations took precedence over humanitarian.

That agricultural settlement was the best way to make the Jews "productive,"[10] and would perhaps even lay the basis for a Jewish Soviet state,[11] was for a period of time officially recognized. On June 15, 1926 the Presidium of the Central Executive Committee of the USSR gave its approval to a plan by KOMZET, submitted late in 1925, "for the transfer to agriculture of 100,000 Jewish families, to take place in the course of a few years."[12] This would have added about half a million Jews to the number already engaged in agriculture, concentrating about one-quarter of the entire Jewish population of the Soviet Union in agricultural occupations. Some Communist officials nursed even more ambitious hopes. Chemeriskii, chief of the Jewish Sections, wrote:

> What is at stake here is nothing more or less than the creation of a great class of Jewish peasants who will make over completely the appearance and economic basis of the Jewish population; on this transformed basis new cultural life will arise, new legal relationships, and new forms of cohabitation within one state. . . .
>
> It must be emphatically reiterated that the range and the pace of rural placement and resettlement depend solely on the [amount of] financial support they receive, since more than enough land is available, and this in large uninterrupted tracts that can accommodate large sections of the Jewish population. The funds required to prepare and settle such extensive tracts of land are not so very exorbitant. At any rate, with a capital of some 20 to 25 million rubles, the KOMZET plan (100,000 families) could be realized to the extent of 150 percent; and in so doing the basis could be laid for solving the problem of territorial autonomy.[13]

This unorthodox enthusiasm for agricultural settlement, however, did not last for any length of time. At the Sixth Conference of Jewish Sections in 1926, their too enthusiastic chief hastily shifted his emphasis from agrarianization to industrialization.[14] It is true that rural settlement was not yet being discarded; a certain falling-off, Chemeriskii said, could be anticipated in the pace of industrial expansion, which would reduce the capacity of industry to absorb additional masses of Jewish *luftmenshn*; when this is the case, "the relative importance of rural settlement will increase."[15] But the prospect of "a great class of Jewish peasants" was now viewed with apprehension. The Jewish peasantry, a new petty bourgeoisie, would be strong enough economically to develop dangerous political aspirations. Against this new petty-bourgeois menace arising from agrarianization a warning call was sounded by the same Chemeriskii:

> Let us throw some light on the basic political and ideological problems connected with the emergence of this class, second in importance

in the Jewish population. . . . Let us confine ourselves to pointing out that this healthiest and youngest stratum of the Jewish petty bourgeoisie becomes, with the first steps it takes after having come into existence, a rallying point for the struggle waged by ideologists of petty-bourgeois nationalism for political influence. It is inevitable that this camp should seek to imbue the peasantry with an up-to-date nationalist ideology which at best renounces its hopes and dreams of a better world in Palestine and [instead] draws its inspiration from the Soviet reality. . . . [But] having cast off Palestinism and Zionism, the petty bourgeoisie and its ideologists attempt to implant that quintessence of all bourgeois ideology in the peasantry, the idea of a national state.[16]

While the organized transformation of the bulk of the Jewish population into wage and salary earners did not get under way until a few years later, proletarianization was already given first place at the Conference of 1926. No workers or artisans already productively employed were to be placed in agriculture. Ester said:

We cannot settle all Jews in the Soviet Union on land. There will be a large number that need not, must not, and shall not settle on land. Jewish workers should not go into farming, or such artisans as are engaged in production and have a possibility to become workers sooner or later. Their road towards socialism is the direct one. For them to become farmers would be the same thing as their going backwards. It would be unnecessary and harmful to direct them into agriculture.

What indeed does agrarianization mean to us? It is a way to transfer to productive occupations those *luftmenshn* who are either non-productive to begin with or have been cast out of production. Those, however, already engaged in productive occupations must not be transferred, and we are not going to do it.[17]

Agricultural colonization and large-scale resettlement, as an answer to the Jewish problem, were clearly relegated by the government to the background. The pace of the recruitment of Jewish families for government-approved farm projects fell off, and in the 1930's the Jewish farm population visibly began to decrease. KOMZET's early plan to raise the number of Jewish farm families to 25 percent of the entire Soviet Jewish population was no longer mentioned.

Increase and Decrease of the Jewish Farm Population

The Soviet census of December 1926 fixed the size of the Jewish peasant population at roughly 155,400,[18] or nearly 6.0 percent of the total Jewish population.[19] The less complete statistics of the OZET showed a Jewish peasant population of 141,780 in 1926; 165,500 in 1927; and almost 220,000 in 1928.[20] The number of Jewish farmers no doubt rapidly increased in the late 1920's, during the initial successes of the government-sponsored resettlement program. But in the 1930's planned resettlement suffered a serious setback. The Soviet census of January 1939 revealed that Jewish farmers with their family helpers and dependents accounted for 5.8 percent of the total Jewish population of 3,020,000,[21] which would make the Jewish farm population 175,000. This, however, included an unspecified number of Oriental Jews, a group counted separately in 1926.[22] The decline was obvious.

The falling-off of Jewish agriculture in the 1930's appears even more precipitous when we regard the statistics on Jewish gainful workers. In 1926, some 38,100 Jewish farms—most of them privately operated—provided work for 38,100 proprietors and 56,400 family helpers, i.e., a Jewish peasantry of 94,500 or 9.1 percent of all gainfully occupied Jews.[23] By October 1, 1930, the number of Jewish self-employed and family helpers in agriculture had risen to 134,100, according to data given in the "Five-Year Plan for Reconstructing the Social Composition of the Jewish Population of the USSR;"[24] at that time farm labor apparently accounted for 10.1 percent of all gainfully occupied Jews,[25] the highest ratio ever recorded. In 1935 the percentage was down to 6.7.[26] By 1939 a further fall had taken place; according to Zinger, who failed to furnish either numbers or percentages for the Jewish farm labor force recorded by the census of January 1939, there were only 25,000 Jewish farm family units in 1939 [27] (as against 38,100 in 1926), all now a part of collective farms. Even if we allow the unlikely number of 3 family helpers to each head of a family (as against 1.5 in 1926), this would still mean a Jewish farm labor force not in excess of 100,000.[28] To make a valid comparison of this figure with that of 1926, an unknown number of Oriental Jewish farmers would have to be subtracted from it. The conclusion is inescapable that the Jewish farm labor force in 1939 had not only fallen far below the peak of 1930, but also below the modest level of 1926.

This striking decline in the role of agriculture in the economic life of Soviet Jews is underscored by detailed data given by Zinger in 1941. As mentioned before, the number of Jewish farms on the outskirts of small towns in the Ukraine had risen to 8,000 by 1928; in White Russia, from 6,500 in 1926 to over 9,300 in 1930, that is, presumably about 7,500 in 1928; the total for both republics in 1928 must have been something like 16,000. In 1939, however, the total number of Jewish suburban farms in the Ukraine, White Russia, and the Western province of the Russian SFSR, was only 7,000.[29] In the space of eleven years, more than half of the Jewish suburban farms had disappeared. In the Crimea, the Jewish farm population increased through the years, with occasional minor setbacks, until 1933, when 5,800 Jewish farmer families comprising some 25,000 persons were counted.[30] Although land still continued to be available, the trend was reversed in the following years, and only 4,992 families comprising some 18,000 persons were left in 1939.[31]

The shrinking of the Jewish population in the rural Jewish national districts of the Ukraine was no less pronounced. Of the three districts, only one, Kalinindorf, kept its predominantly Jewish character, though the proportion of the Jewish population was slightly reduced. The total population of the district on July 1, 1930 was 14,275, of whom 11,745,[32] or 82.3 percent, were Jews; in 1939, the population totaled 16,000, of whom 12,800 were Jews. The Jewish population increased less than the total population, its proportion dropping to 80 percent.[33] The decline was marked in the district of Novo-Zlatopol'ye, where Jews early in 1931 had accounted for 8,349 of a total population of 12,148,[34] or 68.7 percent. Early in 1939 the total population of the district exceeded 15,000, whereas the number of Jews had declined to barely one-half of the total.[35] Things were still worse in Stalindorf, largest of the three districts. There, the total number of inhabitants early in 1931 was 29,874, of whom 14,602, or 48.9 percent, were Jews [36]—plainly insufficient for a "national" district. By early 1939, a sizable drop in the number of Jewish inhabitants had further reduced the ratio: "The Jewish population, some 10,000, makes up about one-third of the district's total population."[37]

For a time, these developments went largely unnoticed in the din of propaganda about the achievements of Jewish colonization in Birobidzhan. But agricultural settlement in actuality had been of secondary importance from the start in the Far-Eastern colonization project, and whatever the accomplishments in Birobidzhan, they did not revive the vanished glory of agrarianization. Resettlement, as an answer to the Jewish problem, was virtually abandoned with the inauguration of Stalin's policy of intensive industrialization. Its place was taken by another form of productivization, the induction of "non-productive" Jews into the growing army of urban wage and salary earners.

Government Plans for Industrial Employment

The "national" theme, as developed at the Sixth Conference of Jewish Sections in 1926, was increasingly elaborated upon as the policy of agrarianization was discarded. Once a sizable Jewish industrial proletariat had been created, the Jewish minority could be "consolidated into a nation" under conditions determined by the rule of proletarian dictatorship. Not that national consolidation was impossible under a system other than the dictatorship of the proletariat; it was possible, but also dangerous and undesirable. Only "in the Soviet context" could "Jewish nationality" realize its progressive potentialities, provided, of course, that there was a native Jewish proletariat to impose its will upon the newborn nation. Semen M. Dimanshtein stated authoritatively:

If under capitalism one or another nationality is retarded in its consolidation as a nation, the proletariat, depending on the circumstances, may raise the question as to whether to fight for its consolidation; in all likelihood, however, the proletariat will oppose such consolidation—anxious lest the struggle for the creation or restoration of a nation be controlled by the bourgeoisie—and will wage its battle on an international basis.

The very same question of the consolidation of a nation is seen in an entirely different light in the Soviet context, in the context of the proletarian dictatorship, when the formation and consolidation of a nation takes place under proletarian leadership.

It is only natural that the question of the consolidation of the Jewish minority into a nation should now arise in our country, for it is no longer the Jewish bourgeoisie that raises it, so as to exploit and enslave the toiling masses, but the Jewish toilers, the Jewish workers, the Jewish Communists, who will make this consolidation serve the interests of the proletarian revolution and Leninist internationalism.[38]

The creation of a proletariat to carry out the national consolidation of the Jews required active efforts by the government to transform large numbers of Jews into wage laborers and industrial workers. But the Soviet government was little concerned with Jewish national problems and for years neglected to make plans for the industrial employment of large numbers of Jews. Such plans were first made when labor shortages in the late 1920's encouraged the mobilization of Jewish manpower reserves.

In the Ukraine, it is true, the first official steps in this direction were already taken in 1926. A lengthy enactment by the All-Ukrainian Central Executive Committee and the Council of People's Commissars of the Ukrainian SSR on May 19, 1926, "concerning measures for the improvement of the condition of the Jewish toiling masses," directed the authorities in charge of industrial production "to prepare and submit for approval to the Council of People's Commissars of the Ukrainian SSR a draft of measures for drawing into productive labor the ruined strata of the Jewish toiling population." The People's Commissariat for Labor was instructed "to prepare measures for drawing the youth among the Jewish poor into industrial plants," paying particular heed to "youths residing in places with a predominantly Jewish population (market towns)."[39] In practice, this meant only that the Soviet administration and industrial management were to look with favor on the efforts of Jews to find employment in industry. The influx into factories continued to take place in a spontaneous and unorganized fashion.

As Zinger put it in 1932, "The beginnings of systematic planning for the employment of the Jewish poor in industry can be said to have been made in 1928–29."[40] The government's role was at first rather negligible. It authorized KOMZET to establish special vocational training classes for young Jews, for which it appropriated the tiny sum of 300,000 rubles; and KOMZET was instructed to organize the "planned transfer" of Jewish youths to the Voikov Metallurgical Works in Kerch (Crimea). Neither of these undertakings worked out too well. Zinger cautiously states that the funds appropriated for industrial training "were used quite successfully in White Russia, and less so in the Ukraine." As for the employment of Jewish workers in the Voikov Works in Kerch, though hailed in the Communist press as an outstanding example of government planning, it in fact took place for the most part in a spontaneous fashion: "Although few workers were recruited for the Kerch plant under the plan, the measure was significant for opening the road to a mass influx of Jewish youth into the plant. As a result, more than a thousand Jews joined the ranks of the workers in the Kerch plant in less than two years, and most of them were hired individually, without any regard to the plan."[41]

The program as a whole was handled in rather a casual way. That it was entrusted to KOMZET, an agency charged with agricultural resettlement, showed the want of a long-range plan for the industrial employment of Jews. Of the year ended September 30, 1930, Zinger said that it showed "the greatest upswing in planned efforts to draw the Jewish youth into industry and building."[42] In the course of the year KOMZET headquarters in Moscow issued over 15,000 orders for admitting Jewish youths into vocational courses and apprentice schools conducted by the various industries and trades; an additional 18,500 placement orders were issued by KOMZET offices in White Russia, the Ukraine, etc. Of the placement orders issued by KOMZET headquarters, the major part (52.4 percent) assigned the young people to building and construction projects.[43] The requirements of the labor market apparently took precedence over the young people's needs and preferences.

A KOMZET order of admittance to vocational training did not, however, ensure the actual placement of the apprentice or trainee. How this worked out may be seen in the case of the Urals. Industrial plants in the Urals had been assigned a high place in the training program for 1930: of 1,798 Jews between the ages of 18 and 30 selected for training on the job, 1,500, or over 83 percent, were to go to the Urals; and of 2,550 Jewish adolescents aged 15 to 18 to be trained in plant schools, 1,220 or nearly 48 percent, were also to go there. But the training on the job had been so poorly planned that KOMZET had to "stop it at the very beginning"; and only 538 of the 1,220 younger apprentices assigned to Ural plant schools were actually sent there, and only 350 stayed on.[44] Meanwhile large numbers of Jews found their way into industry by their own devices.

The Progress of Proletarianization

In 1930, when the planned transfer of Jewish youths fell short of expectations, "spontaneous infiltration into industry resulted in twice as large an increase in the number of Jewish workers."[45] Accordingly, the plans for 1931 were reduced, and the placement of only 12,000 Jewish trainees was called for, as against 33,500 in 1930.[46] But even on this reduced scale the plan was largely unfulfilled. "Later, because of the successful implementation of the Stalin Five-Year Plans and the increased demand for manpower in all sections of the national economy, there was a further growth of Jewish industrial labor as part of the overall process of the country's industrialization and without the application of special measures."[47]

In the course of years the number of Jewish wage and salary earners, particularly in industry, mounted steeply, without any regard to schedules. The total number of Jewish wage and salary earners, which had been 394,000 in December 1926, rose to 562,000 in 1930 and to 787,000 in 1931; wage earners (manual workers) accounted for 38.8 percent, 40.4 percent, and 43.5 percent, respectively, of these totals.[48] Official statements for later years showed an ever increasing Jewish proletariat; yet the data published were so indefinite as to call their reliability into question, although there can be no doubt as to the general trend. The total number of Jewish wage and salary earners as of January 1, 1933 was placed at "no less than 900,000, of whom no less than 50 percent are manual workers."[49] In 1935, the number of Jewish wage and salary earners was said to exceed 1,100,000, the number of wage earners being slightly above that of the salary earners (non-manual workers).[50]

More detailed, though incomplete, statistics occasionally published in Soviet sources would seem to indicate that the total number of Jewish wage and salary earners in 1935 was smaller, and that the proportion of wage earners among them was not above 50 percent, but below. Even so, the nine-year increase is prodigious. The total number of Jewish wage and salary earners apparently increased more than two and a half times from 1926 to 1935, and the number of manual workers alone must have trebled, if not more. The bulk of the "non-productive" Jewish population had in truth been proletarianized. In the late 1930's, when no major population surpluses remained to be absorbed into the ranks of manual and non-manual workers, the increase slowed down. At the same time many of those who had joined the ranks of wage earners in the preceding years, having acquired higher skills, improved their knowledge, or undergone training within industry, were upgraded and promoted to be non-manual workers. In addition, the proportion of the more educated among the young people seeking employment rose continuously from the late 1920's on, because of the great increase in the number of urban secondary schools and institutions of higher learning, a development from which the almost exclusively urban Jewish population profited. As a result, the proportion of manual workers among all Jewish wage and salary earners declined. At the time of the census of 1939 it had dropped to less than 43 percent,[51] whereas in the early 1930's it had been in the neighborhood of 50 percent.[52]

No trustworthy statistics on Jewish labor as recorded by the census of 1939, have been released. The number of Jewish manual workers is said to have reached 600,– to 650,000;[53] if manual workers accounted for 43 percent of the total, there must have been as many as 1,400,000 or even 1,500,000 Jewish wage and salary earners in all, a total accounting, according to Zinger, for 71.2 percent or all gainfully occupied Jews,[54] as against 38 percent in 1926 and 25 percent in 1897.[55] Even though these figures seem too high,[56] it cannot be doubted that by 1939 the process of "industrialization" or "proletarianization" had virtually reached its natural limit, and that most of the floating "non-productive" Jewish population had been recruited for hired work in industry, transportation, commerce, and the public service.

The Atomizing Effect

The success of proletarianization failed to lay the basis for a "consolidation of the Jewish minority into a nation."[57] Quite the contrary, it scattered the Jewish masses across the Soviet Union, broke family and communal ties, and thrust the migrants into an alien cultural and linguistic environment. This was the consequence not only of the spontaneous but also of the planned resettlement of Jews. Such relocation of Jewish manpower as did take place under official auspices was done clumsily and inefficiently. Zinger, for example, describes the transfer of adolescent Jewish trainees to the Ural industrial plants in 1929 and 1930, when the program was at its peak, as follows:

> The main cause of all the trouble attending the transfer to the Urals was the dispersal of the adolescents over a great number of plants. . . . When the transferred youths were placed in 25 different communities, it was inevitable that complications should arise in the arrangements for settling them. It must be kept in mind that these youths, many of whom are under 18, come from remote market towns in the West, find themselves in utterly unfamiliar conditions, and often have an inadequate mastery of the Russian language, etc. Under these circumstances, it was essential to place the young people in a limited number of plants so that they might accustom themselves as painlessly as possible to their situation, and so as to simplify the problem of their care

and maintenance. That none of this has been done is the chief reason for their coming back.[58]

Thus the Jewish migrants had not only to adapt themselves to a strange environment and to suffer the consequences of bureaucratic mismanagement; they were also completely isolated from each other and submerged in an indifferent mass. In the totalitarian climate that increasingly prevailed, the Jewish communality, the nation or would-be nation, was completely submerged. The effect of proletarianization was to dissolve most of the bonds uniting members of the Jewish minority, to atomize the Jewish community, and to isolate the Jewish individual.

NOTES

1. Ya. Kantor, *op. cit.*, p. 56
2. *Ibid.*
3. *Ibid.*, pp. 64f.
4. See p. 117.
5. Agurskii, ed., *Di Idishe Komisariatn . . .*, p. 214.
6. *Ibid.*, p. 216
7. *Ibid.*, p. 214.
8. Yu. Gol'de, *Zemel'noye ustroistvo trudyashchikhsya yevreyev* [*Rural Placement of Toiling Jews*], Central Publishing House of the Peoples of the USSR, Moscow, 1925, pp. 5 and 45–54.
9. *Ibid.*, pp. 69–74.
10. Chemeriskii, *Di Alfarbandishe Komunistishe Partay (Bolshevikes) un di Idishe Masn*, p. 17: "In view of the present pace of the development of our industry and the great reserves of manpower in the countryside—[it was expected that large numbers of workers who had fled to the villages during the Civil War would return to the cities]—it must be said that the highway to the productivization of the Jewish masses is the transformation into peasants of as many of them as possible."
11. See pp. 118ff.
12. Appendix to M. I. Kalinin and P. G. Smidovich, *O zemel'num ustroistve trudyashchikhsya yevreyev v SSSR* [*On the Rural Placement of Toiling Jews in the USSR*], ed. KOMZET, Moscow, 1927, pp. 55f.
13. Chemeriskii, *op. cit.*, pp. 53f.
14. See pp. 126ff.
15. *Alfarbandishe Baratung fun di Idishe Sektsies fun der A1KP/B (Dekabr 1926)*, p. 103.
16. *Ibid.*, pp. 47f.
17. *Ibid.*, p. 129.
18. The figure is based on a projection of census data referring to 87.3 percent of the Jewish population of the USSR; cf. L. Zinger and B. Engel, *Idishe Bafelkerung fun FSSR in Tabeles un Diagrames*, Tables I-2, II-7 and III-8.
19. L. Zinger gave a figure of 5.9 percent in his *Yevreiskoye naseleniye v SSSR*, p. 35. The discrepancy was caused by Zinger's computing the ratio from rounded-out projected totals rather than from the recorded basic data.
20. Zinger and Engel, Table VII-15; D. A. Baturinskii, *Zemel'noye ustroistvo yevreiskoi bednoty* [*Rural Placement of Indigent Jews*], ed. OZET, Moscow, 1929, pp. 14f.
21. L. Zinger, *Dos Banayte Folk*, pp. 39 and 49.
22. Natives of the Caucasus, the Crimea, and Central Asia speaking Iranian (Tat, Parsi) or Turki (Jagatai) dialects. Their total number in 1926 did not exceed

80,000 (cf. Zinger, *Yevrieskoye naseleniye v SSSR* p. 8, and *Dos Banayte Folk*, p. 36; also Zinger-Engel, *op. cit.*, Table 1-2). Agriculture and horticulture were among the major occupations of the Oriental Jews.

23. Zinger-Engel, *op. cit.*, Table III-8; Zinger, *Yevreiskoye naseleniye v SSSR*, p. 35; *Dos Banayte Folk*, p. 87f. Zinger placed the percentage for the same year, 1926, at 8.3 in an article in *Emes* (October 9, 1937) and in a table included in *Dos Banayte Folk*, p. 46, without explaining the discrepancy. In addition to the self-employed and family helpers, some 6,100 Jewish wage and salary earners were employed in agriculture in 1926, i.e., an additional .6 percent of Jewish gainful workers (cf. Zinger-Engel, *op. cit.*, Tables IV-9 and V-11; Zinger, *Yevreiskoye naseleniye v SSSR*, p. 63).

24. Zinger, *Yevreiskoye naseleniye v SSSR*, pp. 137ff.

25. This is the percentage Zinger gives in his article, "Di Sotsiale Rekonstruktsie fun der Idisher Bafelkerung in FSSR," in *Emes*, October 9, 1937, whereas in the source cited in the preceding note 11.1 percent was given, evidently too high as measured against the 1926–1930 increase in the total number of gainfully occupied Jews.

26. Zinger, in *Emes*, October 9, 1937.

27. Zinger, *Dos Banayte Folk*, p. 89.

28. In addition to the self-employed and family helpers, the Jewish peasant population total of roughly 175,000 included not only the dependents of those working on the farms, but also persons of peasant descent who were beneficiaries of pensions and scholarships, or temporarily employed outside of agriculture (cf. Zinger, *Dos Banayte Folk*, p. 49), and presumably also members of farmers' families serving in the armed forces. The number of Jewish agricultural wage and salary earners in 1939, not included in the total of the peasant population, has not been revealed.

29. Zinger, *Dos Banayte Folk*, p. 89.

30. D. Barshchevskii, "Zemel'noye ustroistvo trudyashchikhsya yevreyev" ["Rural Placement of Jewish Toilers"], in *Sovetskoye Stroitel'stvo*, January 1934, p. 87.

31. Zinger, *Dos Banayte Folk*, p. 90.

32. I. Sudarskii, *Kalinindorfer Rayon*, *Emes* publishers, Moscow, 1932, p. 22.

33. Zinger, *Dos Banayte Folk*, p. 94.

34. I. Sudarskii, *May-Zlatopoler Rayon*, *Emes* publishers, Moscow, 1933, p. 7.

35. Zinger, *Dos Banayte Folk*, p. 96.

36. I. Sudarskii, *Stalindorfer Rayon*, *Emes* publishers, Moscow, 1933, p. 21.

37. Zinger, *Dos Banayte Folk*, p. 97.

38. S. Dimanshtein, "V otvet na vopros, predstavlyayut li Soboi yevrei v nauchnom smysle slova natsiyu" ["In Reply to the Question, 'Are the Jews, Scientifically Speaking, a Nation?'"], in *Revolyutsiya i Natsional'nosti*, October 1935, p. 77.

39. The text of the enactment is given in Zinger, *Yevreiskoye nasaleniye USSSR*, pp. 152ff.

40. *Ibid.*, p. 132; "1928–29" means the "economic year" ended September 30, 1929.

41. *Ibid.*

42. *Ibid.*

43. *Ibid.*, pp. 104–111.

44. Zinger (*op. cit.*, pp. 109f.) tells of a conference called by the Ural Provincial Committee of the Communist Youth to discuss the poor results of the placement of Jewish trainees. The lack of preparation and the marked reluctance of local management and labor to accept the newcomers, were especially criticized. Similarly, Kantor (*op. cit.*, p. 142) described conditions in heavy industrial plants in the Ukraine: "The first groups of Jewish youths to be transferred to Dnepropetrovsk and the Donets Basin suffered considerable losses, and the transfer itself was generally accompanied by serious difficulties and complications. Not only had the workers of the plants and mines to which the Jewish poor were being transferred not been prepared for accepting them into their midst, but even the plant organizations had no conception of the essence and political significance of this work. And the management of the plants had made no arrangements whatsoever for receiving [the new-

comers]: no dormitories had been provided, nor was there any plan for employing the new workers. In consequence, the Jewish workers who arrived—mostly young people—were very poorly housed as well as paid. Moreover, they were usually assigned to unskilled labor, and their earnings were not enough to pay the cost of their food, for the Jewish workers were not accustomed to manual labor and were unable to meet the work quotas. And there were manifestations of antisemitism, and Jewish workers were even baited."

45. Zinger, *op. cit.,* p. 112.

46. *Ibid.,* p. 114.

47. Zinger, *Dos Banayte Folk,* p. 29.

48. Data for 1926 and 1930, from Zinger, *Yevreiskoye naseleniye v SSSR,* pp. 34 and 38; for 1931, from Zinger, *Natsional'nyi sostav proletariata SSSR* [*National Composition of USSR Proletariat*], *Vlast' Sovetov* publications, Moscow, 1934, pp. 86f.

49. Kantor, *op. cit.,* p. 149.

50. Zinger, in *Emes,* October 9, 1937.

51. Zinger, *Dos Banayte Folk,* p. 50.

52. See p. 169.

53. L. Zinger, *Dos Ufgerikhte Folk, Emes* publishers, Moscow, 1948, p. 39.

54. Zinger, *Dos Banayte Folk,* p. 49.

55. See p. 20.

56. Zinger's figures would mean that over 2.1 million Jews were gainfully occupied, which would leave only about 900,000 Jewish dependents. But the known data on the distribution of the Jewish population by sex and age, and on the proportion of working Jewish women, indicate that there were many more dependents among the Jews of the USSR, and considerably fewer breadwinners.

57. See n. 38 *supra.*

58. Zinger, *Yevreiskoye naseleniye v SSSR,* pp. 109f.

CHAPTER XIII

Birobidzhan

Considerations of Far Eastern Strategy

Birobidzhan occupies a special place in the Soviet program for the "productivization" of the Jewish masses. It was intended to be the locale of both agrarianization and industrialization. Its political importance was underlined by the decision to use Jewish colonization of this almost uninhabited region as a means for bringing about the national consolidation of the Jewish people on Soviet soil.

The project grew out of attempts made as early as 1926 to find a suitable area for the large-scale agricultural resettlement of destitute Jewish city-dwellers. Economic considerations prevailed with the KOMZET technicians; the political leadership of the "Jewish apparatus" at first touched upon the possibilities of the future center of Jewish resettlement as a national territory only with hesitation and reluctance. The "national" inspiration was furthered by the chairman of the Presidium of the Central Executive Committee of the Soviet Union, Mikhail I. Kalinin, whose prestige, as titular head of the Soviet state, was enough to lend the project great encouragement.

Addressing the first convention of OZET on November 17, 1926, the "Soviet president" thus started the legend of a Jewish national home on Soviet soil:

> The Jewish people faces a great task, that of preserving its nationality, and this requires the transformation of a considerable part of the Jewish population into a compactly settled agricultural peasantry numbering in the hundreds of thousands at least. Only on this condition can the Jewish masses hope for the survival of their nationality.[1]

In the early summer of 1927 a mission was sent out to reconnoiter the remote and inhospitable Far Eastern area of Birobidzhan; in six weeks' time the mission completed its task, and in January 1928 KOMZET requested the government to set aside the area for Jewish colonization. On March 28, 1928 the request was granted by the Presidium of the Central Executive Committee of the USSR; in April the first groups of settlers set out for Birobidzhan. It was of course impossible thoroughly to explore, in six weeks, a territory larger than Belgium or the combined areas of Connecticut and Massachusetts, consisting almost entirely of virgin forest and swamp, without roads, and virtually uninhabited.[2] The haste with which everything was done showed that more than a concern for the plight of the Jewish masses in White Russia and the Ukraine was involved.

Birobidzhan is a border province, and the infiltration of Chinese settlers across the border was causing the government grave concern. Soviet spokesmen began to stress the urgency of colonizing the frontier at top speed. Statements to this effect, which were never given any great publicity, may be found in a number of Soviet publications of the period. Thus, reporting to the KOMZET on July 12, 1928, Abram N. Merezhin, its Deputy Chairman, emphasized the importance of settling Birobidzhan within ten to fifteen years in order to keep out a flood of Chinese: "In about ten to fifteen years a dense mass of Chinese will have moved close to the Amur and Sungari rivers. The Manchurian population will then have reached about thirty million. Hence the question is whether it will be possible to people the Amur area of Birobidzhan within the coming ten or fifteen years. If it is peopled in time, the immigration of Chinese agriculturists will have been made impossible."[3] The Soviet writer Viktor Fink, who accompanied the mission of ICOR—the American pro-Soviet Association for Jewish Colonization in Russia—to Birobidzhan, said: "Aside from a solution to the 'Jewish question,' the Central Executive Committee outlined in this connection the solution of another, no less important problem, that of populating—or to be correct, assimilating by the Soviet state—the vast spaces of the Far East, the continuing emptiness of which whets the appetite of our imperialist neighbors."[4] Similarly, Yurii M. Larin, the noted Soviet economist, declared that a rapid colonization of Birobidzhan was necessary in order to eliminate one of the "factors that inevitably lure Japanese imperialism to the Soviet Far East."[5]

Under the terms of the act of March 28, 1928, Birobidzhan was given over to the KOMZET "to meet the requirements of the close settlement of Jewish toilers on free land" in the area.[6] Non-agricultural immigration was envisaged on a minor scale only. Agricultural settlement was to extend over a large, uninterrupted territory and only Jews were to be admitted as settlers. The authorities were directed "to stop further allotment of land in the Birobidzhan district, except on applications certified by KOMZET." Finally, the government promised to consider the establishment of a Jewish regional administration. Paragraph 5 said: "If the results of the close settlement of Jewish toilers in the area designated in Paragraph 1 prove favorable, the possibility of establishing a Jewish national unit of regional administration shall be considered."

The First Six Years

When colonization of Birobidzhan began, its extent and pace were still in dispute. The report of the mission of 1927 had expected preparations for the allotment of land to take up all of 1928; it added that it would not be possible to send Jewish settlers to Birobidzhan before 1929. The mission recommended that 1,000 Jewish families be moved in 1929, 2,000 families in 1930, and 2,000 to 3,000 families annually thereafter.[7] Actually, the dispatching of settlers followed immediately in the wake of the government's announcement of March 1928, at a time when no arrangements had been made for sheltering the settlers or giving them land. Competent Soviet officials thought that the Jewish colony in Birobidzhan would grow rapidly. Interviewed in October 1929 by the representatives of the American ICOR, Aleksei I. Rykov, chairman of the Council of People's Commissars of the Russian SFSR, said that at the end of the First Five-Year Plan (September 30, 1933) Birobidzhan's Jews would number close to 60,000;[8] thus they would have constituted the great majority of the region's population.

The majority of the settlers who arrived during the first two years, untrained for such work, were unable to endure the rigorous climate and unaccustomed labor in swamp and forest. Some went back—a trip of thousands of miles—while others looked about in the larger cities of the Far East, such as Khabarovsk, Vladivostok, etc., for something to turn their hand to. At the end of 1928, only one-third of those who had arrived during the year remained; the same thing was repeated in 1929. But the few who stayed on were not "settled on the land." Most of them had no choice but to wait around at Tikhon'kaya (later Birobidzhan City), the major railroad station in the region, or in other semiurban communities near the railroad. New arrivals, because land suitable for settlement had neither been allotted nor even surveyed, were kept for months at Tikhon'kaya. The life of the Jewish settlers at this waystation was wretched.[9]

Things improved slightly in 1930 and 1931. The number of arrivals increased, and the number of departures fell off somewhat, though the rate still remained inordinately high. By the end of 1931 the total number of Jews in Birobidzhan was no more than 5,125, in a total population of 44,574. Though the act of March 1928 had barred the area to non-Jewish settlers, they not only continued to come in, but the number of such newcomers even exceeded that of the Jewish settlers staying on.[10] In the fall of 1931 the Presidium of the Central Executive Committee of the Russian SFSR worked out a number of measures to implement the act of March 28, 1928. The economic development of the area was to be "speeded up considerably" by the establishment of large industrial plants processing locally available raw materials (iron ore, graphite, timber, and other construction materials); by an increase in the number of artisan establishments and collective and state farms; and by the building of railroads and the reclamation of the soil. These efforts if successful, were to culminate, at the end of 1933, in the establishment of a "Jewish autonomous unit of regional administration, as part of the Far Eastern Region."[11] The growth of the population was estimated as shown in Table XVIII.[12]

TABLE XVIII

GROWTH OF POPULATION OF BIROBIDZHAN

End of Year	Total population	Thereof; Jews	Non-Jews
1931 (actual)	44,574	5,125	38,449
1932 (plan)	61,555	17,920	43,635
1933 (plan)	80,065	31,100	48,965

In two years the Jewish population was to increase sixfold, by almost 26,000, while the non-Jewish population was to increase by only 9,500, including a natural increase of 2,500. The total exclusion of non-Jewish settlers was no longer contemplated. The government had likewise abandoned its original intention of making farmers out of most of the Jewish settlers. The total number of Jews to be settled in Birobidzhan in 1932 was fixed at 14,000 [13] (including dependents), but of these only 6,200, or 44.3 percent, were to be assigned to farms [14] (3,900 to collective, and 2,300 to state farms).

These figures were revised in the spring of 1932, when the Central Executive Committee of the USSR decided that Jewish migration to Birobidzhan had to be accelerated.[15] In discussing this decision, Dimanshtein said that by the end of 1933 the number of Jews in Birobidzhan would be "about 50,000,"[16] i.e., 19,000 more than the plan of 1931 had contemplated; this estimate was based on the assumption that a total of 20,000 Jewish settlers would be attained by the end of 1932—again in excess of the plan's figure (17,920). At the same time the authorities of the Far Eastern Region concocted still another plan, a far more ambitious one, which looked forward to a total population of 300,000 by the end of 1937, including 150,000 Jews.[17]

The reality was something else. Only 9,000 Jewish settlers arrived in Birobidzhan in 1932, rather than 14,000 or more, and only 3,000 stayed on; "in 1933 the reflux even exceeded the influx of migrants."[18] The Jewish population of Birobidzhan at the end of 1933 was neither 50,000 nor 31,000, but 8,200.[19] Its reaching 150,000 in a few years was out of the question. The movement of Jewish settlers into Birobidzhan is shown in Table XIX.[20]

TABLE XIX

MOVEMENT OF JEWISH SETTLERS INTO BIROBIDZHAN

Year	Arrived	Departed	Net Increase
1928	950	600	350
1929	1,875	1,125	750
1930	2,560	1,000	1,560
1931	3,250	725	2,525
1932⎰ 1933⎱	11,000	8,000	3,000
Total	19,635	11,450	8,185

What the total number of Birobidzhan's inhabitants was by the beginning of 1934 has not been revealed. As it already exceeded 44,000 at the end of 1931, it would seem warranted to assume that in the two succeeding years it approached 50,000. At the time the area was established as a Jewish autonomous province (May 1934), its Jewish population must thus have been far below even 20 percent of the total. A Jewish majority—the legal requirement for making the area a Jewish autonomous province—not only did not exist, but was inconceivable, unless there was a radical change in the methods of colonization.

"Recruitment"

Resettlement of the needy Jewish population of the decayed Ukrainian and White-Russian *shtetls* on the virgin land of Birobidzhan could have succeeded, in spite of the climate and great initial hardships, if enthusiasm had not been wanting in the Jewish settlers to make their sacrifices bearable, and if the work of preparation had been reasonably adequate.[21] If a spirit of pride and devotion had been inculcated in the Jewish youth, hundreds and even thousands of hardy pioneers could have been trained to go out to clear the land, build the roads, and improve the soil of Birobidzhan.[22] The cultivation of such a spirit of the *khaluts*, however, was no object of the Communist administrators of the Birobidzhan project, and certainly not of the local officials. Jewish national motives were occasionally appealed to, but reluctantly and without real conviction. The Communist leadership was unwilling to permit the colonization of Birobidzhan to become a national movement of the Jewish people in the Soviet Union, nor was the smallest attempt made to establish special autonomous Jewish agencies for directing the transfer of the Jewish population and the planning and implementation of the settlement program.

Indeed, when the Jewish Autonomous Province (JAP) was created

on May 7, 1934, after six years of failure and mishap, the entire colonization program became less rather than more "national." Whereas Birobidzhan had been originally intended as a place of rehabilitation for the
uprooted and impoverished populace of the *shtetl,* now the selection
of Jewish settlers was determined by utterly different considerations.
Now settlers were sought among Jewish workers already employed in
industry, Jewish farmers already engaged in farming, and Jewish artisans
already securely established in large urban communities and doing more
or less "productive" work. Now "recruitment" replaced the voluntary
migration of earlier years. The pressure of "public opinion" and "social
organizations" was openly brought to bear to recruit colonists. Com-
menting on the Central Executive Committee's decision to make Birobidzhan an autonomous Jewish province, Semen M. Dimanshtein, chief
official spokesman in those years on Jewish matters, stressed the changed
nature and meaning of the colonization program:

> The resettlement of Jewish workers and toilers in Birobidzhan no
> longer has its sole warrant in the necessity of making these people
> participate in productive work, for that is a matter that we have al-
> ready settled for the most part. A great proportion of those now
> settling in Birobidzhan consists of workers or artisans who have been
> *recruited,* and who go there to take specific jobs. . . . This is a higher
> stage as compared to the previous activity of KOMZET. . . .[23]

No doubt was left as to the government's reasons for this change in
purpose: "To every thinking participant in socialist construction the
great importance of defending the Far East against foreign intervention
is absolutely clear. The settlement of the area with trustworthy and
responsible people is a basic requirement in strengthening the defenses
of our Far Eastern frontier."[24] The entire work of the resettlement
agencies was increasingly concentrated on recruitment, and in 1936 all
other methods for finding colonists for the JAP were discarded.[25] At a
plenary session of OZET early in 1936, S. Ye. Chutskayev, who was
chairman of the KOMZET and a member of the Presidium of the Central
Executive Committee of the USSR, sternly condemned all voluntary and
spontaneous ("self-acting") migration to Birobidzhan, and insisted that
recruitment was the only proper way. A resolution to this effect was
adopted by the session. An official commentator remarked on the resolution as follows:

> Particular attention should be paid to the plenary session's decision
> stating that the recruitment of manpower and better qualified personnel
> must be conducted chiefly in the big industrial cities, where there are
> large numbers of Jewish workers in the plants. Resettlement previously
> aimed at settling in the new places those elements that could not make

a living at home and required organized assistance to improve their condition; at the present stage it is no longer a question of how to take care of the needs of this or that migrant, but of how to meet the skilled labor requirements of the industrial plants of the JAP, and of how to supply the necessary number of agriculturists for the free land of the province. . . .

With respect to agricultural resettlement, the plenary session advocated the dispatching to the province of experienced *kolkhoz* foremen, *kolkhoz* rank-and-filers, tractor drivers, etc., to be taken from suburban and other Jewish collective farms.[26]

In the light of this pronouncement, the proclamation of Jewish autonomy in Birobidzhan, where Jews remained an inconsiderable minority, is seen to be a mere façade covering over the semicompulsory colonization of the region by Jewish industrial workers, artisans, and farmers, who were taken from their old jobs and places of work and sent to the Far East. It was also planned to send non-Jewish immigrants to advance the colonization of Birobidzhan. The influx of non-Jewish settlers had already been foreseen in the plan estimates for 1932 and 1933. In 1934 the admission of an increasing number of non-Jews was an accepted fact. In his aforementioned comment on the establishment of the JAP, Dimanshtein stated:

> The republics must give up those of their people who are best fitted to take part in the new and difficult work of construction in the Far East. In this connection, it must be emphasized that the slogan, "All USSR is building the JAP," also implies that, along with the Jewish settlers, who are primarily the ones to be sent there, it is essential to supply non-Jewish personnel to help fulfill the faster the plans for developing this rich and opulent frontier region.
>
> Our goal is not the establishment of a Jewish majority in the JAP. We are convinced that this will come about in the natural course of resettlement; yet this is not our major goal, for such would conflict with our internationalism. Our first endeavor is to widen and strengthen socialist construction. . . .[27]

The idea of "Jewish nationhood," to which lip service continued to be officially paid, ceased to have any influence on the actual conduct of the resettlement program.

1934–1939: Jews Remain a Minority in the JAP

Recruitment might have been expected to hasten appreciably the transfer of Jewish settlers to the Far East. Though a slight improvement did take place, the actual increase in the number of Birobidzhan's Jewish residents in the years following the establishment of the JAP was far below what had been envisaged. Indeed, the discrepancy was so striking that, having published its plan estimates, the government discontinued the release of annual statistics on migration. As planned, the number of Jewish arrivals in Birobidzhan was to have been: 1934, 9,000; 1935, about 14,000 (3,500 families); 1936, about 20,000 (5,000 families);[28] and 1937, 9,354;[29] that is to say, over 50,000 in four years. The Jewish population of the JAP was to have risen to something like 60,000 by the end of 1937. But in reality there were only "about 20,000" Jews in the JAP in early 1937,[30] as against 8,185 at the end of 1933. The net increase in three years was less than 12,000, and this in spite of a strenuous campaign of propaganda.

To correct the mistakes of earlier years, Communist propaganda this time emphasized the importance of Birobidzhan as a Jewish province. Thus the establishment of the JAP was announced in 1934, and directives "concerning Soviet, party, and cultural activities in the JAP," issued by the Presidium of the Central Executive Committee of the USSR on August 29, 1936, eloquently extolled the realization of Jewish statehood:

> For the first time in the history of the Jewish people its burning desire for the creation of a homeland of its own, for the achievement of its own national statehood, has found fulfilment. . . .
> The Presidium of the CEC of the USSR is firmly convinced that all workers and *kolkhoz* farmers of the JAP, all Jewish toilers of the Soviet Union, and the organizations of the Soviet public will bend every effort to the speediest accomplishment of the tasks connected with the further development and strengthening of national Jewish Soviet statehood in the USSR.[31]

But such statements, which did not fail to have their effect on foreign Jewish opinion, had little connection with the reality. Even in law, the Soviet constitution recognizes only Union and Autonomous Republics, but not national autonomous provinces, as enjoying statehood. Such propaganda, however, was deemed necessary to facilitate the recruitment of Jewish settlers, especially for Birobidzhan's collective farms. The proportion of the JAP's farm population was declining, and the province could not feed its growing population unless agricultural colonization was increased. The Central Executive Committee's directives of August 29, 1936 demanded "that the attention of the provincial authorities be centered primarily on agricultural resettlement."[32] Again, reference was made to the importance of strengthening "Jewish statehood."[33] And again, the estimated annual rates of immigration to the JAP, especially of agriculturists, were set very high. In six years—from 1937 through 1942—Birobidzhan was to absorb "no less than 150,000 new immigrants," among whom "no less than 40 to 50 percent [were to be] *kolkhoz* farmers."[34] It was not indicated how many of these prospective immigrants were to be Jews.

This was in 1936. But in 1937 the entire leadership of the JAP was destroyed by the purges. Not that the JAP had been singled out in this respect; the purges struck every Soviet and party organization in the country without exception. In Birobidzhan, however, this virtually decapitated the party organization and the administration.[35] Yesterday's beloved leaders were publicly exposed as enemies of the people and proscribed as spies and Japanese agents.[36] New officials came to replace them, but irreparable damage had been done to the work of resettlement, and the progress (such as it was) of the young Autonomous Province seriously arrested. All immigration plans were disrupted and the colonization of the region set back for years.

Following the purge, the publication of any precise and detailed information on the Jewish Autonomous Province ceased almost completely.[37] The periodical, *Revolyutsiya i Natsional'nosti*, issued by the section for minority affairs of the Central Executive Committee of the USSR, and *Tribuna*, the OZET magazine, both of which had often, though not regularly, reported on Birobidzhan, were discontinued early in 1938.[38] The last sources of information dried up with the abolition of KOMZET in the summer of 1938 and the suppression of *Emes* shortly thereafter. The Census of January 17, 1939 disclosed only the total number of inhabitants of Birobidzhan, which was given as 108,419.[39] How many of these were Jews remained a closely guarded secret. Lev. Zinger, Soviet authority on Jewish statistics, who had access to unpublished census materials, steadfastly refrained from so much as hinting at the size of the Jewish population of the JAP, although the two books on Jewish problems in the Soviet Union which he published after 1939[40] dealt extensively with Birobidzhan. In a regional breakdown of the Jewish population of the USSR that he made, figures were given for individual republics with less than 2,000 Jewish inhabitants; the Jewish province was not mentioned at all. The meaning of this omission is obvious. The number of Birobidzhan's Jewish residents remained low, and the rate of increase of the Jewish population lagged behind that of the province's total population.[41]

Indirect evidence of the size of the Jewish population of the JAP may be found in the circulation statistics of Birobidzhan's newspapers, which in 1939 still made part of the official records of the Book Chamber of the USSR. A total of 6 newspapers were published in the JAP in 1939: two, *Birobidzhanskaya Zvezda* in Russian and *Birobidzhaner Shtern* in Yiddish, with a province-wide circulation; and four, all in Russian, for individual districts. Of the provincial papers, *Zvezda* had a circulation of 14,700, and *Shtern*, 1,500.[42] Since the one Yiddish-language newspaper of a "Jewish Autonomous Province" must have had a considerable number of required official subscribers, its genuine circulation would appear to be extremely low indeed. Of course, the ratio of the *Shtern's* circulation to the *Zvezda's* (1 to 10) does not exactly reflect the ratio of the Jewish to the non-Jewish population; the proportion of Jewish residents was probably higher, though still far below expectations.

As noted above, the Jewish population of the JAP had increased, in the three years from December 31, 1933 to early 1937, to something in the neighborhood of 20,000, an average annual increase of less than 4,000. There is no indication whatsoever that the increase in 1937 and 1938 was at a higher rate. But even assuming an undiminished increase in 1937–38, Birobidzhan's Jewish population at the time of the census of 1939 must still have been below 30,000, that is, around 25 percent of the total number of inhabitants of this Jewish province. Thus, after eleven years of widely publicized endeavor, the "Jewish nation on Soviet soil" embraced less than one percent of the Jewish population of the Soviet Union.

The Failure of Agricultural Settlement

Rural resettlement proved even less satisfactory than the Jewish colonization of Birobidzhan in general. At the time of the establishment of the JAP in 1934, of a total of some 8,000 Jewish inhabitants, only about 1,500,[43] or less than one-fifth, were on collective farms. The resettlement program for the period of the Third Five-Year Plan (1938–1942), prepared in 1937 by the planning authorities of the JAP and the Far Eastern Region, contemplated a total immigration to the JAP of 100,000, including 6,500 families, i.e., some 25,000 persons, to be settled on collective farms; the establishment of 50 to 60 new collective farms with 100 to 150 families each was envisaged.[44] The plan's estimate of the number of Jews among the new settlers was not disclosed, but it may be assumed that it was to be considerable.

Jewish agricultural settlement in the JAP, however, went forward slowly in the late 1930's, perhaps even more slowly than had been the case in the years before. More or less detailed information on the results achieved by 1939 was given in a pamphlet issued late that year by the *Emes* publishing house in Moscow for the use of new Jewish settlers. According to this pamphlet, only 2 out of the 18 Jewish collective farms operating in the JAP in 1939 had come into existence after 1937. These two *kolkhozes*, established as part of the Third Five-Year Plan's resettlement program, together comprised a mere 91 families, or 379 persons.[45] No change took place in the next two years. Zinger, who summarized the situation existing on the eve of the German-Soviet war (1941), found only the same 18 Jewish collective farms among the 60 *kolkhozes* of the JAP.[46]

In only two of the province's five districts had Jewish collective farms succeeded more or less in achieving economic stability: the five Jewish *kolkhozes* (with 257 families) in the Birobidzhan district, hinterland of the city of Birobidzhan and main source of the provincial capital's food supply; and four Jewish *kolkhozes* (with 160 families) in the Stalin district along the Amur River, where they were able to ship agricultural produce by boat to Khabarovsk, Vladivostok, and other big cities. Together, these nine Jewish collective farms sheltered and fed 417 families; of these, 364 were in seven *kolkhozes* furnishing data on the number of inhabitants: 1,348 at the time.[47] Even if one assumes that in the two remaining *kolkhozes*, the number of whose members was not disclosed, there were as many as 3.7 persons per family on the average as in the others, the combined population of these nine securely established collective farms could not have been more than 1,550.

Of the three other districts of the JAP, each in 1939 had three Jewish collective farms. In the Leninskoye district they had not gone beyond the "organizing stage"; and in the Bira and Smidovich districts the Jewish farmers raised almost no grain crops, concentrating chiefly on vegetables and dairy products. The *Emes'* pamphlet failed to give either the number of families or of persons in these *kolkhozes*, save in one instance, the Kuibyshev *kolkhoz*, in the Leninskoye district, which sheltered only eleven families.[48] Insecure and weak as they were, however, they could not possibly have supported as many families as those more advantageously located in the Birobidzhan and Stalin districts—perhaps little more than 300, and in all likelihood less. The total number of families in the 18 Jewish *kolkhozes* of the entire province of Birobidzhan was thus perhaps 700 or so, at most 750, and the number of all Jewish settlers with dependents on JAP collective farms cannot have exceeded 3,000. Some Jewish settlers may have been employed by one or another of the state farms (*sovkhoz*); but since there is no mention anywhere of Jewish *sovkhoz* workers in the JAP, their number must have been insignificant. All in all, only a small proportion—apparently less than 15 percent—of the Jewish population of the JAP had settled on the land before the war.

Agrarianization, then, proved to be no answer to the socio-economic problem of the *shtetl*—not even for that fraction of the Jewish population in Birobidzhan. But if farming sustained no more than 15 percent of the JAP's Jewish residents, what about the remaining 85 pecent? Birobidzhan's industries were still in their beginnings in 1941, and Jews were far from predominating among the JAP's industrial wage and salary earners. The bulk of the Jewish population had of necessity resumed their "petty-bourgeois" or semibureaucratic occupations in the service trades, government offices and stores, public services, and small-scale artisan production. Instead of a socially rehabilitated Jewish nation, the JAP saw the recrudescence of the unhealthy socio-economic structure of the semi-Sovietized Jewish towns of the Ukraine and White Russia. The only difference was a greater proportion of Jews in the administration, especially in the city of Birobidzhan, where the percentage of Jews among the inhabitants is much higher than in the province as a whole.

Prewar Birobidzhan neither solved the Jewish problem nor developed a national culture with which to "preserve the Jewish nation" against the overwhelming assimilatory effects of industrialization and proletarianization.

Wartime Embargo and Postwar Migration

To judge from Soviet silence on the matter, Jewish migration to Birobidzhan must have been severely limited or halted altogether immediately after the signing of the Hitler-Stalin Pact (August 23, 1939)—the latter hardly created a climate favorable to Jewish colonization of the Far Eastern frontier; not a single Jewish collective farm was established in the JAP in 1939–1941, although the Five-Year Plan for 1938–1942 called for intensive (Jewish and non-Jewish) agricultural colonization. Military considerations precluded the carrying-out of long-range and costly projects near the Manchurian border; moreover, it would have been perilous to cumber the railroads of Eastern Siberia with settlers and their impedimenta. With the outbreak of the war (if not sooner), the transfer of Jewish—and perhaps also non-Jewish—migrants to Birobidzhan was definitely stopped. In contrast to what pro-Soviet propagandists outside the Soviet Union maintained, one of the highest Communist officials in the JAP, A. Bakhmutskii, Secretary of the Provincial Committee of the Communist Party and JAP member of the Supreme Soviet of the USSR, admitted after the war that "immigration to our province was suspended during the war years."[49]

Moreover, there are indications that the Jewish population of the JAP decreased during the war. There is little doubt that the Jewish farm population of Birobidzhan shrank considerably. An otherwise optimistic report by Shifra Kochina, a member of the Supreme Soviet of the USSR and renowned for her agricultural achievements in the Valdhaym *kolkhoz* in the JAP, stated in 1946: "The only difficulty that confronts us in the *kolkhozes* is a shortage of people. I can name a number of *kolkhozes* ('Kaganovich,' 'Kirov,' etc.), where the number of Jewish families is no more than ten."[50] The *kolkhozes* referred to—located in the Birobidzhan district of the province—had been among the best and soundest before the war, the Kaganovich *kolkhoz* having 47 Jewish families in 1939 and the Kirov *kolkhoz*, 67.[51] If the best collective farms thus lost 75 to 85 percent of their families during the war, what remained of Birobidzhan's Jewish farm population of some 3,000?

Not only the farm population, Jewish and perhaps non-Jewish as well, suffered a serious reduction in numbers. Kochina's report of 1946 stated that housing facilities sufficient to put up 11,000 new settler families existed in the JAP; and in the same issue of *Eynikayt*, Bakhmutskii claimed that in the cities, in the workers' developments, and in the villages of Birobidzhan there were enough vacant buildings to house "several times ten thousand new settlers."[52] Since it is inconceivable that there could have been any substantial building during the war, this plethora of housing must have been the result of large population losses. It seems a fair guess that by the end of the war the JAP was left with no more, and probably less, than 20,000 Jewish residents. Industry, too, must have suffered large losses in manpower; between 1940 and 1945 the gross output of government-operated factories declined by one-third.[53]

Not until the second half of 1946 did the government authorize the resumption of organized Jewish resettlement in the JAP. The first party of recruits—over 300 persons—left Vinnitsa, in the Ukraine, in December 1946 and arrived in Birobidzhan in January 1946.[54] Individual migrants and small groups started out for the Far East on their own initiative at an earlier date. Bakhmutskii related in May, 1947:

> Apart from the comrades from Vinnitsa, a considerable number of settlers (about 500 families) came to our province last year from other places, arriving individually and in groups. Several dozen families migrated from the Crimea (Dzhankoi, Azov, and other districts), and many came from the provinces of Kiev, Dnepropetrovsk, Zhitomir, Poltava, Kemerovo, and Novosibirsk, and from the Central Asian republics. . . . Every day letters arrive from Jews in different parts of the Soviet Union saying they want to move to the JAP. Group applications have been filed by over 200 families in the province of Kiev, over 100 families in Zhitomir, and 50 families in the provinces of Poltava, Dnepropetrovsk, Odessa, Kemerovo, and the Crimea.[55]

The first contingent from Vinnitsa was followed by two more from the same province, and by several from Kherson, Nikolayev, Dnepropetrovsk, and the Crimea. Up to July 1948, the arrival of nine organized parties of Jewish settlers was recorded, adding up to 1,770 families.[56] Spontaneous, unorganized migration apparently took place on a larger scale. According to what Bakhmutskii wrote in April 1948, the total number of Jewish migrants arriving "in the last one and a half or two years" was over 20,000.[57] This was doubtless an exaggeration. By this time, some 1,500 families had been brought in by the government, that is, about 6,000 people at best, and official immigration, by May 1947, accounted for 500 families, or about 2,000 persons; this would mean, if the figure of 20,000 was correct, that unofficial immigration, chiefly of individuals, from May 1947 to April 1948 amounted to at least 12,000, which is hardly credible. But even allowing for exaggeration, it seems well established that thousands of Jews came to Birobidzhan in 1946–1948 without official approval or authorization. This spontaneous movement assumed proportions unheard-of in the history of the JAP. It is a safe estimate that Birobidzhan's Jewish population virtually doubled in the postwar years; the total number of Jewish residents in mid-1948 may well have been in the neighborhood of 35,000.

All the official parties of Jewish immigrants came from the Ukraine and the Crimea and most of the individual settlers as well; those among the latter who came from Western Siberia (Kemerovo and Novosibirsk) and Central Asia obviously were wartime refugees. Since few survivors were left in the provinces that had been occupied by the Nazis, the Jews who descended upon Birobidzhan in 1946–1948 must have been discharged servicemen, former evacuees, and slave laborers who had been carried off to Germany, people, that is, who had returned to their homes in 1944 and 1945 and found life there unbearable. Such people could not help reacting with heightened sensitivity to the hostile or indifferent manifestations of the local population; they could no longer endure antisemitism either in its overt or disguised form, or the far more widespread aloofness and lack of interest in the Jewish tragedy, usually coupled with an unwillingness to pay any attention to resurgent antisemitic tendencies.[58] Thus, it was not the "non-productive" and helpless who fled to Birobidzhan, but people well equipped mentally and physically to start a new life, including quite a few possessing jobs, an adequate income, apartments, etc. The new settlers were in most instances far better suited to be pioneers than the destitute *luftmenshn* of the prewar *shtetl*. It might seem that a new era loomed on Birobidzhan's horizon.

The Future of Jewish Birobidzhan

The spontaneous nature of the new movement left its mark even on the most uninspired official statements. Interviewed by the editors of *Eynikayt*, Abram Yarmolitskii, Deputy Chairman of Birobidzhan's Executive Committee, summed up his impressions of a trip to the Ukraine and the Crimea to make arrangements for immigrant transports as follows:

> Wherever I went I found the Jewish population tremendously interested in the JAP. Indeed, this was more than merely an interest. Many laboring people—*kolkhoz* farmers, workers, employees, intelligentsia—expressed their ardent desire to take an active part in the building of Jewish statehood in the USSR, and are merely waiting for an opportunity to resettle. Of course, this is wintertime, and many families, especially those with small children, have put off their departure till spring. But there are more than a few enthusiasts whom the winter has not deterred; 252 families went along with the Crimean transport, 248 with the Kherson transport, and 114 with the one from Nikolayev—a total of 614 families.
>
> The composition of the migrants gives us the greatest satisfaction.

Among the 614 families referred to, we have 255 families of *kolkhoz* farmers, who have brought along all their property and possessions, and who plan to reinforce the existing *kolkhozes* and to start new ones. . . .[59]

This desire to "build Jewish statehood" is apparent in many other *Eynikayt* reports of conversations and interviews with settlers awaiting their turn, preparing to depart, or already on their way to Birobidzhan. Official propaganda is not likely to have filled the heads of Ukrainian and Crimean Jews with notions of a "Palestine in Birobidzhan," or to have encouraged Jewish nationalism in the place of Soviet patriotism. The concern with Jewish statehood was undoubtedly a reflection of the heightened national consciousness of the Jewish survivors, which the authorities apparently were content to have express itself in pioneering.

How strongly the survivors wished to escape the scenes of Jewish slaughter may be gathered from the astonishingly high proportion of farmers among the new settlers of Birobidzhan. The farmers of the Ukrainian and Crimean *kolkhozes* certainly stood in no need of land to till; what they sought on the banks of the Amur River was—the Jewish province, though perhaps not so much statehood as a Jewish environment far removed from the places that had been the shambles of their people. Of the 1,500 Jewish families that the first six transports (1947 through January 1948) brought to the JAP, 400 joined *kolkhozes;* these families had come chiefly from the provinces of Kherson, Nikolayev, and the Crimea, which before the war had been Jewish agricultural centers.[60] Of the 1,770 families in the nine transports that reached Birobidzhan in the period January 1947–June 1948, 830, or almost one-half, joined collective or state farms or farm equipment centers.[61] This was something new in the history of Birobidzhan and could have been the economic basis for a stable national community.

This promising development, however, was cut short in the summer of 1948. The exact date of the shift in official policy cannot now be determined; but from July on *Eynikayt* ceased to report any further movement of settlers to Birobidzhan, organized or individual. With the suppression of *Eynikayt* in December 1948, the Jewish Autonomous Province has been shut off entirely from the outer world. In the summer and fall of 1949 even the Jewish Communist press in the United States was forced to admit its complete lack of information.

Whatever the effect on Birobidzhan of this latest reversal of policy, prospects of a renascence of cultural life in the Jewish Autonomous Province had in any case been dim for years. The original intention of elevating Yiddish to the status of an official language was hardly realized in more than name only. Prior to the war Soviet publications noted an increasing tendency on the part of the official agencies of the JAP to discard Yiddish; even Jewish collective farms and producer cooperatives preferred to keep records and conduct correspondence in Russian. Pointed statements were made about the neglect of Jewish schools.[62] At the end of the war no Jewish schools were left in Birobidzhan, and the Jewish theater performed more plays in Russian than in Yiddish, according to news from the JAP received in Moscow in 1945 by Szmerl Kaczerginski.[63]

The postwar influx of Jewish settlers must have increased the need for Jewish schools. Yet no reference to Jewish schools actually in operation in Birobidzhan is to be found in *Eynikayt*. In 1946 loud publicity was given by the Jewish Communist and pro-Communist press in this country to a directive of the Council of People's Commissars of the Russian SFSR of February 26, 1946, "concerning measures for the consolidation and further development of the economy of the JAP," which among other things instructed the People's Commissariat for Education to supply the JAP with 50 Jewish teachers of mathematics, physics, literature, history, etc.[64] This, however, did not mean, as the pro-Soviet publications would have had their readers believe, that the teachers were to serve on the staffs of Jewish schools. It was intended that they teach in the general schools of the province.[65] Indeed, the directive was issued at a time when Jewish immigration to the JAP was still under the wartime embargo and a mass influx of Jewish settlers was not anticipated.[66] What concerned the authorities was the general shortage of teachers in the Far East; the "Jewish" motive was intended to make assignments in the unattractive border region seem tempting to national-minded Jewish teachers in other parts of the country.

A similar misunderstanding was created by an unofficial report from Soviet sources carried in the American Yiddish-language press late in 1949, which said that 25,000 children were enrolled in Jewish schools in Birobidzhan. Actually this figure—a round one—referred to all the students of the JAP, Jewish and non-Jewish.[67] The Soviet government has never disclosed how many of Birobidzhan's students are Jewish, or the number or percentage enrolled in Jewish schools or in special classes with Yiddish as the language of instruction. Nor do American publications devoted to Birobidzhan contain such information. All this may safely be taken to indicate that Jewish schools in the JAP are now virtually nonexistent, and that the use of Yiddish as the language of instruction in non-Jewish schools in Birobidzhan is negligible.

Jewish publications in Birobidzhan shared the fate of Jewish schools. Before the war the province had one Yiddish-language newspaper, the *Birobidzhaner Shtern*. Whether it has actually gone out of existence we do not know, but for years it has neither been mentioned nor quoted in any other Soviet or foreign publication. Even if the *Shtern* continues to be printed, it is certainly not read outside of Birobidzhan, and its cultural influence in the JAP, to judge from its prewar circulation of 1,500, can scarcely be significant. A modest literary "almanac," *Birobidzhan*, was launched after the war and four issues have appeared, the last in 1948; it has not been heard from since.

Jewish immigration to Birobidzhan may be resumed again, but it is scarcely conceivable that the Jewish Autonomous Province will ever become a center of Jewish cultural life.[68]

NOTES

1. *Pravda*, November 26, 1926.

2. The area of Jewish colonization in Birobidzhan, under the act of 1928, totaled almost 15,000 square miles, with a population of 32,245, according to A. Kantorovich, *Perspektivy Birobidzhana* [*Prospects of Birobidzhan*], Emes publishers, Moscow, 1932, pp. 4 and 16.

3. A. N. Merezhin, *O Birobidzhane* [*In Re Birobidzhan*], ed. KOMZET, Moscow, 1929, p. 10.

4. Viktor Fink, "Birobidzhan," in *Sovetskoye Stroitel'stvo*, May 1930, p. 117.

5. Yurii Larin, *Yevrei i antisemitizm v SSSR* [*Jews and Antisemitism in the USSR*], Moscow, 1929, pp. 184f.

6. The act was reprinted in several places. See, e.g., Merezhin, *op. cit.*, pp. 76f., or, in Yiddish, Dimanshtein, ed., *Idn in FSSR*. p. 177.

7. Prof. B. D. Bruk, "Predvaritel'nyi svodnyi otchet ekspeditsii" ["Summary Preliminary Report of the Mission"], in V. R. Vil'yams, ed., *Birsko-Bidzhanskii raion Dal'ne-Vostochnogo Kraya. Trudy ekspeditsii 1927 goda* [*The Bira and Bidzhan District of the Far Eastern Region. Papers of the Mission of 1927*], Part I, Moscow, 1928, p. 80.

8. *Barikht fun der Amerikaner ICOR Ekspertn-Komisie*, ed. ICOR Association, New York, 1930, p. 107.

9. Viktor Fink (*op. cit.*, pp. 118f.) said of the conditions he witnessed in the fall of 1929, when visiting Birobidzhan with the ICOR mission:

"In the settlement near the Tikhon'kaya terminal of the Ussuri Railroad, the gateway so to speak to Birobidzhan, the Jewish settlers have collected in a bottleneck. They live in a barracks. In an incredibly crowded and dirty place, dozens of people who are no kin to each other—unmarried men, young women, old people, large families with babies—lie around helter-skelter in double-decked wooden bunks. The Birobidzhan settler barracks, I venture to say, would disgrace a jail. Instructions are that the settlers are not to stay in the barracks more than three days. Actually, they hang around for two or three months, first, because the land has not been prepared for settlement, and secondly, because there are no roads. Birobidzhan is just not the Crimea, where you can walk long distances, live in a temporary hut, or even sleep under the sky in summer. You need solid buildings in Birobidzhan, and you have to build roads through the swamps and taiga. As long as neither has been done, people cannot leave Tikhon'kaya. . . .

"The barrack-dwellers develop a peculiarly sinister way of life. Some contrive, while still in the barracks, to obtain settler loans and credit; they live on this money and never bother to go out and look at the land. Others, less ingenious, live in extreme poverty. I have seen a family so sunken in misery that other settlers were moved by pity to take up a collection for these people, though they themselves are half starved. . . . Single women, finding themselves helpless, are driven to prostitution. Some go to Khabarovsk for this purpose; but in September–October 1929 several Jewish women practised prostitution even in Tikhon'kaya. . . ."

No word of these desperate conditions found its way into the report of the ICOR mission.

10. Birobidzhan's total population in 1928 was 32,245; it rose to 38,000 by the end of 1930 (an increase of 5,755), and 44,574 by the end of 1931 (an increase of 6,574).

The Jewish population reached 2,672 in 1930, and increased by 2,453 in 1931. See Kantorovich, *op. cit.*, pp. 78f.

11. Directive of the All-Russian Central Executive Committee of September 30, 1931, in *Revolyutsiya i Natsional'nosti*, October–November 1931, pp. 73f.; cf. Dimanshtein, ed., *Idn in FSSR*, p. 179.

12. Kantorovich, *op. cit.*, pp. 78f.

13. The rate of departure was to be brought under 12 percent, which would have given a net increase in 1932 of 12,557. (*Ibid.*, pp. 77f.)

14. The others were to be assigned as follows: industry, 3,775; producer cooperatives, 2,700; transportation, 500; professionals and white-collar workers, 525; students, 300.

15. Directive of the CEC of the USSR of April 7, 1932, in *Tribuna*, 1932, no. 10–11 (April 20), pp. 8f.

16. S. Dimanshtein, "Yevreiskoye natsmen'shinstvo na novom etape" ["The Jewish National Minority at a New Stage"], in *Revolyutsiya i Natsional'nosti*, May 1932, p. 89.

17. D. Barshchevskii, "15 let Oktyabrya i yevreiskoye zemleustroistvo" ["Jewish Rural Settlement in the Fifteen-Year Period after October"], in *Tribuna*, 1932, no. 27 (November 7), p. 8.

18. *Emes*, November 30, 1934, as quoted by Jacob Lestschinsky in *Dos Sovetishe Identum*, pp. 230f.

19. Of these, "some 1,500" were on collective farms according to Kantor, *op. cit.*, p. 126.

20. The table is from Kantor, *op. cit.*, pp. 118f.; it is not clear whether the net increase includes children born in Birobidzhan; the natural increase, however, must have been so small as scarcely to affect the statistics.

21. Viktor Fink tells of a conversation he had in the fall of 1929 with the chairman of the exceptionally successful "ICOR" cooperative: "Another reason why we are successful, the chairman said, is that conditions were favorable for us from the start: a passable road that wasn't too far off and houses ready to be occupied." (*Yevrei v taige* [*Jews in the Taiga*], Federatsiya Publishers, Moscow, 1930, p. 134.) Even this model cooperative, however, was tempted to engage in "organizational experiments," and a major crisis followed in 1931–33; "surgery" had to be used, according to Kantor (*op. cit.*, pp. 125f.), to save it.

22. How much more could have been accomplished had the political approach been different may be seen from the example of the "ICOR" cooperative, the only collective farm in Birobidzhan to have weathered without loss the hard times of 1928 and 1929. Its members were the first graduates of the Jewish Agricultural School in Kurasovshchina (White Russia), idealistic sons and daughters of pre-Soviet Jewish peasants, who went to Birobidzhan inspired by the slogan "Onward to the land of the Jews!" See Abram N. Merezhin's address to the plenary session of the Central Council and Central Board of OZET, in *Tribuna*, 1929, no. 3 (February 1), p. 13.

23. S. Dimanshtein, "Yevreiskaya avtonomnaya oblast'—detishche Oktyabr'skoi revolyutsii" ["The Jewish Autonomous Province, Offspring and Ward of the October Revolution"], in *Revolyutsiya i Natsional'nosti*, June 1934, pp. 13f. Emphasis Dimanshtein's.

24. *Ibid.*, p. 14.

25. Together with recruitment, forced labor would seem to have been introduced into Birobidzhan during the period of the Second Five-Year Plan (1933–1937). Adolph Held, who visited the JAP on behalf of American Jewish labor organizations in the summer of 1936, reported that the new railroad terminal in Birobidzhan City was being built by inmates of a forced labor camp located in the vicinity, under the supervision of a prisoner who had also drawn up the plans for the terminal (*Jewish Daily Forward*, September 8, 1936). A news item referring to a "special NKVD brigade" concerned with the colonization of the JAP (*Emes*, June 20, 1937) has been recorded by Gregory Aronson, *Di Idishe Problem in Sovet-Rusland*, New York, 1944, p. 140.

26. S. Gorfinkel', "K itogam plenuma Ozet" ["Adding Up the Results of the OZET Plenary Session"], in *Revolyutsiya i Natsional'nosti*, March, 1936, pp. 36f.

27. Dimanshtein (as quoted *supra* n. 23), p. 21.

28. Figures for 1934–1936, from the directives of the Presidium of the CEC of the USSR of March 27, 1936, in *Revolyutsiya i Natsional'nosti*, May 1936, pp. 93f.

29. S. Ye. Chutskayev, "Desyat' let Birobidzhana" ["Ten Years of Birobidzhan"], in *Vlast' Sovetov*, 1938, no. 7 (April), p. 18.

30. *Ibid.*, p. 16. Data issued by the planning authorities, quoted in *Emes*, June 3, 1937, indicated a Jewish population at the time of 18,000, or 23.8 percent of the total population of 76,500.

31. *Revolyutsiya i Natsional'nosti*, November 1936, pp. 146f

32. *Ibid.*

33. See, e.g., S. Dimanshtein, "Prezidium TsIK SSSR o YeAO ["The Presidium of the CEC of the USSR on the JAP"], in *Revolyutsiya i Natsional'nosti*, October 1936, pp. 54f.: "It is for the leaders of the JAP and the organizations in charge of assisting Jewish resettlement to learn the lessons of the charges made at the meeting of the Presidium of the CEC of the USSR by Comrade Kalinin, who accused them of underestimating the importance of agriculture and of not paying sufficient attention to the land settlement of Jewish migrants as a means for solidly establishing Jewish statehood. It is imperative that everything be done in order to expand the resettlement of Jews and their placement in agriculture. The basic task is to obtain, by virtue of collective work in agriculture, a physically and morally healthy generation of new human beings that will have cast off the special vestiges of the past. . . ."

34. *Ibid.*, p. 55.

35. Cf. Aronson, *op. cit.*, p. 127.

36. The KOMZET chairman Chutskayev wrote: ". . . Difficulties were aggravated and multiplied the more by the wrecking activities of the Trotskiite-Bukharinite and bourgeois-nationalist bandits, who had come from counterrevolutionary Jewish parties (Zionists, Bundists, etc.). All these contemptible schismatics deliberately ruined year in, year out the plans for the economic integration and settlement of the province, neglected the needs of the settlers, and thus contributed to their mass exodus. The wreckers' activities were particularly felt in the agricultural colonization of the province and in the setting-up of collective farms, where they aimed at sabotaging all plan objectives. The Trotskiite-Bukharinite bandits, inveterate enemies of the people, had built their nests all through the Far East, and particularly in the JAP, insidiously plotting to wrest this prosperous region from the USSR and hand it over to fascist interventionists." (*Op. cit.*, pp. 17f.)

37. This is not meant to imply that the JAP was henceforth passed over in silence. Quite the contrary; propagandistic publications and press releases continued to be issued in great quantities, though thoroughly purged of facts and especially statistics.

38. The chief editor of the two periodicals, Semen M. Dimanshtein, Commissar for Jewish National Affairs, secretary of the Central Board of the Jewish Sections of the Communist Party, chief of the Division of National Minorities of the party's Central Committee, president of the Central Council of OZET, ranking staff member of the section for minority affairs of the Central Executive Committee of the USSR, was accused late in 1937 of introducing "counterrevolutionary, nationalist, Bundist contraband" and removed from office in January 1938. He "vanished" and has not been heard of since.

39. *Izvestiya*, June 2, 1939.

40. Zinger, *Dos Banayte Folk; Dos Ufgerikhte Folk.*

41. If the Jewish population had increased more rapidly than the general population, at least the percentage rates of increase would have been made public. This would not have betrayed any official statistical secrets, for Soviet authorities customarily compute percentages of change in terms of a base year, the essential statistics for which are withheld. The absence of these percentages indicates an adverse trend.

42. *Yezhegodnik Periodicheskikh Izdanii*, 1939, [Periodicals' Yearbook, 1939], All-Union Book Chamber, Moscow, 1939, p. 31.

43. See n. 19 above.

44. B. Troitskii [changed from Trotskii], "Di Vikhtigste Fragn funem Dritn Fin-fyor far der Idisher Avtonomer Gegnt," in *Emes*, June 3, 1937.

45. A. Gilman, *Vos Darf Visn an Ibervanderer vegn der Idisher Avtonomer Gegnt, Emes* publishers, Moscow, 1939, pp. 24 and 26f.

46. Zinger, *Dos Banayte Folk*, p. 99.

47. Gilman, *op. cit.*, pp. 23-30.

48. *Ibid.*

49. *Eynikayt*, February 1, 1947.

50. *Ibid.*, March 21, 1946.

51. Gilman, *op. cit.*, pp. 26f.

52. A. Bakhmutskii, "Di Kraft fun der Stalinsher Natsionaler Politik," in *Eynikayt*, March 21, 1946.

53. G. Koptelev [chairman, Provincial Planning Commission, JAP], "Ufshtayg fun der Virtshaft un Kultur," in *Eynikayt*, April 19, 1947.

54. *Eynikayt*, January 1 and May 22, 1947.

55. A. Bakhmutskii, "Mir Vartn af Aykh, Naye Ibervanderer," in *Eynikayt*, May 24, 1947.

56. M. Levitin [chairman, Provincial Executive Committee, JAP], "Di Ibervan-derung in der Idisher Avtonomer Gegnt," in *Eynikayt*, July 22, 1948.

57. A. Bakhmutskii, "In der Eynhaytlekher Sovetisher Felkermishpokhe," in *Eyni-kayt*, April 10, 1948.

58. See Part II, "Antisemitism in the Soviet Union," Chap. VI.

59. *Eynikayt*, January 18, 1948.

60. *Ibid.*, March 30, 1948.

61. Levitin, *op. cit.*

62. For details based on reports in *Emes* and *Tribuna*, see Lestschinsky, *op. cit.*, pp. 237-243.

63. S. Kaczerginski, *Tsvishn Hamer un Serp. Tsu der Geshikhte fun der Likvi-datiie fun der Idisher Kultur in Sovet-Rusland*, Editions Grohar, Paris, 1949, p. 83. It is not quite clear whether the information about the schools referred to the city or the province of Birobidzhan; Kaczerginski quoted his informants as saying that only 10,000 to 11,000 Jews remained in Birobidzhan, which is likely to have been a reference to the city only. It is possible that there may have been a few small Jewish schools or Jewish sections in Russian schools in the vicinity of one or another of the larger *kolhozes*.

64. *Eynikayt*, February 28, 1946.

65. Nothing was said about Jewish schools, or the assigning of teachers to Jewish schools. See *Eynikayt*, March 3, 1946.

66. As noted before, the first official contingent of Jewish settlers did not arrive in the JAP until January 1947, ten months after the directive had been issued. (See n. 54 above.)

67. This is clearly apparent, for example, in the *Ambidjan Bulletin*, vol. VIII, no. 4, (December 1949). While an editorial, paraphrasing a report from Moscow, says on p. 3 that "about 25,000 children in the Jewish Autonomous Region attend 144 schools in which Yiddish is the language of instruction," a report from Birobid-zhan on p. 6 flatly contradicts this by stating that in 1948 there were altogether 139 (primary and secondary) schools and 5 technical colleges in operation in the JAP, and that the former had an enrollment of 17,600. This report from a Jewish source in Birobidzhan made no reference either to Jewish schools or to the use of Yiddish as a language of instruction.

68. As this book was going to press, the newspaper *Haaretz*, Tel Aviv, in its issue of March 29, 1951, carried a survey of recent developments in Birobidzhan, based on original sources including official reports presented by Pavel Simonov, Secretary of the Communist Party in Birobidzhan, to a regional conference of the party in Khabarovsk, Siberia. The *Haaretz* survey contained the following information: There are now 130,000 inhabitants in the autonomous province, 30 per cent of them

Jews. There was no large-scale immigration during the past two years, although a few hundred Jews, mostly relatives of old residents, joined the Jewish population. Many more Jews were settled in other parts of Siberia, especially around Krasnoyarsk, and the newspaper concluded that the idea of large-scale Jewish settlement in Birobidzhan was given up by the authorities. A comprehensive purge among local Communist leaders, and especially among Jewish Communists, was conducted during 1949 and 1950. Among those purged were S. Kushnir, former first secretary of the Communist Party in the territory, Bakhmutskii, its former second secretary, Silberstein, former chairman of the Executive Committee of the local Soviet, Goldmacher and Leah Lishnianskaya, former deputies of the Supreme Soviet, Wattenberg, who had been a secretary of the American Birobidzhan Committee before he emigrated to the Soviet Union, and many others. All of them were accused of "Jewish nationalism" and "cosmopolitanism" and relieved of their duties. Russians were appointed to positions formerly held by Jewish Communists; other Jewish Communists, recently brought over from European Russia, serve as their assistants. The local Yiddish newspaper, *Birobidzhaner Shtern*, was discontinued and its staff arrested. From the reports it was not clear whether Yiddish was still taught in the schools, or used in cultural life; no information was given about religious life. *Haaretz* concluded from the evidence that the Soviet leaders decided to discontinue former Jewish colonization and that the official liquidation of the Jewish Autonomous Territory was held up only for reasons of public relations outside the country.

CHAPTER XIV

The War and After

De-Nationalization on the March

The outbreak of the Second World War found the dislocation of the
Jewish population of the Soviet Union progressing at full speed. The
migratory movement depleted the Jewish communities in the areas of the
former Pale of Residence and carried increasing numbers of Jews to
regions where only a few had lived in pre-revolutionary times. In part
this was a natural reaction against the traditional concentration of Jews
in the congested western and southwestern provinces; but it was also a
part of the greatly increased mobility of the Soviet population in general.
As a result of the social upheaval caused by full-speed industrialization
and the collectivization of agriculture, enormous numbers of people were
on the move. The population census of January 17, 1939 revealed notable
changes as compared with the previous census of December 17, 1926.
Many millions had moved from the countryside to the cities, and from
west to east, towards the less populated lands of the Urals and Siberia.
Jewish migration followed this eastward trend. In 1926, 73.9 percent of
all Soviet Jews lived in the Ukraine and White Russia; in 1939, only 63.2
percent. Almost two-fifths of the total Jewish population had moved
out of the Pale.[1]

This scattering of the Jewish population was bound to have a de-nationalizing effect that could have been checked only if the Jewish group had
been able to preserve its cohesion and independent cultural life in the
new places whither it went. But there were no autonomous Jewish organizations to perform these functions. In official eyes the very idea of a
Jewish national consciousness was an undesirable, if not criminal, heresy.
What the Jewish press said in Yiddish was largely identical with what
all other Soviet newspapers and periodicals said in dozens of other languages. Jewish publications in Russian, which had exerted a great influence
on Jewish life in the Tsarist period, as well as in 1917–18, and which
could have played a large role as media of Jewish culture in this time of
dispersion and mounting linguistic assimilation, were even worse off than
those in Yiddish. Even government-supervised Jewish publications in
Russian were deemed inopportune. The only periodical of this kind which
survived for a number of years, OZET's *Tribuna*, had but limited im-

portance as an organ of Jewish interests, in spite of the fact that it appeared for a while under the title, "Tribune of Soviet Jewish Public Opinion"; it was discontinued in January 1938, and no Jewish publication in Russian has since been permitted to appear. Also in 1938 the last remaining institutions of Jewish public life, OZET and KOMZET, were dissolved, and the sole Yiddish-language newspaper of nationwide circulation, *Emes*, was suppressed.

Deprived of Jewish organizations, publications, and schools, the scattered Jewish islets outside of the old ghetto areas were exposed to the full impact of the community-destroying, de-nationalizing process. It was also becoming less and less possible to maintain group identity and cohesion in the old regions of Jewish settlement. In those places, too, a migratory movement set in in the 1920's and 1930's and a considerable portion of the Ukrainian and White-Russian Jewish population migrated from smaller cities and semirural townships with Jewish majorities or pluralities to larger, especially the largest, urban centers. This trend, occasionally termed "metropolitanization," deepened the effects of dispersion on cultural and communal life.

Loss of a group's cohesion and national identity—de-nationalization—is not synonymous with its integration in the surrounding majority people —assimilation. Assimilation signifies so complete an acceptance and integration of the minority by the majority group that the latter does not feel the former to be aliens in any significant way. Full assimilation usually lags far behind de-nationalization; the history of the Jewish people since the Emancipation in many countries is typical of this lack of synchronization. The history of the Soviet Jews has not been essentially different. While their de-nationalization advanced by leaps and bounds, the disjoined elements of the Jewish collectivity were not fully absorbed in the Soviet community at large.

Genuine and complete assimilation may be welcomed as beneficent, accepted as unavoidable, or else rejected on principle. But there can hardly be a difference of opinion as to the pernicious consequences of one-sided de-nationalization. It takes something away without giving anything in return. It places "the intruders" in an inferior position and produces intergroup tensions.

The war pushed the process far ahead and magnified its damaging effects. The provinces that came under the heel of the Wehrmacht soon after the commencement of Nazi-Soviet hostilities in June 1941, were the very ones in which vestiges of the Jewish community and culture still existed. The holocaust not only physically destroyed the least de-nationalized sections of the Jewish community, but also eliminated the only significant surviving centers of Jewish life. This weakened the cohesion and cultural allegiance of Jewish groups in other parts of the Soviet Union.

Wartime Dispersion

The scattering of the Jewish population in the war years, it can now be stated beyond the shadow of a doubt, was not the consequence of its hasty evacuation from areas threatened by the German advance. The story of the Soviet government's rescue of the Jews was concocted for foreign consumption. Government evacuation of the Jewish population, who stood in especial jeopardy, took place only in a few instances. Only a fraction of the survivors owe their lives to any special solicitude on the government's part. The great majority of the Jewish population of the German-occupied areas were neither encouraged nor given an opportunity by the Soviet authorities to flee—most of them perished. Evacuation operations followed a schedule of priorities based on administrative and economic considerations.

First to be evacuated were the personnel of important government institutions and administrative agencies, often with their families; the personnel of large industrial plants; some agricultural establishments; and the dependents of commissioned officers and military officials. This involved the removal of millions of people. The number of Jews among the evacuees cannot be exactly computed. In all likelihood, Jewish evacuees must have numbered several hundred thousand. A certain, apparently smaller, number of Jews fled on their own from areas threatened by the advance of the German armies. In addition, several hundred thousand Jews were deported from Soviet-occupied Poland to Central Asia and to the northern provinces of the Russian SFSR in 1940–41. All in all, the number of Jews in those parts of the Soviet Union never reached by the German offensive—about 900,000 to 1,000,000—is likely to have been doubled as a result of evacuations, deportations, and flight.[2]

Jews were evacuated *en bloc* only in the case of some Jewish collective farms, when entire villages were removed with the *kolkhozes*. This, however, happened infrequently; in the Ukraine and White Russia all Jewish *kolkhozes* were apparently left behind, suffering wholesale extermination. In the case of White Russia, there does not seem to have been a single report in the Soviet press of the rescue of either *kolkhozes* in a body or of individual members. Semiofficial wartime reports holding out the hope that many Jewish farm colonies in the Ukraine survived,[3] were disproved by information coming to light after the war. Thus, of 103 Jewish families in the *kolkhoz* village Nay-Vitebsk in the Jewish national district of Stalindorf, only 10 survived, while 93 families (271 persons) were killed by the Germans on May 29, 1942.[4] In the Jewish village Nay-Kovno, also in the district of Stalindorf, nobody survived—the entire Jewish population was exterminated on May 25, 1942.[5] Of the Kalinin district, formerly the Jewish Kalinindorf, in the province of Kherson, which had a large

Jewish farm population, a Soviet report says: "The fascist bandits killed about 5,000 Jews. As soon as the province was liberated, evacuated *kolkhoz* farmers, some of them Jews, started trekking back from all parts of the country. By now [May 1946] some 250 Jewish families have returned to the district."[6] That is, some 700 people remained out of a prewar population of many thousands; even this number of survivors is high in comparison with other reports from the Ukraine.

Only the Jewish agricultural regions in the Crimea came off somewhat better. The Crimea was occupied much later than White Russia and the Ukraine, the population was not taken by surprise, and several Jewish *kolkhozes* could be evacuated in a body. The extent of the evacuation can be judged from information collected by a representative of the Jewish Antifascist Committee, S. Gordon, who visited the district in the summer of 1945, when most of the evacuees had already returned to their villages.[7] The smallest loss of human life was reported by the Molotov *kolkhoz*, which before the war had consisted of 110 families; in the middle of 1945, 83 families numbering 197 persons had returned, but many more evacuees and discharged servicemen were expected, and the *kolkhoz* management anticipated a population of 350 to 400, i.e., almost as many as before the war.[8] This, however, was an exception; other Jewish villages in the Crimea suffered heavy losses. In the ICOR *kolkhoz*, of 126 families 43 survived, counting as family units even single orphaned children aged 7 or 8. More than this number had been evacuated, but the *kolkhoz* was overtaken by the Nazis in the Kuban region, where 20 families perished.[9] A third Crimean *kolkhoz*, Mayfeld, had 61 surviving families (counting single survivors as families), out of a prewar total of 160.[10] If these *kolkhozes* may be considered as representative, one can perhaps say that about half the Jewish farm population of the Crimea, which in 1939 was made up of nearly 5,000 families,[11] was evacuated.

Those *kolkhozes* in the Jewish national districts which were lucky enough to be evacuated could look forward to a resumption of their life after the war. In some instances their members remained together, or at least were able to keep in touch with one another, and there was not that sense of utter loss and isolation which overwhelmed other survivors.

Political Neglect and the Revival of National Feeling

Uprooted and often separated from their families, as a rule the evacuees were cut off from any kind of Jewish life. Most of the Jewish administrative, cultural, and communal institutions still in existence before the war had been in the Ukraine and White Russia. These were destroyed by the Nazis. The Jewish press, schools, libraries, community centers, agricultural colonies, Soviets, courts, and district administrations—all were abandoned to the invaders' fury. Only single Jewish institutions were saved, chiefly theatrical companies. The Minsk theater was evacuated to Novosibirsk,[12] the Kiev theater to Dzhambul,[13] and the Jewish theater in the former Polish city of Lvov (Lwów, Lemberg) to Alma-Ata.[14] Not a single Jewish newspaper or publishing house was evacuated either from the Ukraine or White Russia; only the *Emes* publishing house in Moscow was transferred to the Urals.

Although there was a noticeable concentration of Jewish evacuees, refugees, and released deportees in a few cities of Central Asia, there were no significant manifestations of Jewish cultural life in these centers, contrary to wartime reports from semiofficial sources occasionally carried by the Jewish press outside the Soviet Union. That the displaced and dispersed Jewish community had no life—either cultural or communal—of its own during the war is unanimously confirmed by many Soviet and Polish Jews who left the Soviet Union after the war; though these eyewitnesses differed politically, they did not differ on this. Additional evidence has been supplied by professional observers—newspapermen, diplomats, etc.—stationed in or visiting the Soviet Union during the war, including persons sympathetic to the Soviet government and fully persuaded of its active championship of the interests of the Jewish minority.

Thus the Palestinian writer Solomon Itzhaki accepted at face value propaganda stories about the Soviet Union's rescuing Jews *en bloc* from imperiled areas.[15] Yet Itzhaki found it impossible to disregard facts given him by a friend, an outstanding Jewish journalist from Poland attached to the Polish Consulate in Kuibyshev in 1941 and 1942, who was able to make several trips to Central Asia. Itzhaki's informant gave the lie to the late Shakhno Epshtein, then secretary of the Jewish Antifascist Committee, who had "said in Tashkent that in all the regions to which the Jews have been evacuated, there are many Jewish national theaters; books in Jewish were published even in 1942; Jewish schools operate normally in Siberia and Uzbekistan."[16] He investigated the story on the spot, and reported as follows: "While it is true that in Tashkent and Bukhara performances are given at the Jewish national theaters, the performances are in Russian; although more than half a million copies [of a book] were printed in Jewish, the book was a new biography of Stalin; while several Jewish schools have been opened in distant territories, instruction is in Russian; not a single Jewish newspaper has been published for more than a year, etc., etc."[17]

Other reports are much the same. It would of course have been unrealistic to expect the Soviet government to support a program of Jewish national reconstruction in the midst of the war; even if Bolshevik intentions had been better, it is unlikely that a great deal could have been accomplished. But the war cannot explain the failure to establish Yiddish-language schools and newspapers in areas with large numbers of Jewish refugees.

The Soviet government also refrained from launching a political offensive in support of the Jewish people, chief target of the Nazi fury, which it certainly could and should have done. Nazi propaganda, penetrating far into the Soviet interior with the tale that Hitlerite Germany was fighting to save the world from Jewish domination, called for an answer from the Soviet leadership openly and unconditionally espousing the cause of the Jewish people, coupled with an energetic campaign against antisemitism. The Soviet government not only did not do this, but, afraid that Hitlerite propaganda might undermine military and civilian morale with its legend of "the Jewish war," took pains to conceal the fact of the Nazi extermination of Jews from the Soviet public, and persisted in describing all Nazi atrocities as having been inflicted upon "Soviet people" in general.[18]

For the same reason, antisemitism was passed over in silence. It was apparently thought to be inopportune to stress the incompatibility of Communism with anti-Jewish discrimination. The unexampled tragedy that befell the Jewish people went unnoticed, no popular sympathy was extended to the Jewish survivors, and the special needs and wants of the Jewish remnants remained unknown to the population at large and were treated with indifference by the inefficient bureaucracy, to whose care they were entrusted. No consideration was given the masses of Jewish evacuees, refugees, deportees or any other Jewish civilians; their mere presence aroused antagonism.

This callous attitude evoked feelings of hurt and bewilderment in many Soviet Jews. Nazi horrors had made them keenly aware of their Jewishness, and they were prey to the tormenting thought that, as a group, they were unwanted even in the Soviet Union. Their sensitivity to hostility or even mere indifference was heightened; they suffered emotional anguish, strong feelings of estrangement, and there was frequently an articulate upsurge of Jewish national feeling. All documents describing the wartime experiences of Jews in the Soviet Union—letters, memoirs, testimonials of Displaced Persons—bear the imprint of this emotional crisis.

The Soviet government was not unaware of the state of mind of its Jewish citizens, as it was not unaware of the horror aroused in the world by Nazi massacres. Press and radio were off and on permitted to record expressions of Jewish national solidarity by well-known Soviet personalities, and statements stressing the common interests of Jews in different countries, were given wide publicity. The very official *Pravda* carried the following profession of faith by Ilya Ehrenburg, a leading Soviet writer and propagandist: "I grew up in a Russian city. My mother tongue is Russian. I am a Russian writer. Like all Russians, I am defending my homeland. But the Nazis have made me remember something else, too. My mother was called Khana. I am a Jew. I say it with pride. We are those whom Hitler hates the most, and this adorns us."[19]

Outside of the Soviet Union its participation in the war against the Axis had given rise to certain illusions. Many believed that the Soviet dictatorship had come to a crossing of the roads, and that its alliance with the democratic powers would last beyond the war and cause it to temper its totalitarian rigors. The Soviet leaders for their part were not averse to experimenting with a Jewish organization that might enlist the support of foreign Jewish groups for Soviet policies.

The Plan of Erlich and Alter

The idea of a political body that would speak for the Jewish people of Eastern Europe was not of Soviet origin. True, the Jewish Antifascist Committee (JAC) which made its public appearance in the spring of 1942 was sponsored and directed by the government. But this was a perversion of the program of Jewish political action outlined in the fall of 1941 by a non-Soviet group. The Communist contention that theirs had been the initiative, and that the JAC was begotten at a "public gathering of representatives of the Jewish people" in Moscow, on August 24, 1941, is without foundation. A lengthy description of the meeting, which took more than a full page in next morning's *Pravda*, made no reference to plans for establishing any Jewish organization whatsoever. The gathering appealed to Jews throughout the world not to despair, not to await destruction passively, but to take an active part in the war against Hitlerite Germany. Not a single word was said about the establishment of a Jewish committee.

A detailed plan for constituting a Jewish war committee was drawn up somewhat later by the leaders of the Jewish Socialist Bund of Poland, Henryk Erlich and Victor Alter, both of whom had been released from prison in Moscow early in September 1941. How the plan was conceived, and what happened after it had been submitted to the Soviet government, we know from a number of documents drafted in October 1941 or shortly thereafter and published in this country in 1943: letters by Erlich and Alter to Lavrentii P. Beriya, People's Commissar for the Interior (chief of the NKVD), and to Stalin himself, the chairman of the Council of People's Commissars; an outline of the activities to be performed by the committee; and the draft of an appeal to the Jewish masses in Poland.[20] The documents reveal that Erlich and Alter were received by Beriya after their release, and that in the course of a lengthy conversation an agreement was reached to seek the establishment of a Jewish committee to foster the fight against Nazism. Following the agreement with the People's Commissar for the Interior, an organizing group was constituted and "a number of conferences" were held; it was decided to request official authorization for the immediate establishment of a Jewish Anti-Hitlerite Committee "on the territory of the Soviet Union." The signatories of the request asked Beriya to expedite the decision.

The organizational plan was discussed in greater detail in a letter addressed to Stalin, of which a copy was sent to Beriya. The Jewish Committee was to be made up of representatives of the Jewish population of the Nazi-dominated countries, such as Poland, Czechoslovakia, Germany, Austria, Rumania, etc., as well as of Jewish representatives from the USSR, the United States, and Great Britain. In addition, honorary membership was to be extended to the ambassadors of Great Britain, the United States, and Poland, and to individuals prominent in Soviet life (scientists, artists, writers, etc.). The Committee was to mobilize Jews throughout the world for the struggle against Hitlerism, to organize aid and assistance to the Jewish masses in countries under Nazi control, and a relief service for Jewish refugees in the Soviet Union. After preliminary negotiations in September and early October 1941, the plan was endorsed by the official Soviet representative, Beriya.

The request for the authorization of a Jewish committee which Erlich and Alter had addressed to the head of the government went unanswered. On December 5, 1941, in the small hours of the morning, Erlich and Alter were arrested; in the same month they were shot. Their execution was not acknowledged until the spring of 1943, when Soviet Ambassador Litvinov, since removed from public office, admitted it in a letter to William Green, President of the American Federation of Labor.

Jewish Antifascist Committee—Weapon of Soviet Propaganda

For several months after the execution of Erlich and Alter the Soviet press omitted all reference to a Jewish committee of any kind. Then, on April 6, 1942, the Jewish Telegraphic Agency's correspondent in Moscow learned that an anti-Nazi "Committee of Soviet Jewish Intellectuals" had been formed,[21] and on April 7 the newly founded organization, announced as the "Jewish Antifascist Committee," issued an appeal to the Jews of the world.[22] On April 23 the existence of the JAC was officially acknowledged at a press conference for foreign correspondents in Kuibyshev by Solomon A. Lozovskii, deputy chief of the Soviet Information Bureau.[23] After a second "public gathering of representatives of the Jewish people" in Moscow on May 24, the first plenary session of the JAC assembled on May 28. How the Committee was founded, and who determined its composition and program, remain a mystery.[24]

It was made clear that the JAC was to devote itself chiefly to influencing Jewish opinion outside the Soviet Union, but not so much in order to safeguard Jewish interests or help the Allies as a whole to win the war, as to enlist support for the Soviet Union in particular. It was not intended to organize relief for Jews on Soviet soil, or even for the Jewish citizens of the USSR: the Committee's chief purpose was to obtain moral and material help for the Red Army. In the appeal of May 24, the Soviet Union was called the first force in the war against Hitlerism, and Soviet Jews were praised for the example they set the Jewish people: "We Jews of the Soviet Union have set you an example. . . . If all freedom-loving peoples were to do what the Soviet people are doing, fascism would soon be smashed to bits," said the appeal at a moment when Hitler's second Russian offensive was sweeping everything before it. "The Red Army is the hope of all mankind," proclaimed the appeal— "Jews throughout the world! Let us collect money, buy a thousand tanks and five hundred airplanes, and ship them to the Red Army!"[25] The first issue of the Committee's newspaper, *Eynikayt*, led off with an article by the chairman, Solomon Mikhoels, the renowned actor, entitled "1,000 Tanks and 500 Bombers."[26]

This interpretation of the objectives of an organization called upon to speak for the Jewish people at the moment of its greatest agony was too shallow to be accepted without objection. Criticism was voiced within the Committee itself at its first session. The Soviet press did not report the speeches of the critics, but it did report the reply made to them by the Committee's secretary. Shakhno Epshtein harshly censured "a tendency now in evidence" to burden the JAC with tasks that "have nothing to do directly with the fight against fascism."[27] This meant all specifically Jewish questions, and even problems of relief and rehabilitation. The critics' objections were overridden.

The JAC in practice was not so much a fund-raising agency for the Red Army as an instrument of propaganda. In comparison with what the Red Army needed and what the Soviet Union received from its allies, voluntary contributions by the Jewish public "throughout the world" (which is to say, the U.S.A.) could only have a negligible influence on the military strength of the Soviet Union. But fund-raising campaigns were an excellent means for spreading Soviet propaganda, and had the additional advantage of paying the way of the JAC. By the spring of 1944, the JAC had collected two to three million dollars in the United States.[28] No information has ever been published as to how this amount was spent.

The regular activities of the JAC were characterized by Shakhno Epshtein in an article on the eve of the Committee's second plenary session (February 1943) as follows: "The basic activity of the JAC was directed towards enlightening the Jewish popular masses in all countries about the great historical accomplishments with which Soviet reality is replete. The Committee did this in writing, dispatching daily by cable, and frequently through special mailing facilities, newspaper material, reports, short stories, songs and even lengthy plays; and it did it orally by means of four weekly radio broadcasts to foreign countries, especially to England and the United States."[29] No change occurred in the character of the JAC's activities in the years that followed.

The activities of the JAC were again criticized by members at its second plenary session, and this once the criticism found its way into the press. The writer David Gofshtein insisted that preparations be made to rebuild the cities and market towns of provinces retaken from the Germans by the Soviet armies. D. Shchupak, chairman of the "Naylebn" *kolkhoz*, urged the Committee actively to prepare for the reconstruction of the Jewish collective farms of the Ukraine and the Crimea. I. Nusinov, a professor of literature, said: "The Committee must not concern itself with propaganda only. . . . The Committee, for instance, should assist the evacuees to make a new life for themselves." This suggestion was seconded by Perets Markish, the poet. In reply to these criticisms of "the Committee's functions and program of activities," Chairman Mikhoels said, mildly: "There is a kernel of truth in the view that the Committee has not yet become, for the entire country, that living center of the Jewish population which it should be. People send letters and complaints to us from different parts of the country; the dispersed Jewish population is searching for the address [of a Jewish organization to which to appeal in their need]; we cannot ignore such things."[30]

Yet this did not bring about a change in the activities of the JAC. Emphasis continued to be placed exclusively on propaganda. What is more, the Committee's campaigns showed less and less interest in the struggle against Hitlerism and fascism, and were given over increasingly to denunciations of all those who criticized Soviet policies, and in particular of the "Jewish fascists" of the New York *Jewish Daily Forward* and the American labor unions. At the third—and last—plenary session of the JAC, in April 1944, no mention was any longer made of Jewish problems; nothing was said about the urgent necessity of assisting Soviet Jews (let alone Jews in other countries). JAC representatives who had returned from a trip to the United States proudly told of their refusal to accept help from American Jewish relief organizations so long as the latter insisted that their funds be spent solely in relieving the distress of Jews— the announcement was made that the JAC had succeeded in persuading the Joint Distribution Committee to assist all evacuees "regardless of nationality."[31] The JAC thus not only persisted in its refusal to organize relief for the Jews of the Soviet Union, it also barred those outside the Soviet Union—for the most part American and British Jews—from coming to the relief of Soviet Jews unless all distressed Soviet citizens shared in the Jewish contributions.

The Vilna Jewish writer and scholar Szmerl Kaczerginski, who was in close contact with the leaders of the JAC in 1944 and 1945, has supplied interesting details about the political atmosphere in which the Committee had to work. Kaczerginski spent the years of the Nazi occupation first in the Vilna ghetto, and later fighting with the anti-Nazi partisans. After the Red Army drove the Germans out of Vilna in July 1944, he was among the first to set to work to rebuild the Jewish community. While he had no illusions about the attitude of the local Soviet authorities (whose arbitrary rule he had had an opportunity to observe before—in 1939–41), he believed that the government in Moscow favored Jewish cultural reconstruction, and that the JAC was influential enough to prevail against the indifference of the local officials. He was full of hope when he went to Moscow in 1944 to appeal to the higher authorities, and not until his return to Vilna, when all hope of Jewish reconstruction had been frustrated, did he give up and decide to escape abroad. In Moscow, Kaczerginski soon found out that the main function of the JAC, which received its directives from Lozovskii, the actual head of the Soviet Information Bureau, was foreign propaganda, and that the Committee was not permitted to do any work inside the Soviet Union or to have local offices in the Soviet provinces: "The sole purpose of the work of the Committee was to send propaganda material abroad."[32]

Conversations with leading Jewish writers, as well as with officials of the JAC, confirmed his gloomy impressions. The view that "the Committee does not fulfill its true obligation towards the surviving Jews of the Soviet Union," was shared by none other than Ilya Ehrenburg. "This is not a Jewish but an anti-Jewish committee," Kaczerginski was told by Ehrenburg, whose words he reproduces in Russian. Ehrenburg's critical attitude led to disputes with Epshtein and Fefer, and finally resulted in Ehrenburg's virtual retirement. "This had nothing to do with the fact that his signature continued to appear with those of other members of the Committee so long as it existed. For this Lozovskii did not have to ask [Ehrenburg's] permission."[33]

The summary suppression of the JAC in 1948 by the Soviet authorities in itself was scarcely a loss to the Jewish population of Russia, but it was indicative of an ominous political trend.

The Postwar Desert

As the German armies retreated, small groups of Jews began to reappear in the southern and southwestern provinces: discharged soldiers, returning evacuees, and farther to the west the few who had hidden in the woods. With the end of the war, the movement increased and a noticeable Jewish population, though much smaller than before the war, began to collect in the larger cities, passing by the *shtetls* which had been the scenes of wholesale slaughter.

The Jews who returned had lost most of their relatives and friends, were surrounded by the ruins of their prewar existence, and were haunted by a sense of loss and of isolation from the Soviet community at large. The absence of all Jewish communal ties, activities, and institutions estranged them from the surviving fragments of the Jewish community in other places as well. It is now apparent that neither a Jewish culture nor a Jewish community was revived in the years that followed the end of the war. No Jewish village or town Soviets have been restored, either in the Ukraine, the Crimea, or White Russia. The five Jewish national districts of the Ukraine and the Crimea have disappeared without a trace; even their names have been obliterated.[34] There are no Jewish schools, newspapers, or any manifestations of Jewish cultural activity. All that remains of the once dynamic cultural life in the traditional area of Jewish settlement are a few theaters; and the solitary issue of a literary periodical, *Shtern*, published in the Ukraine in 1947 and officially discontinued thereafter, is the only reminder of the once flourishing Jewish life of the Ukraine.[35]

The Jewish public school has almost completely disappeared. Apart from Birobidzhan, there are hardly half a dozen Jewish schools in the Soviet Union, including the annexed territories of Lithuania, Eastern Poland, Bessarabia, Bucovina, etc. Occasional reference has been made to a school in Vilna, Kovno, and Chernovtsy (formerly Cernauti or Czernowitz); there may be one or two more, though neither careful search through the columns of *Eynikayt* nor repeated inquiries addressed to the Jewish Communist press in the United States have revealed their existence.

Soviet educational policy would no longer seem to favor Jewish schools. The reluctance of the administration in practice has been illustrated by Kaczerginski in his story of the first attempts to get a Jewish school started in liberated Vilna. Permission was obtained from the Soviet authorities to open a school of four grades, "and who knows whether the school could have opened at all had it not been for the efforts of some Jewish army officers." Enough Jewish teachers had returned to Vilna to set up regular classes. When, however, the budget for the following year was submitted to the authorities, the school was refused permission to institute a fifth grade for children graduating from the fourth. The representatives of the faculty were told by the People's Commissar for Education that the children could continue their studies in Russian or Lithuanian schools. "We learned later that the four grades had been permitted only on the ground that the younger children did not know any language but Yiddish. Within the accepted curriculum they were supposed to acquire enough Russian and Lithuanian in the four-grade school to dispense with a Jewish school thereafter." Similarly, the newly established home for Jewish orphans was authorized to admit children who had survived ghettos, camps, and hiding places, but not to admit those who had spent the war years in evacuation centers in the Soviet interior. Children who had learned to make themselves understood in Russian, and who were not to be exposed to the "nationalistic" influence of a (Soviet) Jewish orphanage, were placed in Lithuanian institutions.[36]

The complete lack of information on Jewish schools in postwar Soviet Jewish publications would seem to indicate that Soviet administrators in general oppose Yiddish schools for children who know another language. And except for the few who survived the war years in "family camps" protected by Jewish guerrillas in the White-Russian woods, and the still fewer survivors of German slave labor camps, it may well be that there is scarcely a Jewish child alive who has not picked up a second language, either in Russian evacuation centers or concealed in the homes of non-Jewish foster parents. Soviet officials apparently saw no reason why they should take pains to reverse this assimilatory process.

Efforts to revive the Yiddish-language press met with an even colder official reception. Again Kaczerginski's personal experience is instructive:

> For several months (in 1944 and 1945) another Jewish writer and I rushed from one agency to another, and even succeeded in approaching the highest authorities in Lithuania as well as in Moscow, seeking authorization to issue at least one publication in Yiddish. (From the Moscow publishing house *Emes*, we had got hold of type stored in Leningrad.) Yet everywhere we met with refusal. Nor did Fefer's and Mikhoels' intercession with [Politburo member Lazar M.] Kaganovich, while I was in Moscow in 1945 seeking permission to issue at least one daily newspaper and one Yiddish monthly for the Jews of Russia, do any good. Kaganovich's promise to take the matter up with Zhdanov bore no fruit, as may be inferred from subsequent events.[37]

At the time the request was made, *Eynikayt*, the small Yiddish-language newspaper published thrice weekly by the Jewish Antifascist Committee, was still appearing in Moscow. But even this official propaganda sheet was suddenly discontinued late in 1948. With the possible exception of a small local paper in Birobidzhan, there is not a single Yiddish publication now appearing in all of Russia. It need hardly be added that the importation of foreign Yiddish-language publications, including those put out by Jewish Communist or pro-Soviet groups in America, remains prohibited.

"Cosmopolitanism"

In the first postwar years the Soviet government's policy on Jewish matters did not differ essentially from what it had been in the last decade before the war. It remained indifferent to special Jewish problems, which the war had multiplied enormously, but it continued to profess allegiance to the principle of racial and national equality. It frowned on racial prejudice and discrimination, although little was done to combat the growth of antisemitic tendencies. Government decisions or the lack of decisions on issues affecting the Jewish population continued to be determined by the prewar approach with its characteristic neglect of the special problems and needs of the Jewish minority.

For quite a while, this essential core of postwar policy was hidden from view. As the rift between the wartime Allies came into the open, Soviet foreign policy concentrated more and more on embarrassing the major Western powers; for this the Jewish-Arab conflict in Palestine was a godsend. Though an inveterate foe of Zionism, Moscow did not hesitate to champion the Jewish cause in Palestine so long as this added to the difficulties of the British in the Middle East and embarrassed the United States. Public opinion was impressed by Moscow's "friendly" attitude to Jews: for a time no obstacles were put in the way of Jews wishing to leave the satellite countries and go to Palestine.

A change came about with the establishment of the independent State of Israel on May 14, 1948. The Soviet government was the first to grant Israel *de jure* recognition. But Jewish nationalism now became doubly suspect—as an ideological deviation and as a treasonable manifestation of sympathy with a foreign country. The Soviet government was certainly not ignorant of the bonds of sympathy and commiseration that united many Jews in various countries—not excluding the Soviet Jews—with the victims of the European holocaust, and it knew what Israel represented in their eyes. It was inclined to distrust a national group thus implicitly asserting a claim to existence transcending the Soviet system.

How the Soviet regime differentiated between its foreign and domestic attitude towards Israel can be seen in an incident described by Edmund Stevens, for fifteen years, until the summer of 1948, Moscow correspondent of the *Christian Science Monitor:*

> With the State of Israel an accomplished fact Soviet policy-makers saw the chance to gain a foothold in the Middle East. Accordingly, Israel received a favorable press, and party lectures were organized on the subject.
>
> After one such lecture in Moscow, a man in the audience got up and asked the speaker how Jews wishing to emigrate to Israel should make their applications. Instead of answering, the speaker launched

into a violent tirade, saying that such a question was unworthy of a loyal Soviet citizen, who should prize his birthright too much even to think of wanting to emigrate, and that the very idea was treasonable. Others in the audience rallied to the questioner's support: Had not Soviet citizens of Polish and Czech extraction been allowed to leave under repatriation agreements with the respective countries? Why not a similar agreement with Israel?

When members of the Israel Legation, headed by Mrs. Golda Myerson, reached Moscow, they received a tremendous spontaneous ovation from the local Jews, first at the synagogue, then under the windows of their Metropol Hotel rooms—something without precedent in Soviet history. Immediately the legation was flooded with inquiries about how to get to Israel. . . .[38]

While official statements were still assuring the Israeli government of the friendship of the Soviet Union, Ilya Ehrenburg had made it abundantly clear, in September 1948, that in Soviet eyes Israel was merely another bourgeois state, and one moreover whose destiny was shaped by "the intrusion of Anglo-American capital." Since Israel's ruling class was likely to "betray national interests for the sake of the dollar," the Soviet Union, Ehrenburg said, would have to support the struggle of the Israeli "working people . . . against the greed of their own bourgeoisie, for whom a war is first of all a means of making money." Moreover, there was no such thing as a Jewish nation internationally. "Jewish laboring people, like all other laboring people, are strongly attached to the soil on which they were born and on which they grew up. . . . The Jewish Tunisian and the Jew who lives in Chicago, speaks American, and also thinks American, have little in common." The only bonds uniting the Jews of different countries had been forged by antisemitic persecution, but the only certain answer to antisemitism was in "the triumph of socialism over capitalism." Not only was it impossible for a Jewish state to eradicate antisemitism, but Palestine itself had been preserved from destruction during the war by "the victory of the Soviet people over the fascists." The "lot of people who bear the yoke of capitalist exploitation," as do the working people of Israel, can never tempt the Soviet Jews, who are "citizens of a socialist society" united by "comradeship in arms" with the whole Soviet people and bound by the "graves of their beloved" to "every inch of Soviet soil." If Jews living in different countries had anything at all in common, it was the desire to put down racial persecution; to bring this about they must join the "progressive" forces and look for leadership "to the Soviet Union, which marches in the van of mankind on the road to a better future."[39]

To look to Israel, to feel an allegiance to a "mystic" Jewish nation united across the boundaries of existing states, was to lack in loyalty to the Soviet Union and to bow to "Anglo-American capital"—to "speak English" instead of "Russian," as Ehrenburg put it when he snubbed Israel's special envoy to the Soviet Union, Mrs. Golda Myerson, at a reception arranged by General Walter Bedell Smith, the American Ambassador in Moscow. General Smith introduced Ehrenburg to the Israeli envoy, "and after some conversation through an interpreter, Mrs. Myerson asked him if he spoke English. Ehrenburg, who speaks excellent French, looked at her for a moment and then replied in Russian: 'I do not speak English, and I have no regard for a Russian-born Jew who *does* speak English.' "[40] As long as Jews outside the Soviet Union preferred not to "speak Russian," they were in the enemy camp.

Lenin's and Stalin's old formula was reinthroned. What in earlier years had been merely "reactionary" or "refined nationalism" was now "scientifically" exposed as "cosmopolitan nationalism" at the service of the enemy.[41] The struggle against "cosmopolitanism" was initiated on a nationwide scale and is being waged on various "sectors" of the "ideological front." A joint session in Moscow in April 1949 of the Scientific Council of the Pacific Institute and the Board of the Moscow Branch of the Oriental Institute, USSR Academy of Sciences, to cite a characteristic example, heard B. V. Lutskii, historian and political scientist, formulate the objectives of the "struggle against manifestations of bourgeois cosmopolitanism in the science of the Orient" as follows: "The pressing task of Soviet Orientalists working in the Near Eastern field is to unmask and demolish the cosmopolitan ideology of 'a single Jewish nation,' which Lenin and Stalin in their time made the subject of annihilating criticism."[42]

End of the Road

Throughout the war appeals "to Jews the world over" had been the stock in trade of the Jewish Antifascist Committee. But the notion of a Jewish nation transcending existing boundaries was now branded as subversive and treasonable. At the end of 1948 the Jewish Antifascist Committee was disbanded and its newspaper, Eynikayt, suppressed;[43] the same action, for reasons that may be conjectured about, was taken against the twenty-year-old Moscow publishing house Emes, and it was dissolved.[44] These things were kept secret, not a word about them appearing in the Moscow press; the USSR Embassy in Washington promised to make inquiries in Moscow,[45] but nothing ever came of it.

Half a year later, the New York Communist Morgn Frayhayt, nettled by the constant queries of the non-Communist press, finally admitted to the suppression of the JAC. N. Buchwald, its press reviewer, wrote: "It stands to reason that the Jewish Antifascist Committee for quite some time already had no place in the new situation. It had been a wartime body with the specific purpose of helping to mobilize the Jews outside the Soviet Union for the common struggle against fascism. Its disbandment, therefore, is not 'persecution,' but merely a part, so to speak, of the process of social 'reconversion.' "[46] Two months later, a more concise explanation was offered by the Communist writer Moshe Katz in *Idishe Kultur*, the monthly periodical of the Communist-controlled All-World Jewish Cultural Association (YKUF): "This Antifascist Committee was dissolved at the end of last year because, as a channel of communication with Jews in the capitalist countries, it no longer had a function."[47] After four more months B. Z. Goldberg, editor of the New York daily, *Der Tog*, and member of the editorial board of *Idishe Kultur*, confirmed both the dissolution of the JAC and the extinction of the Soviet Jewish press:

> While we are at a loss to understand why, except for Birobidzhan, there is no longer a Jewish press in the Soviet Union (and we must express our hope that it will soon be appearing again), it is plain to us why the Antifascist Committee has been dissolved. At a time when the Soviet Union must prepare for war, and when for security's sake it shuts all doors against the outside world, it is not to be thought that a Jewish Committee in Moscow should keep in contact with the entire world.[48]

The details of what actually happened have not been disclosed.[49] The JAC's no longer serving any practical purpose in peacetime was a reason that could not possibly have held for *Eynikayt*; the need for a Yiddish-language newspaper was no less pressing after than during the war. It is also impossible to conceive why the *Emes* publishing house was suppressed; for more than two decades it had been printing official Soviet publications, and had no connection with the JAC. The Soviet government chose to keep silent about these suppressions out of a reluctance to confront foreign Jewish opinion with the implications of its reversal of policy. Ehrenburg's article attacking Israel as a bourgeois state in the clutches of Anglo-American imperialism and denying the existence of a Jewish nation—and even more the fact that it had been published in *Pravda*—had already caused confusion and consternation among Jewish Communists and fellow travelers outside of the USSR, and the Soviet leadership would seem to have preferred to let time pass before confirming Ehrenburg in practice.

For quite some time the impression seems to have obtained even among Jewish Communists outside of the Soviet Union that Ehrenburg's article did not really express the official Soviet attitude. Thus, Moshe Katz, a professional interpreter of Bolshevik theory in the American Jewish Communist press, as late as January 1949 openly argued against what he described as "Ilya Ehrenburg's private views on the national and Jewish questions, views moreover that are incorrect."[50] Quoting abundantly from Lenin and Stalin, Katz argued that although Jews lacked "a number of features characteristic of a fully developed nation," they were nevertheless a separate people, and that national ties uniting Jewish groups in different countries, instead of weakening, had grown stronger in recent decades; "a closer relationship" had developed "between the Jews of the Soviet Union and the Jews of America, between Soviet and American Jews and Israel, between Israel and the Jews of Eastern European and Western Asiatic countries."[51] Ehrenburg's "theorizing on the Jewish problem," he said, "is not clear, is not in the spirit of the Leninist-Stalinist attitude to the national question, and at the present moment can lead to harmful misunderstandings."[52] All this Katz retracted a few weeks later in a penitent letter to the editor of *Morgn Frayhayt*.[53] His retraction, however, did not help to dispel the confusion.

A conviction that the traditional Leninist hostility to Jewish national aspirations had been supplanted by a "pro-Jewish" policy growing out of Stalin's endorsement of national cultures, was too firmly entrenched in Jewish Soviet sympathizers to permit an easy acceptance of Ehrenburg's assault on the "mystic notion" of a "world-wide Jewish nation." The attack created dismay and disbelief even in the strongly pro-Communist leadership of the YKUF. As late as June 1949, nine months after the publication of Ehrenburg's article in *Pravda* and *Eynikayt*, the YKUF periodical *Idishe Kultur*, disregarding the public retraction by Moshe Katz, a member of its editorial board, printed a lengthy historical and doctrinal answer to Ehrenburg by the noted Polish historian, Dr. Raphael Mahler, who, though not a Communist, firmly believed that Soviet policy was pro-Jewish. Mahler, buttressing his article with quotations from Lenin and references to Jewish cultural activities in the Soviet Union, sought to disprove Ehrenburg's denial of the national essence of Jewish solidarity.[54]

Although Mahler erred in his appraisal of Jewish culture in the USSR, his interpretation of the implications of Ehrenburg's position was very much to the point. "If one accepts the view," he wrote, "that the Jews are a distinct people and that Jewish culture is a distinct national culture, then one cannot break the Jewish people up into some hundred separate ethnically Jewish groups. . . . If one denies that Jews in all countries are a people, a global people, then one must go on to the further conclusion that the Jews are not a distinct people anywhere, in any country, and that they lack completely a national culture of their own."[55] This conclusion was indeed difficult to escape. It took Moshe Katz five months to produce a rebuttal, in which an array of quotations from Stalin was brought up in support of Ehrenburg's views.[56] But the doubts in the minds of YKUF's leaders proved so potent that the editors of *Idishe Kultur* ventured to dissociate themselves from the Ehrenburg position in a note appended to Katz's article, saying that "the majority of the editorial board is not in agreement with the contentions and conclusions of Comrade Moshe Katz."[57] And in a leading article in the following issue of the periodical, Ehrenburg's arguments were flatly contradicted by B. Z. Goldberg, member of the presidium of the YKUF.[58] At the national convention of the YKUF, however, held in New York on January 27–30, 1950, Dr. Mahler was publicly rebuked for having communicated to the convention a message of greeting from the Center for Progressive Culture in Israel (Merkaz L'Tarbut HaMitkademet) that warned the YKUF against tendencies characteristic of old Jewish Sections of the Communist Party of the Soviet Union ("rickety Yevsekism"). This was censured as "Red-baiting" and "an attack on world peace," and a special resolution of disapproval was passed over a few dissenting votes.[59] The resolution, however, was "softened" by an amendment introduced by B. Z .Goldberg.[60]

Alarming rumors about the fate of Soviet Jewish writers in one way or another connected with the JAC, *Eynikayt*, or the *Emes* establishment, began to circulate soon after their suppression. On April 1, 1949 a report from Brussels in the *Jewish Daily Forward* said that five prominent Jewish writers, Itsik Fefer, Perets Markish, Der Nister, S. Halkin, and David Bergelson, had been jailed, and that all but Bergelson had been accused of "pro-Zionist sympathies." A few days later a dispatch from Paris, purporting to quote "reliable diplomatic sources," added the name of the Polish Jewish poet M. Broderzon to the list of those arrested. Early in May it was reported in London that Leyb Kvitko and L. Goldberg also were in prison. None of these reports has been confirmed by Soviet authorities, and none has been denied. American Jewish organizations and publications untiringly addressed inquiries to the Communist press about the reasons for the dissolution of the JAC, *Eynikayt*, and *Emes*, the fate of the Jewish writers reported to be jailed, the utter lack of information on Jewish schools and Jewish national life in Birobidzhan, the rumored growth of antisemitism, etc. All this, however, was to no purpose. The Communist newspapers and periodicals only discharged broadsides against the "malicious Soviet-baiters" who asked such questions.

Silence was broken for the first time by N. Buchwald's aforementioned press review in *Morgn Frayhayt*, which finally confirmed the fact of the suppression of the JAC by Soviet authorities. Buchwald, while arguing at great length that Soviet-baiters did not deserve any information, admitted for the benefit of "decent people" that he had no information to impart, that no communications had been received from the Soviet

Union on any of the issues under discussion, and that what was going on inside the Soviet Union could only be conjectured at. A process of "social reconversion" to postwar conditions was under way, he wrote, adding: "We can assume that the process of switching the social forms of Jewish life over onto the postwar track has not yet been completed. . . . And when the final transformation will have taken place, we shall surely learn about it—not through private channels, but openly from Soviet publicity. So far we know only that the haters of the Soviet Union spread idle rumors and odious lies."[61] These vague references to "reconversion" and "transformation" merely augmented the confusion and anxiety.

But once silence had been broken, it was impossible to let matters simply rest. The June issue of *Idishe Kultur* carried an announcement from the editors that said: "In the following issue of *Idishe Kultur* we will print articles on the alleged antisemitism in the Soviet Union, and on the rumors that are being spread about the condition of Jewish culture and Jewish writers in Soviet Russia." And an unsigned editorial, taking to task "new vile slanders" by the [New York] *Daily News*, the *Forward*, and the "Dubinsky machine," concluded: "We understand the motives underlying this vile campaign, and we must combat it and prove the absurdity of such charges against the Soviet Union."[62] But nothing was said nor were any charges disproved either in the following or any other issue of the periodical. *Idishe Kultur* confined itself to printing a single article on the subject in August, in which Moshe Katz once more "unmasked" the interest which American Jewish opinion took in events affecting the life of Jews in Russia as part of the cold war against the Soviet state. He expressed his confidence that in the Soviet Union "nothing can happen which is directed against the Jewish people, its culture and literature, or against its writers on the sole ground that they are Jewish"; but he admitted that he was in no position to say what might have happened to them on other grounds. Katz stated: "We have so far refused to 'confirm' the rumor [about the imprisonment of the Jewish writers] simply because we have not the slightest reason to do so. And we have not found it possible to 'deny' it simply because we do not have the necessary facts. The only thing we can say is: having no first-hand news, we do not know if anything has happened to any of the Jewish writers in the Soviet Union . . . We are cut off from them by circumstances neither of our making nor of theirs."[63]

Thus even the pro-Soviet groups in this country were denied any information by Soviet authorities on the fate of Jewish culture and its outstanding representatives in the Soviet Union. Moreover, Katz disclosed that even the shipment of manuscripts of Soviet Jewish authors to the United States had been discontinued with the disbandment of the Jewish Antifascist Committee and its literary commission. Again the reason was the cold war, and all this was "of course, chiefly the fault of the anti-Soviet slanderers in the ranks of the Jewish Labor Committee, the American Jewish Committee, etc.," to whom for good measure Katz hastened to add Sholem Asch and the American PEN Club.[64] Yet the cold war had in no way interfered either with the transportation of passengers, mail, and freight, or with the cable services and diplomatic communications between the Soviet Union and the United States.

The suppression of the last Jewish newspaper of any importance, the dissolution of the only noteworthy Jewish publishing house in the Soviet Union, and the impenetrable official silence on all matters of Jewish interest, permit of only one interpretation. Sometime in 1948 it was decided to put an end to everything that in any way could stimulate or keep alive the national consciousness of Soviet Jews, so that they might ultimately disappear as a separate national group. Certainly, Jews will continue to live in the Soviet Union, and Jewish religious congregations may even exist, but there will be no "Jewry," no Jewish nation, no Jewish community or culture.

The true meaning of the disappearance of the Jewish people as a national entity has been obscured and distorted by news and rumors concerning a postwar wave of antisemitism. Antisemitism is no new phenomenon in the Soviet Union. It is incompatible with the official Soviet ideology, but the government in the past has had occasion to tolerate antisemitism for its own reasons, and over long periods of time the bureaucratic inclination to ignore or deny it prevailed. Not until the late 1930's, however, was it possible to discern antisemitic traces in public life, and it was not until after the war that antisemitism began to color certain government actions. But such traces of official antisemitism as may now exist in the Soviet Union have no necessary connection with the latest development of the Soviet policy on the Jewish problem, which would have taken the same course regardless.

Underlying and ultimately determining Soviet policy is the denial of the existence of a Jewish nationality. For a period of time this traditional doctrine had chiefly an ideological significance; it did not bar the way entirely to the development of Soviet Jews as a nationality, nor did it necessarily prevent the Jewish minority from enjoying the rights accorded by the Soviet Union to other nationalities. This has now changed. Communist policy on the Jewish problem is again one with Communist dogma. The wheel has come full circle, and for the rulers of the Soviet Union the Jewish people is once more a vestige and an anachronism—only now a much smaller vestige than in the days when Lenin lived, and a much more impotent anachronism.

NOTES

1. See Chap. I above.

2. See Appendix for details and source references.

3. E.g., a dispatch from Kuibyshev, April 28, 1942, said: "A number of Jewish colonists from the Nazi-occupied Ukraine are now settled in the Saratov district on the Volga river, where they have been enabled by the Soviet authorities to establish collective settlements" (*JTA Daily News Bulletin*, April 29, 1942). It is now apparent that "a number" in such dispatches meant "a few."

4. *Eynikayt*, June 16, 1945.

5. *Ibid.*

6. *Ibid.*, May 16, 1946.

7. Cf. his articles in *Eynikayt*, July 14, 17, and 24 and August 16, 21, and 25, 1945.

8. *Eynikayt*, July 14, 1945.

9. *Ibid.*, August 16, 1945.

10. *Ibid.*, July 24, 1945. Cf. Zinger, *Dos Banayte Folk*, p. 90.

11. *Ibid.*

12. JTA dispatch from Moscow, May 6, 1942.

13. JTA dispatch from Kuibyshev, March 21, 1943.

14. JTA dispatch from Tashkent, September 30, 1942.

15. "It is a fact," he wrote, "that no less than 70% of the Jews were rescued from the claws of the Nazis through the Soviet might. In dozens of cities and towns—especially in the Ukraine [sic] and Bessarabia—Jews were the first to be evacuated. . . ." See Solomon Itzhaki, "Jews in Soviet Russia. A Personal Report," in *Congress Weekly*, vol. 9, no. 32 (October 30, 1942), p. 12.

16. *Ibid.*, p. 11.

17. *Ibid.*

18. See pp. 334ff.

19. See Ehrenburg's address to the first "public gathering of representatives of the Jewish people" in Moscow, on August 24, 1941, in *Pravda*, August 25, 1941.

20. *Unzer Tsayt*, July 1943, pp. 26–30.

21. *JTA Daily News Bulletin*, April 7, 1942.

22. Cable from Kuibyshev in *Naylebn*, May 1942, p. 13.

23. Questioned about antifascist committees operating in the USSR, Lozovskii mentioned five: The All-Slav Committee, commitees of Soviet women, of the Soviet youth, and of Soviet science, and the JAC. Of the latter Lozovskii said: "Jews have formed an antifascist committee in order to help the Soviet Union, England, and United States of America put an end to the bloodthirsty rage of Hitler and the other fascist apes who fancy themselves a master race." (*Izvestiya*, April 24, 1942.)

24. Later, at the second plenary session of the JAC in February 1943, its secretary, Shakhno Epshtein, defying the facts, stated that although the Committee did not appeal to Jewish world opinion until April 1942, it actually had been set up following the first "public gathering of representatives of the Jewish people" (August 24, 1941), and that "in fact its activity had begun in February 1942." (*Eynikayt*, March 15, 1943).

25. *Izvestiya*, May 26, 1942, and *Eynikayt*, June 7, 1942.

26. *Eynikayt*, June 7, 1942.

27. *Ibid.*, June 17, 1942.

28. In a report submitted to the third plenary session of the JAC in April 1944, Shakhno Epshtein (*Eynikayt*, April 13, 1944) stated that "close to $2,000,000" had been raised in support of the Soviet Union by Jewish organizations in the United States. In the transcript of the session's proceedings, published as a pamphlet a year later—*Yevreiskii narod v bor'be s fashizmom. Materialy III antifashistskogo mitinga predstavitelei yevreiskogo naroda i III plenuma Yevreiskogo Antifashistskogo Komiteta v SSSR*, Moscow, 1945, p. 88—the same report by Epshtein mentioned "about $3,000,000."

29. *Eynikayt*, February 7, 1943.

30. *Ibid.*, March 15, 1943.

31. Reporting to the plenary session on his trip to America, Itzik Fefer said: "In their conferences with us, the 'Joint' in America, the Association of Jewish Organizations in England, etc., said they wanted to help only the Jewish population of the USSR. We did not deem it possible to single out Soviet Jews in this respect from the fraternity of peoples making tremendous sacrifices along with us in the war." (*Yevreiskii narod . . .* , p. 119.) And Epshtein in his report stated: "The most important event in the matter of help for the evacuated population of the USSR is the successful outcome of the negotiations of Comrades Mikhoels and Fefer with the 'Joint,' the latter having begun to put into effect its decision to help, through the 'Red Cross,' the evacuated population regardless of nationality." (*Ibid.*, p. 88.)

32. S. Kaczerginski, *Tsvishn Hamer un Serp*, pp. 51f.

33. *Ibid.*, p. 56.

34. A complete listing of districts is given in connection with the apportionment of seats for the Supreme Soviet for the elections of 1937, 1945, and 1950 (*Pravda*, October 12, 1937; October 17, 1945; January 12, 1950). All administrative districts are listed twice, as part of the constituencies of the Soviet of the Union (SU), and as part of the constituencies of the Soviet of Nationalities (SN). In 1937 the Jewish national districts were listed as follows: Stalindorf in the 388th SU and 33d SN constituencies; Novo-Zlatopol'ye, 385th SU and 35 SN constituencies; Kalinindorf, 434th SU and 36th SN; Larindorf (Crimea), 338th SU and 390th SN; Fraidorf (Crimea), 338th SU and 394th SN. None was listed either in 1945 or 1950.

35. In Moscow six issues of the literary almanac *Haymland* appeared. None has been published since 1948.

36. Kaczerginski, *op. cit.*, pp. 47ff.

37. From a letter by Kaczerginski, quoted by Jacob Lestschinsky, "Zaynen Ale Felker Take Glaykh in Sovet-Rusland," in *Jewish Daily Forward*, May 2, 1948.

38. *Christian Science Monitor*, January 10, 1950.

39. Ilya Ehrenburg, "Po povodu odnogo pis'ma" ["On the Subject of a Letter"], in *Pravda*, September 21, 1948.

40. Walter Bedell Smith, *My Three Years in Moscow*, Philadelphia and New York, 1950, p. 275.

41. An illustration is the attack launched in February 1949 against a literary glossary compiled for the second edition of the *Great Soviet Encyclopedia*, then in preparation. The authors of the glossary had committed "atrocious mistakes that cannot but arouse profound indignation"—they had taken for granted the existence of an international Jewish literature. The following bill of particulars was drawn up in an article by Ye. Koval'chik, "Bezrodnyye kosmopolity" ["Cosmopolitans without Ancestry"], in *Literaturnaya Gazeta*, February 12, 1949:

"The cosmopolitan, objectivist views of the authors of this glossary were particularly evident in their way of treating Jewish literature, and in the names they included in the corresponding section. The authors have appended the very 'curious' note, saying: 'This glossary encompasses the *whole* of Jewish literature.' Modern Jewish literature in the glossary occupies as much space as the Uzbek, Kazakh, and Georgian literatures together.

"The authors of the glossary mock the principle of party allegiance and Soviet patriotism. Embracing 'the whole of Jewish literature' regardless of differences between countries and government systems, they espouse the puny cosmopolitan, bourgeois-nationalistic idea of an allegedly 'world' Jewish literature, which plays into the hands of the enemies of our Homeland. Their glossary lists Soviet writers side by side with contemporary dyed-in-the-wool businessmen of America, Palestine, and other countries. It is impossible to call this conception anything but servile submission to hostile bourgeois-nationalist theories."

42. *Voprosy Istorii*, historical periodical of the USSR Academy of Sciences, 1949, no. 3, p. 158.

43. The first news of the suppression of the JAC and *Eynikayt* appeared in print in the New York *Jewish Daily Forward* on January 3, 1949, on the authority of the

Voice of America, which in turn relied on "a trustworthy source." The next day the *Forward* received confirmation from "highly responsible diplomatic sources in Washington." Also, on January 4 a similar story was carried by the *JTA Daily News Bulletin.*

44. Reported by the *Forward* and the JTA on January 4, 1949, and confirmed by General Smith in *The New York Times,* November 23, 1949, and by Edmund Stevens in *Christian Science Monitor,* January 10, 1950.

45. The Embassy was questioned about the truth of the report by the JTA; its answer was that "it would make inquiries to Moscow regarding [it]." *JTA Daily News Bulletin,* January 4, 1949.

46. N. Buchwald, "In der Idisher Press. Vekhentlekhe Iberzikht," in *Morgn Frayhayt,* June 2, 1949, p. 2, col. 5.

47. Moshe Katz, "Farvos Shrayen Zey Take?" in *Idishe Kultur,* vol. XI, no. 7 (August 1949), p. 12.

48. B. Z. Goldberg, "Velt-Problemen fun YKUF," *op. cit.,* vol. XI, no. 11 (December 1949), pp. 4f.

49. A Jewish officer of the Soviet Army, just arrived in Vienna, told this story to a correspondent of the New York *Morgn Zhurnal:* On December 4, 1948 a detachment of the political police invaded the premises of the JAC and *Eynikayt* in Moscow. A minute search was conducted, manuscripts and documents were seized, and the premises placed under seal. Itsik Fefer, secretary of the JAC and editor of *Eynikayt,* was arrested; but some days later he was released. (*Morgn Zhurnal,* January 7 and 9, 1949.) The dissolution of the JAC would seem to have been an act of police repression rather than the regular dissolution of an outlived organization.

50. Moshe Katz, "Yisroel un dos Idishe Folk," in *Idishe Kultur,* vol. XI, no. 1 (January 1949), p. 2.

51. *Ibid.,* pp. 4f.

52. *Ibid.,* p. 1.

53. *Morgn Frayhayt,* March 29, 1949. A lengthy comment was appended to the letter by the executive committee of the Morgn Frayhayt Association. The publishers confessed their failure to disseminate Ehrenburg's views and said that in consequence they had made the mistake of not waging an aggressive fight againt Jewish "bourgeois nationalism." The statement added—possibly for the benefit of Moscow—that these grave errors had been committed despite the fact that Alexander Bittelman, at the November 1948 national conference of the Association, had correctly interpreted the conclusions to be drawn from Ehrenburg's article. It should be noted that Mr. Bittelman is not only the executive secretary of the Morgn Frayhayt Association, but also a member of the governing body of the American Communist Party. Cf. also the editorial in *Morgn Frayhayt,* March 31, 1949.

54. Raphael Mahler, "Di Alveltlekhkayt fun Idishen Folk un Mdinas Yisroel," in *Idishe Kultur,* vol. XI, no. 6 (June 1949), pp. 7–15.

55. *Ibid.,* p. 12.

56. Moshe Katz, "Idishe Marksistn un dos Idishe Folk," *op. cit.,* vol. XI, no. 10 (November 1949), pp. 38–45.

57. *Ibid.,* p. 38.

58. B. Z. Goldberg, *op. cit.,* pp. 3ff.

59. *Morgn Frayhayt,* January 31, 1950.

60. *Ibid.,* February 3, 1950.

61. Buchwald, *op. cit.,* p. 48.

62. "Di Naye Viste Farlowmdungen," *Idishe Kultur,* vol. XI, no. 6, p. 2.

63. See n. 47 above.

64. *Ibid.*

APPENDIX

Evacuation and Re-Evacuation of the Jews in the War

The size of the present-day Jewish population of the Soviet Union cannot be exactly determined. The last general census was taken in January 1939, and immediately thereafter—in 1939 and 1940—the Soviet Union annexed new territories having large Jewish populations. In 1941 the Nazi invasion began, and the German armies seized all the lands annexed by the Soviet Union in 1939–40, as well as those Soviet provinces in which the great majority of Soviet Jews were concentrated. With few exceptions, those Jewish inhabitants of the invaded regions who stayed behind when the Red Army retreated were exterminated. In the main, only those survived who fled or were evacuated, or who had been deported, before the German invasion, from the annexed areas to the remote Soviet interior. The number of the deported (which is difficult to establish) hardly affects the calculation of the size of the postwar Jewish population, for the bulk of the Polish, Lithuanian, and Rumanian deportees who survived the privations to which they had been exposed left the Soviet Union—some followed in the wake of the Soviet armies, and most chose to be repatriated after the cessation of hostilities. Only a small group of deportees from Lithuania, Latvia, and Estonia stayed on in the Soviet Union. A few Soviet citizens claiming foreign descent also were repatriated.[1] The number of Jews evacuated by the Soviet authorities can only be roughly estimated; nor is it possible to state definitively how many did in fact escape.

Size of Jewish Population in Occupied Areas

At the time of the German invasion of the Soviet Union the total population of the country, including the newly annexed provinces, was approximately 200 million.[2] The total number of Jews within the pre-annexation boundaries of the USSR was probably somewhat in excess of 3,100,000.[3] The Jewish population of the regions annexed in 1939–40 was roughly as shown in Table XX.

In the enlarged area of the USSR, the Jewish population—exclusive of some 400,000 refugees from German-occupied Western Poland, most of whom were among those deported on the eve of the German invasion—thus totaled about 5,000,000. The total population of the provinces occupied by the Germans was 88 millions:[5] 23 millions in the annexed provinces and 65 millions in the old Soviet areas. The overwhelming majority of Soviet Jews lived in regions that came under the heel of the invader. The German armies took all of the Soviet-annexed territories, all

TABLE XX

JEWISH POPULATION OF SOVIET AREAS
ANNEXED IN 1939-40

AREA	Number of Jews[4]
Eastern Poland	1,309,000
Lithuania	155,000
Latvia	95,000
Estonia	5,000
Northern Bucovina and Bessarabia	330,000
Total (approximately)	1,900,000

of the Ukraine and White Russia, and a number of provinces of the Russian SFSR. The total number of Jews living in the occupied areas before the war can be estimated to have been as shown in Table XXI.

TABLE XXI

JEWISH POPULATION OF AREAS OCCUPIED
BY GERMAN ARMIES

Area	Number of Jews
White Russia and Ukraine	1,908,000[6]
Occupied provinces of the Russian SFSR	over 250,000[7]
Annexed regions	over 1,900,000
Total	4,058,000 to 4,100,000

Of the pre-annexation Jewish population, more than two-thirds resided before the war in areas occupied by the German forces; and of the Jewish population after annexation, no less than four-fifths had their homes in the occupied area.

Evacuation

During the war exaggerated rumors about the evacuation of civilians from Nazi-held areas were circulated inside and outside the Soviet Union. The view prevailed in the American press that the Soviet government, in addition to evacuating the personnel of government services, industrial establishments, etc., had taken effective steps to save the Jewish population in particular from the danger that threatened. Similar notions found their way into serious studies by authors free of pro-Soviet illusions. As late as 1948, Eugene M. Kulischer stated:

In fact, the government took care to prevent a general population displacement, which would have obstructed the highways, and, furthermore, resulted in a mass influx to an area unable to house and feed them. Only a small part of the rural population was evacuated. In urban centers factories were removed, together with skilled and many other workers. Besides, officials and a large proportion of the Jews were evacuated to save them from German atrocities.[8]

Yet the Soviet sources available outside of the Soviet Union did not mention any governmental decrees or directives relative to evacuation, nor were there any statements by Soviet leaders on the nature and scope of the evacuation program. The only exception was a radio broadcast by Stalin on July 3, 1941, in which he proclaimed the strategy of "scorched earth" (without, however, using that term):

> When detachments of the Red Army are forced to retreat, it is essential that all railroad rolling stock be driven off, that not a single locomotive or railroad car be left to the enemy, and that the adversary find not a kilogram of bread or a liter of fuel. The *kolkhoz* farmers must drive away all their cattle and deliver their grain for safekeeping to government authorities, who will transport it to districts behind the lines. All valuable property, including non-ferrous metals, grain, and fuel, that cannot be removed, must be destroyed without exception.[9]

Actually, the term "scorched earth" does not properly describe the meaning of this policy. To judge from descriptions of evacuation in the newspapers and works of fiction, what the Soviet authorities aimed at was not so much wholesale destruction as the removal of anything that the enemy could have used—first of all factories producing goods essential to the war effort, and their indispensable personnel. Men capable of bearing arms were also to be evacuated. In this plan there was no place for the evacuation of Jews as such. In all the Jewish literature on the war there is only the one reference by Moshe Kaganovich to a decree by the Soviet government ordering the evacuation of the Jewish civilian population.[10] But there is no trace of such a decree either in *Izvestiya* or in any other Soviet publication, and it can be assumed that the author was merely repeating one of the many rumors current in the years of the war. None of the Communist writers who so eagerly seized on the émigré Kaganovich's laconic statement could quote from the decree or indicate where and when it was issued;[11] his book remains their only authority.

The true picture of evacuation has to be pieced together from the various accounts of eyewitnesses. Everywhere there seems to have been a great deal of confusion in the evacuation. No uniform procedures had been worked out. In provinces nearest the western border, which were invaded in the early days or weeks of the German-Soviet war, operations were chaotic and on a very limited scale. The farther the province from the border, the more organized the procedure of evacuation and the more people there were saved.

In the Annexed Territories

In the regions annexed by the Soviet Union in 1939 both the local authorities and the population at large were taken unawares by the German attack. Parts of the Jewish population, especially refugees from Western Poland, had been deported to the Soviet interior before the outbreak of hostilities. Planned evacuation, in any degree, was impossible. Small groups fled eastwards to escape the Nazis, but mostly to no avail; fugitives traveling on foot or in carts were overtaken by motorized detachments of the advancing German army and were forced to turn back. Dr. Dworzecki, a Jewish physician who witnessed the German invasion and later, after having lived through most of the dramatic history of the Vilna ghetto, joined the partisan movement, has told of the tribulations of fugitives in the Vilna region. Bombed by German planes in the very first days of the war, the city of Vilna was immediately abandoned by the Soviet forces. The retreating army was followed by thousands of Vilna's residents, mostly Jews:

> Tens of thousands left Vilna at that time. Only isolated individuals succeeded in reaching the Soviet Union. All vehicles had been seized by the armed forces, which were being evacuated at full speed. Of the civilian population only a few who carried membership cards in the Communist Party were permitted on the railroad trains. Thousands walked on foot along highways and bypaths. German tanks overtook them. Some of those attempting to escape were killed on the roads, and corpses remained unburied in the woods and on the fields. All others returned to Vilna, worn out, starved, exhausted, desperate. . . .[12]

The Soviet government not only did not help to evacuate the Jews, or the civilian population in general, it actually stood in their way. Another eyewitness, who also lived through the period of agony of Vilna's Jews and, having escaped to the woods, played a leading role in the reconstruction of Jewish community life in the first year of liberation, said in his chronicle: "Several tens of thousands of Jews try to leave for the interior of the country. Part of them are turned back by [Soviet] frontier guards. They are returning to Vilna."[13] On the third day of the war Vilna was taken by the Nazis. The Jewish population was almost completely exterminated. In other border regions things were scarcely different. A Jewish journalist and educator from Kaunas (Kovno) wrote:

> Because of the hasty evacuation of the military and the government agencies, there was a marked shortage of transportation for the civilian

population. This was one of the reasons why only small groups of Lithuanian Jews were able to be evacuated in time.

It must also be noted that Soviet frontier guards did not permit refugees from the Baltic countries and from regions annexed by the Soviet Union after the beginning of the Second World War to cross over into the territory of Russia proper. Many refugees had therefore to return to the places they had come from, although these had already been occupied by the Germans.[14]

A Jewish agronomist, also from Kaunas, having obtained a car, drove to the frontier of Latvia and Soviet White Russia, which he reached northeast of Dvinsk. He, too, discovered that the Soviet guards barred the way over the frontier:

> This is where the calamity, the great calamity starts. We are not permitted to go farther. There are already hundreds of refugees from Lithuania and Latvia near the border, and their number increases from one day to the next. But regardless of how much they implore the Soviet guards, this is the one answer they get: "No one is to cross—those are orders. Move back twenty steps, if you don't we'll shoot. Get moving —one, two, fire!"
>
> For twelve long terrible days and nights we have stayed near the border. Meanwhile thousands of refugees have crowded together here. Droves of people, mostly Jews, but here and there non-Jews too, lie around in near-by ditches, woods, and fields and beg for permission to continue their trek so that they may save their lives. They are not allowed to pass. Only Communists, party members with the proper documents, may cross. We others are not kosher, we have no right to be saved, although we have been Soviet citizens for over a year. . . .
>
> Not until the Germans had reached a point some six to eight miles from the Latvian-Russian [White-Russian] border did the frontier guards suddenly disappear, and not until then did we have a chance to proceed. But how far can one flee when the dreadful enemy is so close.[15]

Neither the narrator nor his companions in distress succeeded in getting very far. Most were overtaken by the Nazis.

In the Polish provinces the Jewish population was struck with particular severity. In Lvov, the retreating Russian army "did not even have a chance fully to evacuate, along with the combat forces, the new Russian population that had recently immigrated."[16] Of the Jewish population, about 10,000 had been deported previously to the Soviet Union;[17] several thousand Jewish youths had been drafted into the Red Army; and a small number had somehow managed to flee east before the entry of the German troops. The rest remained in the captured city. By June 21, 1941 the number of Jewish inhabitants, which had been around 90,000 in 1939, had increased, owing to the influx of Jews from the smaller towns, to some 160,000, and on August 28, 1941, according to the German-appointed *Judenrat,* Lvov still had approximately 150,000 Jews, all of whom fell into the hands of the executioners.[18] There manifestly had been no evacuation at all.

Somewhat more detailed data are at hand for the city of Bialystok. Here the course of the evacuation resembled events in Vilna and Kaunas rather than in Lvov;[19] the catastrophe was not a complete one, yet the outcome was appalling. According to Dr. Datner, who after the war was chairman of the Jewish Committee of the province of Bialystok, in the middle of 1946 there were only 900 survivors of a Jewish population of 50,000.[20]

In Eastern Poland as a whole, of the Jewish population of 1941 (excluding those who had been deported to the Soviet Union), only a fraction survived. Only a few had fled or had been evacuated to the Soviet Union. Most of the survivors had either escaped to the woods and joined the partisans, or had been taken as slave laborers to Germany, a number of them living to see the day of liberation.

In the Rumanian provinces of Bessarabia and Northern Bucovina, deportations of Jews to the Soviet Union commenced on the very eve of the German attack on Russia and were continued, thanks to bureaucratic inertia, after the war had started. This was the origin of the rumor, circulated abroad, that said a planned and systematic evacuation of Jews was taking place. An eyewitness of the German occupation, Tanya Fuks, a Jewish educator from Poland, has related the following about the invasion of Cernauti (Czernowitz):

> In the confusion and disorder of the first days of the war, the "undesirable elements" were still being deported. Soviet officials, prominent Communists who wished and had to be evacuated, protested: "What are you carrying off these rich people for? You had better give us transportation so we can escape." And in fact many of them did not manage to get out of the German-Rumanian encirclement in time.[21]

While the deportation of the "undesirables" went on, there was, of course, no evacuation of the bulk of the endangered population.

In Soviet White Russia

A few days after the commencement of operations the German armies reached the old Soviet border and crossed into pre-1939 Soviet territory All of White Russia was shortly overrun. Evacuation in White Russia proceeded in the same haphazard fashion that had been the case shortly before in Eastern Poland. The fate of Minsk, capital of White Russia, is characteristic. Nothing was done to evacuate civilians not possessing special priorities. The removal of military installations and government agencies again was conducted with frantic haste; the mass of the people was abandoned to its fate.[22] The events can be retraced in Ehrenburg's novel

Storm,[23] and in a number of memoirs. When, soon after the capture of the city by the Germans, the Jews were confined to a ghetto, there were behind its walls some 75,000 to 80,000 people,[24] as against the 90,000 Jews of prewar Minsk.[25] When account is taken of the Jews who had been drafted (though there had been no time to complete the mobilization), the maximum number of Minsk's Jews who either escaped by their own efforts or were evacuated with their government agencies must have been between 12,000 and 15,000.

How small a part of the Jewish population was able to escape from the other important cities, may be judged by the tiny number of Jewish survivors who returned to Gomel, Vitebsk, Bobruisk, and Mogilev in 1946, a considerable number of them being discharged servicemen.[26] For purposes of comparison, in the absence of official data for 1939–1941, the figures of the census of 1926 must be adjusted for probable population increases.[27] While the increase of the Jewish population did not keep pace with the high rate of increase of the total population, there is no doubt that the number of Jews in the major urban centers had increased considerably.[28] In 1926 a total of 167,000 Jews lived in the capital and the abovementioned four cities. These five cities thus accounted for 41 percent of White Russia's Jews, and it may be assumed that by 1939 this proportion had risen to three-fifths or even two-thirds. This would make for a total of 225,000 to 250,000; without Minsk, some 135,000 to 160,000. Estimates for 1939 based on this assumption, together with purely theoretical population projections computed according to the rate of increase of the total population, are compared in Table XXII with the known figures for 1926 and 1946:

TABLE XXII

JEWISH POPULATION OF WHITE RUSSIA'S
MAJOR CITIES, IN THOUSANDS [29]

City	1926	1939		1946
		Projection (Assuming general rate of increase)	Estimated Actual Size	
Gomel	37.7	63.0	48 to 53	3.0
Vitebsk	37.0	62.7	45 to 52	.5
Bobruisk	21.6	35.4	22 to 28	6.5
Mogilev	17.1	33.9	20 to 27	8.0
Total	113.4	195.0	135 to 160	18.0

Needless to say, the proportion of survivors, as got from the figures of the table, is highly approximate. It is not known how many evacuees failed to return and how many servicemen had not yet been discharged in 1946. While these surviving former residents of the four cities should be added to the number of residents for 1946, a certain number of new residents—Jews from near-by villages and smaller towns who for various reasons chose to settle in the larger cities after the war—should be deducted. Assuming that these corrections would on the whole cancel each other out, the proportion of Jewish survivors can be estimated as follows: Gomel, 5 to 6 percent; Vitebsk, 1 percent; Bobruisk, 25 to 30 percent; Mogilev, perhaps 30 to 35 percent.

In smaller places the proportion of survivors was apparently equally varied. In Mosyr', which had 5,901 Jewish residents in 1926 and probably less in 1939, there were some 500 Jews left in the winter of 1945–46; Shklov, with 3,179 Jews in 1926, had about 1,000 Jews alive in 1945–46 [30] —the percentage of survivors was thus about 10 in the former, and 25 to 35 in the latter village. There were rare exceptions where the greater part of the Jewish population of this or that small town was lucky enough to escape. Such was the case in Chechersk, in the district of Gomel, where 400 Jewish families lived before the war: "Because the Red Army delayed the Germans near Propoisk, the Jewish population of Chechersk was able to get away; only about 150 Jews—old people, women, and children— remained behind in the town." All those left behind (apparently less than 10 percent) perished, but it has not been disclosed how many of those who escaped did actually survive; in August 1946, three years after the liberation, the town again had over 100 Jewish families (of a presumably smaller average size) composed of ex-evacuees and discharged servicemen.[31]

No statistics have ever been published on the total number of Jews who survived. The People's Commissar for Foreign Affairs of the White-Russian SSR, Koz'ma Kiselev, has been quoted as stating: "Almost the entire Jewish population of White Russia was exterminated; of 800,000 people exterminated by the Nazis in White Russia, more than one-half were Jews."[32] He also said that "in Minsk 80 percent of the entire Jewish population was annihilated during the German occupation, in Gomel 90 percent were murdered, while in Orsha practically all the Jews were killed."[33] Interviewing the People's Commissar, the correspondent of *Morgn Frayhayt* asked him pointblank how many White-Russian Jews had survived. "Perhaps a hundred thousand, Kiselev replied in a low voice, we don't know." The correspondent of the Communist paper concluded: "A hundred thousand—this then is the maximum number of survivors of a Jewish population of half a million living in White Russia for dozens of generations; the German beast annihilated 80 percent of White-Russian Jews."[34]

The People's Commissar's estimate embraced not only the Jewish inhabitants of old Soviet White Russia, but also those of the former Polish provinces of Western White Russia; moreover, the total of survivors also included those who had fought in the ranks of the Red Army and of the partisan movement. It can be safely inferred that of the 375,000 Jews who lived in Soviet White Russia before 1939, some 75,000, perhaps less, escaped extermination, or no more than 20 percent.

In the Ukraine

Many of the larger Ukrainian cities were not occupied until several weeks after the beginning of the invasion, and some not until months later. Thus there was ample time to prepare for evacuation and to carry it out in an orderly manner; it should also have been possible to take special measures to rescue the imperiled Jewish population. And yet there are fewer press reports of evacuation in the Ukraine than in White Russia. Not a single news item mentioned any special evacuation of Jews, although the evacuation of government agencies and industrial establishments was more thorough, a large part of their personnel, often accompanied by their families, being removed.

A large number of Jews were employed in the government as professional and semiprofessional workers in the administration and in economic affairs, or were manual workers in heavy industry. As a result, the percentage of the evacuated who were Jews seems to have been more than proportionate to the number of Jews in the Ukraine's urban, let alone total, population. Another contributing factor was the non-compulsory character of the evacuation in many instances; employees of essential plants and government offices were permitted, but not ordered, to leave. While many non-Jews preferred to stay behind, quite a number of Jews availed themselves of the opportunity and left.

Of the many Soviet novels and short stories describing wartime experiences, there are some that deal with evacuation, a few in great detail. But there is no reference anywhere to a special evacuation of Jews. Ehrenburg's *Storm*, which explicitly describes the experiences of Jews in Kiev on the eve of and in the first stages of the war and luridly portrays the Babii-Yar holocaust, has nothing to say about evacuation. Valentin Katayev's ambitious novel, *For the Power of the Soviets*,[35] unfolds a detailed panorama of life in wartime Odessa. The narrative begins a week before the outbreak of hostilities and continues through all the phases of the war until the city's liberation, but only a few lines deal with evacuation in general; nor is anything said about evacuation of Jews in particular, or about Jewish attempts to escape from the city, which it took the enemy some time to encircle.

Industrial evacuation from the Donets Basin in the fall of 1941, on the other hand, is described in Fadeyev's *Young Guard*,[36] Perventsev's *Test*,[37] and Galin's *In the Donets Basin*.[38] Many interesting details on the evacuation of the Stalin Metal Works in Stalino are given by Galin, who served as correspondent for the Donets region in the early months of the war and returned to its pits, blast furnaces, and steel works in the train of the Red Army in the summer of 1943. The plant he describes was one of the largest, employing 10,000 workers and more before the war; but only "one and a half thousand workers, with their families, left for the Urals" when the plant was removed.[39] Neither Perventsev nor Galin mentions the evacuation of any civilians other than those employed in the Metal Works. In this respect Fedeyev's novel was more informative. The evacuation of government offices, industrial plants, and collective and state farms, and the mass flight of the people, were depicted on almost an epic scale.[40] But the novel did not so much as hint at the escape or evacuation of Jews.

In contrast to the silence of Soviet newspapers, periodicals, and books, statements to the effect that the Soviet authorities had been at pains to help the Jewish population leave the Ukraine before the arrival of the Germans, were frequently made outside of the Soviet Union; occasionally these were echoed by serious and otherwise reliable informants. In 1946, for example, the bulletin of the Hebrew Sheltering and Immigrant Aid Society (HIAS) carried an article that said: "There is no doubt that the Soviet authorities took special care to evacuate the Jewish population or facilitate its spontaneous flight. Apart from officials, industrial workers and employees, all Jews were privileged. . . . The Soviet authorities provided thousands of trains, especially for the evacuation of the Jews, realizing that they were the most endangered part of the population."[41] Such reports were given ready credence, although no facts had been adduced in corroboration, and although the Soviet press, including its Yiddish section, consistently avoided the subject. Only outside of the Soviet Union was an attempt made to furnish a semblance of evidence. Thus, B. Z. Goldberg, back from a trip to the Soviet Union in 1947, in an article bearing the promising title, "How Jews Were Evacuated in Soviet Russia During the War," wrote:

> It is essential to know what was the policy of the government and how it was carried out in most cases, or in the most typical cases. This is what I inquired about in my talks with various people, Jews and non-Jews, army people and evacuees. They all replied that the policy was to grant the Jews priority, to get them out as soon as possible, so that the Nazis would not kill them. And a number of Jews confirmed . . . [the fact that] Jews had been urged and warned [to leave], and that they had been the first to be removed. During the evacuation there was an understanding that Jews were to be removed soon after

the women and children. A number of Jewish evacuees who left the Soviet Union have conceded as much.[42]

Mr. Goldberg, however, quoted only one such corroborating report by a Rabbi Shekhtman from Kiev:

Long lines of cars, coupled to engines, were waiting near the station, and in the street militia men were distributing "passes," or tickets entitling one to transportation: "Take these and leave the city by train!" But the crowd made no haste to leave. People did not believe that the enemy would ever take Kiev. Jews were told: "You are Jewish, you will be among the first victims, you had better leave." Twice people came to Rabbi Shekhtman's place to tell him: "Leave the town, *batyushka* [little father], you are a Jew, you will be the first to be killed—here is the ticket, just leave!" He did in fact leave, accompanied by those of his family who were not engaged in war work.[43]

The story is full of absurdities—officers distributing tickets in the street, people addressing a rabbi as if he were a Greek Orthodox priest (not even members of the Catholic or Protestant clergy are called *batyushka*), etc.[44] This was the only instance in which an attempt was made to illustrate the alleged Soviet solicitude for the Jews by a concrete and specific case.

The only way for determining the number of those who escaped or were evacuated from the Ukraine is by examining the scattered and inexact data on the number of Jews who returned to individual Ukrainian cities after their recapture by the Soviet Army.[45] In many instances such information has been supplied by the Soviet Yiddish-language press, but the data are not such as to inspire great confidence. Too often exaggeration, prompted by the transparent desire to conceal the true scope of extermination, is obvious.

Postwar efforts to make the public believe that a large part of the Jewish population had been rescued go back to 1945. Seeking to refute the pessimistic view expressed in the New York *Forward*, Itsik Fefer, in a message to the American Committee of Jewish Writers, Artists and Scientists in October 1945, stated that Odessa again had a Jewish population of 45,000; Kiev, 50,000; Berdichev, 10,000, etc.[46] But a few months earlier *Eynikayt* had recorded only "about 10,000" Jews in Kiev,[47] and half a year later it found only 6,000 Jews in Berdichev.[48] All subsequent reports were marred by similar contradictions and exaggerations. When B. Z. Goldberg, ten months after Fefer's message, cabled that the number of Jews in Kiev (175,000 before the war) was again "about 100,000" in August 1946;[49] when a report in *Eynikayt* in April 1946 referred to 80,000 Jews in Odessa [50] (180,000 before the war) and seven weeks later Goldberg spoke of "almost 100,000" (and raised the prewar size of the Jewish population to 260,000);[51] or when Dnepropetrovsk (100,000 Jews before the war) was said to have 50,000 Jews in June 1946;[52] then it is hardly possible to credit any of these contradictory and confused "statistics." These high figures were the less credible in that more than a few surviving evacuees and refugees, as will be shown below, did not return to their native places.

The large cities no doubt attracted survivors who before the war had resided in the smaller towns or villages; yet Soviet sources likewise attributed an improbably high number of Jewish residents to the smaller urban communities. Thus, the city of Vinnitsa, with 21,816 Jews in 1926 and scarcely more than 25,000 or 28,000 in 1939, was occupied by the Germans at the very beginning of the war, when the chances of escaping were virtually nonexistent; but as early as September 1945 the Jewish population was said to have again reached 14,000;[53] and in May 1946, 18,000.[54] Zhitomir, with about 30,000 Jews before the war, was credited with 10,000 to 12,000 Jews in August 1945,[55] and with 16,000 in August 1946.[56] More plausible figures were given for Berdichev, which in 1926 had 30,812 Jews, in 1939 perhaps 35,000, and in March 1946 some 6,000;[57] here, too, Mr. Goldberg, in August 1946, gave a figure twice as large— 10,000 to 13,000.[58] The statistics for Mogilev-Podolsk—15,000 before the war and 3,000 in April 1946[59]—and for Belaya-Tserkov'—15,624 in 1926, scarcely more in 1939, and 1,000 in May 1945[60]—also are plausible.

To estimate the total number of survivors in the Ukraine on the basis of such figures as these is no easy matter. In the smaller cities and townships, and especially in the rural communities, the proportion of Jews overtaken and killed by the Germans was very high; in the Ukraine west of the Dneiper it was probably no lower than in White Russia. In the larger cities the chances of escape were better; since a major part of the Jewish population was concentrated in larger communities, the total number of Jews who were able to flee or be evacuated was not so low as it was in White Russia. It would seem safe to assume that about one-third of the Jewish population of the Ukraine, but scarcely more, escaped. The Jewish population of the Ukrainian SSR numbered 1,533,000 in January 1939, and after allowing for those drafted into the Red Army, about 1,400,000; it must then be assumed that no less than 900,000, and perhaps more, perished in the Ukraine.

In the Russian SFSR

A wide strip of the Russian SFSR, chiefly along the frontiers of White Russia and the Ukraine, was also occupied by the Germans; but those determined to leave had had more time to make their arrangements and find transportation. However, there is hardly any mention of evacuation and flight from these provinces either in works of fiction or in memoirs. Tat'yana Lagunova's memoirs, *In the Forests of Smolensk*,[61] only told how cattle were driven to the east. Ignatov's *Notes of a Partisan*,[62] which described life in Krasnodar (Northern Caucasus) in the months before the capture of the city, omitted all mention of evacuation and said only a few words about the flight of the local population. Kalinin's *Comrades* [63] dwelt at length on the retreat of the Red Army in 1942 from Taganrog, Rostov and the province of the Don, without referring to the evacuation of civilians; the escape of the local people, which took place on a large scale, was chronicled along the same lines, though with less artistry, as the exodus from the Donets Basin in Fadeyev's *Young Guard*. This writer has found only one literary work making any extensive reference to evacuation from RSFSR provinces, *The Heroic Deed of Sebastopol*,[64] by Borisov, who repeatedly touches upon the organized evacuation of civilians, mainly women and children; this was motivated by the need to clear the fortified city of non-combatants.[65] There was no reference either to the evacuation or to the escape of Jews.

This, of course, does not mean that there was no evacuation. It was in fact carried out on a larger scale and with greater efficiency than in the Ukraine or White Russia, and this increased the number of Jews who were rescued. From frequent references in the Jewish press it may be inferred, for example, that the removal of Jewish agricultural colonies, as part of the general evacuation of the Crimean collective and state farms,[66] was on a much larger scale than anywhere in the Ukraine. Also, more Jews escaped from these regions by their own efforts. This was especially the case in Rostov, which was captured twice, early in November 1941 and again in the summer of 1942. The first occupation took Rostov's Jews by surprise, and the bloody lesson of the few days under the Nazi heel was sufficient to cause a mass exodus when the second capture threatened. Apparently, about half the Jewish population fled or was removed in 1942; of the 40,000 Jewish inhabitants of prewar Rostov, 18,000 were exterminated on the spot.[67] It is not possible to ascertain whether all those who left the city reached safety, or whether part of them were overtaken and annihilated elsewhere, as was the lot of some of the evacuees from the Crimean farm colonies,[68] or of 6,000 Jewish intellectuals from Leningrad killed near Mineral'nyye-Vody (Northern Caucausus).[69] No information has been released on evacuation or escape from other provinces in the Russian SFSR, such as Smolensk, Bryansk, Kursk, Voronezh, etc.

The scarcity of information requires particular caution in the summing-up of the results. Of an estimated 250,000 to 275,000 Jews in the Nazi-occupied provinces of the RSFSR,[70] more than one-half may be assumed to have escaped the invaders. Thus the number of Jews that perished was at least about 100,000, which very likely is too low an estimate.

Summing Up

In the Ukraine, no less than 900,000 Jews perished; in White Russia, no less than 300,000; in the occupied parts of Russia proper, no less than 100,000. The total number of the Jewish dead, excluding those of the annexed areas, would thus approximate 1,300,000 of a total of 3,100,000, and may very likely have been considerably higher. The birthrate declined during the war and could hardly be expected to have exceeded the rate of mortality, which the war casualties and the greater incidence of disease and malnutrition among evacuees and refugees caused to rise. In consequence, the number of Jewish survivors from pre-annexation Soviet territory cannot have been more than 1,800,000 at the end of the war.

The additional Jewish population which the Soviet Union acquired through annexation in 1939 and 1940 was almost totally exterminated. The majority of those who survived, among whom former deportees from Eastern Poland were particularly numerous, preferred not to stay in the Soviet Union, and were repatriated to Poland or Rumania in 1944–1946. There is no indication that the number of Jewish natives or ex-residents of the annexed areas on the Eastern border who chose to become Soviet citizens during or after the war exceeded, or even approached, 50,000.

Careful analysis of all available evidence leads one to the conclusion that at the close of the war the Jewish population of the Soviet Union, including non-repatriated survivors from the annexed areas, could not have much exceeded a total of 1,850,000.

Aftermath

The Jewish evacuees and refugees began their trek back home even before the end of the war; once the war had ended, the tide swelled. This has been confirmed by a multitude of reports; it has also been emphasized by a delegate of the British Soviet Society, Sarah Wesker, who visited the Soviet Union in 1946:

> They want to go back to their old centers—in the Ukraine, White Russia, etc., where they lived before the war.
> Is this not natural? Maybe some relations are still alive, maybe some of their property is still intact.
> And many say: "If we have to build again from the very bottom, then why not where we have lived all our lives?"
> This was the dominant note struck by many Jews with whom I conversed (in good homely Yiddish) in the USSR.[71]

Similar statements were so frequent in the Soviet Yiddish-language press that it came to be generally accepted that all refugees and evacuees, with a few exceptions, returned to their prewar localities. Yet, though the great majority did return, many did not. This shows a new trend in the geographical dispersal of the Jewish population which must not be overlooked.

Before the termination of hostilities and for several months thereafter, return to the liberated regions was, as a rule, permitted only upon a special call from the local authorities.[72] Rigid enforcement of this rule was, of course, impossible. From numerous stories in Soviet newspapers, it would appear that the "unauthorized" reflux of evacuees—not only Jews, but principally non-Jews in fact—was considerable.[73] Generally return without special permission was not authorized until August 1945; from then on, organized re-evacuation was carried through by special trains. Its start was reported late in August from Kazakhstan and Uzbekistan. A correspondent from Tashkent wrote:

These last days the mass re-evacuation of Uzbekistan's Jewish population has begun. In addition to those hundreds and thousands who move westward with the regular railroad traffic, special trains for the re-evacuated are now being dispatched from time to time.[74]

This Tashkent correspondent witnessed the departure of a special train that took 2,500 Jews from Tashkent to the Ukraine and White Russia; several more special trains were scheduled for the following weeks. Similar reports abounded. Public interest was focused on re-evacuation, and for a while the fact went unnoticed that a large part of the evacuees and refugees remained behind. Attention was drawn to this in July 1945 by the Kazakhstan correspondent of *Eynikayt*, who pointed out that while the majority had left or were about to leave, "part of the Jews undoubtedly will remain as permanent residents in Kazakhstan," where they had "found their second home."[75] In November a report from the Urals said that "quite a number of Jews are going to stay here forever."[76] Similar news came in December from the Turkmen Republic:

Evacuation brought a substantial Jewish population here that has settled in all parts of the Republic. . . . Jews from the Ukraine, Bessarabia, and the Crimea have been working here. A large part of them have already gone home, but many have remained for good. Jews are now a considerable percentage in Turkmen industry, on collective farms, in the government services of the Republic and of the individual provinces. You will find them in the workshops of the industrial combines, at the oil wells, in the People's Commissariats of the Republic, in government and party offices.[77]

In 1946 such reports became more frequent. So far as one can judge, the Moscow correspondent of *Morgn Frayhayt* was fully justified in writing:

The great and overwhelming majority of Jews evacuated to Central Asia, Siberia, and the Urals have returned to the cities and towns of the Ukraine, White Russia, Moldavia, Lithuania, and Latvia. But many thousands of Jews have grown such deep roots in their new homes that they never even think of leaving. Here they have become true residents, passionately attached to their new homes.[78]

The correspondent listed a number of the new centers of Jewish population, such as Alma-Ata, Dzhambul, Chkalov (formerly Orenburg), Sverdlovsk (formerly Yekaterinburg), Chelyabinsk, Molotov (formerly Perm), Krasnoyarsk, Tomsk, Irkutsk, etc. The total number of Jews who settled in these remote regions cannot be determined. There are perhaps a hundred thousand of them, or even more.[79]

NOTES

1. The Polish-Soviet agreement on population exchanges provided for the repatriation of Jews from provinces included in postwar Poland, as well as of those who had been residents of provinces which the Soviet Union retained after the war, i.e., Polish White Russia, the Polish Ukraine, and Polish Lithuania. A number of Bessarabian Jews were likewise allowed to go to Rumania. The repatriates were permitted to take their families with them even when these included native Soviet citizens. In addition, a number of Soviet citizens of Polish, Rumanian, or Lithuanian descent obtained—either legally or illegally—recognition as aliens entitled to repatriation.

2. The USSR's population in 1939 was 170,500,000; it may be assumed that by mid-1941 it had increased by 6 to 7 million, perhaps more. The regions annexed in 1939-40 had a population of about 23,000,000. See the Bol'shaya Sovetskaya Entsiklopediya's supplementary volume: Soyuz Sovetskikh Sotsialisticheskikh Respublik, Moscow, 1946, p. 49.

3. The census of 1939 showed 3,020,171 Jews (Zinger, Dos Banayte Folk, p. 126.) From January 1939 to June 1941 the natural increase can be estimated to have been at least 100,000 These figures refer only to persons who told the censustakers they were Jews, and do not include an unknown number of persons of Jewish parentage who considered themselves Russians, Ukrainians, White Russians, etc., which has been estimated at 250,000 to 300,000. (See Jacob Lestschinsky, "Idn in Sovet-Farband: 1946," in Idisher Kemfer, September 27, 1946, p. 95.

4. Statistics on the Jewish population of those parts of Poland which the Soviet Union occupied in 1939, and annexed later, vary according to the source. According to a German study, of the 3,155,000 Jews listed by the Polish population census in 1931, 1,901,000 lived in the provinces occupied by Germany in 1939, and 1,254,000 lived in the provinces occupied by the Soviet Union. (See Peter Heinz Seraphim, "Die Judenfrage in General-gouvernment als Bevölkerungsproblem," in Die Burg, Krakau, October 1940, p. 60.) Thus, 39 percent of Poland's Jews were in the Soviet zone. By September 1939 the total number of Jews had risen to 3,340,000 (Dr. Filip Friedman, Zaglada Zydów Polskich w okresie okupacji niemeckiej 1939-1945, Federation of Polish Jews, Munich, 1947, p. 5), so that the Soviet share should have been about 1,303,000. Lestschinsky (op. cit.) estimated the number of Jews in Soviet Poland at 1,300,000. The Institute of Jewish Affairs ("Jews under Soviet Rule" in Jewish Affairs, August 1941, p. 2) arrived at the somewhat higher figure of 1,270,000 without Vilna, this city being transferred to Lithuania soon after the Soviet occupation of Eastern Poland; at the time the district of Vilna had an estimated Jewish population of over 80,000. The figure of 1,309,000 given here is from an official Polish source (Concise Statistical Year-Book of Poland, Polish Ministry of Information [London], December 1941, p. 10).

Data for Lithuania (without Vilna), Latvia, and Estonia are from *The American Jewish Year Book, 1947–48*, p. 740; for Northern Bucovina and Bessarabia, from the issue of *Jewish Affairs* referred to above.

5. As stated by the Extraordinary State Committee for the Ascertaining and Investigation of Crimes Committed by the German-Fascist Invaders, in *Pravda*, September 13, 1945.

6. The figure for the Ukraine and White Russia is that of January 1939, on the assumption that migration eastwards, which had reduced it from 1,981,000 to 1,908,000 between 1926 and 1939 (Zinger, *Dos Banayte Folk*, p. 36), continued, though at a slower pace. From the late 1920's to the mid-1930's migration from the Ukraine and White Russia exceeded the natural increase of the Jewish population. Later, however, especially in the Ukraine, expanding industry began to absorb a greater number of Jews, and migration fell off perhaps to a point below the rate of natural increase. The Jewish population of White Russia and the Ukraine might have been somewhat larger in mid-1941 than in January 1939, but it was certainly not smaller.

7. Statistics on the Jewish population of the occupied provinces of the Russian SFSR are not available for 1939, for census figures for the individual republics have not been broken down by provinces. In 1926, the number of Jews in the provinces of Pskov, Novgorod, Smolensk, Bryansk, Orel, Kursk, Voronezh, and the Don, and in the Crimean Autonomous SSR, totaled 184,000. Between 1926 and 1939 the total Jewish population of the Russian SFSR increased by almost two-thirds, from 566,900 to 948,000 (*op. cit.*, p. 126); it can therefore be assumed that on the eve of the invasion the number of Jews in these provinces was at the very least 250,000. Moreover, other provinces, with relatively few Jews, were invaded in part. The actual Jewish population in the occupied parts of the Russian SFSR thus probably was in excess of 250,000, perhaps 275,000 or more.

8. Eugene M. Kulischer, *Europe on the Move: War and Population Changes 1917–47*, New York, 1948, p. 260.

9. J. V. Stalin, *O velikoi otechestvennoi voine Sovetskogo Soyuza* [*Remarks on the Soviet Union's Great War for the Fatherland*], Moscow, 1946, p. 14.

10. See p. 325.

11. E.g., Moses Miller in *Soviet Antisemitism—the Big Lie*, New York, n.d. [1949], p. 21.

12. Mark Dworzecki, *Yerusholayim d'Lite in Kamf un Umkum*, Paris, 1948, pp. 23f.

13. S. Kaczerginski, *Tsvishn Hamer un Serp*, Paris, 1949, p. 27.

14. Josef Gar, *Umkum fun der Idisher Kovne*, Federation of Lithuanian Jews in the American Zone of Germany, Munich, 1948, pp. 31ff.

15. Yankev Rasen, *Mir Viln Lebn*, New York, 1949, pp. 22f.

16. Stefan Szende, *Der letzte Jude aus Polen*, Zurich–New York, 1945, p. 136 (British edition: *The Promise Hitler Kept*, London, 1945, p. 124).

17. Friedman, *op. cit.*, p. 7.

18. *Ibid.*

19. Yisroel Kot, *Khurbn Byalostok*, Buenos Aires, 1947, pp. 11–17; Rfoel Rayzner, *Der Umkum fun Byalostoker Idntum*, Bialostoker Centre in Australia, Melbourne, 1948, pp. 34–36; Dr. Szymon Datner, "Der Khurbn fun der Idisher Byalostok un di Arumige Yishuvim," in *Byalostocker Shtime* (Byalostocker Landsmanshaft in America, New York), September–October 1946, p. 20.

20. Datner, *op. cit.*, pp. 18f.

21. *A Vanderung iber Okupirte Gebitn*, Buenos Aires, 1947, p. 112.

22. The order had been given to evacuate the Minsk prison. Political prisoners were shot on the spot, but the criminals were marched out of town, under a strong escort of armed guards. The marching crowd, however, was soon stopped by German planes. The guards ran off in all directions, and so did some of the criminals, while others decided to go back to Minsk. The story has been told by Herschel Vaynraukh, an inmate of the Minsk prison who was able to join the non-political prisoners when they were marched out of jail, in *Blut oyf der Zun*, New York, 1950, pp. 100ff. The killing of the Jewish poet Zelik Akselrod, a political prisoner in the

Minsk jail, has been confirmed by F. Grim (Moyshe Grosman) in his *In Farkishuftn Land fun Legendarn Dzhugashvili*, Paris, 1949, vol. 2, pp. 8f.

23. Ilya Ehrenburg, *Burya*, Moscow, 1944.

24. G. Smolyar, in *Fun Minsker Geto*, Moscow, 1946, p. 15, estimated the population of the ghetto at 80,000. A slightly different figure was given by Koz'ma Kiselev, White Russia's People's Commissar for Foreign Affairs, to an interviewer, Moshe Katz. According to him, there were 75,000 Jews in the ghetto of Minsk, but the Germans later brought in more Jews from the surrounding towns, so that its population numbered 100,000 as early as July 1941. Cf. *Morgn Frayhayt*, May 23, 1945.

25. The census of 1939's figures on the Jewish population by individual cities have never been released. From 1926 to 1939 Minsk's total population rose from 131,528 to 238,772 (*Vsesosoyuznaya perepis' naseleniya 17-go dekabrya 1926 goda*, Central Statistical Office, Moscow, 1928, vol. X, p. 214; S. Sul'kevich, *Naseleniye SSSR*, 1939, p. 32). If the Jewish population—53,686 in 1926—had increased in the same proportion, it would then have slightly exceeded 97,000 in 1939. During this period the Jewish population of White Russia decreased both absolutely and relatively—from 8.2 to 6.7 percent of the total population (Zinger, *Dos Banayte Folk*, p. 40). But the Jewish population was not only tending away from White Russia; it also was moving from the smaller to the larger cities of White Russia, and the percentage in Minsk apparently declined less than in the White-Russian SSR as a whole, so that the number of Jews in the capital city may be estimated at roughly 90,000.

26. Data obtained by B. Z. Goldberg in Minsk from Grigorii Eidunov, referred to as "the Vice-President of the White-Russian Republic." (*Der Tog*, March 10, 1946.)

27. Census data for 1926, from *Vsesoyusnaya . . .* , vol. X, pp. 214ff.; 1926–1939 rate of increase for individual cities computed from data in Sul'kevich, *op. cit.*, pp. 33f.

28. See n. 25 above.

29. For source references, see notes 25 to 27 above.

30. Data for 1926, from *Vsesoyuznaya . . .* , vol. X, pp. 216ff.; the number of survivors from Goldberg, *op. cit.*

31. D. Katsovich, "Menshn fun Chechersk," in *Eynikayt*, August 15, 1946.

32. Dispatch from San Francisco by M. Dantsis in *Der Tog*, May 25, 1945.

33. Statement at a press conference in San Francisco, *JTA Daily News Bulletin*, May 25, 1945.

34. Dispatch from San Francisco by Moshe Katz in *Morgn Frayhayt*, May 25, 1945.

35. *Za vlast' sovetov*, Moscow, 1949.

36. Aleksandr Fadeyev, *Molodaya gvardiya*, Moscow, 1947.

37. Arkadii Perventsev, *Ispytaniye*, Moscow, 1944.

38. Boris Galin, "V Donbasse," in *Novyi Mir*, October–November 1946.

39. *Ibid.*, p. 19; cf. p. 26.

40. Fadeyev, *op. cit.*, pp. 16–20, 32–35, 40–47. In obvious imitation of Tolstoi's *War and Peace*, Fadeyev sought to interpret the vast chaotic trek as an ordered operation growing out of thousands of individual volitions: "What to the surface view of the individual drawn into this current of retreat and perceiving what occurred inside him rather than the events around him seemed a haphazard and senseless manifestation of panic, was actually the movement, unprecedented in range, of huge masses of people and material values set in motion by the complex and organized mechanism of war moving according to the will of hundreds and thousands of big and little people."

41. Eugene M. Kulischer, "Three-Fifths of Europe's Jews Now in the USSR: War Shifted Jewish Population Eastwards," in *Rescue*, Information Bulletin of the Hebrew Sheltering and Immigrant Aid Society (HIAS), vol. III, no. 7–8 (July–August, 1946), p. 2. A few months later Julius Silverman, M.P. and member of a British labor delegation that toured the Soviet Union, wrote: "Realizing the special danger of the Jews, the Soviet authorities granted them priority in evacuation in areas in which the Germans were advancing. Many Jews thus escaped the fate which befell the

great mass of Jewry in the rest of Europe, but many stayed on to do their jobs, refusing to accept special treatment." (*Morgn Frayhayt*, November 12, 1946.)

42. *Der Tog*, February 21, 1947.

43. *Ibid.*

44. The Shekhtman story, incidentally, was told by Mr. Goldberg once before (*Der Tog*, June 13, 1936). At that time the rabbi was only a *zeydenyu* (grandpa).

45. The majority of Jewish evacuees and refugees—but by no means all—returned to their homes.

46. Itsik Fefer, "Sovetn Rateven Ondertalbn Milyon Idn–'Forverts' Kon Es Nit Fartrogn," in *Morgn Frayhayt*, October 21, 1945. This was in reply to the *Jewish Daily Forward*, July 1, 1945. See also *Morgn Frayhayt*, October 14, 1945.

47. *Eynikayt*, May 29, 1945. Fefer, incidentally, had told the Presidium of the Jewish Antifascist Committee as early as August 1944 that the number of Jews in Kiev was nearly 30,000; this was reported in the same *Eynikayt*, August 24, 1944.

48. *Eynikayt*, March 5, 1946.

49. *Der Tog*, August 15, 1946. Statistics on the prewar Jewish population of Kiev, Odessa, and Dnepropetrovsk are from *Jewish Affairs*, August 1941, p. 3. For other cities, whose prewar population cannot be established from the sources indicated in notes 51 through 61 below, the census figures of 1926 have been used, together with rough estimates for 1939.

50. Kh. Vaynerman, "Odes Vet Ufgeshtelt," in *Eynikayt*, April, 9, 1946.

51. *Der Tog*, June 1, 1946.

52. S. Ortenberg, "Dnepropetrovsk," in *Eynikayt*, June 27, 1946.

53. Avrom Kagan, "Vinitser Eyndrukn," in *Eynikayt*, September 20, 1946.

54. B. Z. Goldberg in *Der Tog*, August 29, 1946.

55. Avrom Kagan, "Zhitomirer Bagegnishn," in *Eynikayt*, August 14, 1945.

56. *Der Tog*, August 29, 1946.

57. Avrom Kagan, "Tsu a Nay Fridlakh Lebn," in *Eynikayt*, March 5, 1946.

58. *Der Tog*, August 29, 1946.

59. N. H. Kats, "Mogilev-Podolsk. Rayze Notitsn," in *Eynikayt*, April 4, 1946.

60. A. Blonder, "Belotserkov Lebt Uf," in *Eynikayt*, May 24, 1945.

61. Tat'yana Lagunova, *V lesakh Smolenshchiny*, Moscow, 1945.

62. Petr Ignatov, *Zapisky partizana*, Moscow, 1944.

63. Anatolii Kalinin, *Tovarishchi*, Moscow, 1945.

64. Boris Borisov, "Podvig Sevastopolya," in *Znamya*, March 1950.

65. *Op. cit.*, p. 112. The removal of women and children began on the very first day of the war, June 22, 1941, when no one expected the city ever to fall to the enemy.

66. See p. 198.

67. V. Vatin, "Rostov Vet Ufgerikht," in *Eynikayt*, May 29, 1945.

68. See p. 198.

69. See p. 339.

70. See n. 7.

71. *The Daily Worker* [New York], October 13, 1946.

72. B. Slutskii, "Aheym!" [Letter from Kazakhstan], *Eynikayt*, August 23, 1945.

73. The general Soviet press discussed this phenomenon as early as 1944; there was perturbation over the heightened mobility of manpower. When it transpired that many of the evacuated plants would not be returned to their original locations, production and office workers in many places abandoned their jobs and started trekking home, which seriously disrupted operations. See, e.g., *Pravda*, September 7 and 24, and October 1, 1944; *Izvestiya*, October 24, 1944.

74. V. Ortenberg, "Zay Gezunt, Uzbekistan," in *Eynikayt*, August 23, 1945.

75. B. Slutskii, "Idn in Kazakhstan," in *Eynikayt*, July 3, 1945. See also his "Alma-Ata," in the issue of January 19, 1946. Similarly, the deputy chairman of the Presidium of the Supreme Soviet of the Kazakh Republic, dealing with the "Rebirth of the Kazakh People" (*Eynikayt*, February 15, 1947), said of the new Jewish residents: "In the years of the war tens of thousands of people—Russians, Ukrainians,

White Russians, Jews—were evacuated from the western provinces to Kazakhstan.
. . . After the war thousands of Jews stayed for good in the prosperous republic,
and they work here in the factories and plants, in producers' cooperatives and scientific institutes, displaying model work heroism."

76. B. London, "Idishe Kulturarbet in Magnitogorsk," in *Eynikayt*, November 3,
1945.

77. *Eynikayt*, December 20, 1945.

78. S. Rabinovich, "Naye Idishe Yishuvim Zaynen Oysgevaksn in Sovet-Farband," in *Morgn Frayhayt*, December 22, 1946.

79. In the fall of 1946 Jacob Lestschinsky estimated the number of Jewish refugees
and evacuees who "still remained" in Siberia and Central Asia at approximately
250,000 to 300,000, and assumed that up to 250,000 might possibly settle as permanent
residents ("Idn in Sovet-Farband: 1946," in *Idisher Kemfer*, September 27, 1946,
p. 98). The present writer would make a somewhat lower estimate.

Part Two

ANTISEMITISM
IN THE U.S.S.R.

CHAPTER I

The Emergence of Popular Antisemitism

Antisemitism in pre-revolutionary Russia was part and parcel of the government's general policy. It was traditionally the official creed of a part of the aristocracy, was supported by sections of the state official-dom, and in some places had infected the urban middle classes. But the government's anti-Jewish campaigns found little echo among the people. Even the pogroms of the 1880's and early 1900's, which the Tsarist ad-ministration deliberately instigated, attracted little popular support, and this chiefly among debased elements in the cities. Compared with the anti-Jewish violence that swept Russia's southwestern provinces in 1918–1920, not to speak of the horrors of German National Socialism, these early pogroms which so stirred the conscience of the world were rela-tively limited affairs.[1]

Antisemitism in the Soviet era, on the other hand, was neither instigated nor countenanced by the government. It first appeared during the Civil War, growing by leaps and bounds wherever the fighting raged. For the counterrevolutionary forces it was an effective political weapon. Follow-ing in Tsarist footsteps, they identified the Jews with "revolutionists and troublemakers," but whereas Tsarist antisemitism had failed to win popu-lar response, now, in the turbulence and terror of social revolution and civil war, reactionary propaganda was successful in sowing distrust and in alienating the masses from the new revolutionary regime. Antisemitism in 1918–1920 conquered large sections of the urban and rural populations in the southern and southeastern provinces. Pogroms raged in cities and villages. The Soviet government was determined to smash this dangerous weapon of the counterrevolution, and as early as July 1918 declared war on antisemitism and "outlawed" instigators of and participants in pogroms.[2] In the confusion of war, however, the government's announce-ment failed to attract wide attention.

Resurgence of Antisemitism in the Mid-1920's

Open antisemitism subsided at the end of the Civil War. In the early years it seemed to many, not only among the Communists in Russia but also in Jewish groups abroad closely following events in the Soviet State, that the triumph of the revolution had put an end once and for all to this evil. Antisemitism, it was now widely thought, was a ghost of the past that the socialist rationalization of society would forever exorcise.

This optimism was soon proved illusory. Antisemitism reappeared widely in the mid-1920's. The Soviet press, without intentionally seeking to hush it up, at first failed to note or adequately to appraise the significance of the recurrence of antisemitic manifestations. In 1926 the alarm began to be sounded. Mikhail I. Kalinin, chairman of the Central Executive Committee of the Soviets and titular head of the Soviet state, replying in the press to a letter by a young Crimean Communist perturbed by the establishment in the Crimea of Jewish agricultural settlements, wrote:

> There are lots of letters and written questions addressed to speakers at public meetings, signed and unsigned, referring to the Jewish question in general and to the transfer of Jews to the Crimea in particular. Some are clearly reactionary and antisemitic; others, like Comrade Ovchinnikov's letter, sincerely endeavor to find out why the Soviet Government befriends the Jews. Incidentally, this is very characteristic: according to Comrade Grandov [editor of *Bednota* (*The Poor*), a newspaper published by the Central Committee of the CPSU for the rural poor], among the letters written by farmers to *Bednota* one did not notice any at all about the Jewish question, and such letters only recently began to make their appearance in connection with the transfer of Jews to the Crimea.[3]

Kalinin did not clearly differentiate between the two currents of antisemitic feeling that he mentioned. "Public meetings" would mean first of all workers' meetings in industrial plants, whereas it was peasants who would resent the establishment of Jewish agricultural colonies. He mentioned a third group, the intelligentsia, when he discussed the rise of antisemitism at the First Convention of the OZET (Association for the Rural Placement of Jewish Toilers in the USSR) in November 1926:

> Why is the Russian intelligentsia perhaps more antisemitic today than it was under Tsarism? It is a natural development. In the first days of the revolution the mass of urban Jewish intellectuals and semi-intellectuals threw itself into the revolution. Members of an oppressed nation, a nation that never had any share in the government . . . they naturally flocked to the revolutionary work of construction, of which administration is a part. . . . At the very time when large sections of the Russian intelligentsia were breaking away, frightened by the revolution, at that very time the Jewish intelligentsia were pouring into the revolutionary stream, swelling it in a high proportion as compared with their numbers, and starting out to work in the revolutionary administrative organs.[4]

Kalinin simplified matters considerably. The unexpected resurgence of anti-Jewish feeling took the Soviet leadership unawares. In their perplexity they even occasionally gave vent to utterances that appeared to excuse antisemitic resentment and to blame Jews for an excessive eagerness in taking advantage of their newly acquired rights. Thus in the same speech Kalinin said:

> For the Jewish people as a nation this phenomenon is of immense, and I must say negative, importance. When in one plant I was asked, "Why are there so many Jews in Moscow?" I answered: "If I were an old rabbi heartsick over the fate of the Jewish nation, I would hurl forth an anathema against those Jews who come to Moscow to take Soviet jobs, for they are lost to their nation." In Moscow Jews mix their blood with Russian blood, and from the second or at least the third generation on, they are lost to the Jewish nation, having become outright Russifiers.[5]

This, coming from a Communist leader, was not only proof of perplexity, but singularly ill-judged. Kalinin was himself unquestionably free of antisemitic bias. But uneducated workers were scarcely interested in the Jewish people's "losses"; what was bound to impress them was this "anathematization" of Jews flocking to the Soviet capital, and they were likely to interpret an insidious reference to Jews looking out for Soviet jobs, as well as remarks about Jewish and Russian "blood," in the old familiar antisemitic way.

Workers' Antisemitism

Antisemitic whispering was accompanied by antisemitic violence. The Communist Party was alarmed, for antisemitism seemed to have penetrated into the ranks of industrial workers, who before the revolution had been largely free of racial prejudice. In the daily press as well as in special pamphlets, numerous antisemitic incidents involving workers and even members of the Communist Party were reported. How far the epidemic had spread it is impossible now to determine, for only incomplete information is available[6] that hardly lends itself to quantitative analysis. Quotations from Soviet publications, however, convey its emotional climate and shed some light on those social aspects of the phenomenon which struck Soviet opinion at the time as representative and important.

In *Against the Antisemites* (1928), Mikhail Gorev told of the response elicited by a series of articles on antisemitism which he had written for *Komsomol'skaya Pravda*, the Moscow paper of the Communist Youth Association. "Dozens of letters," he said, were received "daily" in the editorial office. "I had apparently touched upon a sore and vital point, speaking aloud what many comrades had been worrying about." Gorev wrote of these letters:

All these letters said that antisemitic feelings had lately reappeared [*sic*] among certain groups of workers, that antisemitism was penetrating the Komsomol [Communist Youth Association], and that even some of the party members were falling prey to it.

"In our place, Kanavino (province of Nizhnii-Novgorod)," writes B. Solovetskaya, "antisemitism is increasing daily, and not only among non-party people but, regrettably, also among Communists."

Comrade Gufeld from Smela (Cherkasy district) relates:

"In 1925–1926 I worked in the Smela sugar refinery. Antisemitism there was widespread. More than once a green 'Jewboy' was put on the running gear and the carriage made to roll full speed, and then the 'Jewboy' was ordered to jump off the racing wheels. Then another entertainment was invented—dousing 'Jewboy' greenhorns with hot water. Or the fellows would form two lines, and yelling and shouting hurl the Jew back and forth between the lines. When work clothes were to be distributed the stockkeeper simply announced: 'No work clothes for long-nosed Hayyims and Hershs, they can go out and peddle.' "

An utterly scandalous occurrence that took place in Kharkov, at the First-of-May Government Distillery No. 2, is reported by another correspondent, Comrade Rais:

"This happened to me during lunch recess. I got to talking to a Komsomol member, but he rebuffed me right away. 'You're a Jew, you have no business mixing in the conversation.' An argument started. I reasoned with him, telling him it was wrong to talk that way. He just laughed at me, then started yelling: 'What do you want, you dirty kike-face? What business have you got here? So you want a separate Jewish republic? Want to take the Crimea? We won't stand for it.'

"Other workers, older ones, gathered around us. A member of the Komsomol shouted at me: 'So you want to go to school, to the university? You won't make it.' Another Komsomol member, Anikiyev, a candidate for membership in the CP of the Ukraine and a Workers' Faculty student at the Agricultural Institute, came by. He was even more pleasant: 'You dirty kike-face, what do you want here? Came here to take our living away from us? Well, you damn kikes, we won't let you alone. A pity it's no longer 1920—I'd have seen to it that your goose was cooked. You are speculators, all of you. And on top of that, you've got the nerve to come and work here!' "[7]

This abuse would seem to have touched upon the main points of conflict. The economic recovery that took place in the mid-1920's had placed higher education within the reach of many young workers. By taking courses given by the so-called "workers' faculties" of institutions of higher learning, they were able to make up the schooling that they lacked and upon graduation were eligible to matriculate at universities and institutes of technology. Conversely, many young people, chiefly children of lower-middle-class families, were barred from universities because of "non-proletarian descent," and these flocked to the plants. Once they had become workers, they too could be selected for admission to workers' faculties by their trade unions, factory organizations, etc., and in this roundabout way acquire a higher education. Among those of lower-middle-class origin were numerous Jews, whom the "genuine" workers distrusted as "bourgeois" and whom their fellow scions of the middle class regarded as "too smart" or "too influential." Resentment against "non-proletarian intruders" and "careerists" turned against the Jews in general, although most of the latter never dreamed of a university education, having gone into industry for the simple reason that they no longer could make a living by the traditional Jewish pauper occupations—store-keeping, peddling, etc. Newcomers to the factories, marked out by their appearance and behavior, the Jewish workers were met with hostility by those very Young Communists whom the government regarded as the progressive leaven in a mass of backward workers of rural or lower-middle-class origin.[8]

The Young Communist "vanguard" had reached adolescence during the Civil War or even later. These Soviet youngsters were ignorant of the egalitarian traditions of a free labor movement and looked with suspicion on anyone that seemed alien and different. The strength of anti-semitic feeling in the ranks of the Komsomol alarmed the Soviet leadership, and the Communist press vigorously exposed and castigated the Youth Association's shortcomings in counteracting the spread of prejudice. Aleksandr Chemeriskii, Secretary of the Central Board of Jewish Sections of the Communist Party, wrote in 1929:

In the Mechanical Works No. 13 in Bryansk, a gang of young workers constantly baited a young Jewish worker, Furmanov. In the gang there were six Young Communists, of whom two were board members of the Komsomol cell. The cell paid no attention to these goings-on. . . . In general, antisemitic feeling runs very high in this plant. Recently an informal discussion was held with workers on the subject, and this is what Comrade Ilenkov, who conducted the forum on behalf of the Bryansk District Committee, CPSU, writes about it:

"The workers who attended the discussion may be divided into three groups of different strength: (1) Those strongly contaminated with antisemitic prejudice. This is an active group—they asked questions, objected, made speeches, wisecracked, etc. (2) The bulk of the audience, who tacitly agreed with the arguments and speeches of the former. (3) A tiny minority, who timidly tried to reason with the first group.

"*Party and Komsomol people in the audience kept silent. The secretary of the Komsomol cell behaved as if the cat had got his tongue. The impression was obtained that they were all in agreement with the anti-Jewish statements.*" . . .

The daily paper of the All-Ukrainian Trade Union Council is in receipt of local reports pointing to an increase in antisemitic feeling among more backward groups of workers. Antisemitism is particularly widespread in plants whose operations are closely connected with the rural economy, especially in the sugar refineries and distilleries. Thus, a group of hoodlums at the Brailov refinery (in the Vinnitsa district) locked up Etin, a Jew, in the sulphuric acid shop, from which he was rescued in a severely poisoned condition. At the Lantsutskii refinery (in the Shepetovka district) a gang of antisemites over a period of time abused the Jew Kurzh, who as a result fell mentally ill. At the Uladovka refinery (in the Vinnitsa district) antisemites beat up the worker Shveirud, who had been nominated as a candidate for the works council. At the Boguslav broadcloth factory a Jewish apprentice, Bursuk, was the victim of repeated baitings and beatings by a group of hoodlums.[9]

Another Communist writer compiled a long list of antisemitic acts:

Here are some facts on the activities of antisemites among workers, facts that have come to light during the last two or three months:

"Now don't you get scared, I'll be there to protect you when a little pogrom starts up"—so the sales clerk Galperin was "innocently made fun of" by his fellow employees at the Mostorg store in Krasnaya Presnya [a borough of Moscow]. The fun ended in Galperin's being beaten up by the sales clerk Golubkov. When it was suggested that Golubkov be fired, the works council chairman Kuz'michev (a member of the CPSU) declared: "We won't allow Russians to be fired on account of a kike."

A man who agrees with Kuz'michev is Chikhachev, manager of the Novo-Bogoyavlensk factory. "Antisemitism is no cause for dismissal," he said, when the board of the Komsomol cell suggested discharging antisemitic workers who had persecuted a young technical engineer, Gurevich. To "get" the engineer they hated, some of the workers had mixed sand and wood shavings in the motor lubricant. It was only an accident that saved the factory from catastrophe. Gurevich had to go. The antisemites are triumphant.

At the "Labor's Will" cannery in Kerch a gang of workers hounded the unskilled worker Gutmanovich, a Jew, whipping him with a wire-coil. . . . In the presence of the works council chairman, the antisemite Pichugin shouted in front of a crowd of workers: "If they don't kick this Jewboy out of the plant, I'll strangle him." The shop meeting, attended only by cronies of the antisemitic hoodlums, decided that Gutmanovich had not been persecuted, that they had only been "joshing one another."

A different reaction on the part of proletarian public opinion was recorded in connection with a similar incident. Antisemites in the "Red Progress" plant (Bol'shoi Tokmak, in the Ukraine) had long abused the worker Reznik. They pelted him with bolts and wrenches, blinded him with wood shavings, and threatened to kill him, cut his throat; finally, Komsomol member Gleikh beat up Reznik in the shop while the crew looked on. A shop meeting attended by 1,400 workers denounced the antisemitic hoodlums and demanded that they stand trial before a court of their fellow workers. Only the Komsomol cell lagged behind, confining itself merely to reprimanding Gleikh.

At the "Metal Worker" plant in Pskov, Komsomol member Trofimov for a long time systematically baited another Komsomol member, Bol'sheminnikov, a Jew. A group of Komsomol members repeatedly approached the board of Komsomol cell on the matter, but the board failed to act. On February 14, Trofimov brutally struck Bol'sheminnikov down with an ax. The murderer proudly told his cronies: "I did it after all, I finished off that Jewboy." When questioned by the authorities, he said: "I killed him because I am a Russian and he was a Jew."[10]

Even in Leningrad, old citadel of the labor movement, antisemitic violence flared up in the factories. A pamphlet issued by the publishing house of *Krasnaya Gazeta*, a local newspaper of the Communist Party, cited the following facts:

At the "Lit" plant, antisemites egged on by a training foreman started the thing, shouting at Jewish workers, "You damn kikes." Then the slogan, "Kill the kikes, save Russia," was painted on lavatory walls. As this went unpunished, they threw bricks at Comrade Meller, then Comrade Yelashevich, then at several other Jews.

And here is another case, also from Leningrad. At the Marty plant, wisecracks and jokes on Jewish subjects were widely circulated among Young Communists, even among active members. Small wonder that a board member of the plant organization threatened a Jewish Komsomol member who took the floor against him: "If you dare take the floor one more time, I'll get you, you kike." Small wonder that a number of workers in this plant baited and beat up a Jewish Komsomol member while other Komsomol members looked on and laughed encouragement.[11]

Jew-baiting and antisemitic violence, it is plain, were not confined to backward regions, to the "non-proletarian" countryside or to the traditionally antisemitic Ukraine. All incidents reported by the Soviet press took place in industrial plants, with Young Communists—"even active members"—again and again singled out as having initiated or encouraged the persecution of their Jewish fellow workers.

Collegiate Antisemitism

As noted before, prejudice among young workers was to some extent the result of a conviction that Jews used the factories as a stepping stone to admission into institutions of higher learning. Often the prejudice did not abate when these youths themselves entered the universities, institutes of technology, surveying schools, conservatories of music, etc.[12] Numerous instances of violence, and even bestiality, were reported. The following are taken from *Komsomol'skaya Pravda*:

> At the Surveying Institute (in Kharkov), the Jewish Workers Faculty student Sh. was obstinately hounded for months, constantly, day in and day out, behind the closed doors of the student dormitory. Among his fellow students Sh. lived the life of a hunted animal. Every one of his steps, gestures, casual remarks brought down upon him an avalanche of coarse taunts and vile abuse.
>
> Lyashenko, a young surveying student and member of the Komosol, abused Sh. simply because the latter happened to be the only Jew in the dormitory. Another surveying student, Mikula, an intimate of Lyashenko's, was not behindhand. Sh., a harmless fellow, and perhaps too timid, was . . . kept awake at night, forced to lie in bed with his eyes wide open. To awaken him, they hit him on the head with a ruler, doused him with icy water, prodded his bare heels with a pair of compasses. The result of this persecution was that Sh. suffered repeated and protracted fainting fits. He was hardly recognizable after this—he had aged, shrunk, become an invalid with shaking hands. The hoodlums went on abusing Sh. One day Lyashenko slapped his face. This won Mikula's praise who repeated the experiment. The next day Sh. was beaten up. The third day they struck Sh.'s face not with bare hands but with a dirty galosh.
>
> At the same Institute, hoodlums beat up a pregnant Jewish girl student, trampling on her belly with their feet. In the Kharkov "student city," in the dormitory in Building No. 11, another gang of hoodlums beat a sixteen-year-old music student, Arkadii Reikhel, into unconsciousness.[13]

Kharkov was not the only place. Antisemitism was reported to exist in many universities. A JTA cable from Moscow, dated May 28, 1928, said:

> Reports [in the Soviet press] from various parts of the country say that the custom of referring to a Jew as a "*zhid*" [Russian equivalent for "Yid" or "kike"], with a contemptuous accent, has become common among students in Soviet educational institutions.
>
> *Oktyabr'*, a Yiddish Communist paper in Minsk, avers that the term "*zhid*" is frequently applied to Jewish students who seek to enter the White-Russian Music Conservatory. The paper charges the dean of the Conservatory, Prokhorov, with deliberate discrimination against Jewish students.
>
> The Kharkov *Shtern* cites a number of incidents showing the intense antisemitism prevalent among students of the Kharkov Technological Institute, despite the fact that the Communist Youth Organization has a membership of 400 at the Institute and exercises a strong influence.

Even the Communist students are affected by antisemitism and often ask why no *numerus clausus* against Jewish students is introduced.[14]

The revival of the idea of the *numerus clausus* was particularly striking. For decades limitation of the number of Jewish students had been one of the chief weapons in the Tsarist government's anti-Jewish campaign and a target of much liberal criticism. That the idea should now be taken up by the elite of the Soviet youth was ominous. The Kharkov case was not unique. A JTA dispatch from Moscow, dated October 21, 1929, reported:

> The introduction of a *numerus clausus* for Jewish students in Soviet universities was demanded at a meeting of Communist students in Kiev. The request had been previously discussed at a meeting of the Executive of the Komsomol.[15]

Time and again it was the Young Communists who were in the forefront of the antisemitic agitation. Press reports of antisemitism in elementary and secondary schools were less frequent. The family, whose parents belonged to an older generation, bred much less antisemitism in its children than did industry in its youthful workers.[16] Nevertheless, Soviet opinion ignored antisemitism's connection with Soviet industrialization and proletarianization, and the antisemitic outbreaks were blamed on "backward elements."

Antisemitism, an Urban Growth

The Communist leadership was especially disturbed by the amount of antisemitism in revolutionary Moscow, capital of the Soviet state and seat of the government and party. A rare "survey of antisemitism among trade union members" was made by the Moscow City Trade Union Council for the month of February 1929; whether similar surveys were made for other months cannot be ascertained, and even the survey of February 1929 was apparently never printed in full. Excerpts from it were printed in a book on antisemitism by Yurii M. Larin, an outstanding Soviet economist and a member of the Central Executive Committee and of numerous planning and legislative bodies, who was one of the few Communist writers to pay serious attention to antisemitism. The survey said:

> Antisemitic feeling among workers is spreading chiefly in the backward section of the working class that has close ties with the peasantry, and among women. . . . Often workers heard to make antisemitic remarks fail to realize the counterrevolutionary meaning of antisemitism. Many facts reveal the presence of Komsomol and party members among the antisemites.
>
> Talk of Jewish domination is particularly widespread. The offensive

taunting, aping, and ridiculing of working Jews are frequent occurrences. The telling of all kinds of jokes about Jews is common. Antisemitic administrators use their positions to persecute and badger Jews to the point where they quit. Vicious antisemites try to provoke Jews into fighting and beat them up.

Antisemitism sometimes takes the form of shouted curses, threats, and pogrom-like instigations, as well as anonymous inscriptions and threatening letters. In meetings and discussions and at public lectures instances of antisemitic heckling, speeches, and questions are becoming numerous. Speeches and written questions holding with the notion that it is only the Greek Orthodox religion which the Soviet government combats are frequent. . . . There are cases in which Jews who had been abused kept silent about it and made no appeal to any organization, apparently from fear of persecution or because they did not expect to receive much support.

Trade unions have failed to wage an organized struggle against antisemitism. Quite often local trade union organizations fail to bring antisemitic tendencies out into the open soon enough, fail to react to manifestations of such tendencies, and avoid taking the necessary steps to overcome them. Instances of a conciliatory and inexcusably tolerant attitude to manifestations of antisemitism have been observed in the lower levels of trade unions. Occasionally, these organizations attempted to hush up instances of antisemitism.

Still, a minor change has been discernible of late. The advanced strata of workers give evidence of conducting a deliberate struggle against displays of antisemitism by individual comrades and reactionary elements.[17]

The trade unions agreed with the government in attributing the increase in prejudice to backward elements from the countryside newly employed in urban industry; in addition, women were singled out for blame. But in the many press reports of antisemitic incidents women were mentioned only rarely, nor do these corroborate the charge that the backward elements accused of spreading the infection were of rural origin. In all the available source material there are only casual references to happenings involving the farm population.

The antisemitic wave of the mid-1920's did not originate in the villages. Rural newcomers to industry occasionally clashed with proletarianized Jews, newcomers themselves. As a rule, however, it was either the status-conscious, class-indoctrinated youth who resented the influx of "socially different Jews," or vociferous and self-assertive elements long established in the cities who were the very opposite of country yokels. Antisemitism originated to a large extent among dispossessed urban groups, people, that is, who, their families having lost their middle-class independence, saw themselves reduced to working for a wage or salary in factories and offices.

The villagers had little chance to influence the urban workers, whereas the newly proletarianized urban groups were a dangerous source of intellectual and emotional contamination. Better educated, they were more articulate and persuasive, and their fallen status and sense of grievance exacerbated their hostility to their Jewish fellow workers. The latter, often insecure in their unaccustomed role of proletarian, were vulnerable to attack.

To what extent the politically better-educated urban workers—Komsomol and party members—proved susceptible to prejudice can be gathered from Larin's account of a "seminar on antisemitism" that he conducted in August 1928 at party headquarters in one of Moscow's boroughs. The seminar was attended by several scores of workers employed in different factories, among them advanced party members, active members of the Komsomol, and sympathizers—that is to say, precisely those from whom the party, Komsomol, and the trade unions recruited their more active elements. The instructor was asked many questions, most of which revealed antisemitic bias. The following are representative of the 66 which Larin recorded:

Why is it that Jews don't want to do heavy work?

Why were the Jews in the Crimea given good land, while the land the Russians get is not so good?

How is it that Jews always manage to get good positions?

Why was the opposition within the party made up of Jews to the extent of 76 percent?

Why are there so many Jews in the universities? Isn't it because they forge their papers?

Won't the Jews be traitors in a war? Aren't they dodging military service?

Should a person who jokingly uses the term "zhid" be called an antisemite? How do such jokes have to be judged in general?

Should not the cause of antisemitism be looked for in the [Jewish] people itself, in its ethical and psychological upbringing?[18]

Conniving Officials

Anti-Jewish feeling made itself felt sooner in the Soviet administration, especially of smaller cities, than in the industrial working class. Its social origin, as traced above, explains why. Reports of incidents in industrial plants were not frequent in the Soviet press until 1926, but already in 1925 the newspapers were full of stories about the antisemitic leanings of local officials and agencies, particularly in the Ukraine. Some of the provincial Soviet administrations had apparently retained their antisemitic propensities in a latent form from the days of the Civil War. Economic recovery engendered social conflicts in which this feeling found expression. In 1925 the Jewish Telegraphic Agency cabled from the Soviet Union reports of quite a number of occurrences of this kind. Thus, a cable from Moscow (June 20, 1925) said:

> The existence of antisemitism on the part of the Soviet administration in the small towns mainly populated by Jews was admitted by a member of the special commission which was appointed to investigate this condition.
>
> A Jewish member of this commission writing in *Emes* admits that "antisemitism is practised openly in numerous places."[19]

Another dispatch from Moscow (September 4, 1925) reported:

> Complaints of mistreatment of the Jewish population in the smaller towns and villages were voiced in various parts of the Soviet Union. Expressions of these complaints are found in almost every issue of the Yiddish Communistic press. . . .
>
> Mistreatment of even Jewish invalids in the government invalid homes, terrorization of the Jewish population to such an extent that, according to a recent issue of *Der Shtern*, Jewish Communist paper in Kharkov, when three members of Kiev militia were arrested for frequent mistreatment, abuse and acts of terror, no one was willing to testify against them out of fear of revenge.[20]

Six weeks later a JTA report from Kharkov (October 19, 1925) said:

> . . . Open charges against local Communist authorities of violating the Soviet law in their attitude toward the Jewish population were made at the [Ukrainian] conference of the *Yevsektsiyas*, the Jewish sections of the Communist party.[21]

Instances of open anti-Jewish discrimination in the allocation of living quarters,[22] in tax assessment,[23] and even in state employment agencies,[24] became more and more numerous. In some cases personnel departments of government agencies and government-operated industrial establishments were reported to discriminate against Jewish employees. "When personnel was reduced and efficiency measures were introduced into the organization, Jewish employees were oftener discharged, and met with much more difficulty in finding new jobs, than was the case with employees who were Ukrainians, Great Russians, etc."[25] Local party officials refrained from acting against the antisemites and tacitly acquiesced in their misdeeds. Larin writes:

> This, for example, is from a recent newspaper clipping: "Comrade Denisov, manager of the personnel desk of the Krasnaya-Presnya borough division of the [Moscow] Real Estate Administration, has very decided opinions on the Jews. He quotes, eloquently, the antisemitic slogan, 'Kill the kikes, save Russia'; occasionally, when he has had one drink too many, he races round the building, shouting: 'I am going to shoot all those kikes.' The District Control Commission [of the party],

regarding [these charges] as borne out by the evidence, decided to reprimand Denisov and have him removed from his job." And that is all that happened.[26]

Another instance, also reported by Larin:

At a meeting on antisemitism called by *Nasha Gazeta* [Moscow newspaper of the Union of Government and Commercial Employees] in the spring of 1929 such facts as the following were cited: The [Communist] cell at the Naphtha Syndicate offices "warned" (just warned— that is all) a woman, a party member since 1919, for having said to non-party people that there are cases where Jews kidnap Christian children to make matzoth out of their blood.[27]

Another Soviet writer quoted a correspondent from Starobino near Slutsk (in the province of Minsk):

Achinskii, a Jew, was a few days late in reporting to the Military Board for registration; in punishment, he was sentenced to one month's compulsory labor in the district militia. After having served two weeks, Achinskii submitted a letter from the Peasant Committee certifying that he was poor and the only breadwinner in the family, and that the family was literally starving. Instead of replying, instead of (for all the difference it made to him) turning down the application in a civilized fashion, militia officer Potapov started yelling: "Makes no difference, you'll go on working. Going to croak? Well, good riddance, there will just be one kike less in Russia." That is the way a Jew is treated in a Soviet office by a police bully who has managed to worm his way into the militia. But this is nothing to be surprised at. Here in Slutsk a trade school student, one Vecher, a member of the Komsomol, rushed down to the market place yelling: "Kill the kikes, save White Russia." And this with the Komsomol emblem on his chest! Why should he worry—he is still a member of the Komsomol.[28]

Toleration of antisemitism by inferior party officials, especially in industrial plants, assumed such menacing proportions that a warning signal was sounded in *Pravda* (the only editorial, so far as can be ascertained, ever to have dealt with antisemitism):

More and more frequently reports of manifestations of antisemitism are appearing in the press. . . . In investigating plants in which antisemitic acts occur we are invariably [*sic*] confronted with the dangerous fact of the connivance of the local party, trade union, and Komsomol organizations; this alone makes it possible for the antisemitic campaign of persecution to go on unpunished for months and years.

The tortured worker finds no protection; antisemitic slang becomes current in the shops; and the officials of the cells, works councils, and the Komsomol prefer not to "meddle" in an unpleasant business, prefer not to start "trouble," etc.[29]

The Dagestan Case

In some instances local party units not only tolerated but took an active part in the persecution of Jews. Such was the case, apparently over many years, in the Dagestan Autonomous Soviet Socialist Republic (a part of the Russian SFSR), in the northern Caucasus. It is true that Soviet reports of the persecution of the native Dagestanian Jews (the so-called Mountain Jews) did not accuse the party, but only "Dagestan's highest governmental agencies" (i.e., the Presidium of the Central Executive Committee and the Council of People's Commissars). But these high agencies of the administration were entirely the creatures of the party and could do nothing of which the latter disapproved; they were also largely composed of members and officials of the party.

The story of the Jewish farmers and artisans of the mountain villages of Dagestan deserves being told in detail:

> During the winter of 1917–18 Mountain Jews returning from the army took an active part in establishing the Soviet government in Dagestan, made up more than 70 percent of the Red Guards at that time (according to data of the Dagestan Control Commission), and took up arms to defend the Soviet Government against the White armies. When the Whites . . . got the upper hand, a number of Jewish mountain villages were sacked and burned, their lands seized and distributed among neighboring Moslem villages, and their inhabitants—those who were not killed—banished to the cities. . . . In these cities they [now] live in misery, most of them hiring themselves out in near-by vineyards and orchards, or working as journeymen, and some as peddlers, etc.
>
> The forced transfer of the Mountain Jews to the cities in the Caucasus Mountains gave rise to antisemitic feeling among the urban lower middle class, because of competition in commerce, handicrafts, and for jobs. The local Soviet bureaucracy, closely connected with petty and middle-bourgeois city-dwellers, actively supports "our own people" (co-religionists, fellow tribesmen) against the "strangers." . . .[30]

Most of the members of the local government were city-bred Moslems and Russians, among whom there were apparently quite a few former Tsarist officials who had been violently antisemitic and prominent in the uprisings of 1917–18 against the Soviet regime in the Caucasus. The active antisemitism of the Whites may have accounted for the Mountain Jews' sympathetic response to the Soviet regime in its early stages; it is probable, however, that the Communist Control Commission greatly exaggerated the percentage of Jews among the Red Guards of Civil War days.

For years the Mountain Jews appealed to the higher Soviet authorities for protection against the local administration. In 1926 their complaints came to the attention of the Department of Nationalities of the Central Executive Committee of the Russian SFSR, which requested an explanation from the Central Executive Committee of the Dagestan ASSR. The latter appointed a commission of investigation and on the basis of its report enacted certain measures. But these remained a dead letter. What followed has been described by the Commission for the Rural Placement of Jews (KOMZET), in a memorandum submitted to the government on February 28, 1928:

This [lethargic] attitude towards the results of an investigation carried out by a commission appointed by the Presidium of the Dagestanian CEC itself, was all the more peculiar as shortly before (in 1926) an anti-Jewish pogrom had erupted in Makhach-Kala, the capital of Dagestan, and found an immediate echo in other cities of Dagestan. The pogrom turned on the accusation that Jews had used the blood of Moslems, and had apparently been organized beforehand; this would explain how it came to break out at the same time in different places. . . .

Having failed in all their efforts in Dagestan, the Jews of eight mountain villages elected a spokesman, Antilov, a farmer, to go to Moscow, where he was to approach the All-Russian [RSFSR] CEC. The upshot was that in February 1927 the Presidium of the All-Russian CEC commissioned Comrade Ostrovskii to go to Dagestan to investigate the situation of its Mountain Jews.[31]

The conclusions of the investigation were as follows:

(a) The antisemitic misdeeds of the administration, murder and violence went unpunished; complaints were fruitless, for they were neither acted upon nor passed along.

(b) The cultural, medical, etc. needs of the Mountain Jewish population were neglected, in spite of instructions from the central authorities; there were attempts to mislead the central authorities with incorrect information.

(c) The rights of national minorities to organize Soviets of their own in places where their populations were concentrated were violated.

(d) The repeated refusal to employ Mountain Jewish workers was more than accidental.

(e) The attitude of the local Soviet administration to the Mountain Jewish population was negligent, rude, and knowingly opposed to established policy.

(f) All these illegal acts and deviations were tolerated by Dagestan's government leaders, although they were informed in time of everything that took place.

The material amassed in the course of the investigation by the commissioner of the All-Russian CEC contains a written report to the effect that the former [Tsarist] administrator of the mountain village of Dzharach, Achgar-Bek Novruz-Bek-Ogly, who during the Civil

War had the Mountain Jews' defense militia shot as Bolsheviks, now serves with the Derbent city militia. Nothing was done about this report.

Minutes of the meeting of the Mountain Jews of Derbent on July 31, 1926 (attended by the chairman of the Municipal Soviet and a representative of the Dagestan CEC) state that Mountain Jews in most instances were under an administration run by remnants of [the White General] Denikin's gangs, and that the Dagestanian CEC, though informed of this, had done nothing about it. And so on and so forth.[32]

Following the commissioner's investigation, the Presidium of the CEC of Dagestan decreed a series of measures to restore the rights and liberties of the Dagestanian Jews. Again nothing happened. KOMZET's memorandum said:

Comrade Galulayev, chief delegate of the Dagestan People's Commissariat for Workers' and Peasants' Control and a member of the party, sent a written report to Moscow, pointing among other things to the following:

(a) The interest of Dagestan's highest government agencies in the fate of the Mountain Jews, which the arrival of Comrade Ostrovskii had aroused, was short-lived, and was soon followed by a reaction that in the Derbent district took the form of *revenge* for the unpleasantness temporarily occasioned [by the Jews].

(b) Those individuals and agencies on whom depends the implementation of the measures [of reform] display a *clearly inimical* attitude, or at best a lack of interest, and in consequence the directives are not being carried out.

(c) At the center of the area of settlement of Mountain Jews—the Derbent district—the oppressive treatment of the Mountain Jewish masses by Soviet authorities is *persistently* maintained. . . .[33]

The agent of the People's Commissariat also stated that the Jewish farmer Antilov, who had gone to Moscow to plead the cause of Dagestan's Jews, was jailed upon his return and held for trial. The court, however, did not find him guilty.

In February 1929—two years after sending its special commissioner to Dagestan—the Presidium of the CEC of the RSFSR decided once again to ameliorate the lot of Dagestan's Jews.[34] But what, if anything, was done we do not know, for no information has been made public.

NOTES

1. For the decisive role of the government in pre-revolutionary antisemitism, see Mark Vishniak, "Antisemitism in Tsarist Russia," in Koppel S. Pinson, ed., *Essays on Antisemitism* (Jewish Social Studies Publications, No. 2), 2d ed., New York, 1946, pp. 121ff.

2. *Izvestiya*, July 27, 1918.

3. M. Kalinin, "Yevreiskii vopros i pereseleniye yevreyev v Krym" ["The Jewish Question and the Resettlement of Jews in the Crimea"], in *Izvestiya*, July 11, 1926.

4. *Pervyi Vsesoyuznyi Syezd OZET v Moskve, 15-20 noyabrya 1926 goda. Sten-*

ograficheskii otchet [*First All-Union Convention of OZET in Moscow, November 15-20, 1926. Stenographic Transcript*], Moscow, 1927, p. 65.

5. *Ibid.*

6. Most reports of antisemitic incidents were published in local newspapers, which are virtually unobtainable outside of the Soviet Union, as well as in the Soviet Yiddish press and the *Komsomol'skaya Pravda*. Complete files of the two latter for the 1920's do not exist in this country. In addition, there are the Jewish Telegraphic Agency's dispatches from the Soviet Union, drawn from press reports, especially in the Yiddish newspapers, and passed by the censor; since Soviet censorship never permitted news not printed in one or another Soviet publication to be cabled abroad, the JTA's dispatches may well be considered semiofficial.

7. Mikhail Gorev, *Protiv antisemitov. Ocherki i Zarisovki* [*Against the Antisemites. Stories and Sketches*], Gosizdat (State Publishers), Moscow and Leningrad, 1928, pp. 9ff.

8. For additional illustrations, drawn from local Soviet newspapers, as well as from observation, see *Red Russia*, London, 1932, pp. 72ff., by Theodor Seibert, a German correspondent in the Soviet Union from 1926 to 1929.

9. A. Chemeriskii, "Antisemitizm orudiye kontr-revolyutsii" ["Antisemitism, Tool of Counter-Revolution"], in *Kommunisticheskaya Revolyutsiya*, periodical of the Agitation and Propaganda Department of the Central Committee, CPSU, 1929, no. 5 (March), pp. 68f. Original emphasis.

10. G. Nagornyi, "Na bor'bu s antisemitizmon" ["Let's Fight Antisemitism"], in *Kommunisticheskoye Prosveshcheniye*, issued by the Main Office for Political Education, People's Commissariat for Education of the RSFSR, May 1929, pp. 32f.

11. Yefim Dobin, *Pravda o Yevreyakh* [*The Truth about Jews*], Leningrad, 1928, p. 5

12. Cf. Yurii Larin, *Yevrei i antisemitizm v SSSR* [*Jews and Antisemitism in the USSR*], Government Publishing House, Moscow—Leningrad, 1929, p. 133.

13. Dobin, *op. cit.*, pp. 3f.

14. *The Jewish Daily Bulletin*, May 29, 1928.

15. *Ibid.*, October 22, 1929.

16. Cf. Gorev, *op. cit.*, pp. 10ff.; also JTA dispatches from Leningrad, June 5, 1928, and from Moscow, June 7, 1928, in *The Jewish Daily Bulletin*, June 6 and 8, 1928.

17. Larin, *op. cit.*, pp. 238f.

18. *Ibid.*, pp. 241ff.

19. *The Jewish Daily Bulletin*, June 22, 1925.

20. *Ibid.*, September 5, 1925.

21. *Ibid.*, October 20, 1925.

22. JTA dispatch from Moscow, October 26, 1926.

23. Discrimination against Jews by tax collectors was easily disguised. Former "exploiters," in which category there were many Jews, were deprived of civil rights, and such second-class citizens could hardly expect fair treatment.

24. JTA dispatch from Moscow, June 7, 1928.

25. G. Ledat, *Antisemitizm i antisemity* [*Antisemitsm and Antisemites*], Priboi publications, Leningrad, 1929, p. 52.

26. Larin, *op. cit.*, p. 276.

27. *Ibid.*, p. 281.

28. Gorev, *op cit.*, p. 10.

29. "Vnimaniye bor'be s antisemitizmom" ["Attention to the Fight Against Antisemitism"], in *Pravda*, February 19, 1929.

30. Larin, *op. cit.*, p. 128.

31. *Pravda*, June 23, 1928. The memorandum appeared as an article signed by Larin. It was reprinted in Larin's book with some deletions, where it was stated for the first time that it was an official memorandum by the KOMZET.

32. *Ibid.*

33. *Ibid.* Emphasis *Pravda's*.

34. Larin, *op. cit.*, p. 133.

Chapter II

Antisemitic Grievances and the Jewish Reality

Social Antagonisms under the NEP

The New Economic Policy (NEP) introduced in 1921 relaxed the rigid governmental control of the economy that had characterized the period of "War Communism" and made concessions to private enterprise. But this private enterprise, after the havoc of revolution and civil war, was not of the solid but of the speculative and unstable kind which, apart from intrinsic risks, was constantly menaced by prosecution and socialization. The NEP by its very nature appealed to lower-middle-class elements uprooted by the revolution, people having personal and family connections with the new bureaucracy, which to a large extent had also been recruited from the disintegrating middle class. These "Nepmen" —a few big speculators and numerous small-fry middlemen, retailers, and peddlers—enjoyed a hectic and ephemeral success in the period of relative prosperity that ensued.

The misery and hunger of the Civil War had been a universal leveler. But the NEP brought what then passed for luxury to a few Nepmen and privileged members of the ruling party and government. This was resented not only by the dispossessed upper and middle classes, but by the workers as well. The "capitalist sector" of Soviet society became the object of the scorn and hatred of large sections of the "proletarian vanguard." Party and Komsomol people saw their privileged position menaced by "concessions to capitalism."

Resentment turned into aggression and, inevitably, the Jewish "intruders" were singled out. Jews now enjoyed full civic rights, were employed in the government, and could go anywhere in Russia. Had they not conspicuously profited from the revolution? Were they not now profiteers of the NEP? Were they not turning to personal advantage whatever rights and liberties they had been granted?

Antisemitic agitation and incitement were prohibited as counterrevolutionary. But the genteeler and less aggressive forms of prejudice could be expressed without fear of punishment. One such typical expression deserves to be mentioned. In a public discussion in Moscow on December 2, 1926, a repentant anti-Soviet émigré, Professor Jurii V. Klyuchnikov, who had been permitted to return to Russia to join the staff of the People's Commissariat for Foreign Affairs, said:

The February [1917] revolution had already established equal rights for all citizens of Russia, among them the Jews. The October revolution went even farther. The Russian nation displayed self-denial. A definite disproportion was created between the numerical strength [of the Jews] in the [Soviet] Union and the position which Jews came temporarily to hold in the cities. . . .

You can see how all over Moscow small bread and sausage booths, run by Jews, have been set up. Here you have the main source of dissatisfaction: here we are in our city, and along come people from somewhere else crowding in on us. When Russians see how Russian women, old people, and children freeze in the streets for nine or eleven hours, how in the soaking rain they are bent over the stands of the Mossel'prom [government-operated chain stores], and when they see these rather warm [Jewish] booths with their bread and sausage, they feel some discontent. . . .

You can't disregard this. These things have to be taken into consideration. It is natural that people in big cities should feel some alarm, since the proportion between the number [of Jews] and the population is not maintained at all in the government, in the organization of daily life, or in other things. Well, if we didn't have a housing shortage in Moscow—but crowds of people are jammed together in places where one just can't live, and at the same time you see people from other parts of the country coming here and taking up apartment space. They are out-of-town Jews. . . .

What is involved here is not antisemitism, but an increase in national discontent, national sensitivity, and vigilance of other national groups. You can't shut your eyes against it. What a Russian might tell another Russian he won't tell a Jew. The masses say that there are too many Jews in Moscow. Bear this in mind, but don't call it antisemitism.[1]

Following Klyuchnikov's catalogue, the chief grievances against the Jews can be summed up as follows:

(1) Jews were accused of enjoying a privileged position. It was not enough, their accusers argued, that the February revolution had granted Jewish citizens full civic rights, the Bolsheviks went "even farther," driving the "Russian nation" to "self-denial" and bestowing upon the Jews "disproportionate" privileges. They figured more than their numbers warranted in the government and administration.

(2) Jews were blamed for their business activities and the wealth these brought them. In the period of the NEP a limited freedom of commercial activity was promised private operators, who often had plenty of merchandise that they disposed of quickly, whereas government stores and open stands were poorly stocked, ill-managed, and inefficient. Those who operated these government outlets fared no better than the consumers. Who then was to blame but the independent re-

tailer, the "speculator," the Jew? Was it not the Jew who sat in a warm and sheltered booth, waiting on affluent customers, while Russian sellers froze behind their open stands and Russian buyers queued up in the rain and cold?

(3) Jews invaded the large cities and aggravated the housing shortage. This was only one aspect of their general "intrusiveness."

Two additional charges may be added to Klyuchnikov's list:

(4) Jews were said to shirk hard work and manual labor; instead they monopolized positions in the administration and public services, usurped the professions, or turned to commerce and illicit speculation.

(5) Though accused of shirking manual labor, Jews were blamed for grabbing up the good land, which by rights should have gone to the "genuine" farmers. The government did indeed allocate land to Jewish settlers, especially in the Crimea, Russia's "southern paradise." To the antisemitic mind this was but another instance of the "privileged treatment of the Jews" by the Soviet state.

Though it is not the purpose of this study to refute the arguments of Soviet antisemites, we shall do well to look into the actual position of the Jewish minority in Soviet society.

Jews in Party and Government

Bolshevism from its inception in the early 1900's lacked support among the Jewish workers, artisans, and intellectuals, though numbers of them were active in the anti-Tsarist underground. The Bolshevik leaders were well aware of this, and one of their doughtiest factional fighters once went so far as to call the Mensheviks "a Jewish faction." The incident has been preserved for posterity by none other than Stalin. Reporting on the London Convention of the Russian Social Democratic Workers Party in 1907, Stalin, who had attended the convention as a delegate of the Caucasian Bolsheviks, said to his local organization:

> No less interesting was the composition of the convention according to nationality. Statistical analysis has shown that in the Menshevik faction the majority were Jews, the next larger group Georgians, and then Russians. Conversely, the overwhelming majority of the Bolshevik faction were Russians. . . . Commenting on this, one of the Bolsheviks (Comrade Aleksinskii, I think) jokingly said that the Mensheviks were a Jewish faction, while the Bolsheviks were truly Russian, and so it might be a good idea for us Bolsheviks to start a pogrom within the party
> This composition of the factions is not hard to explain. The centers of Bolshevism in the main are districts with large industries, purely Russian districts except for Poland, while the Menshevik districts—where production is on a small scale—are populated by Jews, Georgians, etc.[2]

This "joke" of Grigorii A. Aleksinskii's, who deserted Bolshevism at the start of the First World War and during the Civil War joined the forces of counterrevolutoin and antisemitism, hardly calls for comment. But it should be noted that Stalin's explanation was questionable in all respects but one. This one respect was the small number of Jews in the Bolshevik movement. Jewish liberals, democrats, and revolutionists proved to be even more averse to Bolshevism during the revolution of 1917–18, in spite of the fact that some outstanding people among them later went over to the Bolsheviks and played a prominent role in subsequent events. Even in later years, after the Soviet regime had been firmly established and all opposition crushed, Jewish membership in the Communist Party was small.

Twice—in 1922 and 1927—party members and candidates were canvassed as to their nationality. Jews were found to constitute 5.2 percent of the members and probationers of the Communist Party of the Soviet Union (CPSU) in 1922, and 4.3 percent in 1927,[3] as against 1.8 percent in the total population. But the population of the USSR in those years was overwhelmingly rural, whereas the Communist Party was (and still is today, though to a lesser degree) a party of the city. Since the Jewish rural population was negligible, a true comparison must measure the percentage of Communists who were Jews against the percentage of the urban population who were Jews. This comparison is shown in Table I.

TABLE I

JEWISH CITY-DWELLERS IN THE USSR AND JEWS IN THE CPSU, 1926–1927 [4]

Area	Percent Jews Within Urban Population (1926 Population Census)	Percent Jews in the Communist Party (1927 Party Membership Census)	
		Members	Probationers
USSR	8.2	4.9	3.2
Thereof:			
Russian SFSR	3.1	2.7	1.4
Ukrainian SSR	22.7	13.1	10.0
White-Russian SSR	40.2	26.6	18.6

The percentage of the members of the Communist Party who were Jews was everywhere substantially below the percentage of city-dwellers who were Jews. Still lower was the percentage of Jewish candidates for party membership admitted on probation, an indication that the proportion of Jewish party members was on the decrease.[5]

In the early years of Soviet rule the small number of Jews in the Communist Party was obscured by the relatively greater prominence of Jewish officials as compared with Tsarist times, when Jews had been excluded from the government and public service. A Jew in public office did not go unnoticed anywhere, not to speak of Jewish members of the central government and famous leaders of the Communist Party.

Moreover, the Soviet bureaucracy constantly increased in size with the enlargement of its functions, and the number of government employees of every nationality multiplied. The predominantly urban Jewish group being on the average better educated and having a higher proportion of professional, commercial, and clerical people, was well represented in it. Likewise the insignificant attraction of the Communist Party for the Jewish masses was masked by the notably higher proportion of Jews holding party office, especially in White Russia and the Ukraine, where the native non-Jewish population was a minority in the cities and the proportion of intellectuals and technicians of all kinds who were Jews had even prior to the revolution exceeded the proportion of the total population that was Jewish.

The consolidation of the Soviet system resulted in a rapid increase of the representation of other minority nationalities in party and government, and as early as the mid-1920's the proportion of Jews in positions of prominence began to decline. Data from official sources for 1925–26 are given in Table II.

TABLE II

JEWS HOLDING HIGH PARTY AND SOVIET OFFICE, 1925–1926 [6]

	Total Number Office-holders	Thereof Jews	
		Number	Percent
Central Committee, CPSU, members and alternates	104	11	10.6
Central Control Commission, CPSU, members and alternates	162	13	8.0
Presidium of the Central Executive Committee, Russian SFSR	37	2	5.4
Council of People's Commissars, Soviet Union	12	None	None
Council of People's Commissars, Russian SFSR	14	None	None
Chairmen of CPC's and CEC's of national republics, chairmen of provincial Executive Committees	88	1	1.1
Presiding judges of provincial tribunals	66	4	6.1
Provincial public prosecutors	66	3	4.5
Presidents of industrial trusts	54	4	7.4
Leading officials of the central agencies of cooperatives	194	21	10.8

Thus, the executive branch of the Soviet government (the Councils of People's Commissars of the USSR and the RSFSR) contained not a single Jew. Even in the Central Committee and the Central Control Commission of the CPSU, which in the 1920's were still largely made up of the old Bolsheviks of the anti-Tsarist underground, the percentage of Jewish members and alternates was about the same as the percentage of Jews in the urban population of the Soviet Union—in the Central Committee somewhat more, in the Central Control Commission slightly less. Of the members of the Presidium of the Central Executive Committee of the Russian SFSR, 5.4 percent were Jews; for the Soviet Union, data from another source show that of 833 members and alternates of the Central Executive Committee, 46, or 5.5 percent, were Jewish.[7] The proportion of Jews among the chiefs of the regional administration at the medium and higher levels was negligible. Even among the heads of Soviet industry there were fewer Jews than corresponded to their number in the cities; the popular notion of the "Jewish control" of economic life was without foundation. While no exact data are available for later years, it would appear that the percentage of Jews holding high office in the government and party positions declined considerably through the late 1920's and after.

"Invasion of the Cities"

It is obvious from the foregoing that Jews held no monopoly of government employment or party office. Nor was the increase of the population in the cities to be attributed to a "Jewish invasion." Moscow and Leningrad are cases in point. Moscow's population of 1,700,000 in 1917 shrank considerably during the Civil War, then rose again when peace was restored. By 1923 Moscow had over 1,500,000 inhabitants; by 1926 the two-million mark was passed. Only a tiny fraction of the increase was accounted for by Jews. In 1923 the number of Jews in Moscow was 86,171, or 5.7 percent of the city's population; in 1926 it was 131,200, or 6.5 percent. In three years the city had acquired an additional population of more than 500,000, while the Jewish population increased by only 45,000. And yet these were the years of exodus from the small cities and market towns of the old Pale. Leningrad showed a similar trend. From some 2,500,000 in 1917, Leningrad's population dropped below 1,000,000 during the Civil War; it was again over the one-million mark in 1923, and approached 1,700,000 in 1926. From 1923 to 1926 the number of Jews in Leningrad rose from 52,374, or 4.9 percent, to 84,500, or 5.0 percent. While the city gained over 600,000 inhabitants in three years, the Jewish population increased by little more than 32,000.[8]

When the Five-Year Plans caused a general rush to the cities in the early 1930's,[9] the percentage of inhabitants of large cities who were Jewish began to decline. Between 1926 and 1939 the percentage of the total population of the Soviet Union that was Jewish declined slightly, from 1.82 to 1.78. While the total number of city-dwellers had grown tremendously (32.8 percent of the USSR population living in cities in 1939 as against 17.9 percent in 1926), the percentage of city-dwellers who were Jews declined from 8.2 in 1926 to 4.7 in 1939.[10]

The geographical dispersal of the Jewish population assumed significant proportions. From 1926 to 1939 the total Jewish population of the Soviet Union increased 12.7 percent; in the Ukraine and White Russia, however, the Jewish population declined 3.7 percent, whereas the number of Jews outside the Ukraine and White Russia rose 59.1 percent.[11] The Soviet Union's Jews had been on the move since the early days of the revolution; the development in 1926–1939 merely continued and reinforced this trend. What irked the antisemites was not so much the number of Jews in the cities as their appearance in places where they had never existed before. As early as 1926 a large proportion of Jews were recorded by the census as having been established less than six years in their places of residence: in the Ukraine, 38.6 percent of all Jewish inhabitants; in White Russia, 42.3 percent; in Leningrad, 65.6 percent; in Moscow, 69.8 percent. Of these Jewish newcomers, who had come to their new places of residence after the Soviet revolution, many in 1926 were very recent arrivals, having been less than three years in the places in which they resided at census date: in the Ukraine, 20.8 percent of all Jewish inhabitants; in White Russia, 23.0 percent; in Leningrad, 34.5 percent; in Moscow, 26.5 percent.[12] After 1926 the stream of Jewish migrants, which in the early 1920's had flowed ostensibly towards the capital cities and other large centers, spread more evenly over urban communities and new industrial settlements of different sizes.

In the overcrowded cities Jews represented only a fraction of the newcomers clamoring for food, clothing, and a place to sleep. By rights, considering their small numbers, they should have gone unnoticed in the metropolitan crowd. But the rancorous eye of prejudice was always quick to spy them out.

"Non-Working Jews"

Jews were conspicuous, after the revolution and the destruction of the ghetto, not because they "shirked work," but because they were forced in large numbers to take up proletarian occupations and thus figured as strangers and aliens in their new social environment. Countless Jewish traders, middlemen, and artisans went to work for a wage in the 1920's, especially in the latter half of the decade, the proportion of Jewish manual workers increasing considerably. But compared with the newly proletarianized peasant from the countryside, who was utterly lacking in all industrial skills, the Jewish hand could pass for skilled and semiskilled, qualified for the better job,[13] and was looked upon as having a higher social standing.

While the Jewish office and factory worker gradually came to predominate in the Jewish population, and while the "non-working Jew" was more and more relegated to the realm of myth, the tardy assimilation of Jews into their new spheres of activity continually revived the old antisemitic stereotypes. In great measure this was owing to the haste with which non-proletarian Jews were turned into wage and salary earners. Table III illustrates the rapidity of the process in the late 1920's.

TABLE III

JEWISH WAGE AND SALARY EARNERS, 1926–1931 [14]

Area	December 1926 Thousands	April 1931 Thousands	Increase April 1931 over December 1926	
			Thousands	Percent
Ukraine				
Wage earners	93.2	195.0	101.8	109.2
Salary earners	126.5	189.0	62.5	49.4
Total	219.7	384.0	164.3	74.8
White Russia				
Wage earners	25.2	52.0	26.8	106.3
Salary earners	25.5	34.8	9.3	36.5
Total	50.7	86.8	36.1	71.2
Other Republics				
Wage earners	34.6	95.0	60.4	174.6
Salary earners	89.0	221.2	132.2	137.2
Total	123.6	316.2	192.6	155.8
USSR Total				
Wage earners	153.0	342.0	189.0	123.5
Salary earners	241.0	445.0	204.0	84.6
Grand Total	394.0	787.0	393.0	99.7

In less than four and a half years the number of Jewish wage and salary earners virtually doubled. The increase was highest outside of the former Pale and reflected not only the advance of proletarianization, but also the scattering of the ghetto population of the Ukraine and White Russia. The proportion of Jewish wage and salary earners outside the former ghetto area rose from 31.4 percent of the total in 1926, to 40.2 percent in 1931. But while in the Ukraine and White Russia the increase in the number of wage earners (manual workers) substantially exceeded the increase in the number of salary earners (mostly non-manual workers), the number of new Jewish salary earners in other parts of the Soviet Union was more than twice that of new Jewish wage earners, notwithstanding the higher rate of increase of the latter. For the Soviet Union as a whole, therefore, the increase of Jewish salary earners was greater than that of Jewish wage earners. Although the gain of 123.5 percent in the number of Jewish manual workers contradicted the anti-semitic charge that Jews shirked hard work, the fact remained that a large part of the Jewish proletariat was made up of white-collar workers. The growth in the number of white-collar workers was not a specifically Jewish phenomenon, but a general consequence of the political and economic structure of the Soviet Union and the burgeoning of the bureaucracy. "Salary earners" were mostly recruited from the cities, and Jews were relatively prominent among them for the simple reason that over four-fifths of the Jewish population lived in cities.

"Soft Jobs"

In 1926, 61.2 percent of all Jewish wage and salary earners were non-manual workers, i.e., for the most part government employees. In the Soviet Union as a whole, salary earners in 1926 accounted for 23.2 percent of all Jews gainfully occupied.[15] But of all the Jews gainfully occupied in Moscow, 50.1 percent were salary earners; in Leningrad, 40.1 percent; in the Kharkov district, 43.5 percent; and in all cities with more than 100,000 inhabitants, 35.0 percent.[16]

The progress of proletarianization in the late 1920's changed things somewhat. By 1931 the proportion of the non-manual workers among Jewish wage and salary earners had dropped to 56.5 percent; but this was counteracted by the continued increase in the number of Jews in white-collar occupations outside the old Pale. From 1926 to 1931, as shown in Table III, the total number of Jewish salary earners in the Soviet Union rose 84.6 percent; but the increase was 137.2 percent outside the Ukraine and White Russia, as against 49.4 percent in the Ukraine and 36.5 percent in White Russia. Of all Jewish salary earners 36.9 percent lived outside the Pale in 1926, but as many as 49.7 percent in 1931. Changes in the distribution of Jewish wage and salary earners are shown in Table IV.

TABLE IV

JEWISH MANUAL AND NON-MANUAL WORKERS
PERCENT DISTRIBUTION, 1926–1931 [17]

Area	Percent Wage Earners		Percent Salary Earners		Ratio Wage Earners to Salary Earners	
	1926	1931	1926	1931	1926	1931
Ukraine	42.4	50.8	57.6	49.2	.73	1.01
White Russia	49.9	59.9	50.1	40.1	.98	1.49
Other Republics	28.0	30.0	72.0	70.0	.39	.43
USSR Average	38.8	43.5	61.2	56.5	.63	.77

In 1931 the majority of Jewish labor in the Ukraine and White Russia no longer consisted of white-collar workers. Outside of the Ukraine and White Russia, however, 70 percent of the Jewish wage and salary earners were still non-manual workers in 1931, although the number of Jewish manual workers in this area almost tripled between 1926 and 1931.[18] Nationally, the ratio of wage earners to salary earners rose from .63 to .77.

This process expressed itself in a marked regrouping of the Jewish working class in the Ukraine and White Russia: the number of Jews employed in industry, construction work, etc. (where many more wage than salary earners are employed) increased relatively, and the number of Jews employed in government offices and trade (which employ salary earners for the most part) decreased relatively. But in the first half of the 1930's this development was reversed, and by 1937 the percentage of Jewish wage and salary earners employed in industry, construction work, etc. had decreased, the percentage employed in government offices and trade had increased. These two contrary developments are shown in Table V.

TABLE V

PERCENT DISTRIBUTION OF JEWISH WAGE AND SALARY EARNERS, NON-FARM, BY ECONOMIC DIVISION, 1926-1937 [19]

Economic Division	Ukraine			White Russia		
	1926	1931	1936–37	1926	1931	1936–37
Industry	44.2	51.7	37.1	48.4	58.0	45.6
Construction work	1.3	8.9	4.5	2.5	8.0	2.4
Transportation	3.7	3.9	2.0	2.9	4.8	3.7
Administration, public services, commerce, communications	50.8	35.5	56.4	46.2	29.2	48.3
Total, Non-Farm	100.0	100.0	100.0	100.0	100.0	100.0

We have no such data for Jewish manual workers and salaried employees for the entire Soviet Union. Zinger mentions that the ratio of the number of Jewish manual workers to salaried employees throughout the country in 1939 was approximately 3 to 4,[20] i.e., manual workers constituted somewhat less than 43 percent of the Jewish workers. This indicated an insignificant decline in the proportion of manual workers within the Jewish working class as compared with 1931's 43.5 percent (Table IV). The same author reports that the total number of Jews employed in large industry and construction work reached something like 700,000 in 1939.[21] But in his most recent work he gives the more cautious estimate of 600,000–650,000 Jewish manual workers in industry and construction work.[22] If we were to accept the latter figure, the number of salaried employees must be estimated at 800,000 or higher, and the total number of manual workers and salaried employees at almost 1½ million, while the aggregate number of gainfully employed Jews must be set at about 2 million, i.e., about two-thirds of the total Jewish population—which is a rather improbable figure for a predominantly urban population.

Zinger's most recent data must therefore be approached with caution. But, with all due allowance, they still seem to permit of certain conclusions.

It seems indisputable that in the Ukraine and White Russia, where the principal mass of the Jewish population was still concentrated, the ratio of workers within the Jewish working class declined markedly during the 1930's. But at the same time this ratio remained constant or almost constant for the Soviet Union as a whole. And that could have been possible only through a continuous increase in the ratio of workers within the Jewish working class in those parts of the Soviet Union where the Jewish population had until recently been quite small, but which swelled in the 1920's and 1930's as the stream of migrants from the areas of the old Pale poured in.

"Land Grabbing"

From 1924 on, the Soviet government actively sponsored the settlement of destitute Jews on the land. The Jewish farm population and the acreage under cultivation by Jewish individual and collective farms began to show considerable increases, as indicated in Table VI.

TABLE VI

JEWS IN FARMING, 1913–1928 [23]

Year	Jewish Farm Population, Including Dependents Number	Area Under Cultivation, Jewish Individual and Collective Farms, Hectares*
1913	52,758	119,403
1923	75,911	153,298
1924	94,158	162,875
1925	120,288	270,533
1926	141,780	375,296
1927	165,500	488,054
1928	ca. 220,000	642,054

* One hectare equals 2.471 acres.

The reaction of the countryside was not hostile. There is no recorded opposition to the Jewish suburban farms that predominated in the early years. The larger Jewish settlements at first tended to arouse the neighboring peasants' distrust, but soon came to be accepted on their merits and were even viewed with a certain degree of sympathy by the near-by non-Jewish farming communities. Discussing Jewish farm settlements in the Ukraine and White Russia, a Soviet Jewish author wrote in 1928:

At first . . . the attitude of the peasants was not so much hostile as skeptical: "What kind of farming people are they? Surely they won't work themselves, they'll go in for speculation." But this attitude soon vanished as the peasants became convinced that the Jewish toilers really work the land themselves, with their own hands and in the sweat of their brow, suffering great privations; relations grew still better when they saw that the Jewish novices made use of more up-to-date farming methods.[24]

Similarly, another authority stated:

According to the unanimous testimony of various missions that visited the colonies, the attitude of the peasants roundabout to the resettlement of Jews was neighborly and benevolent. This, however, was not the case at first. The Ukrainian and White-Russian peasants at first distrusted the new settlers. Used as they were to seeing the Jew as a trader, middleman, or at best a craftsman, native peasants did not believe in the Jews' ability to farm the land, or in the seriousness of their intentions. But by and by the doubts were dispelled. As they saw how former traders and middlemen worked the soil in the sweat of their brow, how they built houses, dug wells, etc., as they came to believe that the Jews sow and reap and bring in the harvest by their unaided efforts, the Ukrainian and White-Russian peasants began to show respect for their new fellow farmers, hardworking people like themselves. In a number of instances neighboring peasants have taken up the agrotechnical devices applied in Jewish colonies.[25]

Indeed, there was little reason to expect an anti-Jewish reaction from the rural population, for the Jewish settlements were and remained tiny islands in the vast peasant sea. Moreover, the Jewish settlers were generally given uncleared land, which took nothing away from anyone, and clearing it for cultivation was a costly and back-breaking task:

Actually most of the land placed at the disposal of Jewish settlers is hardly suited for cultivation and they have to work hard and suffer much before they succeed in surmounting nature's obstacles.

In the Crimea Jews are allotted land not in the south, where the climate is beneficent, but in the north, where the settler finds arid steppeland, the winds rage, the soil is highly saline and you have to dig 30 to 40 sazhen [210 to 280 feet] to reach potable water, etc.

Conditions are virtually the same in the Stepnovsk district in the North Caucasus, and in the Kizlyar district in Dagestan.

In White Russia Jewish migrants and settlers have to drain marshland, uproot tree stumps, etc.[26]

"The Jewish Crimea"

Only when wide publicity was given in 1925 and 1926 to plans for settling Jews in large numbers in the Crimea, the "Russian Riviera," did antisemitic tongues begin to wag. And yet the lot of the first Jewish settlers in the Crimea was far from enviable. A narrow coastal strip of southern Crimea, about one percent of the peninsula's total area, is the Riviera; only in the adjacent uplands—19 percent of the total area—are conditions especially favorable for the cultivation of the soil. The remaining four-fifths of the peninsula, beyond the mountains, is mostly an arid and wind-swept steppeland, and there it was, in the even more inhospitable northern and northeastern districts, that the Jewish settlers were sent.[27]

These facts were stressed in all Soviet publications dealing with the antisemitic epidemic of the mid-1920's. It is conceivable that the plight of the Jewish settlers was deliberately exaggerated in such publications— to disarm antisemitic propaganda; but this surely does not apply to reports and monographs not intended for publication. Such reports, prepared by the American Joint Distribution Committee (JDC) and agronomists of the American Jewish Joint Agricultural Corporation (Agro-Joint) as well as a KOMZET memorandum of 1925 addressed to the Council of People's Commissars of the Russian SFSR and dealing with the "allocation of 40,000 desyatin [108,000 acres] of land in the northern part of the Crimean ASSR for the settlement of Jews from other parts of the USSR," have been preserved in the private archives of the late Dr. Joseph B. Rosen, then JDC representative in the Soviet Union, later director and field representative of Agro-Joint. The picture emerging from these documents fully justifies the description of conditions in Soviet pamphlets.

Because of unfavorable farming conditions the Crimean steppe always had been thinly populated, and a terrible famine in 1921, which reduced the total population of the peninsula by one-fifth, further diminished the number of steppeland farmers. Prior to the revolution peasant farms in the northern Crimea had been underdeveloped; a substantial part of the land was owned by big estates which employed migratory workers from the Ukraine. After the revolution the private estates were seized by the government, and as migratory workers no longer came, cultivation ceased on many of the former estates. In all of the Crimea total acreage under cultivation in 1916 had amounted to 2,100,600 acres. In 1924 only 1,053,000 acres were under cultivation, or 50.1 percent of 1916 acreage. At the same time acreage under cultivation in the Ukraine had already been restored to 91.0 percent of the pre-revolution level.[28] Unless revived by new settlers, Crimean agriculture certainly could not have been expected to reach even the low prewar levels. The prewar migratory workers, who had been given land in their native regions and no longer came south in search of work, had to be replaced.

Placement of new settlers met with obstacles. The reclamation of land for agriculture was a costly affair. On the other hand, the Crimean administration did not particularly welcome the arrival of Jewish settlers. When in January 1925 it was decided to grant 108,000 acres of land to Jewish settlers and KOMZET sent an official to survey available land in cooperation with the Crimean agricultural administration, the People's Commissariat for Agriculture of the Crimean Autonomous Republic consented to the allocation of only 34,560 acres, reserving the rest for native Crimean Jews should they desire to become farmers. Of the 34,560 acres allotted, KOMZET in its memorandum accepted only 22,000 acres, "of mediocre quality," and rejected the rest as unsuitable for cultivation.

In subsequent years, especially 1929 and 1930, more acreage was given the Jewish settlers, but crops were poor and returns meager.[29] In spite of the combined efforts of KOMZET, OZET, and Agro-Joint, the transfer of Jewish settlers to the Crimea fell short of the plan, and after 1930 the acreage allotted to Jewish settlers in the Crimean steppe was reduced.[30] On January 1, 1932, a total of 5,122 Jewish farmer families were counted in the Crimea,[31] as against an estimated 16,000 which the Jewish land allotment could have supported. Prospective settlers were not tempted: "If, as planned, a few thousand more Jewish families are transferred to the Crimean ASSR in the years to come . . . about 6,000 lots or over 120,000 hectares [nearly 300,000 acres] of land will still lie unused," Zinger stated in 1933.[32]

To make the area suitable for cultivation considerable funds had to be appropriated. In 1926, President Kalinin had frankly stated: "You can't just put the settlers on the land; to put them there you have to invest at least several hundred rubles per desyatin [2.7 acres]; neither the Soviet government nor the population . . . has that much money. But such amounts may be raised abroad, and the Jews do raise them."[33] A few months later, at the first OZET convention in November 1926, Kalinin appealed to "the national feeling of Jewish capitalists":

> The Jewish people faces a great task, that of preserving its nationality, and this requires the transformation of a considerable part of the Jewish population into a compactly settled agricultural peasantry numbering in the hundreds of thousands at least. . . .
> This calls for substantial funds. The government for its part makes every effort to provide at least some material assistance. . . . But, on the other hand, the government does not prevent Jewish settlers from accepting help . . . from Jewish capitalists abroad. . . . Here different interests . . . coincide—the masses' interest in their preservation as a nation coincides with the national feeling of Jewish capitalists who, although they are capitalists and enjoy all advantages, still can't sleep in peace when they know that the people of whose blood they are, suffers and is miserable. . . .[34]

By 1929, a total of 22,500,000 rubles had been spent on the agricultural placement of Jews in the Soviet Union; of this amount, 16,700,000 rubles, or 74.2 percent, had been raised and donated by Jewish organizations abroad, whereas only 5,800,000 rubles, or 25.8 percent, had come from Soviet sources.[35] Far from robbing the non-Jewish peasants of fertile land, Jewish farm settlements increased the area of cultivable land in the

Soviet Union largely at the expense of foreign Jews.[36] In the Crimea itself the brunt of the arduous labor of the reclamation of its barren steppes was borne by Jewish colonists. Though more satisfactory results were obtained in later years, the Crimea never became "a paradise for Jews," and even the most antisemitic soon forgot to repeat the tales about "Jewish land-grabbing" and "the Jewish Crimea."

NOTES

1. Quoted from a stenographic transcript given in Larin, *op. cit.*, pp. 124f. Parts of the transcript were published in the Moscow newspaper *Rabochaya Moskva*, December 7, 1926.

2. J. V. Stalin, *Sochineniya* [*Works*], vol. 2, Moscow, 1946, pp. 50f. First printed in *Bakinskii Proletarii*, Bolshevik underground publication, Baku, June 20, 1907.

3. *Statisticheskiye materialy po yevreiskoi demografii i ekonomike* [*Statistical Materials on Jewish Demography and Economy*], ORT Documentation Series, Issue 4, mimeog., Moscow, March 1929, p. 29.

4. Party membership data, from *Statisticheskiye materialy . . .* , p. 28; population data from L. Zinger, *Yevreiskoye naseleniye v SSSR. Statistiko ekonomicheskii obzor* [*Jewish Population in the USSR, Statistical and Economic Survey*], Moscow—Leningrad, 1932, p. 11.

5. No comprehensive data on the distribution of CPSU members and probationers by nationality are available for later years. Without indicating a source, Zinger stated that in 1932 Jews accounted for slightly more than 4 percent of the total number of the party members and probationers. See L. Zinger, *Dos Banayte Folk*, Emes publishers, Moscow, 1941, p. 54.

6. A. Yenukidze, V. Knorin and K. Mal'tsev, ed., *K perevyboram sovetov. Sbornik statei i materialov* [*Preparing for Soviet Elections. Articles and Materials*], Government Publishing House, Moscow—Leningrad, 1927, p. 64.

7. Larin, *op. cit.*, pp. 114f. No figures were given for the Presidium of the CEC.

8. Data from the Urban Census of 1923 and the Population Census of 1926; total population, from *Bol'shaya Sovetskaya Entsiklopediya* [*Great Soviet Encyclopedia*], vol. 36, p. 489, and vol. 40, p. 377; Jewish population, from L. Zinger, *Materialy i issledovaniya obyedinennoi statistiko-ekonomicheskoi komissii pri pravlenii Vserossiiskogo ORT* [*Materials and Inquiries of the Joint Statistical and Economic Committee, All-Russian ORT Administration*], Issue I, Moscow, 1928, p. 41, and *Yevreiskoye . . .* , p. 18. A more spectacular growth took place in the subsequent years. According to S. Sul'kevich, *Naseleniye SSSR* [*USSR Population*], Moscow, 1939, p. 32, Moscow had over 3,500,000 inhabitants in 1936, and 4,137,018 in 1939; and Leningrad, over 2,700,000 in 1936, and 3,191,304 in 1939. This, of course, was accompanied by a substantial increase in the Jewish population; official data on the number of Jewish inhabitants, however, were no longer made public.

9. Some 18,500,000 villagers had moved to the cities between 1926 and 1939. An additional 5,800,000 inhabitants of rural communities had been added to the urban population through reclassification of places which could no longer be regarded as rural. Cf. Sul'kevich, *op. cit.*, p. 15.

10. Zinger, *Dos Banayte Folk*, pp. 35 and 39; Sul'kevich, *op. cit.*, p. 15.

11. See pp. 15ff.

12. Zinger, *Yevreiskoye . . .* , p. 18.

13. According to Zinger, 50 percent of all Jewish wage earners in 1939 were skilled, 40 per cent semiskilled, and only 10 percent unskilled (*Dos Ufgerikhte Folk*, Emes publishers, Moscow, 1948, pp. 41f.) The percentage of Jewish skilled and semiskilled may not have been as large in the 1920's. Jewish artisans in the Pale rarely had a chance to develop high mechanical skills. Yet they were far better used to handling tools than the illiterate peasantry who passed through the factory gates in the 1920's

and after. Under Soviet conditions this was a considerable qualification. In addition, the degree of literacy among Jews was far above that of the Soviet population as a whole, not to speak of those rural elements first cast out of the Sovietized countryside. Cf. also Zinger, *Yevreiskoye* . . . , pp. 30ff. and 55ff., and *Dos Banayte Folk*, pp. 50 and 63ff.

14. Based on data in L. Zinger, *Natsional'nyi sostav proletariata SSSR* [*National Composition of USSR Proletariat*], Moscow, 1934, pp. 85ff.

15. See p. 20.

16. Zinger, *Yevreiskoye* . . . , pp. 52f.

17. Computed from the figures given in Table III.

18. Cf. Table III.

19. For 1926 and 1931, Zinger, *Natsional'nyi* . . . , p. 88; for 1936–37, Zinger, *Dos Banayte Folk*, p. 62. Figures for the latter period adjusted to eliminate agricultural labor, which had not been included in the totals for the earlier years.

20. Zinger, *Dos Banayte Folk*, p. 50.

21. *Ibid.*, p. 60.

22. Zinger, *Dos Ufgerikhte Folk*, p. 39.

23. Data taken from D. A. Baturinskii, *Zemel'noye ustroistvo yevreiskoi bednoty* [*Rural Placement of Indigent Jews*], publications OZET, Moscow, 1929, pp. 14f. Baturinskii assumed, as did others, that the figures for 1913 approximately described the situation prevailing on the eve of the Soviet revolution. Cf. Yu. V. Gol'de, *Zemel'noye ustroistvo trudyashchikhsya yevreyev* [*Rural Placement of Toiling Jews*], Moscow, 1925, pp. 7ff.

24. M. Kamenshtein, *Sovetskaya vlast', yevreyskoye zemleustroyeniye i OZET* [*The Soviet Government, Jewish Land Settlement, and OZET*], OZET publications, Moscow, 1928, p. 48.

25. Baturinskii, *op. cit.*, p. 19.

26. Kamenshtein, *op. cit.*, pp. 47f.; cf. Baturinskii, *op. cit.*, p. 16.

27. For the Crimean geography, see *Ekonomiko-geograficheskiye ocherki SSSR* [*Outlines of the Economic Geography of the USSR*], vol. 9, *Krymskaya ASSR* [*Crimean Autonomous Soviet Socialist Republic*] by B. Shustov, Gosplan publications, Moscow–Leningrad, 1927, p. 17.

28. Samuil Ye. Lyubarskii, a JDC agronomist, in a memorandum to the staff of KOMZET on the "Mission to the Crimea, January 17 to 31, 1925," p. 16-a. (The memorandum is in Dr. Rosen's files.)

29. This point was repeatedly stressed in reports drawn up by Agro-Joint officials in 1927–1929. A number of such documents have been preserved in Dr. Rosen's files. Conditions apparently improved in later years.

30. The total land fund for Jewish settlements in the Crimea was 852,000 acres in 1930, but only 789,000 acres in 1932, according to an article by Zinger in *Revolyutsiya i Natsional'nosti*, February 1933, p. 65.

31. *Ibid.*, p. 66.

32. *Ibid.*, p. 65.

33. M. Kalinin, "Yevreiskii vopros i pereseleniye yevreyev v Krym" ["The Jewish Question and the Resettlement of Jews in the Crimea"], in *Izvestiya*, July 11, 1926.

34. *Pervyi Vsesoyuznyi Syezd Ozet v Moskve, 15–20 noyabrya 1926 goda. Stenograficheskii otchet* [*First All-Union Convention of OZET in Moscow, November 15–20, 1926. Stenographic Transcript*], Moscow, 1927, pp. 66f.

35. Baturinskii, *op. cit.*, p. 17.

36. It would seem that some Jewish organizations (the JDC for one, later the Agro-Joint) also extended financial assistance to non-Jewish farmers. Samuil Ye. Lyubarskii stated: "We must consider, in view of present conditions, that at the same time as Jewish settlers are being taken care of, assistance will have to be provided for the local non-Jewish population, and that this will require no less than 33.5 percent of the budget." ("Attracting Jews to Agriculture and the Establishment of Jewish Agricultural Settlements in the Crimea," p. 28, a report made in Russian in 1924 to the JDC. A copy has been preserved in the files of Dr. Rosen.)

CHAPTER III
The Fight Against Antisemitism

Antisemitism a Punishable Offense

In the battles of the Civil War antisemitism was a weapon that served the counterrevolutionary forces well. Thus it was strongly impressed upon the Soviet government that antisemitism was a dangerous enemy of the state threatening even the preservation of Soviet rule. Beyond this, however, the government leaders did not think about the problem.

In the Soviet Union both legal repression and political education were used to fight antisemitism. The belief is widespread outside of Russia that each and every display of antisemitic feeling exposes the culprit to severe punishment, and that jibes and insults, let alone physical assault and vandalism, are given short shrift in Soviet courts. The actual situation is more complex. Antisemitic acts are indeed culpable, but the punishment meted out is not of the exceptional character it has been reputed to be.

This misconception grew in part out of the much publicized "outlawing of pogromists" by a Soviet order first published (undated) in the government newspaper *Izvestiya* on July 27, 1918,[1] in the section devoted to "Government Activities and Ordinances." It is worth while to recall the important passages of the order:

FROM THE COUNCIL OF PEOPLE'S COMMISSARS

According to information reaching the Council of People's Commissars, counterrevolutionists in many cities, particularly in the neighborhood of the front, carry on a pogromist agitation which leads to local attacks on the working Jewish population. Bourgeois counterrevolution catches up the weapon that the hands of the Tsar let slip. . . .

In the Russian Soviet Federated Socialist Republic, where the principle of the self-determination of the laboring masses of all peoples is established, there is no place for national oppression. The Jewish bourgeois is our enemy, not as he is a Jew but as he is a bourgeois. The Jewish worker is our brother.

Incitement to hatred of any nation whatever is intolerable, shameful, and criminal.

The Council of People's Commissars declares that the antisemitic movement and anti-Jewish pogroms are fatal to the cause of the workers' and peasants' revolution, and appeals to Socialist Russia's laboring people to combat this evil with all its means. . . .

The Council of People's Commissars directs all *sovdeps* [Soviets of Workers', Peasants', and Soldiers' Delegates] to take such steps as will effectively destroy the antisemitic movement at its roots. It is herewith ordered that pogromists and persons inciting to pogroms be outlawed.

The government itself did not attribute to this document the exceptional importance which later writers on the subject thought it had. It was primarily an appeal to the population and to local administrative bodies; the unpretentious heading—"From the Council of People's Commissars"—would indicate that it was not an official decree. Moreover, the last paragraph, which gave the statement its statutory character (though the term "outlawed" is very vague), was missing from the text submitted for signature to Lenin, who was the chairman of the Council of People's Commissars. Semen M. Dimanshtein, Commissar for Jewish National Affairs, and Anatolii V. Lunacharskii, at that time and for many years thereafter People's Commissar for Education, later described what took place. The draft of the document was handed to Lenin by Yakov M. Sverdlov, chairman of the Central Executive Committee. "Lenin read it and in his own hand added in red ink" the last paragraph.[2] That is, the last and crucial paragraph was in the way of an afterthought.

The order of July 27, 1918 hardly influenced the administration and the courts in their prosecution of antisemitic agitators; it was not even included in the official *Collection of Laws and Government Ordinances*, which at the time was issued several times a month. The "outlawing of pogromists" was apparently regarded as a wartime necessity and was forgotten when the Soviet government came to draw up the first Criminal Code of 1922. The Criminal Code did not neglect to condemn "agitation and propaganda arousing national enmities and dissensions," the punishment for which was a minimum of one year's solitary confinement, and in time of war, if the offense was flagrant, death.[3] This provision also applied to antisemitic propaganda, though antisemitism was not itself specifically condemned. Acts of violence against Jews, including pogroms, were not singled out by the code, but came under its general interdiction against assault and abuse.

A special "Statute on Crimes against the State," issued on February 25, 1927 [4] and later incorporated in the Criminal Code, broadened the provision against the incitement of national enmities to include the "dissemination, manufacture, or possession of literature" so tending. Section 59–7 of the present Criminal Code reads:

Propaganda or agitation aimed at arousing national or religious enmities and dissension, as well as the dissemination, manufacture, or possession of literature of such nature, shall entail:
Loss of freedom for a term of no less than two years.

Such actions in time of war, or during popular disturbances, shall entail:

Loss of freedom for a term of no less than two years, accompanied by forfeiture of all or part of the delinquent's property; and if there are aggravating circumstances, severe penalties including the supreme measure of social protection—death by shooting, accompanied by forfeiture of property.

In a special decision of March 28, 1930 the Supreme Court of the Russian SFSR ruled that Section 59–7 of the Criminal Code was not applicable to "attacks on individual members of national minorities following personal conflicts with such individuals." All such attacks were to be punished under the statutes governing insult and abuse (Sec. 159), or, "if accompanied by hooliganism," under Section 74.[5]

Leniency in Criminal Prosecution

In practice, Section 59–7 of the Criminal Code has been infrequently invoked, nor in general have severe sentences been meted out for antisemitic offenses. Press reports of the judicial proceedings against antisemites are few; as a rule, only extreme cases of violence are taken notice of. The Soviet press, including the legal journals, has refrained throughout the years from describing the salient facts of Soviet judicial practice with respect to antisemitic crimes, nor is any such description to be found in textbooks of Soviet law or legal reference books. This writer has discovered only one survey of court proceedings against antisemites, covering only one year—that ended September 30, 1928—and one region—the city and province of Moscow. Written when the first wave of antisemitism was at its height and the government was taking a firm stand against it, this unique and neglected document deserves to be quoted at length.

We have collected [wrote the author] all cases of antisemitism dealt with by the People's Courts of the province of Moscow in 1927–28. These cases were subjected to meticulous study, the results of which we can now offer to the reader.

The most noteworthy fact is the extremely small number of cases. In the period dealt with there were altogether 38 proceedings at law involving antisemitism. Of these, only 4 took place in district areas; all others were in the city of Moscow. People's Courts in other districts reported that no action involving antisemitism had been or was now on their dockets.

The insignificant number of cases of antisemitism dealt with by People's Courts is very characteristic. It indicates that only a small number of those committing antisemitic offenses were brought to trial—either when the injured person had no other recourse and had to appeal to the court for help, or when . . . the case was so "big" that it stood out by its repulsiveness. . . .

As a rule, antisemitic manifestations are ignored by those in whose midst they take place; antisemitism is not sufficiently opposed by those who witness it. This is apparent from the data. In 34 out of 38 cases, proceedings were initiated on the complaint of the injured party, though most cases of antisemitism occurred in surroundings that by no means can be considered secluded. . . .

A great number of cases (about 35 percent), it would appear, were not confined to verbal abuse, but were usually accompanied by counterrevolutionary incitement to pogroms. Vicious hooliganism occurred, and individuals were singled out for particular abuse and antisemitic attack. This included cases of beatings in homes, open assaults on and beating of Jewish passers-by in the street, abuse and insult, persistent hounding, and attempts to force people out of their apartments, etc. . . .

Here are some examples. One Kramskoi, a teamster who had been repeatedly tried and subjected to administrative punishment for hooliganism, persistently abused a Jewish invalid living in the same apartment. Not satisfied with this, he broke into his neighbor's room and, carrying out a real pogrom, wrecked the furniture with an ax. The court pronounced him guilty under Section 74-2 of the Criminal Code and sentenced him to six months' confinement, to be followed by deportation (People's Court of the borough of Krasnaya Presnya).

A woman teacher, Shakalinis, a former houseowner, together with her son, a Komsomol member, systematically persecuted Jews with whom she shared an apartment. They were fined by the People's Court of the borough of Sokol'niki.

Korneichev, a driver, assaulted a doctor walking on the street in the very heart of Moscow and beat him up to the accompaniment of shouted pogromist incitement. Confinement for one and a half months (People's Court of the borough of Bauman).

A worker, Pokrovskii, constantly vilified a Jewish fellow worker operating a lathe next to him. This harassment, accompanied by threats of violence, went on over a long period until the persecuted worker appealed to the court. (And where, during all that time, were the local party, union, and social organizations?) The court sentenced Pokrovskii to one month's compulsory labor.

It would be easy to cite many more examples. . . .

Penal practice in all such cases may be summarized as follows: of 70 defendants, 30 were fined, 12 were sentenced to compulsory labor, 14 to loss of freedom, 3 to a public reprimand, and 10 were acquitted. The crimes committed were dealt with under the terms of Section 146 [assault and battery], 159 [insult and abuse], and 74 [hooliganism], of the Criminal Code.[6]

One can see that even at a time when antisemitism was being sternly denounced, antisemites were coming off rather lightly at the hands of the courts. In 38 trials involving 70 defendants, only 14 out of the 60 persons convicted were sentenced to imprisonment. What at that time was called "compulsory" (later "corrective") labor entailed no detention; persons so sentenced continued to work at their regular jobs, forfeiting a part of the regular wage (up to 25 percent) and some social insurance claims.

The Soviet press seldom mentioned cases where severer penalties were imposed on antisemites; leniency was the rule in most of the judicial proceedings reported. A case that was appealed provides a telling illustration. Larin writes:

> In practice, even the courts are tolerant of antisemitic manifestations; this attitude is apparently a part of a still widespread tolerance shown to instances of the moral breakdown of everyday life ("We are no monks"). Here is an example, taken from *Komsomol'skaya Pravda*, of a trial in Moscow in 1929. The People's Court of the 14th Precinct of the borough of Krasnaya Presnya tried the two Krasins, father and son, on charges of antisemitism. The sentence of the court reads: "Besides assaulting the persons of the Fridmans, mother and son, the defendants, carrying out a pogrom in the Fridman apartment, wrecked the door and broke dishes, in witness whereof there is a document on file drawn up by the board of the housing cooperative; it has been established by testimony of witnesses that Krasin is an antisemite." In punishment the People's Court imposed six months of compulsory labor. It is known that compulsory labor does not involve arrest, but usually means only that a certain percentage of the individual's salary is deducted by the government as a fine. This is all the punishment antisemites incur for a "pogrom" involving the wrecking of a door, beatings, etc.
>
> But the most remarkable feature is the later history of the case. The Moscow Provincial Court voided the verdict and ruled that the [penalty], as represented by a six-month term at compulsory labor, was too lenient, having been imposed without properly considering the social danger inherent in the criminal acts committed by the defendants. . . . The Provincial Court therefore referred the case for re-trial to another Precinct Court of the same borough.
>
> And after all this, the People's Court for the 12th Precinct of the borough of Krasnaya Presnya decided to uphold that very sentence of six months' compulsory labor which had been imposed by the borough's 14th Precinct Court.[7]

This case, so far as one can judge, was not unique. Soviet judges in the late 1920's were apparently little inclined to treat antisemites as "outlaws."

"Chauvinism"

In the early 1930's antisemitism was superseded officially by a broader legal concept. Judges were directed to concentrate their efforts on the repression of nationalist bigotry in general, called, in the official jargon, "great-power and local chauvinism"; to what extent antisemitism was involved in "chauvinist" offenses was no longer recorded. The new concept stigmatized all acts of oppression or discrimination against any of the numerous minority peoples living on Soviet soil. After hearing Stalin's report on the activities of the party's Central Committee, the Sixteenth Convention of the CPSU (June and July 1930) voted a resolution deploring the "revival, within the party, of nationalist deviations towards great-power and local chauvinisms," and appealing to all party members to combat chauvinism, particularly the Great-Russian kind.[8]

This shift in emphasis was the result of new frictions caused by the mass recruitment of backward minority peoples into industry, where hard working and living conditions were the rule. Smoldering resentments led to violent clashes between the old hands and the new, and among the new groups of Tatars, Bashkirs, Kirghiz, Uzbeks, etc.—and Jews.

In combating "great-power chauvinism" in general, the government neglected the specific threat of antisemitism. Neither in his major report nor in his concluding remarks at the Sixteenth Party Convention did Stalin so much as mention the problem. In the extensive debate on Stalin's report, no mention was made of the attacks on the Jewish minority, and one delegate (Gei, from White Russia) drew the Convention's attention to the danger of "Jewish chauvinism."[9] In a resolution dealing with the "tasks of trade unions in the period of reconstruction,"[10] the Convention, among other things, called for an intensified fight against antisemitism, which, however, had been mentioned neither in the comprehensive report on union problems made by Nikolai M. Shvernik, then First Secretary of the All-Union Central Trade Union Council, nor in his reply to the comments of delegates discussing the report from the floor; in the debate a single speaker (Stasova, a delegate from the Central Committee of the International Workers Aid) cited an incident involving the persecution of a Jew by fellow workers as one of many examples of chauvinism illustrating the need for more "education in internationalism."[11]

Following the Sixteenth Convention, the repression of great-power chauvinism was energetically carried out for a number of years. Culprits were usually indicted for hooliganism, assault and battery, and insult and abuse; only in a few cases was Section 59–7 on the "arousing of national enmities" invoked. The application of different sections of the Criminal Code to offenses involving racial enmity had been determined by the aforementioned decision of the RSFSR Supreme Court.[12] Though voluminous information was published on the prosecution of chauvinism, action under this head against antisemitism was rarely mentioned in the press. In part this is owing to the abatement of the antisemitic epidemic in the early 1930's. And such antisemitic acts as did occur were not singled out by the courts from the multitude of chauvinist offenses.

Political Education

The legal repression of antisemitism is necessarily of limited efficacy. In times of social upheaval, when customary forms of social life are smashed and traditional social ties broken, prosecution and punishment may play an important part in the fight against antisemitism; but they certainly cannot destroy it at its roots. The rulers of Soviet society were well aware of this. But to appreciate the necessity of combating antisemitism by political and educational measures is one thing, and to realize those measures in practice is another.

In 1918 a program for combating antisemitism was incorporated in a decision of the Executive Committee of the Moscow Soviet (then called the Council of People's Commissars of the City and Province of Moscow).

Information having been received of pogromist agitation of an antisemitic nature taking place in Moscow and the province of Moscow and of the recorded facts of anti-Jewish pogroms in some cities of the province of Moscow, BE IT RESOLVED:

(1) To urge all Soviets of Workers' and Soldiers' Delegates in the province of Moscow by circular letter: (a) to call special sessions of the Soviets to discuss the Jewish question and the fight against antisemitism; (b) to initiate in print and by word of mouth a campaign against antisemitic agitation, and to organize public meetings and lectures; (c) to give serious heed to the reactionary and bigoted antisemitic agitation carried on by the clergy, and to combat with the utmost energy its counterrevolutionary activities and agitation.

(2) Not to create a special Jewish fighting organization.

(3) To give wide publicity to all well-established facts about pogroms.

(4) To direct the Commissariat for Jewish Affairs to draw up, within seven days and in cooperation with the Military Commissariat, a series of preventive measures to be taken against anti-Jewish pogroms; the Commissariat shall report thereon to the Council of People's Commissars of the City and Province of Moscow.[13]

The practical consequences of this decision we do not know; so far as can be ascertained, no special Soviet sessions or public meetings and lectures on antisemitism were recorded by the press. The "well-established facts about pogroms" did not appear in print, nor did any proposals by the Jewish Commissariat for preventing pogroms. In the confused circumstances of the spring of 1918, the practical effect of the decision was to prevent the creation of a Jewish defense militia.

Only the spectacular rise of antisemitism in the mid-1920's roused the government from its torpor.[14] In August 1926, in the Party Life section of *Pravda*, a trenchant article appeared by M. Ryutin, one of the leading officials of the Communist Party in Moscow:

> So far we have paid virtually no attention to antisemitism in our educational work—or at any rate very little attention.
>
> Let us see. In our newspapers covering the entire period of the proletarian revolution you will find scarcely two or three articles on antisemitism. Do we have even so much as one or two pamphlets explaining the nature of antisemitism to workers and peasants in an easily understandable manner? Do the curricula of our schools for political instruction contain a section on the necessity of popularizing our attitude to antisemitism? There is nothing of the sort. This is why our party rank-and-filers often do not know how to give a satisfactory answer to nonparty workers who bring the matter up. Moreover, our rank-and-filers, talking to workers who at times backslide into nationalism, are unable to reason the problem out and sometimes fall victims themselves to such attitudes. . . .
>
> Starting in the fall, we will have to deal with this problem much more seriously in our party activities. . . .[15]

But no visible change took place, and meanwhile the tide of antisemitism rose. At last, the Propaganda Department ("Agitprop") of the Communist Party's Central Committee decided on emergency measures in May 1928. They were summed up as follows in an official release:

> (1) The problem of fighting antisemitism is to be included in the party's educational curriculum. It is necessary to improve the internationalist education of the youth in secondary schools.
>
> (2) Among current publications there are too few works of fiction and too few political pamphlets on the problem. It is necessary to expose the class background of antisemitism more systematically and on a wider scale, using for this purpose fiction, the stage, the screen, the radio, and the daily press.
>
> (3) The party must create an atmosphere in which antisemitism will be socially scorned. Virulent antisemitism must be punished by expulsion from the party.[16]

The Propaganda Department demanded a discussion of the matter in the Central Committee, and for this purpose a subcommittee was appointed to draft the detailed program of an educational campaign against antisemitism. A JTA dispatch said about the subcommittee's conclusions:

> [The draft] provides for a systematic campaign by trained personnel. Lectures on the Soviet nationalities policy and on the issues of antisemitism are to be made a special subject in the curricula of the schools

and colleges. The entry of Jewish workers into industry and the Jewish back-to-the-land movement are to be emphasized.

The campaign against antisemitism is to be introduced into school books, motion pictures, the press, and literature. . . . Public debates on antisemitism are to be held and excursions to the Jewish colonies arranged. A campaign against antisemitism is also to be conducted in the Red Army and in the trade unions.

The highest [party] penalties are provided in the program recommended by the committee for those who have been found guilty of antisemitic practices, and particularly for those who oppose . . . Jewish colonization. . . . The trials of those persons are to be public.[17]

Whether the Central Committee of the CPSU ever discussed the draft, and whether a decision was made as to how antisemitism should be fought, cannot be determined; nothing of this appeared in print, either in 1928 or later. Action against antisemitism continued to be neglected in the party's educational work. With a few exceptions, *Pravda* refrained from printing articles on antisemitism;[18] even periodicals issued by the party's Central Committee for party staffs and active members ignored the matter for the most part. During the most active period of antisemitism (1926–1930), the fortnightly *Bol'shevik*, a periodical of the Central Committee devoted to expounding and popularizing official doctrine, did not publish a single contribution on antisemitism. In the course of five years a single— and rather inadequate—article appeared in *Sputnik Agitatora* [*The Organizer's Vademecum*], another fortnightly publication of the Central Committee.[19]

Programs of Action

It is impossible to suppose that, for the period under review, this inactivity on the part of the leadership was intentional. But the party was often irresolute and lethargic and fought antisemitism only when flagrant instances came to light; its activities seldom rose above the local level.[20] So far as the decisions of higher political bodies are concerned, a somewhat more extensive campaign against antisemitism was waged in the Ukraine and White Russia, where the bulk of the Jewish population was concentrated and where antisemitism had struck deeper root. An ambitious program for the Ukraine was outlined in May 1928 by a special conference convened by the Agitation and Propaganda Division of the Central Committee of the Communist Party of the Ukraine. As it gives a fair idea of the official approach, the document is worth being quoted in full:

The fight against antisemitism must be conducted by means of propaganda, agitation, and education. Party and non-party masses must be made to understand that the fight against antisemitism is part of the fight against the monarchist and bourgeois nationalist groups. It is necessary to familiarize the masses with the Soviet government's policy on nationalities and with the steps taken to create sound economic conditions for the declassed Jewish poor.

Talks on antisemitism must be given in elementary party schools, circuit and local rural schools, evening schools, and in institutions of higher learning; that part of the curriculum of political indoctrination dealing with the Soviet government's policy on nationalities must be enlarged.

The Central Committee of the Komsomol will draw up instructions and prepare materials on antisemitism, and will introduce such materials into the courses of education in internationalism given to Komsomol members and Pioneers.

The cultural department of the All-Ukrainian Trade Union Council, the Political Office of the Ukrainian Regional Army Command, and the Main Office for Political Education are directed to draw up concrete instructions as to how campaigns against antisemitism shall be conducted among workers, soldiers of the Red Army, farmers, and the institutions and organizations supervised by these bodies.

The All-Ukrainian Moving Picture Administration will prepare appropriate moving pictures.

Excursion trips of workers' delegations from Kharkov plants to Jewish colonies have yielded satisfactory results. The workers were able to familiarize themselves with the situation of the Jewish masses and the conditions under which they work. This lesson will have to be continued. Similar delegations from other industrial centers must be organized. It is also desirable that delegations composed of poor peasants be arranged.

Charges of antisemitism brought against party members must be tried publicly.

In addition, it is necessary to provide for public-opinion trials of antisemites and antisemitism.[21]

Late in 1928 antisemitism in White Russia came to a head in the case of the hounding, over a period of months, of a Jewish woman worker by the crew of the Oktyabr' factory in Borisov district. The party leadership was alerted, and the highest organs of the party in White Russia—the Board of the Central Committee and the Presidium of the Central Control Commission—drafted a program of action. In many respects it was similar to the resolution of the Ukrainian conference; but instead of emphasizing long-term educational plans, the White-Russian program concentrated on immediate political action:

The Board of the CC and the Presidium of the CCC . . . set the following tasks before the Communist Party (Bolsheviks) of White Russia for fulfilment:

(a) Strengthen the education of the masses in internationalism and make known to them the class nature of antisemitism and other forms of national dissension, which are attempts on the part of capitalist elements to split the unity of the working class. Every party member, every Komsomol member, every worker active in public life must be made to react vigorously to each and every manifestation of anti-semitism.

(b) Use repressive measures against antisemites carrying on overt antisemitic propaganda.

(c) Pay more attention to the fight against antisemitism in the schools; the education of the students in internationalism must be promoted; antisemitic instructors must be eliminated.

(d) Special attention must be paid to plants located outside of large cities. District committees of the party are directed to investigate the organization of mass activities in industrial plants with a view to their expansion, and to strengthen the leadership of party and trade union organizations in such plants.

The Communist Group in the White-Russian Trade Union Council shall see to it that the cultural mass activities of the unions in industrial plants are expanded.[22]

The results of the program were apparently unsatisfactory. A strong appeal to revive the campaign was issued by the Secretariat of the Central Committee of the White-Russian Communist Party about a year later:

The Secretariat notes that a number of social, trade union, and party organizations display much too lenient an attitude towards manifestations of antisemitism, failing to realize their counterrevolutionary character. . . .

The Secretariat of the CC of the CP(B)WR directs:

(1) The People's Commissariat for Education and the Communist Group in the White-Russian Trade Union Council to foster activities promoting education in internationalism and knowledge of the party's policy on nationalities, and to organize such activities in a more systematic way. With respect to education in internationalism, the People's Commissariat for Education shall within a month's time prepare, and direct the schools to carry out, a program embodying concrete steps and instructions;

(2) The organs of the judiciary to enlarge rather than restrict the scope of the fight against antisemitism, and to prosecute not only individuals [guilty of specific acts], but also those who inspire them;

(3) Party organizations and trade unions to initiate a campaign pointing out the damage caused by a conciliatory attitude towards minor manifestations of antisemitism in daily life, and to combat such manifestations not only in the courts, but also by educational means.[23]

In spite of all resolutions, decisions, and directives, public action against antisemitism was weak and sporadic. Many of these programs never went further than their being written down. Larin in 1929 attacked the influential party organizations for having failed to wage an intensive campaign against antisemitism, and said: "This timid reluctance to 'hammer away at the Jewish question' (in order, it is said, 'not to provoke still more antisemitism') actually results, along this sector of the ideological front, in obscuring the struggle against bourgeois counterrevolutionary sabotage."[24]

Pedagogical Efforts

Official directives and resolutions had least effect on the schools, which in general paid scant heed to the party's appeal to combat prejudice. No attempt was made to treat antisemitism and its implications in school and reference texts. Publications devoted to the philosophy and science of education ignored the subject entirely. Thus, an encyclopedia of education issued at the very time when antisemitism became a major phenomenon in Soviet life, *Pedagogicheskaya Entsiklopediya* (vols. 1–3, Moscow, 1927–1929), neither mentions antisemitism nor considers the means afforded by the schools to eradicate it, not even in sections describing the role, in education, of the Communist youth and children's organizations.

No noticeable effort was made to combat prejudice in the works of fiction of the time, or in theatrical or screen productions.[25] Hardly anything is known about the activities of Red Army political and educational officers in combating antisemitism in the ranks.

The official rejection of antisemitism by the party also failed to influence the daily practice of the Communist youth organizations. It is true that *Komsomol'skaya Pravda*, daily newspaper of the Communist Youth Association, was more eager to expose and attack antisemitic practices than was its party counterpart or any other Soviet publication; but local Komsomol organizations in most cases did nothing, even when acts of violence and persecution occurred against their Jewish members. At a conference of the Komsomol in 1929, Rakhmanov, a secretary of its Central Committee, said:

> What arrangements do we make to combat antisemitism within the Association? How do we fight the evil? At best our Komsomol cells in this or that plant merely pass resolutions declaring that antisemitism must be fought; at worst, the cell tolerates its manifestations; and at the very worst, Komsomol members are themselves guilty of antisemitism and take part in beating up and abusing working people who happen to be Jews. . . .
>
> We not only have antisemites who openly talk and make speeches, we also have—and this is the most dangerous thing in our situation—antisemites in disguise who make use of all sorts of veiled expressions, but who in reality are the most vicious, the vilest antisemites. To fight these disguised antisemites, of whom unfortunately there are many in the ranks of the Komsomol, is a very difficult but necessary task of the Association. . . .

I regret to say that there are even activists of the Association among these disguised antisemites. When told to their faces that they are antisemites, they take offense, threaten to appeal to the Control Commission, brag about their party seniority, etc. But it is a fact, Comrades —there are antisemites among our active members. How do they display their antisemitism? They tell jokes about the Jews, repeat what they claim others said when it is their own opinions which they are voicing. . . .

And another thing. I think it's wrong to assume, as some do in our Association, that it is for the Jews themselves to fight antisemitism. That's not so! The job of fighting antisemitism is the job of our whole Association.[26]

The reports of incidents that continued to come into the editorial offices of *Komsomol'skaya Pravda* showed that the antisemitic mood in the rank and file remained unchanged. Conditions in the Pioneer groups were no better and sometimes worse.[27]

Antisemitism did not fail to infect the trade unions. In the summer of 1929 the Secretariat of the All-Union Central Trade Union Council issued a statement that said: "A great number of revolting antisemitic acts lately taking place in the plants attest to a weak and inadequate education in internationalism and politics in general, and to deficient instruction in the Soviet government's policy on nationalities and the fight against antisemitism in particular." The trade union statement demanded a "vigorous fight against antisemitism, a phenomenon that springs from counterrevolutionary roots," and urged all union bodies to organize meetings and lectures, to publish pamphlets, and to expose publicly all instances of antisemitism. The statement said it was "intolerable" that "persons implicated in antisemitism or persons displaying an indifferent or passive attitude" should "continue to take part in trade union or cultural and educational activities."[28] But apparently they did so continue.

Official documents of this kind were identical in pattern. Their issuance from time to time was almost a routine procedure [29] and they could hardly influence deep-seated passions. Still, constant iteration that the toleration of antisemitism was "counterrevolutionary" could not fail to have a result, limited though it may have been. It restrained the flagrant dissemination of antisemitism and in the early 1930's helped to arrest the epidemic.

Of all the campaigns planned, only two were actually carried out on a significant scale—the publication of books and pamphlets; and the organization of workers' trips to Jewish colonies. Large numbers of publications were issued by government printing houses between 1926 and 1930. This list is impressive;[30] no attempt, however, was ever made to measure and evaluate their effect. Visits to Jewish settlements, though at first effective, in the end proved a failure, for reasons that require a closer examination.

An Experiment in Intergroup Relations

The notion of urban workers' seeing at first hand the Jewish work of rehabilitation and reconstruction in agricultural colonies came from the workers of a Kharkov plant who suggested it early in 1928. Delegates from the plant made a trip to a Jewish farm colony, were impressed by what they saw, and returned vowing to become active fighters against anti-semitism. Their reports made a deep impression on their fellow workers. The experiment, acclaimed by the press and commended by the authorities, was soon emulated by a number of organizations in Kharkov and other Ukrainian cities, as well as in other republics. Excursion trips to Jewish colonies were a favorite means of recreation and education in 1929.[31]

As a rule, visiting delegations were composed of the employees of individual plants, offices, workshops, etc.; and in a few instances of students and soldiers. The following is an instruction sheet issued to parties of Moscow industrial and office workers chosen to visit Jewish settlements in the Ukraine, the Crimea, and White Russia in the summer of 1929:

You are instructed:

(1) To familiarize yourself in detail with the condition of Jewish agricultural settlements, and especially with the land they have been allotted and how they utilize it. You are to find out about:

(a) How Jewish farmers live and work; the kind of establishments and the amount of acreage they have, the progress of harvesting, preparations for sowing; what is being done to carry out Soviet Congress decisions calling for a 35 percent increase in crop yield?

(b) What is the accepted form of enterprise in the colony, collective or individual; how many *kolkhozes,* and of what size; whether tractors and agricultural implements are used; what fertilizer is applied to the soil; the percentage of those in cooperatives, and how the cooperatives function; whether there are social organizations, and how they work; whether farmers hire help; whether there is a tendency to go back to the city; religious attitudes of Jewish settlers; whether there is a cell of the party, of the Komsomol; percentage of party members.

(c) What is the relationship between Jewish farmers and farmers of other nationalities around them?

(d) How are the cultural and commercial needs of the Jewish agricultural masses met?

(e) How do Jewish farmers participate in Soviet construction work?

(f) What steps are being taken to prevent the growth of *kulak* elements in the villages?

(g) What difficulties are encountered in fitting in newly arrived

Jewish settlers without agricultural experience, and how the difficulties are overcome?

(h) Situation of the younger generation, and what is being done in the way of educational opportunities for them?

(2) On behalf of the men and women workers and salary earners of Red Moscow's largest plants and offices you are asked to give our greetings to Jewish farmers, and to assure them that Moscow's working people undertake to aid and assist the Soviet government in every way to help the Jewish poor find productive employment either in agriculture or in industrial plants.

(3) You are to give an accounting to the Jewish agricultural masses, telling them about our gigantic Five-Year Plan and about how we carry out in practice socialist competition in our industrial plants.

(4) You are to tell the Jewish farmers that we conduct a relentless fight against antisemitism, for we know that antisemitism in all its mani-〔e〕stations plays into the hands of the enemies of the Soviet government and of the working people, and that dissension among our nationalities, which we inherited from Tsarist rule, cannot be overcome except by the friendly cooperation of the working masses of all peoples of the Soviet Union.

(5) Upon your return from the Jewish settlements and villages it is your duty to report to plant meetings, conventions of delegates, and other meetings, conferences, and gatherings, on what you saw and learned.

(6) Upon your return from the Jewish settlements it is your duty to utilize our proletarian press—plant bulletin board papers as well as general Soviet, trade union, and party publications—to acquaint working men and women with what you saw and heard in those settlements where, under the guidance of the Soviet government, a new life it being built despite all difficulties and hardships.[32]

This instruction sheet, a fairly typical one, though showing the ambitious aims assigned to the visits, also shows their limitations. The visiting workers could observe Jewsh farmers at work, could, by meeting them in the flesh, find out that the "greedy Jew" was just another hard-working farmer, and could learn a great deal about their lives and hopes and dreams; back in the plants and offices their reports might stir the imagination of the other workers and counteract antisemitic rumors and fictions. But the original core of spontaneous and sympathetic curiosity was overlaid by bureaucratic organization and the clichés of propaganda. What had been unpretentious visits by unpretentious working people in quest of knowledge were turned into "campaigns" that shared the fate of other official campaigns against antisemitism. All real feeling perforce withered in the blast of instructions to praise the "gigantic" achievements of Soviet industry to the Jewish farmers, and the "new life" of the Jewish settlements to the urban workers. In the bear's hug of the bureaucracy these excursions, which had been astonishingly popular for a few months in 1929, were soon stifled.

NOTES

1. Larin mistakenly gave the date of publication of the order as *June* 27, 1918 (*op. cit.*, pp. 8 and 278), and others have perpetuated this error.

2. Anatolii V. Lunacharskii, *Ob antisemitizme* [*On Antisemitism*], Gosizdat, Moscow–Leningrad, 1929, p. 38; cf. S. M. Dimanshtein, "Vvedeniye" ["Introduction"], in N. Lenin, *O yevreiskom voprose* [*On the Jewish Question*], Moscow, 1924, p. 15, and also S. M. Dimanshtein, ed., *Idn in FSSR. Zamlbukh*, Moscow, 1935, p. 17.

3. *Ugolovnyi Kodeks RSFSR* [*Criminal Code of the Russian SFSR*], issued by the People's Commissariat for Justice, Moscow, 1922, sec. 83.

4. *Sobraniye Zakonov i Rasporyazhenii Pravitel'stva SSSR* [*Collection of Laws and Government Ordinances of the USSR*], 1927, no. 12.

5. *Ugolovnyi Kodeks RSFSR* [*Criminal Code of the Russian SFSR*], issued by the People's Commissariat for Justice, Moscow, 1938, p. 148.

6. I. Zil'berman, "Sud v bor'be s antisemitizmom" ["The Courts in the Fight against Antisemitism"], in *Yezhenedel'nik Sovetskoi Yustitsii*, weekly publication of the People's Commissariat for Justice, 1929, no. 4, pp. 83–85.

7. Larin, *op. cit.*, pp. 277f.

8. *XVIyi Syezd VKP(B). Stenograficheskii otchet* [*Sixteenth Convention of the Communist Party of the Soviet Union (Bolsheviks). Stenographic Transcript of Proceedings*], Moscow–Leningrad, 1931, p. 716.

9. *Ibid,.* pp. 140f.

10. *Ibid.,* p. 740.

11. *Ibid.,* p. 672.

12. General rules governing the prosecution of offenses involving great-power chauvinism were laid down by the Supreme Court of the Russian SFSR on April 16, 1931 (see *Ugolovnyi Kodeks RSFSR* [1938], pp. 148f), and by a decision of the RSFSR People's Commissariat for Justice "on the fight of the judiciary against great-power and local chauvinism," issued on December 31, 1931 and printed in *Sbornik tsirkulyarov i razyasenii N. K. Yustitsii RSFSR, deistvuyushchikh na 1 maya 1934 goda* [*Collection of Directives and Interpretative Rulings of the RSFSR People's Commissariat for Justice in Force on May 1, 1934*], Moscow, 1934, pp. 175ff.

13. *Izvestiya*, April 28, 1918.

14. Even the phonograph record of Lenin's speech against Jew-baiting, recorded on March 31, 1919 and so often pointed to by pro-Soviet writers outside the Soviet Union, remained largely unknown to the Soviet public until the mid-1920's. The speech appeared in print after Lenin's death in the Young Communists' *Molodaya Gvardiya*, (February–March 1924, pp. 165f.), but was not included in the first Russian edition of Lenin's Works, of which vol. XVI, containing the 1919 speeches and writings, was issued in 1925; it was later inserted in the second edition: N. Lenin (V. I. Ul'yanov), *Sochineniya*, 2d ed., vol. XXIV, Moscow, 1932, p. 203.

15. M. Ryutin, "*Antisemitizm i partiinaya rabota*" [Antisemitism and Party Activities"], in *Pravda*, August 13, 1926.

16. *Pravda*, May 5, 1928. The release was also carried by OZET's Russian-language fortnightly *Tribuna*, 1928, no. 9, p. 25.

17. *The Jewish Daily Bulletin*, May 17, 1928. Neither *Pravda* nor the OZET's *Tribuna* published the subcommittee's proposals.

18. In addition to Ryutin's article (see n. 15 above), this writer was able to discover only one other in *Pravda* for the entire period of 1926 to 1930—Ye. Preobrazhenskii, "Ob antisemitizme" ["On Antisemitism"] (March 17, 1927)—and one editorial, the above-mentioned one of February 19, 1929. Even if allowance is made for one or another item overlooked, the five-year total can hardly be called impressive.

19. "Natsional'naya politika sovetskoi vlasti i antisemitizm" ["Nationality Policies of the Soviet Government and Antisemitism"], in *Sputnik Agitatora*, 1926, no. 17, pp. 44–57. In addition, there were two book notes on Mikhail Gorev's *Protiv antisemitov*, and one article on a related issue by Yurii M. Larin, "Zachem pereselyayut yevreyev na zemlyu?" ["What Is the Purpose of Settling Jews on the Land?"], 1927, no. 2, pp. 44–66.

20. Instances of local action were reported from different provinces—Tver', Leningrad, Stalingrad, Astrakhan, Poltava. Cf. *Tribuna*, 1928, no. 12, p. 23; no. 16, p. 25; 1929, no. 9, pp. 9f.

21. *Tribuna*, 1928, no. 9, p. 25.

22. *Tribuna*, 1929, no. 1, pp. 32f.

23. *Ibid.*, no. 24, p. 27.

24. *Op. cit.*, p. 280.

25. A comprehensive survey of antisemitism in Soviet literature and drama was made by Leonid Radishchev, *Yad. Ob antisemitizme nashikh dnei [Poison. On Antisemitism in Our Day]*, Priboi publications, Leningrad, 1930

26. *Tribuna*, 1929, no. 5, pp. 3f.

27. See the survey of antisemitism among the Pioneers by I. Bobryshin, "Antisemitizm sredi molodezhi" ["Antisemitism among the Youth], in *Molodaya Gvardiya*, periodical issued by the Central Committee of Komsomol, Februry 1928, p. 159.

28. *Tribuna*, 1929, no. 14, p. 12.

29. Of the many official statements issued in the late 1920's, only one stands out as imaginative and effective: an address issued by the panel on antisemitism of the 1929 All-Union Jamboree of Pioneers. Cf. *Tribuna*, 1929, no. 17, p. 18.

30. The following is a fairly complete catalogue of Soviet writings against antisemitism published in 1926–1930:

M. Ya. Aleksandrov, *Klassovyi vrag v maske. O natsionalizme i antisemitizme [The Class Enemy Masked. On Nationalism and Antisemitism]*, 104 pp., Gosizdat, Moscow–Leningrad, 1929.

M. Ya. Aleksandrov, *Otkuda beretsya vrazhda k yevreyam i komu ona vygodna? [Hatred of Jews—Where Does It Come From?—Whom Does It Benefit?]*, 48 pp., Gosizdat, Moscow–Leningrad, 1929.

G. Alekseyev, ed., *Protiv antisemitizma, Sbornik [Against Antisemitism, A Symposium]*, 240 pp. Zhisn' i Znaniye pub., Moscow, 1930.

S. K. Bezborodov, *Signaly. Ob antisemitizme [Signals. On Antisemitism]*, 59 pp Krasnaya Gazeta pub., Leningrad, 1929.

Yefim S. Dobin, *Pravda o yevreyakh [The Truth about Jews]*, 45 pp., Krasnaya Gazeta pub., Leningrad, 1928.

V. Glebov, *Sovremennyi antisemitizm i bor'ba s nim [Contemporary Antisemitism and the Fight Against It]*, 56 pp., Molodaya Gvardiya pub., Leningrad, 1927.

Mikhail Gorev, *Protiv antisemitov. Ocherki i zarisovki [Against the Antisemites. Stories and Sketches]*, 183 pp., Gosizdat, Moscow–Leningrad, 1928.

Ye. Kochetkov, *Vragi li nam yevrei? [Are the Jews Our Enemies?]*, 20 pp., Moskovskii Rabochii pub., Moscow–Leningrad, 1927.

Yurii Larin, *Yevrei i antisemitizm v SSSR [Jews and Antisemitism in the USSR]*, 311 pp., Gosizdat, Moscow–Leningrad, 1929.

G. Ledat, *Antisemitizm i antisemity [Antisemitism and Antisemites]*, 72 pp. Priboi pub., Leningrad, 1929.

S. G. Lozinskii, *Sotsial'nyye korni antisemitizma v sredniye veka i v novoye vremya [Social Roots of Antisemitism in the Middle Ages and in Modern Times]*, 205 pp., Ateist pub., Moscow, 1929.

Anatolii Lunacharskii, *Ob antisemitizme [On Antisemitism]*, 48 pp., Gosizdat, Moscow–Leningrad, 1929.

L. Lyadov, *O vrazhde k yevreyam [On Hatred of Jews]*, 40 pp., Moskovskii Rabochii pub., Moscow–Leningrad, 1927.

M. Yu. Mal'tsev, *Sud nad antisemitizmom [Antisemitism on Trial]*, 36 pp., Priboi pub., Leningrad, 1928.

Leonid Radishchev, *Stupeni. Protiv antisemitizma* [*Steps. Against Antisemitism*], 40 pp., Molodaya Gvardiya pub., Moscow—Leningrad, 1929.

Leonid Radishchev, *Yad. Ob antisemitizme nashikh dnei* [*Poison. On Antisemitism in our Day*], 125 pp., Priboi pub., Leningrad, 1930.

Yurii Sandomirskii, *Puti antisemitizma v Rossii* [*Avenues of Antisemitism in Russia*], 50 pp., Gosizdat, Moscow—Leningrad, 1928.

Nikolai Semashko, *Kto i pochemu travit yevreyev?* [*Who Persecutes Jews? Why?*], 30 pp., Gosizdat, Moscow—Leningrad, 1926.

G. L. Zhigalin, *Proklyatoye naslediye. Ob antisemitizme* [*Accursed Heritage. On Antisemitism*], 104 pp., Molodaya Gvardiya pub., Moscow—Leningrad, 1927.

[Anonymous] *Ob Antisemitizme* [*On Antisemitism*], 30 pp., issued by the Moscow Committee of the CPSU, Moscow—Leningrad, 1929.

[Anonymous] *Na bor'bu s antisemitizmom. Materialy dlya agitatorov i besedchikov* [*Let's Fight Antisemitism. Materials for Propagandists and Leaders of Discussions*], 30 pp., issued by the Leningrad Provincial Committee of the CPSU, Leningrad, 1929.

[Anonymous] *Komsomol protiv antisemitizma* [*Komsomol against Antisemitism*], 24 pp., Moskovskii Rabochii pub., Moscow, 1929.

[Anonymous] *Ob antisemitizme. Metodischeskoye posobiye dlya dokladchikov i gruppovykh agitatorov* [*On Antisemitism. Handbook for Speakers and Group Propagandists*], 30 pp., Moskovskii Rabochii pub., Moscow—Leningrad, 1929.

31. See the reports in *Tribuna*, 1929, no. 9, p. 27; no. 10, p. 25; no. 11, pp. 3f. and 20ff.; no. 12, p. 4; no. 14, pp. 16, 21; no. 16, pp. 10–19; no. 18, p. 22–23, pp. 26f.

32. *Tribuna*, 1929, no. 14, p. 21. The instruction sheet was signed by the works council officers of several dozen plants and offices.

CHAPTER IV

Decline of the Old and Rise of the New Antisemitism

The Antisemitic Tide Recedes

From the early 1930's on overt manifestations of antisemitism began to disappear. In the first months of 1930 the Soviet press still carried many reports of antisemitic incidents,[1] but as time went by they became less and less frequent. The cessation of press reports of antisemitic incidents was not simply owing to a government order, nor did it on the other hand imply that antisemitism had suddenly disappeared without a trace. But the growth of nationalism, and particularly of "Great-Russian chauvinism," in the 1930's, as has already been said, caused chauvinism in general, rather than antisemitism in particular, to come under official attack. The government apparently chose to minimize the campaign against antisemitism so as to discourage any notion that fighting chauvinism amounted to fighting for Jews. Had antisemitism continued to play the prominent role it had played in Soviet life in the previous half-decade, however, it would surely have had a place, however subordinate, in the government's denunciations of nationalist arrogance.

Inside the Soviet Union in the 1930's the problem of antisemitism was passed over in silence. A few examples will suffice. No reference to antisemitism was made by Stalin at the Sixteenth Convention of the CPSU in 1930, when he spoke on the fight against "great-power and local chauvinism," his example being followed by the delegates who took part in the discussion of his report. This same silence prevailed at the Ninth Convention of the Komsomol in January 1931. Its lengthy resolution "on the building of national cultures in the Soviet Union and the tasks of the All-Union Leninist Communist Youth Association"[2] said nothing about either antisemitism or the Jews.

At the same time a strong statement by Stalin on the subject of antisemitism was quoted by newspapers all over the world in January 1931.[3] In replying to a question from the Jewish Telegraphic Agency, Stalin had said:

> National and racial chauvinism is a survival of the barbarous practices of the cannibalistic period. Antisemitism serves the exploiters as a lightning rod to protect capitalism from the attack of the working people, a wrong path to divert the latter from the right one and lead

them into a jungle. As consistent internationalists, Communists there-fore cannot be but irreconcilable and sworn enemies of antisemitism. Antisemitism, a phenomenon profoundly hostile to the Soviet regime, is sternly repressed in the USSR. Under the laws of the USSR active antisemites are subject to capital punishment.[4]

This statement (which, as we know, overrated the efficacy of the legal repression of antisemitism) was not made public in the Soviet Union until late in 1936,[5] a delay of almost six years. At the time it had apparently not been deemed expedient to draw the attention of the Soviet public to the anti-Jewish variety of chauvinism.

Antisemitism in the late 1920's had spread among groups dispossessed by the revolution, who incited the new industrial proletariat against the "Jewish intruder." With unemployment still widespread, "the Jew," traditionally viewed as a non-worker, was accused of ousting the "genuine" worker and monopolizing the better jobs.

When the Five-Year Plan policy created millions of new jobs, recrimi-nations against Jewish "usurpers" became less frequent and lost their emotional meaning. How swiftly employment increased is apparent from the statistics in Table VII.

TABLE VII

EMPLOYED WAGE AND SALARY EARNERS, ALL SPHERES OF ECONOMIC ACTIVITY [6]

Year	Total Wage and Salary Earners
1929	12,168,000
1930	14,531,000
1931	18,990,000
1932	22,943,000

In three years the number of employed increased by nearly 11 million, or 88 percent. Jobs stood open for anyone who wished to work. The rapid expansion of industrial production, and the emphasis placed by the gov-ernment on the spectacular performances of "shock workers" and on speed-up, piecework records, etc., multiplied the chances for development of young and skilful workers, who could now aspire to the highest wages and positions. Changes in the economy were paralleled by a conspicuous change in the nation's social pattern. In the 1920's Jews had been numer-ous among the Nepmen; Jews also had been conspicuous in small trade as merchants, peddlers, and middlemen. Although the latter far outnum-bered the former and were in general humble people, in the eyes of many urban workers, university students, and especially Young Communists brought up on the simplistic party slogans of class struggle "the Jew" was synonymous with the big "speculator" and NEP tycoon. But as the Five-Year Plans came to triumph, the ground was cut from under the feet of the Nepmen; quite a number of them were "liquidated," and the entire social group disappeared from the Soviet scene. Private trade, though not abolished, lost some of its bad odor, not only because of the disappearance of the profiteering Nepmen, but also because government controls and universal planning severely restricted the scope of speculation. One of the more obvious stimuli to popular antisemitism had ceased to exist.

Another factor also helped greatly to check the spread of antisemitism among industrial workers. Mass recruitment of workers into industrial building and construction radically changed the composition of the labor force and modified the psychological climate inside and outside the plants. Before industrialization many minority nationalities had been scantily represented in the ranks of industrial labor, even in those regions where they made up a large part of the population. But then these predominantly rural or even nomadic peoples were drawn in large numbers into the industrial orbit. The proportion of minority nationals among industrial workers, especially at the new industrial and construction sites, rose notably within a few years. A few examples will illustrate this change.

In Kazakhstan, where a considerable part of the population a short time before had been nomadic herdsmen and where even now nomadic tribes exist, the total number of industrial workers on January 1, 1927 was 12,353; of these, 2,485 were of Kazakh nationality. By February 1, 1933, industrial workers in Kazakhstan totaled 75,972, an increase of more than 500 percent; the number of Kazakh workers had increased elevenfold to 27,642, the proportion of Kazakh workers among those employed in Kazakhstan's plants rising from 20.1 to 36.5 percent. This trend was even more marked in the building trades, where total employment rose from 850 to 96,530, and the number of Kazakh workers from 69 to 36,005; the proportion of Kazakh among Kazakhstan's building workers increased from 8.1 to 37.3 percent.[7] Much the same happened with other minority groups, as evidenced by a comparison of the figures of the census of December 1926 with those of a special survey for August 1, 1934. Uzbeks rose from 26.0 to 37.2 percent of all wage and salary earners in the Uzbek SSR; Tatars from 22.1 to 33.6 percent in the Tatar Autonomous Republic; Chuvash from 13.7 to 24.1 percent in the Chuvash Autonomous Republic. The increase in the number of native building workers in these regions was even more rapid.[8]

Increased industrial employment of minority nationals was accompanied by expanding migration. In many places workers of differing national and cultural backgrounds worked side by side. Frictions were numerous, often arising from the hostile attitude of the larger nationalities, Russians and Ukrainians for the most part; this was the "great-power chauvinism" which so exercised the Soviet leadership in the 1930's. Antisemitism was lost to sight in the upsurge of aggression against members of other ethnic groups, who were often far more remote, culturally, from the Russians and Ukrainians than the Jews, and less familiar with Russian or Ukrainian and White Russian. To a degree, "European" was pitted against "Oriental" or "Asiatic."

A survey of court proceedings against chauvinism in the Lower Volga Region, analyzed in the periodical of the People's Commissariat for Justice in 1932,[9] showed that of those convicted, 73 percent had been working for a wage less than two years.[10] First among the victims of chauvinist violence and abuse were Kalmucks and Kazakh (chiefly working in fisheries), then Jews (in the cities), then Tatars, and in isolated instances Volga Germans; most of the victims were "Orientals." Of the offenses, 47 percent had been committed on construction projects and in *sovkhozes* (government farms), 34 percent in fisheries, 6 percent in other places of work, 4 percent in schools, and 9 percent in places "not connected with production" (housing developments, on the street, or in the market place). While antisemitism still bulked large in the survey of trials in the Lower Volga, acts of anti-Jewish violence were no longer mentioned in other reports of the prosecution of chauvinist crimes, which were often more violent than those tried in the Lower Volga courts.[11] Xenophobic aggression had been deflected into other channels.

The antisemitic tide might not have receded as it did had not the abruptness, speed, and ruthlessness of industrialization and collectivization disrupted the habitual modes of thinking, feeling, and reacting, replacing them with new ones. In the general unsettlement antisemitism failed to perform its habitual psychological function as an outlet for accumulated resentments. This, of course, did not spell the end of antisemitism in Soviet society. The older antisemitism of the previous decade was replacd by a new when the social relationships introduced by industrialization and collectivization grew more stable and new rivalries and conflicts were engendered.

Antisemitism at Its Lowest Point

The curve of antisemitism dropped to its lowest point in the middle of the 1930's. Antisemitic feeling still was present in a subdued form, occasionally breaking out in individual acts of aggression,[12] but it was no longer of great importance and did not attract the interest of official opinion. Unexpectedly, official pronouncements on the subject reappeared in 1935 and 1936 and were given considerable publicity. This change was owing to considerations both of foreign and domestic policy.

Soviet relations with Nazi Germany were strained; in opposing anti-semitism the Soviet government was seeking to enhance its moral authority in world affairs. Internal developments, however, were decisive. In the mid-1930's Bolshevik policy experienced a profound crisis. Conflicting developments came to a head and it was forced to choose between relaxing the dictatorial rule and gradually developing some democratic forms of government and social organization, or consolidating the dictatorship and building a fully totalitarian system stripped of the libertarian, democratic, and Utopian traditions of the early days of the revolution, traditions that time and again had threatened the party machine's absolute rule.[13]

There were still shifts and vacillations in 1935 and 1936. But in 1937 the die was irrevocably cast for totalitarianism. So long, however, as the decision had not been finally taken, the prospect of a democratic future seemed to loom on the Soviet horizon.

In 1936 the new Stalin Constitution was promulgated; it promised universal and equal suffrage and the introduction of the secret ballot, all of which hitherto had been denounced as counterrevolutionary and treasonable. Many began to hope that the grip of the party and bureaucracy might yet be relaxed and a measure of freedom be introduced. In this atmosphere of hope and expectation antisemitism was bound to decline; to denounce it accorded with the prevailing "democratic" mood of the Soviet leadership. Now for the first time the aforementioned reply by Stalin to the Jewish Telegraphic Agency was communicated to the Soviet public in the limelight of publicity. Stalin's statement was read by Vyacheslav M. Molotov, then chairman of the Council of People's Commissars of the Soviet Union, in the course of his speech on the draft of the new constitution at the Eighth Soviet Congress in November 1936. Molotov contrasted Stalin's unequivocal rejection of antisemitism with the "cannibalism" of the Nazis, and then went on to say:

> Whatever may be said by presentday cannibals in the ranks of the fascist antisemites, our fraternal feeling towards the Jewish people springs from the fact that it gave birth to the creator of genius of the ideas of the communist liberation of mankind, Karl Marx, who gained scientific mastery over the supreme achievements of German as well as of other cultures; that the Jewish people along with the most advanced nations produced a great number of outstanding men of science, technology, and art; that it gave many heroes to the revolutionary struggle against the oppressors of the working people; and that in our country it produced and continues to produce more and more fine and gifted leaders and organizers in every sphere of endeavor advancing and defending the cause of socialism. All this determines our attitude to antisemitism and antisemitic bestiality wherever they may arise. . . .[14]

This profession was unusually emphatic, though no more perspicacious in dealing with the antisemitic mentality than all such tributes to "Jewish achievements." But coming from one of the highest figures in the land, it was a firmer pledge to expose antisemitism to public censure than any that had been made in the first half of the decade. This firmness, however, did not last. The changing political situation soon ushered in a different policy.

The Turning Point: the Great Purge

In retrospect, the years 1936–38 seem to be the decisive ones in the emergence of the new social structure of the Soviet Union. Where one party rules, the party itself is inevitably the arena in which opposing social and economic forces clash.

The first big trial of Communist oppositionists (Zinov'yev and others) was staged in August 1936. Old Communist leaders who had been entrusted with high office in party and government were branded as "enemies of the people," traitors, and spies. However, what the choice in favor of totalitarianism implied did not become manifest at once, especially since the new constitution adopted in December 1936 fostered illusions as to the prospects of a turn towards democratization. The ruling clique itself seemed hesitant. But this appearance of uncertainty ended in 1937 when party and government were purged to a degree and with a ferocity exceeding all precedent.[15] In the course of the purge the old Communist Party was destroyed and supplanted by a new one, which retained the name but modified everything else—social basis, ideology, and social and political orientation.

This merciless cleansing ensured the perfect docility of the apparatus as an instrument of social and political domination.[16] That generation of active Communists which had personified the revolutionary and internationalist tradition of the Communist Party was denounced and destroyed. Internationalism, dear to the oppositionists, was stigmatized as the cloak of traitors spying for foreign military intelligence. Russian nationalism, previously censured as Great-Russian chauvinism, seemed vindicated by the government's violent attack on treacherous internationalists. Indirectly and occasionally even directly encouraged from above, it spread rapidly in the Communist Party and in the upper class of Soviet society generally.

Jews in particular were an easy target for attack. The purge struck first of all at the "Old Guard," the surviving revolutionary elite of the old heroic days. The proportion of Jews among these was much higher than in the party as a whole, and especially in the party's younger generation. Many of the most outstanding old Communist leaders castigated at the Moscow Trials as traitors, spies, and assassins had been Jews— Trotskii, Zinov'yev, Kamenev, Radek, and others. Treason, espionage, and other abject crimes were associated in the Soviet public's mind with the names of Jewish leaders who for a while had contrived to rule the Soviet state.[17] The politically uneducated and inexperienced sighed with relief to know that the nation had been cleansed in the nick of time of the poison of "Jewish internationalism."

The reputation of the Jewish minority as a whole suffered noticeably from the effects of the trials. In addition, the purge directly affected a large number of Jewish party people, and especially those to whom the party had entrusted the supervision of Jewish affairs. An entire generation of Jewish political leaders was liquidated, or else vanished from sight. Among them, to mention only a few, were such well-known men as Semen M. Dimanshtein; Professor Liberberg, formerly head of the Jewish Section of the Ukrainian Academy of Sciences, later chairman of the Provincial Executive Committee of the Jewish Autonomous Province (Birobidzhan); Khavkin, secretary of the Birobidzhan Provincial Committee of the CPSU; his successor, Yankel Frenkel; Moisei Litvakov (who died in prison), the editor of *Emes;* several former Bund leaders who, after joining the Communist Party in the early 1920's, had held high positions on the Central Board of Jewish Sections, in KOMZET, OZET, and other Jewish Soviet institutions, among whom were Rakhmiel (Aron I. Vainshtein), Ester (Maria Ya. Frumkina), Aleksandr Chemeriskii, Abram N. Merezhin, G. Lipets-Petrovskii; and scores of others.[18] All were exposed to public scorn and indignation as "enemies of the people" and "traitors."

The Jewish minority, it is true, was not the only one to suffer the decapitation of its political and cultural leadership. The purge destroyed the leaders of all minority nationalities. But in the case of the Jews the destruction went farther. The Great Purge virtually terminated the organized life of the Jewish group as a recognized cultural and ethnic minority.

Apart from the purges, the late 1930's witnessed something of a revival of antisemitism in consequence of the upsurge of nationalist feeling which the government condoned. When the purge exposed Jewish Communist leaders as venal spies; when the entire leadership of Jewish organizations was annihilated; when Jewish institutions, publications, schools, etc. were closed down; then certainly antisemites high and low must have felt encouraged. The recrudescence of antisemitic feeling failed to lead to violent outbreaks of the kind that had taken place in the 1920's, but it was more tenacious and reflected first of all the desire of various sections of the bureaucracy to eliminate Jews from positions of influence and to reduce the proportion of Jews in occupations reserved for the elite.

Antisemitism after the purges, to be sure, was not openly condoned, but neither was it publicly censured. Officially, it did not exist. But such information as we have on the composition of the Soviet elite, indicates a tacit ousting of Jews from many spheres of Soviet life. This might never have gone beyond the stealthy removal of Jewish individuals from influential positions if the purges had not swept away the entire old bureaucracy, replacing it with a new bureaucratic caste based upon a new ideology and hostile to elements likely to disrupt its homogeneity.

Discrimination Against Jews

In Tsarist Russia exclusion of Jews from the government service had been traditional and well-nigh absolute. The tradition was breached but not destroyed by the revolution. Although never as high as antisemites asserted, the percentage of government officials who were Jews increased notably in the course of the first twenty years of Soviet rule. Yet even during that period, certain branches of the government service had been virtually closed to Jews. The railroads are a case in point. As late as 1930 a JTA dispatch from Moscow (June 18, 1930) said:

> Jewish workers are not accepted on the Soviet railways, the Kharkov *Shtern* complains, emphasizing that despite a resolution of the Central Committee of the Communist Party of the Ukraine that Jewish youth be absorbed into the railways system, only 1,581 Jews are employed in the railways out of a total of 181,000 workers.
>
> The *Shtern* points out that there is no prospect of an increase in this insignificant percentage in view of the attitude of local leaders.[19]

Early in 1932 the OZET's *Tribuna* published illuminating information on the employment of Jews by the railroad in the district of Gomel (White Russia). Of 4,314 manual workers employed in all railroad services, including repair shops, only 239, or 5.5 percent, were Jews, and among non-manual workers the percentage of Jews was still lower— 21 out of 1,088, or less than 2 percent. And this in a district with a particularly large Jewish population! In railroad training courses in the district, 811 workers acquired higher skills in 1931; of these, only 10, or just 1.2 percent, were Jews. Only in special railroad schools was the percentage of Jewish students higher—7.2 percent in engineering schools, and 19 percent in schools for the training of skilled railroad workers; but even this was below the percentage of the district's total population that was Jewish. Discrimination against Jews by the administration of the railroads was ascribed by the *Tribuna* to definite antisemitic bias.[20]

In the late 1930's discriminatory attitudes to the employment of Jews became more marked and were no longer confined to individual occupations or administrative departments. In the large cities, where most of the Jewish intellectuals and non-manual workers lived, discrimination began to influence promotions and appointments, especially in the executive, professional, and semiprofessional spheres. The tales of Jewish domination of the professions and government jobs spread anew and, going uncontradicted by the press and the Communist leadership, led to further stealthy, and sometimes open, discriminatory treatment of Jewish employees and jobseekers.

In what numbers did the Jews actually figure in the class of Soviet "intelligentsia," i.e., in the professional and semiprofessional occupations? Complete statistics on Jews are lacking for several occupations; though this makes an exact comparison impossible, a rough statistical picture can be seen in Table VIII.

TABLE VIII

JEWS AMONG USSR PROFESSIONAL AND SEMIPROFESSIONAL WORKERS, JANUARY 1937 [21]

Occupational Group	Total Number	Thereof Jews	
		Number	Percent
Managers of industrial and commercial establishments, government agencies and institutions, plant departments, *sovkhozes, kolkhozes*, etc.	1,751,000	?	?
Graduate engineers, technologists, architects (other than plant and department managers)	250,000	25,000	10.0
Semiprofessional engineering and technical personnel	810,000	60,000	7.4
Agronomists	80,000	1,000	1.25
Agricultural technicians (surveyors, farm technicians, animal breeders, etc.)	96,000	1,000	1.1
Scholars (university teachers, research specialists)	80,000	7,000	8.8
Teachers (other than in universities)	969,000	46,000	4.7
Information, cultural institutions (newspapermen, librarians, professional personnel of cultural institutions)	297,000	30,000	10.0
Art, theater, etc.	159,000	17,000	10.7
Physicians	132,000	21,000	15.9
Semiprofessional medical personnel (nurses, etc.)	382,000	31,000	8.1
Economists, statisticians	822,000	?	?
Accountants, bookkeepers	1,617,000	125,000	7.7
Judges, prosecutors, defense counsel	46,000	?	?
University students	550,000	?	?
Others (incl. "military intelligentsia")	1,550,000	?	?
Grand Total	9,591,000	?	?
Thereof: 11 groups with data on Jews	4,872,000	364,000	7.5

Of those groups of the intelligentsia for which exact data are available, Jews constituted on the average 7.5 percent. At first glance this would seem to be considerably in excess of the proportion of Jews within the total population. But again, it must be kept in mind that the overwhelming majority of those employed in professional and semiprofessional occupations came from the urban population; hence the percentage of the intelligentsia that was Jewish should be compared with the percentage of the urban, rather than of the total, population that was Jewish. In January

1939, according to the census, Jews accounted for 4.7 percent of the urban population, as against 8.2 percent in 1926. Since the total urban population had increased appreciably from January 1937 to January 1939, whereas the number of Jewish city-dwellers increased but insignificantly, it may safely be assumed that Jews accounted for no less than 5 percent of the urban population in 1937 and perhaps for more. Also, the influx of millions of villagers into the cities did not bring about a corresponding increase in the number of city-dwellers qualified to do professional and semiprofessional work.

When all this is taken into consideration, the number of Jews in the professional and semiprofessional occupations cannot be regarded as disproportionate. Even the number of Jewish physicians—15.9 percent—did not seem too high for a profession that, because of legal restrictions in other fields, necessarily absorbed a large proportion of Jewish professionals in pre-revolutionary days. Conversely, the number of Jews among school teachers—4.7 percent—and among accountants and bookkeepers—7.7 percent—seems small.

Table VIII, since it lumps all members of a profession together, sheds little light on the proportion of Jews among the higher-ranking and executive personnel of each occupational division. It tells us nothing about the elimination of Jews from the ranks of the Soviet upper class, and the Soviet press in general refrains from mentioning facts that might elucidate this point. But, of course, it is impossible to suppress all such facts. Let us cite an example from a later period that reflects developments taking place at this time. In 1944 the Soviet government established the USSR Academy of Medical Science; first to be appointed to it were the outstanding medical men of the older generation. Although there had been more than a few Jews among the prominent representatives of Russian medical science in the early years, only 5 Jews were to be found among the 60 members of the new academy whom the Soviet government considered the leading men of the medical profession.[22] This certainly was no mere accident.

Removal of Jews from Public Office

To say that as early as the 1930's there was a definite tendency to thrust Jews into the background in every sphere of public life would be an unjustified exaggeration. Such a tendency, however, was visible in some spheres, particularly where some degree of popular antisemitism was traditional and would have had to have been vigorously opposed. The removal of Jews from positions in the public eye may not have represented direct antisemitic discrimination, but rather a tacit attempt to deprive antisemitic resentments of a visible object. But, as the war was to show, this willingness to conciliate antisemites made them believe that the government was deliberately avoiding a contest, or (which was even worse) that the authorities did not want "to be bothered about the Jews." This conciliation of antisemitism was characteristically manifested in the selection of candidates for high political office.

Elections were held in 1938 in all parts of the Soviet Union to choose members for the Supreme Soviets of the individual Soviet Republics. And since an election in the USSR means voting Yes or No on a ticket bearing the name of one candidate only in each constituency, and since all candidates are carefully selected under the supervision of the Communist Party, the composition of the Supreme Soviets is in no sense accidental.

TABLE IX

JEWS IN THE SUPREME SOVIETS
OF THE INDIVIDUAL REPUBLICS, 1938 [23]

Soviet Republic	Members of Supreme Soviets			Percent Jews within Total Population
	Total	Thereof: Jews		
		Number	Percent	
Russian SFSR	727	30	4.1	.9
The Ukraine	304	2	.7	4.9
White Russia	273	21	7.7	6.7
Azerbaidzhan	310	5	1.6	1.3
Georgia	237	3	1.3	1.2
Armenia	256	None	None	0.05
Turkmenistan	226	3	1.3	.2
Uzbekistan	395	10	2.5	.8
Tadzhikistan	282	11	3.9	.3
Kazakhstan	300	3	1.0	.3
Kirghiz SSR	284	4	1.4	.1
Total	3,594	92	2.5	1.8

In White Russia and the Caucasian republics the number of Jewish members of the Supreme Soviet was more or less proportionate to the number of Jews in the population. These were areas with numerous minorities and with multinational administrations, where the "Jewish question" was only one of many. Among the many nationalities represented in the government the Jewish was not conspicuous, and in White Russia Yiddish was even one of the official languages.

Similarly, in the late 1930's in the Russian SFSR, the major theater of industrialization, Jews were intermingled with dozens of other minority nationalities coming from other parts, and there was no reason to conceal the fact that Jews were often to be found in the highest party positions, or to eliminate high Jewish party officials from also holding office in the more conspicuous Supreme Soviet. Here the percentage of Jewish members of the Supreme Soviet exceeded the percentage of the total, and even the percentage of the urban population that was Jewish.

In the case of the five Central Asiatic republics with their predominantly Mohammedan populations speaking non-Slavic languages, the Russian-speaking Jewish official was primarily a Russian, and it made little difference whether his parents had attended the synagogue or the Greek Orthodox church. In large areas of Central Asia Jews were either completely unknown (hardly accounting, after three decades of widespread migrations, for more than one-tenth of one percent of the population), or else they were natives speaking local dialects and wearing native dress; Jewish Communist administrators or intellectuals wearing European dress were no more identified with the native Jews than were any other non-native officials. That the proportion of Jews in the regional Supreme Soviet was 3 or 7 or 15 times as high as the proportion of Jews in the population failed to draw attention.

But matters were different in the Ukraine, where a population of 31 million (mostly of Slav stock and speaking Slavic languages) included 1.5 million Jews, who were a compact and distinct group comprising more than half the entire Jewish community of the Soviet Union. While in Tadzhikistan, for example, 11 Jewish members of the Supreme Soviet represented a Jewish population of barely 5,200, the Ukraine's 1,533,000 Jews had only 2 representatives in a Supreme Soviet of the same size, or half as many representatives as were given in the Kirghiz Republic to less than 1,900 Jews. This huge disparity cannot be attributed to chance—chance plays no part in elections in the Soviet Union. One can only conclude that the rulers of the Communist Party in the Ukraine deemed it politically inexpedient for Jews to figure among the members of the supreme governmental body.

This was plainly a concession to antisemitism. Such antisemitism must have indeed been strong to force the almost complete elimination of Jews from the Supreme Soviet of the second largest Union Republic. Whether the Communist leadership was simply conciliating popular sentiment, or using it as a pretext to curb "excessive Jewish influence" for its own account, is impossible to establish with certainty. It is likely, however, that certain bureaucratic elements, though not aggressively antisemitic, were content to have Jews absent from high places in the government.

When, following the partition of Poland in September 1939, the Soviet Union began to occupy, annex, or control areas with large Jewish populations, such as the Polish Ukraine, Polish White Russia, Lithuania, etc., its officials, desiring to eliminate all traces of Polish influence, cultivated an extreme nationalism in "the Western Ukraine" and "Western White Russia" (to give them their Soviet names), and the strong antisemitic tendencies of the Ukrainian and Lithuanian nationalists were allowed to manifest themselves unchecked.

Elections to the Supreme Soviet of the USSR were held in the annexed territories on March 24, 1940. Forty-three new members were elected to the Soviet of the Union, and 12 to the Soviet of Nationalities. Shcherbakov, rapporteur of the Committee on Credentials and a member of the Politburo, told the Soviet of the Union: "There are among the elected representatives Ukrainians, White Russians, Poles, and Russians; the nationalities of the representatives personify the Stalinist amity of the peoples of the Western Ukraine and Western White Russia."[24] Similarly, Burmistenko, rapporteur of the Committee on Credentials of the Soviet of Nationalities, stated: "Among the representatives elected to the Soviet of Nationalities there are Ukrainians, White Russians, and Poles."[25] No Jewish representatives were mentioned, and with good reason. The complete list of the new members, printed by the Moscow newspapers,[26] contained not a single Jewish name. No Jewish representative was elected from Bialystok, Grodno, Lvov or Pinsk, cities with large Jewish populations.

Presumably, the leadership in Moscow did not care to antagonize antisemitic elements among the locally influential Ukrainian or White-Russian sympathizers with the Soviet Union; at the same time there may have been antisemitic feeling at the very top of the party machine.[27]

An impression was created in Soviet-occupied areas—whether intentionally or not—that Jews were not welcome in the new administration. Reports to this effect were numerous at the time and found ample corroboration after the end of the war. In February 1940, for instance, the JTA's correspondent in Paris was told the following by a "responsible investigator" just returned from Soviet-occupied Poland:

> Although no Jewish question exists in Russia and no differentiation is made between Jews and non-Jews, there is not a single Jew in an important position in Soviet-occupied Poland.
>
> Jews in East Galicia are being accepted in small numbers into the militia, into the school system and as state engineers. Similarly, colleges which had been closed to Jews are now open to them. But no Jews—not even Jewish Communists—have political influence and not a single responsible position is entrusted to a Jew. All such positions are held by Russians sent from the interior of the Soviet Union or by local Ukrainians.
>
> Illustrative of the situation is the fact that among 1,700 delegates to the Soviet National Assembly [People's Assembly of the Western Ukraine, officially listed as having 1,495 delegates] held last October in Lvov to proclaim Galicia a part of the Soviet Union, hardly twenty delegates were Jews, despite the large ratio of Jews in the population. It is known that when Jewish Communists were nominated by Jewish workers, the Soviet authorities intervened and advised withdrawal of the Jewish candidates and [their] replacement by Ukrainians. In Lvov, whose population is 30 percent Jewish, only two Jews were elected to the local Soviet of 160 members.

Moscow seems to take the attitude that in East Galicia the Ukrainians alone should have political influence and therefore Jews are not admitted to leading positions even when they are Communist party members.[28]

A similar state of affairs was reported in Lithuania and White Russia. More, indeed, was involved than the barring of Jews from government office. The Soviet authorities seemed anxious to avoid anything that could possibly have been interpreted as favoring the Jews. The official use of Yiddish was limited to small sections of the administration. Appeals and proclamations issued in millions of copies to Ukrainians and White Russians ignored the existence of the Yiddish-speaking population. When, later, Russian, Ukrainian, White Russian, Lithuanian, and even Polish were used officially, Yiddish was not. In areas where numerous Yiddish-language newspapers had flourished, only one or two were permitted to appear, with Soviet-appointed editorial staffs and under particularly severe censorship. Jewish political, cultural, and communal organizations were either dissolved or narrowly circumscribed as to their functions. Harsh restrictions were imposed on Jewish schools.[29]

None of this was unmistakable proof of active antisemitism. Not until the war with Nazi Germany did it become tragically plain what the consequences of this conciliation and tolerance of antisemitism were.

NOTES

1. See, e.g., the JTA dispatches in *The Jewish Daily Bulletin*, January 20 and 31, and February 5, 20, and 26, 1930.

2. *IX Vsesoyuznyi Syezd VLKSM. Stenograficheskii otchet* [*Ninth All-Union Convention of the All-Union Leninist Communist Youth Association*], Moscow, 1931, pp. 414-417.

3. E.g., *The New York Times*, January 15, 1931.

4. Translated from the Russian text first published in 1936 (see following note).

5. According to the detailed bibliography of all Stalin's writings and speeches, compiled by the Moscow periodical *Kniga i Proletarskaya Revolyutsiya* [*The Book and the Proletarian Revolution*], December 1939, p. 152, Stalin's statement, "Ob antisemitizme (Otvet na zapros YeTA iz Ameriki)" ["On Antisemitism (Answer to a JTA Inquiry from America)"], was written on January 12, 1931 and first appeared in Russian in *Pravda*, November 30, 1936, when it was quoted in full by Molotov in a speech on the new Soviet constitution.

6. *Sotsialisticheskoye Stroitel'stvo SSSR. Statisticheskii sbornik* [*Socialist Construction of the USSR. Statistical Abstract*], issued by the Central Office for Records and Audits of the National Economy (Central Statistical Office), State Planning Commission of the USSR, Moscow, 1936, p. 508.

7. Zinger, *Natsional'nyi sostav* . . . , pp. 63f.

8. *Trud v SSSR (1934 g.). Statisticheskii sbornik* [*Labor in the USSR (1934). Statistical Abstract*], issued by the Central Office for Records and Audits of the National Economy, State Planning Commission of the USSR, Moscow, 1935, p. xviii.

9. V. Pomerantsev, "Uchastki shovinisticheskoi deyatel'nosti i metody bor'by s neyu" ["The Locale of Chauvinist Activity, and Methods of Fighting It"], in *Sovetskaya Yustitsiya*, 1932, no. 19, pp. 18f. The Lower Volga region at that time included territories on the left and right banks of the Volga River from the province

of Saratov to the Caspian Sea; parts of it were the Volga-German and Kalmuck Autonomous Provinces; its eastern part adjoined the Kazakh Autonomous Republic (since made a Union Republic). Whether the survey referred only to 1931 or to a longer period of time was not disclosed.

10. The majority of those convicted—58 percent—were between 18 and 25 years of age, 6 percent were under 18, and only 36 percent were 25 years and older.

11. Not even such an "expert on Jewish affairs" as S. M. Dimanshtein referred to antisemitism when writing about "great-power chauvinism." Information on ethnic friction may be found, *inter alia*, in the following contributions to Soviet periodicals:

P. Andreyev, "Bor'ba s shovinizmom v Dal'ne-Vostochnom Kraye vedetsya slabo" ["Fight against Chauvinism Weakly Conducted in the Far Eastern Region"], in *Sovetskaya Yustitsiya*, 1931, no. 2, pp. 29–31.

N. Kulagin, "Velikoderzhavnyi shovinizm na Dal'nem Vostoke i bor'ba s nim" ["Great-Power Chauvinism in the Far East and the Fight against It"], *ibid.*, no. 6, pp. 13–17.

F. Makarov, "Bor'ba s velikoderzhavnym shovinizmom na Severnom Kavkaze" ["Fight against Great-Power Chauvinism in the Northern Caucasus"], *ibid.*, no. 19, pp. 16–19.

S. Dimanshtein, "Bol'shevistskii otpor natsionalizmu" ["Bolshevik Repulsion of Nationalism"], in *Revolyutsiya i Natsional'nosti*, April 1933, pp. 1–13.

N. Safarov, "Protiv izvrashcheniya natsional'noi politiki" ["Against Distortion of Nationality Policies"], *ibid.*, pp. 74–77.

I. Smirnov and N. Kulagin, "Sil'neye ogon' po velikoderzhavnomu shovinizmu!" ["Hit Harder at Great-Power Chauvinism!"], in *Sovetskaya Yustitsiya*, 1935, no. 16, pp. 8f.

12. References to antisemitic incidents in 1934 and 1935 in Soviet Yiddish-language publications have been collected by Jacob Lestschinsky, *Dos Sovetishe Idntum*, New York, 1941, p. 263.

13. For a more detailed analysis of this crucial period, see an earlier contribution by the present writer, "Zur Demokratie oder zur plebiszitären Diktatur?" in *Zeitschrift für Sozialismus* (Karlsbad, Czechoslovakia), September-October 1935, pp. 792–801.

14. *Pravda*, November 30, 1936.

15. Walter Duranty, a Moscow correspondent for American newspapers who for many years enjoyed the friendship, protection, and confidence of leading Soviet personalities, wrote:

"The death roll ran into thousands, the number of exiles to hundreds of thousands. These figures cannot be controlled, but it is known that from two-thirds to three-quarters of the leading personalities in Soviet Russia were 'purged,' that is, expelled from the Party and in many cases executed.

"It was no longer a purge of cleansing, as the Party had known them before, but a panic madness which struck right and left almost haphazard. The statistics are appalling:

"Two-thirds of the Soviet diplomatic corps—ambassadors, ministers and counselors of embassy or legation—were 'liquidated,' that is their execution was announced or they simply disappeared.

"Casualties were equally severe in the Army and Navy leadership. It is sufficient to say that of the eight officers of the highest rank who were called as extra judges in the trial of Tukhachevsky and the Generals in June 1937, only one, Marshal Budenny, survived. The others were liquidated except the Cossack Commander, Gorbachev, who died in his bed.

"Of the Council of [People's] Commissars, numbering twenty-one at the end of 1936, only five were left two years later. One, Ordjonikidze, died, and the rest were shot or disappeared.

"In the Central Committee of the Communist Party there were seventy-one members elected at the beginning of 1934. At the end of 1938 twenty-one remained active;

three died naturally; one, Kirov, was assassinated; thirty-six disappeared; one, Marshal Gamarnik, committed suicide; nine were announced as shot.

"In the city of Kiev more than half the members of the local Communist Party were officially declared to have been expelled between August, 1947 and June, 1938. No such announcements were made about the other great cities of Russia, but the proportion of expulsions is known to have been about the same." (*USSR. The Story of Soviet Russia*, Philadelphia–New York, 1944, pp. 227f.)

16. The change in the character of the Communist Party of the Soviet Union is clearly apparent from a comparison of the data on party membership submitted by the Committee on Credentials to the Seventeenth Convention in January and February 1934 (before the purge), and to the Eighteenth Convention in March 1939 (after the purge). The following analysis is taken from an earlier publication by the present writer:

"For years the Communist Party aimed to be and to remain a workers' party, which it actually had been in the years of the revolution, and even attempted to guarantee its proletarian character by provisions in the party's by-laws (which rendered more difficult the admission of non-manual workers as party members). At the same time it cultivated high esteem for the old party membership, for those who had belonged since the first years of the revolution or, particularly, from the time of underground activities prior to the revolution. The Great Purge of 1936–1938 sharply broke with this tradition.

"At the Seventeenth Convention 22.6 percent of the delegates had been party members before 1917 and 17 percent dated their membership from 1917; thus 40 percent had belonged to the party before the time it took power. A total of 80 percent of the delegates had been party members since 1919 or earlier. But five years later, at the Eighteenth Convention, only 5 percent of the delegates had been members of the party in 1917 or before (2.6 percent had joined in 1917, and 2.4 percent in earlier years), and instead of 80 percent, only 14.8 percent dated their membership from 1919 or earlier.

"Perhaps even more impressive are figures for the party as a whole. At the time of the Eighteenth Convention the party had 1,588,852 members (as against 1,872,488 at the time of the Seventeenth Convention, a loss of almost 300,000). Of the 1,588,852, only 1.3 percent, that is, hardly more than 20,000, had belonged to the party in 1917 or before. At the beginning of 1918 the party had numbered 260,000 to 270,000 members, mostly young people. Even taking account of the high mortality during the Civil War, it may be assumed that hardly fewer than 200,000 were alive at the beginning of 1939. But only 10 percent of them had remained in the party.

"The high regard for party membership dating from the heroic period was over. At the Eighteenth Convention it was particularly emphasized that 70 percent of the party membership had joined the party after 1928, and that even of the convention delegates 43 percent belonged to this group. (For delegates to the Seventeenth Convention the comparable figure was 2.6 percent.)

"The report of the Committee on Credentials to the Seventeenth Convention pointed with satisfaction to the fact that 9.3 percent of the delegates were 'workers from production,' i.e., actual, not merely former manual workers. The point always had been mentioned at previous conventions. At the Eighteenth Convention, however, the party had lost interest in the matter. Even the most glorified "Stakhanovist workers"—Stakhanov, Busygin, Krivonos, Vinogradova, Likhoradov, Smetanin, Mazai, Gudov—appeared rather out of place at this convention. All of them now were party members, and some were delegates, but when the convention proceeded to elect the Central Committee of the party, the governing body of 139 (71 members and 68 alternates), not one of the famous Stakhanovists was elected. Logically enough, the convention revised the by-laws and eliminated all provisions aiming to preserve the proletarian character of the party. The Communist Party no longer is a workers' party; to an increasing extent, it has become the party of the officials of the various divisions of the economy and administration." ("Heads of Russian Factories. A Sociological Study," in *Social Research*, September 1942, pp. 330f.)

For additional information, see Gregory Bienstock, Solomon M. Schwarz, and Aaron Yugov, *Management in Russian Industry and Agriculture*, New York, 1944, pp. 28–30; also this writer's article, "VKP na 18-om s'yezde" ["The CPSU at the 18th Convention"] in *Sotsialisticheskii Vestnik*, 1939, no. 6.

17. Already in the late 1920's some Soviet groups were inclined to identify "opposition" with Jews (cf. Larin's list of antisemitic questions, p. 251 above).

18. A more comprehensive list of names has been compiled from Soviet sources by G. Aronson, "Vi azey Stalin Hot Farnikht Kim'at Ale Vikhtige Idishe Komunistn," in *Jewish Daily Forward*, January 8, 1938; personal recollections have been supplied by the expatriate Soviet Jewish writer Herschel Vaynraukh (Vinokur), *Blut oyf der Zun*, New York, 1950, esp. pp. 47ff., 71ff., 190ff., 203ff.

19. *The Jewish Daily Bulletin*, June 30, 1930.

20. *Tribuna*, 1932, no. 3, pp. 10f.

21. Intelligentsia totals are from Molotov's presentation of the Third Five-Year Plan at the CPSU convention in March 1939: *XVIIIyi Syezd VKP. Stenograficheskii otchet* [*Eighteenth Convention of the CPSU. Stenographic Transcript of Proceedings*], Moscow, 1939, p. 310; figures relative to Jews, from Zinger, *Dos Banayte Folk*, p. 106; percentages of Jews in each occupational class computed from Molotov's and Zinger's data. Zinger's assertion that his data refer to the beginning of 1939 is manifestly wrong and probably a misprint; if he were right, the percentage figures for Jews in all groups would be less than those shown in the table, for group totals must have been higher in 1939 than in 1937.

22. *Meditsinskii Rabotnik* [*Medical Worker*], weekly of the People's Commissariat for Public Health of the USSR, November 16, 1944.

23. The figures relative to the membership of the Supreme Soviets and the number of Jews elected are from the official analysis of election returns: *Vybory v Verkhovnyi Sovet SSSR i v Verkhovnyye Sovety soyuznykh i avtonomnykh respublik, 1937–1938 gg. (Tsifrovoi sbornik)* [*Elections to the Supreme Soviet of the USSR and the Supreme Soviets of Union and Autonomous Republics in 1937–1938 (Statistical Résumé)*], Division of Information and Statistics, Secretariat of the Presidium, Supreme Soviet of the USSR, Moscow, 1939, pp. 16f.; percent rato computed. The proportion of Jews within the population of the USSR and of the individual republics, based on the Census of January 1939, from S. Sul'kevich, *Naseleniye SSSR* [*USSR Population*], Moscow, 1939, p. 29, and Zinger, *Dos Banayte Folk*, pp. 38 and 126.

24. *Pravda*, March 30, 1940.

25. *Ibid.*

26. *Pravda* and *Izvestiya*, March 28, 1940.

27. It was rumored time and again that Shcherbakov, the political supervisor of Red Army staffs during the war, was an aggressive antisemite; many Jewish Displaced Persons who had served in the Soviet forces insisted that the rumor was not unfounded. Burmistenko, member of the Politburo and secretary of the Central Committee of the Communist Party of the Ukraine, disappeared after the beginning of the Soviet-Nazi war, and various reports, impossible now to verify, insisted that he had stayed on in the Ukraine to await the arrival of the German army, and that subsequently he became an active collaborationist and Nazi supporter.

28. *JTA News*, February 25, 1940.

29. For the story of the disintegration of Jewish life under the first Soviet occupation, see S. Kaczerginski, *Tsvishn Hamer un Serp*, Editions Grohar, Paris, 1949.

CHAPTER V

Under the Nazi Occupation

Effects of the Hitler-Stalin Pact

After the pact with Germany that the Soviet government signed in August 1939, an attitude of neutrality was officially taken towards the Nazi ideology. The government made it plain that it disapproved of any public denunciation of Nazism, and at public meetings, in the press, and on the radio silence was maintained on Nazism's persecution of the Jews.

The brunt of the political and ideological attack was directed against the democratic countries locked in combat with the Third Reich. To denounce "the ruling classes of England and France" became the daily chore of Soviet political spokesmen and commentators. Thus Vyacheslav M. Molotov, then chairman of the Council of People's Commissars, in a keynote speech on foreign policy before the Supreme Soviet of the USSR on October 31, 1939 said:

> The governing groups of England and France have been trying of late to make themselves out to be fighters for the democratic rights of nations against Hitlerism; thus, the English government has announced that its goal in the war against Germany is nothing more or less than "the annihilation of Hitlerism." It looks as though the English, and along with them the French supporters of war, have declared some kind of an "ideological war" on Germany, something that recalls the old religious wars. Religious wars against heretics and people of another faith were indeed quite the fashion in their time. Those wars, as we know, had the most onerous consequences and resulted in economic devastation and the relapse of nations into cultural savagery. But this was in medieval times. Is it back to these medieval times, times of religious wars and cultural barbarization, that the ruling classes of England and France would drag us once again? At any rate, a war of much greater scope, and much more dangerous for the peoples of Europe and of the entire world, has now been plotted under an "ideological" flag. A war of this kind cannot be justified in any way. Like any other ideology, the ideology of Hitlerism may be accepted or rejected—it is a matter of one's political views. Yet anyone can see that ideology cannot be annihilated by force, cannot be done away with by war. Therefore, to wage such a war as this one for "the annihilation of Hitlerism," which wraps itself around with the false flag of the fight for "democracy," is not only senseless but also criminal. . . .[1]

This attitude of friendly neutrality was maintained with fatal consistency. Throughout the period preceding the Soviet Union's entry into the war, readers of the Soviet press were kept in ignorance of the Nazi anti-Jewish policies; the government's neutrality blinded Soviet Jews to the mortal danger threatening them. When, on June 22, 1941, the Wehrmacht suddenly invaded the Soviet Union, the Jewish population was largely unaware of the persecution and extermination that awaited them; many of those who might have fled, remained where they were and perished. This is apparent both from statistics on the number that survived [2] and from documents captured from German occupation authorities. In a report from White Russia to the representative of the Reich Ministry for the Occupied Areas attached to the Supreme Command of the Army (OKH), an occupation official, Sonderführer S——, wrote in July 1941:

> The Jews are strikingly ill-informed about our attitude towards them and about the treatment Jews are receiving in Germany or in Warsaw, places after all not too remote from them. If they were not, they would scarcely ask whether we in Germany treat Jews differently from other citizens. Although they do not expect to be granted equal rights with the Russians under the German administration, they do believe that we shall let them be if they apply themselves diligently to their work.[3]

This is borne out by the eyewitness reports of Displaced Persons from the Soviet Union, memoirs of prominent Jews who lived through the Nazi occupation in areas that the Soviet armies held in 1939–1941, and even by occasional remarks in Soviet publications.

The marked unpreparedness of the Jewish population was not the only effect of the Soviet-Nazi pact. During almost two years it also sapped the average Soviet citizen's resistance to Nazi antisemitism. The opportunistic policy of neutrality disarmed ideologically the population of the areas that were to be occupied, not only with regard to antisemitism but to everything.

Popular Response to Nazi Incitation

From its very first days the German occupation was accompanied by ferocious anti-Jewish acts. The German authorities were eager to create the impression that the local populaces spontaneously rose against "Jewish Bolshevism." "Liberation from Jewish-Bolshevik oppression" was to be celebrated by outbursts of "popular wrath and ire," i.e., pogroms.

Hardly any reports on what actually happened in the early days of the German occupation were published in the Soviet press, either general or Jewish, either at the time or later. The German press was more communicative, but of dubious veracity, as its information came from official sources interested in magnifying the "liberated" population's hatred of the Jews. In contrast to German press utterances, a number of German secret documents inspire much greater confidence as to their credibility. Some of the secret reports of German occupation officials show that mechanical meticulousness in detail which is the hallmark of German officialdom. Thus a report on the activities of "Action Group A," operating in the Baltic countries, White Russia, and the adjacent districts of the Russian SFSR, addressed to Himmler on October 15, 1941 by SS Brigade Commander Stahlecker, said:

> . . . Native antisemitic forces were induced to start pogroms against Jews during the first hours after capture [of each city by the German army], though this . . . proved very difficult. Following out orders, the Security Police was determined to solve the Jewish question with all possible means and most decisively. But it was desirable that the Security Police should not put in an immediate appearance, at least in the beginning, since the extraordinarily harsh measures were apt to stir even German circles. It had to be shown to the world that the native population itself took the first action by way of natural reaction against the suppression [oppression?] by Jews during several decades and against the terror exercised by the Communists during the preceding period.[4]

The local population's reluctance to begin pogroms caused difficulties that the planners of the anti-Jewish campaigns had not foreseen. The report discussed the situation in the Baltic countries which had been under Soviet rule since 1939:

> Considering that the population of the Baltic countries had suffered very heavily under the government of Bolshevism and Jewry while they were incorporated in the USSR, it was to be expected that after the liberation from that foreign government, they (i.e., the population themselves) would render harmless [do away with] most of the enemies left behind after the retreat of the Red Army. It was the duty of the Security Police to set in motion these self-cleansing movements and to direct them into the correct channels in order to accomplish the purpose of the cleansing operations as quickly as possible. It was no less important in view of the future to establish the unshakable and provable fact that the liberated population themselves took the most severe measures against the Bolshevist and Jewish enemy quite on their own, so that the direction by German authorities could not be found out.
> In *Lithuania* this was achieved . . . by partisan activities in Kovno [Kaunas]. To our surprise it was not easy at first to set in motion an extensive pogrom against the Jews. Klimatis, the leader of the partisan unit . . . who was used for this purpose primarily, succeeded in starting a pogrom on the basis of advice given to him by a small advanced detachment acting in Kovno, and in such a way that no German order or German instigation was noticed from the outside [i.e., by the non-

initiated]. During the first pogrom in the night from 25. to 26.6 [June 25–26] the Lithuanian partisans did away with more than 1,500 Jews, set fire to several synagogues or destroyed them by other means, and burned down a Jewish [residential] district consisting of about 60 houses. During the following nights about 2,300 Jews were made harmless [put to death] in a similar way. In other parts of Lithuania similar actions followed the example of Kovno, though smaller and extending to the Communists who had been left behind.

These self-cleansing actions went smoothly because the Army authorities who had been informed showed understanding for this procedure. From the beginning it was obvious that only the first days after the occupation would offer the opportunity for carrying out pogroms. After the disarmament of the partisans the self-cleansing actions ceased necessarily.

It proved much more difficult to set in motion similar cleansing actions in *Latvia*. Essentially the reason was that the whole national stratum of leaders [the nationalist political leadership] had been assassinated or destroyed by the Soviets, especially in Riga. It was possible, though, through similar influences on the Latvian Auxiliary, to set in motion a pogrom against Jews . . . in Riga. During this pogrom all synagogues were destroyed and 400 Jews were killed. As the population of Riga quieted down quickly, further pogroms were not [deemed] convenient.

So far as possible, both in Kovno and in Riga evidence by film and photo was [secured to prove] that the first spontaneous executions of Jews and Communists [had been] carried out by Lithuanians and Latvians.

In *Estonia*, by reason of the relatively small number of Jews, no opportunity presented itself to instigate pogroms. . . .[5]

In both Latvia and Lithuania the German authorities succeeded in collecting antisemitic gangs willing to kill Jews and sack Jewish districts, with or without orders issued by German commanders. It was these gangs that eagerly supported the Nazis when the policy of the wholesale extermination was put into effect.[6] But it is clear from this report as from others that the bulk of the local inhabitants failed to justify the Nazi chieftains' expectations. An "activity and situation report of the Task Forces of the Security Police and the SD [Gestapo Security Service] in the USSR," referring to White Russia in October 1941, stated:

Now as ever it is to be noted that the population on their own part refrains from any action against Jews. It is true that the population reports collectively of [unanimously bears witness to] the terror [perpetrated by] the Jews to which they were exposed during the time of the Soviet regime, or they complain about new encroachments of the Jews, but nevertheless they are not prepared to take part in any pogroms.[7]

Who the informants were that told the German authorities about a "Jewish terror" during the Soviet era is not mentioned in any of the German documents we now possess; probably such reports originated with local collaborationists posing as spokesmen of the population. No such statements were to to be found in the many files consulted; if really made, such statements were obviously anything but frequent. The German hangmen apparently did not succeed in enlisting supporters even among those who supplied manufactured information. A later report, submitted in August 1942 by an "authoritative informant" (*Vertrauensmann*), a White-Russian resident of Latvia who "for the first time [had] visited former Soviet territory," said:

No Jewish problem exists for the White Ruthenians [so called by the Nazis to emphasize their non-Russian nationality]. This is regarded as a purely German matter, of no concern to the White Ruthenians. Here, too, Soviet education was able to impose its view that racial differences do not exist. All around the Jews are objects of pity and compassion, and the Germans are regarded as barbarians and hangmen, the Jew being held to be as much of a human being as the White Ruthenian.[8]

Although "pity and compassion" may not have been quite so widespread as this would make it appear, the Nazi extermination policies evidently did not meet with the general assent of the White Russians.

Matters were different in the Ukraine. Before the German invasion antisemitic feeling had run higher there than in the northwestern regions. Also, the German army was accompanied by exiled partisans of extreme nationalist Ukrainian groups that had always been violently antisemitic, and these reinforced, especially in the larger cities, the local antisemites. Here and there the local population, to judge from reports, did actually participate in the slaughter. Still, there is no evidence of a general bloodlust.

The report on the operations of the Security Police and SD Task Forces already referred to noted that "the embitterment of the Ukrainian population against the Jews is extremely great, because they are thought responsible for the explosions in Kiev," adding that Jews "are also regarded as informers and agents of the NKVD who started the terror against the Ukrainian people." But then the report described the slaughter carried out by German police detachments in Kiev, Zhitomir, and Kherson without even mentioning the Ukrainian antisemites.[9] This did not mean that Ukrainians did not participate in the slaughter and pillage. So long as relations between the Nazis and the Ukrainian nationalists continued to be friendly (i.e., during the first year of the occupation), the Nazi executioners got assistance from among them. Active participation in acts of terrorism, however, was for the most part confined to gangs recruited from among the old antisemites of Polish Galicia.

In White Russia and the occupied districts of the Russian SFSR, Russian émigrés of Hitlerite or semi-Hitlerite persuasion were imported from Germany or the occupied countries of Western Europe. With the assistance of these Russian-speaking fascists the German command set up local police detachments. In some places these police outdid their masters in terrorizing and slaughtering the Jewish population. In the city of Borisov they killed 6,500 Jews in the course of two days (October 20 and 21, 1941), displaying a savagery which even the Nazi hangmen marveled at.[10] The bloodshed, however, shocked the local people, even those not untainted by prejudice:

> The eyes of the latter [the non-Jews] expressed either complete apathy or horror, because the scenes which took place in the streets were ghastly! The non-Jews may have believed on the evening preceding the execution that the Jews deserved their fate, but on the following morning their sentiment was: "Who ordered such a thing? How is it possible to kill off 6,500 Jews all at once? Now it is the Jews' turn, when will it be ours? What . . . [had] these poor Jews [done]? All they did was work! The really guilty ones are surely in safety."[11]

In this city as in others, the popular reaction to the Nazi atrocities does not seem to have gone beyond mute horror. No instances of active protest are recorded either in Nazi or Soviet sources.[12] A passive attitude seems to have been the rule. But in rural districts the passive indifference of the surrounding population more than once gave way to open hostility. In the Ukraine west of the Dnieper and in White Russia Jewish fugitives, like the guerrilla fighters, hid out in the woods. In these places a large partisan force grew up, and the forests sheltered Jewish partisans as well as non-combatant Jewish fugitives accompanied by their women folk and children. All these people required food, which they often had to take from near-by farms already bled white by the Germans. This naturally led to discord, of which more hereafter.

Civilian Efforts to Rescue Jews

Authentic information about the efforts of the Soviet civilian population to rescue Jews in German-occupied areas is scarce. News items in the foreign Communist press during the war, especially after the end of 1942, gave the impression that Jews in considerable numbers were being rescued by the Soviet people. But these stories lack confirmation. Isolated instances were made much of and unduly generalized. Thus Ilya Ehrenburg, in the preface to the second of his collections of documents on the extermination of Jews in Nazi-occupied provinces, said:

The reader will also be deeply moved to note the facts proving Soviet solidarity and the strength of the fraternal bond of nations, expressed in the efforts of many Russians, White Russians, Poles, and Ukrainians to rescue Jews from slaughter.[13]

Such facts, however, were few. Ehrenburg took pains to record them; but when all the cases of Soviet citizens rescuing Jews which he mentions are added up, there are 10, wherein a total of 24 Jews were saved—and in 2 of these 10 instances (one of which involved 10 individuals) the rescue was apparently contingent upon some sort of payment. In an article for the American press in the fall of 1944, "Little Men in Occupied Russia Helped Rescue Jews,"[14] Ehrenburg gave an abridged version of the cases recorded in his second collection of documents; in addition, drawing on his first collection,[15] he described how 7 Jewish families (30 persons) from the city of Ordzhonikidze (formerly Yenakiyevo) in the Donets Basin had been hidden away in and rescued by a Ukrainian collective farm. The case was probably not unique, but it surely was exceptional, to say the least. Ehrenburg refrained from giving any particulars when he wrote:

> People in Kharkov (the Ukraine), Vilna (Lithuania), and Lvov (Galicia) were executed for saving Jews. This did not deter the noble people. We have kept on record the names of the worthiest of people who justify our faith in man no matter to what tests he may be subjected.[16]

Acts of heroism no doubt did occur, though none of the documents amassed by Ehrenburg mention any instances of the execution of people for coming to the assistance of Jews. A thorough search of Soviet publications has revealed no trace of the record Ehrenburg refers to. The Soviet press itself never published any of the facts which American newspapers reported on the authority of Soviet sources, or any of the stories passed by Soviet censorship for publication abroad. The following dispatch from Moscow is typical of the wartime reports supplied to the American press:

> Hundreds of Russian peasants in White Russia were executed by the Nazis for appealing to the military and police authorities against the extermination of Jews, as reported by refugees returning to liberated Gomel.
>
> In the village of Ushtasha, the peasant population marched in a religious procession, bearing icons and crosses, to Nazi headquarters in a last minute appeal to spare the lives of two hundred Jewish men and women being led from their cells to the execution grounds. The Nazis opened fire on the procession and killed 107 persons, before the demonstrators could flee the hail of bullets.

In Novosedid 145 peasants were killed for protesting the mass execution of Jews.[17]

Stories of this kind would have been widely publicized by the Soviet press, Jewish and non-Jewish, if they had been based on fact. Yet none is to be found in the Soviet press of the period. The above dispatch from Moscow never appeared either in *Pravda* or *Eynikayt*, nor was anything like it mentioned in Ehrenburg's collections. Nor did Soviet publications ever mention any organized efforts to rescue Jews. This writer knows of only one such case, recorded in the chronicle of the Minsk ghetto by the Soviet writer Smolyar. The account reads:

> Comrade Mikhl Gebelev is in contact with a reliable person working in the Department of Education of the occupation's municipal administration. Arrangements have been made with that person to allow us an opportunity to get Jewish children into White-Russian children's homes. A password and a secret code have been agreed upon: if an ostensibly abandoned child is brought to Room 20 in the Municipal Building between 9 and 11 A.M., this will indicate that the child must be rescued and placed in the Municipal Children's Home. For this purpose two women's teams have been set up, one in the ghetto, consisting of Jewish women who will pass the children across the fence, and one outside the ghetto, consisting of White-Russian women who will pick up our children and pass them on to the place arranged for.
>
> Workers employed in the Oktyabr plant live close to the ghetto boundary on Obertkovaya Street. This factory has now been changed over to manufacture supplies for the Hitlerite Air Force. It includes shops where several hundred Jews are at work. Very early every day, before the work gangs start out for the plant, Comrades Rivka Norman, Genya Pasternak, Gisha Sukenik, and others take up their post near the ghetto boundary. They wait for a sign from the other side. On the other side, outside the ghetto, is the home of the Voronovs, a White-Russian family. The father works in the underground printing shop; the son is engaged in conveying men and arms to the partisans; his wife carries parcels to arrested comrades and provides hiding-places for people in danger. At dawn she takes up her post and signals the Jewish comrades if the street is safe and if the children can be smuggled out. In her house Comrades Mariya Ivanovskaya, Tat'yana Gerasimenko, Lelya Revinskaya, and others are ready and waiting. Thanks to this organization, it is possible each time to rescue several children from the ghetto. . . . During the first few weeks they have already succeeded in transferring 70 Jewish children from the Minsk ghetto to White-Russian children's homes.[18]

Despite certain implausible elements,[19] the salient circumstance—that a group of White-Russian women had banded together to smuggle

Jewish children out of the ghetto—is told in such detail as to lend it credibility. Even though the number of children saved may not have been considerable when compared with the number exterminated in this one ghetto, the mere fact of a concerted action by a non-Jewish group to rescue Jewish children is a remarkable manifestation of moral courage and political determination. That such heroism was rare, especially in the Ukraine, is apparent from the tiny number of Jewish survivors liberated by the Soviet armies' advance into the eastern part of the occupied area.

Late in 1943 the liberated Ukrainian provinces east of the Dnieper were toured by Vasilii Grossman, the famous Soviet writer and war correspondent. In a series of articles called "The Ukraine Without Jews," Grossman reported:

> I covered this country on foot and by car from the Northern Donets to the Dnieper, from Voroshilovgrad in the Donets Basin to Chernigov on the Desna River. I went down to the Dnieper and looked from afar at Kiev—and I met but one Jew in all that time. He was Lieutenant Shlema Kapershtein, who had been caught in an enemy encirclement in the Yagotin district in September 1941.[20]

The lieutenant owed his life to a Ukrainian peasant woman who for two years passed him off as a Moldavian refugee. Isolated Jews had been seen in Kharkov and Kursk, so Grossman was told in chance encounters; and he heard from Ehrenburg of a Jewish girl in the northern Ukraine who had been with the partisans. This, according to Grossman, was the sum total of the Jewish survivors in the Ukraine. At about the same time a Jewish army officer made a tour of liberated White Russia and failed to find a single Jew either in Gomel or the neighboring towns.[21] Later, when the Red Army advanced farther west, the picture changed somewhat. The Ukrainian provinces west of the Dnieper and the western part of White Russia are densely forested; the woods gave shelter to fugitives and guerrilla fighters. More Jews survived in those parts than had been thought, in some districts as many as several hundred, and all in all several thousand; but most of these were saved by their own enterprise and endurance, only a few having been aided by the local population.

On the whole, the number of Jews saved by non-Jews in the Nazi-occupied Soviet areas was appallingly low, perhaps less than one-hundredth of one percent of the number of Jews living in this area before the war. This compares very unfavorably with the number of Jews rescued from death by non-Jews in France, Belgium, Holland, and even Poland.

That many more Jews were saved in Western Europe may well be ascribed to the lesser ferocity there of the Hitlerite terror; the French, Belgians, and Dutch were not, in the eyes of Nazi administrators, sub-human scum, as were the Slavs, and were treated more leniently. The higher cultural level of the Western countries may also have had something to do with this. But none of these reasons applies to Poland. Nazi terror was no less severe in Poland than it was in the Ukraine and White Russia; nor was there a substantial difference in culture between the Polish and the Soviet populations. And yet the number, relative and absolute, of Jews rescued by Poles was much higher than that of Jews rescued by the Soviet people. At the time the war started, antisemitism, of course, was neither dead nor forgotten in the Soviet Union. But its extent and depth in the decade preceding the war were much less important in the USSR (save perhaps in certain parts of the Ukraine) than in Poland, where the populace's hostility to Jews was traditional and ingrained. And yet the mass of the people in Poland and the Polish part of Lithuania (Vilna) reacted with much more humanity to the savage persecution of Jews than did the Soviet population.[22]

Only a tentative explanation can be offered. Soviet citizens had been trained for decades to obey official orders without discussion or hesitation; to keep silent in the face of acts of violence; and to suppress all spontaneous reactions that might be construed as rebellious demonstrations against injustice and brutality. Unaccustomed to protest against the rule of force, they remained deaf and dumb before the Nazi terror. Even when horror-struck by the atrocities perpetrated against Jews, they looked on stupefied and could do nothing. This callousness on the part of the population particularly shocked and hurt the most assimilated among the Jewish intellectuals believing in the Soviet ideas of equality and justice, who had felt the closest kinship with Russian and Ukrainian culture and hardly ever thought of themselves as Jews.[23]

The average Soviet individual was incapable of offering independent resistance to the Nazi evil. It rarely occurred to him that something could yet be done at least to save individual Jews; and that to help other human beings was worth the risk of life and limb. This passivity also may have had a farther-reaching psychological effect. Those who stood mutely by while Jews were being carried away to the shambles or killed on the spot, had to justify themselves to their own consciences; this necessity may have ultimately made them resent and hate the victims rather than the executioners.

Another contributing factor may have been the politically neutral, if not openly collaborationist, position that large sections of the population took towards the Nazi authorities. In Poland the mass of the people, including those groups bitterly hating the country's prewar rulers, were unanimous in rejecting and actively opposing the German conquerors.

Such was less generally the case in the Ukraine and White Russia, where many were content passively to await further developments and more than a few were even inclined to welcome the German invaders as liberators from Communist oppression.

In Poland an organized political underground functioned from the very first on a nationwide scale and enjoyed the moral support of almost all the people. In spite of widespread antisemitic feeling, the Polish resistance movement, aptly characterized as "a state within a state," made the protection of Jews a part of the war which it relentlessly waged against the occupying power.[24] In the Soviet Union no such underground organization functioned throughout the German-occupied provinces. To be sure, many were drawn into the resistance movement and helped the partisan guerrillas. But organized resistance was limited to small underground groups in the cities or partisan detachments in the countryside; the defense of the Jewish minority was not regarded as one of their objectives.

The Underground's Reaction to Persecution of Jews

A few of the underground groups in the occupied areas were non-Soviet in persuasion. German documents in the archives of the Yiddish Scientific Institute (YIVO) mention the existence of a strongly nationalist group of Lithuanians; a leaflet issued by this group which the authorities seized in January 1942 protested against the use of Lithuanian auxiliary police detachments to exterminate Jews in Lithuania, Latvia, the Ukraine, etc.[25] This underground group was antisemitic to some extent, and it is not quite clear whether it was protesting against the extermination of Jews, or merely the compulsory participation of Lithuanians in it. "Are we to be Europe's hangmen?" the leaflet asked. But it showed at any rate that even reactionary nationalists were alarmed by the German practices.

It is significant that no such documents issued by the far more numerous pro-Soviet or Soviet-inspired underground groups came into the possession of the Germans. Resistance to the occupiers, which was mainly a matter of the harassment of the German forces by partisan detachments, depended in large measure on Soviet support. The underground organizations received not only assistance, but also guidance and instructions from behind the Soviet front lines. In effect, they were the vanguard of the Red Army in enemy-held areas. A great many leaflets issued by this pro-Soviet underground are preserved (some in the original language, and some in German translation) in the YIVO's collection of German documents. With one exception, all these leaflets, which were distributed in the German-occupied White Russia and the Baltic countries, made no mention of the extermination or even persecution of Jews. In February

1942, to cite an example, a leaflet signed by the Central Committee of the Communist Party of Lithuania was circulated in a number of Lithuanian districts. It said the Germans were plundering the people, committing arson, and killing Lithuanians. They had brought the people unemployment, compulsory labor, typhoid and other epidemics. "They destroy Lithuanian culture, they have banished the Lithuanian language from public life and the radio, by force and guile they Germanize our homeland." The Germans had "annihilated Lithuanian statehood and communal life," the Lithuanians on their own soil were being deprived of all rights, "at every step the Germans offend Lithuanian national dignity." But nothing was said about the annihilation of Jews.[26] In the fall of 1942 a Lithuanian leaflet (probably also printed in Latvian and Estonian) was seized, which over the signatures of a number of Communist and pro-Communist writers of the three Baltic countries denounced German atrocities in Lithuania, Latvia, and Estonia; not a word was said about atrocities against Jews.[27] In the late summer of 1942 the Central Committee of the Communist Party of White Russia issued a manifesto to the population entitled "Liberator Hitler" in which the Führer was called the "liberator from life"; the "liberation" of the Jews "from life" was not mentioned.[28] On the eve of May 1, 1943, an appeal was circulated in White Russia captioned "To the Toiling People of White Russia," and signed by Ponomarenko, secretary of the Central Committee of the Communist Party of White Russia, and Natalevich, chairman of the Supreme Soviet of the White-Russian Soviet Socialist Republic. This official document of the Communist underground denounced the "extermination of our people" by the Hitlerites. "Lately, in the district of Vitebsk alone," said the appeal, "more than 40,000 women, elderly people, and children were killed, burned, and poisoned." That most of those "killed, burned, and poisoned" were Jews was passed over in silence.[29]

In one instance only was this silence broken, in deference to currents of opinion among Lithuanians which it was impossible for the underground to ignore. A declaration of the "League for the Liberation of Lithuania" appeared in the first issue of the Lithuanian underground newspaper, The Fatherland Front, on June 1, 1943; it was clearly of Communist origin, which it not too skilfully masked under a show of Lithuanian nationalism. The declaration admonished Lithuanian policemen and soldiers to resist German attempts to enlist them in the work of extermination "of Jews and other peoples." Like the abovementioned Lithuanian nationalist leaflet, the League said:

> You must realize that the Germans want to destroy the Lithuanian people. First they try to destroy us morally, taking pains to turn all Lithuanians into executioners. Later the Germans will shoot us like

they did the Jews, and will justify their acts to the world by saying that Lithuanians are depraved, hangmen, sadists. . . .[30]

As a rule, the underground groups paid no attention to the Nazis' efforts to destroy the Jewish people as such.[31] The attitude of the underground seems to have been determined by opportunistic considerations like those which prevailed with the Soviet government, and provided a certain justification to the local population for their passivity.

Nevertheless, the anti-Nazi underground did contribute to rescuing Jews from Nazi persecution. Thanks to the guerrillas, individual Jews could lose themselves in the host of partisan fighters in the woods. This, however, was not always possible. Guerrilla fighters were on the whole not especially friendly to Jews, and friction, and even open clashes, sometimes developed when Jews tried to join the partisans.

Jewish Partisan Life

Only recently have the testimony of eyewitnesses and the memoirs of survivors shed some light on Jewish partisan life. Also, additional documentary material can now be consulted, particularly testimonials by Jewish partisans collected in Poland by the Jewish Historical Commission (Centralna Zydowska Komisia Historyczna w Polsce), some of which are in the possession of the YIVO. Much of this testimony refers to the Eastern Polish provinces annexed by the Soviet Union in 1939, and also to Nazi-held Soviet territory.

Two principal problems call for investigation: (1) the relations between Jewish and non-Jewish partisans; and (2) the relations of Jewish partisans and fugitives with the local populations. There is unfortunately little on these matters to be found in Soviet publications. Both Sidor Kovpak,[32] the most acclaimed guerrilla commander, whose division operated in White Russia and the Western Ukraine for over two years, and his chief lieutenant, Petro Vershigora,[33] avoided discussing any Jewish problem in their chronicles, or even mentioning Jewish participants in the guerrilla warfare save in exceptional cases.[34] Soviet Jewish writers dealing with the Jewish resistance or the role of Jews in the partisan movement likewise ignored the problem of Jewish-Gentile relations.[35]

On the other hand, former Jewish partisans in Poland, in Displaced Persons camps in Italy, and in Palestine have done commendable work in collecting original material. Many partisans of the guerrilla fighting in White Russia and the Western Ukraine went to Poland in the final stages or shortly after the end of the war; there, in Lodz in May 1945, they set up a Jewish Federation of Partisans—Partizan-Khayyil-Khaluts (PAKHAKH). The majority of the PAKHAKH members soon moved westward, to Austria, Italy, and France. With them went the

PAKHAKH's Central Historical Commission, under the chairmanship of Moshe Kaganovich, a former partisan from the town of Ivye near Lida. The Commission not only collected documents, but also induced many partisans to write down, or to dictate to it, everything they remembered. The impressive fund of information thus collected has been summed up by Kaganovich in a bulky volume, *The Jewish Share in Soviet Russia's Partisan Movement*.[36]

Kaganovich's work, as the title indicates, is primarily concerned with partisan units that accepted guidance and support from the Red Army and the Soviet authorities; Poland is little touched upon.[37] His attitude towards the Soviet Union is sympathetic and he is not distrustful of Soviet propaganda. This influences his presentation of facts whenever he relies on hearsay, and occasionally leads him into errors of fact and judgment. Kaganovich, moreover, is not always a dispassionate historian.[38] But these faults do not seriously impair his work, for in spite of his uncritical approach to information from Soviet sources, Kaganovich preserves an independent judgment, verifies evidence wherever possible, and bases his conclusions chiefly on personal experience and the testimony of trustworthy informants. His book is a remarkable contribution in more than one respect. With respect to the Jewish problem in the partisan movement in German-occupied Soviet territory, his work is a mine of valuable information. As a rule, the non-Jewish partisans were made up of individuals able and willing to fight. Those unable or unwilling either stayed where they were, or moved to another place if they had reason to fear detection. Jews, however, faced an inescapable alternative; death or flight to the woods. Flight was no outing, and many fugitives perished; but to stay on was certain destruction. You did not consider your military qualifications, but sought only to reach the woods. Jews fled with their families, with the aged and infirm, and with small children escaping from ghettos—sometimes in sizable groups—and from death trains. In the eyes of the non-Jewish partisans those unable to bear arms were only a burden. There were thousands such. Thus Jewish "family camps" came into being in the depths of the forest; and along with these, special Jewish detachments to protect the family camps. The organization of exclusively Jewish partisan units was encouraged by the difficulties Jewish combatants encountered when they sought to join non-Jewish detachments.

Antisemitism among the Guerrillas

Many non-Jewish partisans had been in German war-prisoner or slave-labor camps, where they had been exposed to Nazi propaganda. The after-effects of this were widely felt. According to testimony of former partisans, manifestations of antisemitism among the guerrillas were frequent and at times violent, especially in 1942 and 1943. Kaganovich writes:

To get admitted into the ranks of a Soviet fighting detachment was no easy job. There were some Russian units that did not admit Jews as a matter of policy. They justified this by saying that Jews neither knew how nor wanted to fight.

The first requirement a Jew had to meet to get accepted by a detachment was to have a weapon. Many young Jews had no way of obtaining arms and thus had no choice but to join family camps or family combat units accepting any Jew who managed to escape.

Non-Jews joining a detachment were given arms by the partisans. It often happened that for this very purpose a Jew was deprived of the weapon with which he originally had come to join the detachment, or else was given one inferior to his own. Commanders and political leaders explained these astonishing acts of national discrimination by pointing to overriding political considerations: a Jew had no way out, he could not turn back; but a White Russian, a Pole, or a Ukrainian still had a number of courses open to him—he might join the police or the Vlasov army, or he might take a well-paid job with the Germans that would permit him to rob the population and to benefit from property left behind by the Jews; it was therefore essential to do the utmost in order to draw him into the ranks of the fighters against the German occupation.

To be just, one must note that as more Soviet arms were supplied, the detachments began to admit young Jews fit for combat into their ranks even though they had no weapons. But still, Jews were caught in a vicious circle. Those unfit for combat were reproached with: "What did you come here for? Why aren't you fighting?" And those fit for combat, who wanted to join the detachments, were told: "So you gave your gold to the Germans, and now you want to be with us to save your hides?" Those who came at a later stage were upbraided: "Where have you kept yourselves so far? Working for the Germans? . . ."

What with this attitude to Jewish partisans, it is not surprising that some of the Jews (especially Russian Jews from the eastern provinces) who were able to do so, thanks to their appearance and knowledge of Russian, should have concealed their Jewish origin and passed themselves off as Russians, Tatars, Armenians, etc.

In particular it was the family camps that suffered at the hands of antisemitic partisans.

When the ghetto was liquidated and Jews escaped to partisan areas, they were ambushed by Russian partisans and robbed of every stitch. Thus Jews from Lida who escaped from a train carrying them to Maidanek were robbed by partisans of the Iskra detachment (Novogrudok district). When the family camp in Belitsa had to be transferred to one near the village of Dem'yanovtsy, Jews were attacked enroute and robbed, and some of them severely beaten, by partisans of the antisemitic Voroshilov company, also called the Lida detachment.

There also were instances when Russian detachments ambushed returning Jewish foraging parties and seized the food that the Jews had obtained at the risk of their lives. More than once the [Jewish] detachments commanded by Biel'skii and Zorin were thus made victims of banditry, and detachment commanders were not always able to retrieve the spoils by appealing to the higher partisan command. Often enough such happenings resulted in the loss of lives.[39]

The fact that Jewish fugitives were blamed for escaping to the woods showed how little the guerrillas understood what the occupying power was doing to Jews. Suspicion and distrust of Jews were not confined to partisans who had been indoctrinated in the Nazi camps. A like attitude was displayed by partisans coming from the Soviet Union. Kaganovich recalls "an October night in the Lipichi Forest in 1943" when Jewish fighters had a long talk with Red Army paratroopers just dropped from Soviet planes:

> They fired questions at us. These questions hurt and deeply perturbed us. Instead of sympathy for the few individuals surviving from large Jewish communities, we saw a tendency to hurt and insult us, to throw salt in our wounds. We sought to lift the veil, to conjure up before their eyes the picture of the ghetto, and dwelt on those things which ought to have made them understand the tragedy of our people. . . .[40]

The Soviet soldiers, however, were not impressed with what the Jewish partisans had to tell.

Anti-Jewish preconceptions were so widespread that even charges of collaborationism and espionage on behalf of the Germans found an echo. Some partisans, according to Kaganovich, reasoned as follows:

> How is it that Jews still keep alive in the Lida ghetto in 1943? Why is it that Jews work in shops for the Germans, producing German military supplies? Doesn't this prove that the Jews have collaborated with the Germans? Perhaps the last Jewish survivors in the Lida ghetto do really feel grateful towards their well-intentioned regional official, and do take to the woods in order to spy for him?[41]

Such accusations were made repeatedly. Distrust went so far that in September 1943 a special warning against Jewish spies was made part of an order sent down from headquarters to partisan detachments.[42] Also, a number of Jewish women who had managed to escape from the ghetto in Minsk were accused of having been sent by the Germans to poison the food of the partisans.[43] Such instances, were, of course, extreme, but could never have occurred if antisemitism had not made deep inroads into the partisan ranks. From the material amassed by Kaganovich it would appear that the situation of the Jewish partisans in quite a number of detachments was unbearable. There was outspoken hostility towards family camps and non-combatant fugitives in general, because they were regarded as "superfluous eaters."[44] Jews were killed both in the family camps and in the fighting detachments [45] (in the latter case, on account of arms coveted by non-Jewish partisans). In some of the detachments antisemitism was so virulent that Jews felt they had to leave at once, and actually did escape to other districts.[46] In one case (53d squad of the Shchors detachment, Volch'ya-Nora district), a partisan commander ordered all Jews to leave his district; many of those expelled were lucky enough to reach other districts, but a large number had no other choice but to return to the ghetto, where they perished.[47]

Judging from material now available, of which the above incidents are only a fraction, the bulk of the partisan movement must have been affected in one way or another by antisemitism.[48]

Partisan Assistance to Jews

Nevertheless, there are numerous reports of Jews fleeing to the woods who owed their survival to the assistance and protection given them by partisans. According to Kaganovich, an order from Moscow directed the partisan high command to protect non-combatants (i.e., primarily Jewish family camps); it emphasized that the rescue of "Soviet people" was a major objective of the partisan movement.[49] Whether such an order was indeed issued is doubtful;[50] but the fact remains that several Jewish family camps were protected by non-Jewish partisans. "In the Lipichi Forest," Kaganovich writes, "there were individual Russian detachments that assigned food from their own stocks to feed family camps."[51] In Volhynia, where conditions in general were better, because a large part of the region was under partisan control and a rudimentary local government had been early established by partisan commanders, Jewish family camps were under the protection of detachments that supplied them with food. Two such instances were reported from the Polesye region.[52]

In some cases partisans were said to have invaded smaller towns to set Jews free from ghettos or camps. Kaganovich mentions four such exploits: in Sverzh, where the Zhukov detachment saved 170 Jews; in Kossovo, where some 300 Jews were liberated by the 51st squad of the Shchors detachment; an assault by one of Kovpak's detachments on Skalat, Galicia where several hundred Jews were said to have been freed by partisans; and the capture of Molodechno by the Uncle Vanya detachment.[53]

The facts seem fairly well established only in the case of the attack on Sverzh, which was carried out by a Jewish detachment. The Kossovo affair, where according to Kaganovich the attackers included many Jews (who had proposed the foray), had a different aspect. Testimony by one of the Jews liberated in Kossovo says that the town was attacked by some

300 partisans, who succeeded in driving out the German garrison on August 2, 1942.

> After the battle, which lasted four hours, the partisans again fled to the woods. They took along the younger people from among our [Jewish] workers. They would not consent to take along the older and more infirm Jews, and left them behind in the town. I and my brother went with the partisans to the woods.
>
> Monday morning [August 3] Germans arrived from nearby and shot all the surviving Jews.[54]

Kovpak's attack on Skalat, we know from an eyewitness report, did not result in the liberation of the town's Jewish population; only a small number of Jews attached themselves to the partisans, much against the latter's wishes.[55] As for the capture of Molodechno, Kaganovich's reference is too vague to permit verification.[56] However, other facts have been reported that point to the good record of some partisan groups:

> The Russian partisan movement helped Jews cross over to the Soviet side of the front. The brigades headed by Starek, Dombrovskii, Romanov, Zheleznyak, Dyatkov, and Mel'nik, which operated just behind the German lines, conveyed across them many thousands of Jews who had scattered all over White Russia in their flight from slaughter.
>
> The combined detachments under Major General Fedorov-Chernigovskii (area of operations: Chernigov province, later Volhynia) collected more than 500 Jewish children from family camps in the woods; the detachments took care of these children, supplying them with the necessaries of life. After the Red Army had occupied Sarny (Volhynia), some of these detachments broke through the front lines and sent the Jewish children on to Moscow.[57]

There seems to be a certain amount of exaggeration in these reports. If in fact "many thousands of Jews" and hundreds of Jewish children had been rescued by partisan detachments, there should have been more corroboration for this than there is in the Russian and Yiddish Soviet press, in partisan memoirs, in documents collected by the Jewish Historical Commission in Poland, and in the testimony of numerous Jews who left the Soviet Union after the war. Still, there is no reason to assume that the reports quoted by Kaganovich were made out of whole cloth. To some extent they must have had a basis in fact. And modest as those facts may be, they are not to be underestimated.

On the whole, however, the picture is a depressing one. Most partisan detachments were either blatantly or covertly antisemitic; their leadership did not consistently oppose them in this, and their attitude often found support in the local peasantry, with whom the guerrillas came into sporadic yet frequent contact.

Wavering Partisan Command

Antisemitism in the partisan movement did not escape the notice of the high command directing its operations. When making organizational and operational decisions, partisan commanders often took into account the anti-Jewish attitude of their men:

> Knowing of the strong antisemitic feelings of some of the partisans, the leadership of the Soviet partisan movement considered it necessary to scatter Jews among Russian detachments so that they would not strike the eye, or supply antisemites in the partisan ranks with pretexts for accusing Jews of cowardice whenever a special Jewish detachment would suffer defeat in battle or be compelled to retreat for one reason or another. . . .
>
> In fact, however, Jews, though scattered over a great number of Russian detachments, still attracted attention and aroused the hostility of antisemites.
>
> Jews as a rule were given the more dangerous combat assignments. Jews in Russian detachments, whether they wanted to or not, were assigned the most dangerous duty so as to discourage antisemitic talk about Jewish ineptitude in combat or Jewish cowardice.
>
> Defeat or failure in combat, or in carrying out a diversion, of a Russian detachment, company, squad, or platoon was frequently blamed on Jews. Here too Jews were the scapegoat.
>
> Acts of heroism committed by Jews were often ascribed to non-Jews. Conversely, the failures of non-Jews were frequently imputed to Jews. . . .
>
> During the first half of 1943, the atmosphere in some of the Russian detachments had become so tense that Jews feared to go into combat with their non-Jewish fellow fighters.[58]

Conditions improved by the end of 1943. The ranks of the partisans were swelled by more disciplined elements arriving from the Soviet Union to join detachments behind the German lines. But despite this improvement, the basic situation continued bad to the very end:

> Antisemitism and hatred of Jews were so strong, and at times affected large groups of partisans and even part of the leadership in certain districts to such an extent, as to make it difficult to act against the antisemites.
>
> Time and again a partisan who should have been tried for an antisemitic crime would turn out to be a person of special merit . . . having to his credit many trains derailed and many Germans killed, and basking in the reputation of a hero. To a certain extent detachment commanders were prone to defend and excuse their antisemitic partisans, pointing to general tactical considerations and military requirements. . . .

Responsible leaders of the partisan movement and emissaries of the [Communist] party explained all this as follows: There is a war on, nothing can be done right now. It is impossible to stop the source feeding antisemitism. This is not the time to settle accounts. They [the antisemites] valiantly fight against the occupiers, let's not hinder them. Under the conditions prevailing in the woods it is difficult to maintain strict discipline over so great a number of people. There will come a day when they will have to pay for everything.[59]

Jewish Partisans and the Local Peasantry

One of the sources of partisan antisemitism was the local peasantry. Partisans, as a rule, lived off the land; the peasants who bore the burden of these requisitions had also to endure the repeated requisitioning and outright confiscation of foodstuffs by the German authorities:

> The peasant was caught between hammer and anvil. If he failed to deliver his "quota" to the Germans, his farm was set afire and he was killed for being a "partisan." On the other hand, the partisans, using force, robbed him of everything they needed. . . . Two and a half years of the partisan movement had devastated the peasant economy in partisan districts. In the Lipichi Forest, for example, some villages were left, on the eve of liberation, with just one cow for every four or five farms and one horse for every two or three farms.[60]

The peasants suffering requisitions at the hands of the partisans might feel that the fight against the Germans justified the sacrifice. But they often treated the demands of the Jewish family camps, whose members were not engaged in combat, with open hostility; they bitterly resented their possessions, not only food, but also shoes and clothing, and even women's dresses, being forcibly seized for the use of Jewish "civilians." They inveighed against the Jewish partisans in general, and Jewish foraging detachments in particular. The local peasantry's antisemitism reinforced that of the partisans, who often had close ties with them.

Kaganovich has recorded many instances of antisemitism on the part of local populations. This hostile environment made Jewish life in the woods still more wretched, especially for non-combatants, and increased the number of their casualties. The death rate among Jews in the forests was very high as a result of privations and exposure, punitive raids by the Nazis (with the collaboration of Ukrainian, Russian, and other hirelings), and the depradations of bandits who flocked to the woods and even wormed their way into organized detachments:

> Of the Jews who by superhuman efforts succeeded in escaping from the ghettos in Western White Russia and the Ukraine, only a tiny fraction lived to see the liberation.
> Some 800 Jews escaped from the ghetto in Dzhetl to the Lipichi Forest. Of these, only 250 are alive today.

Of more than 1,000 Jews from the ghetto in Pruzhany who reached freedom, not above 100 have remained alive.

A large part of the Jewish population managed to escape from the Volhynian cities and from Kamen'-Kashirsk, Tutchin, and Sernik in the Polesye region; of these, only isolated individuals are among the living today.

In the city of Mir, 180 Jews fled from the ghetto, but only 40 of them have survived.[61]

Casualties among Jewish partisans were much fewer. The total number of Jewish partisans in White Russia and Western Ukraine has been estimated at 10,000 to 11,000; of these, some 3,000 were killed in battle.[62]

The Aftermath of Liberation

The survivors of the family camps were set free by the advance of the Red Army. New tribulations, however, even then awaited some of the Jewish guerrilla fighters:

Immediately after liberation Jewish partisans were drafted into the Red Army advancing on Germany.

There were instances when after the demobilization of partisan detachments virtually all Jews were sent to the front (the Ordzhonikidze, Red Guard, Victory, etc. detachments). . . . In non-Jewish detachments, as a rule, only those were sent to the front who originally had served in the German Wehrmacht and who had not come to the woods before the second half of 1943—those, in short, who had to atone for their betrayal of the homeland.

Partisans in civilian dress, with guerrilla weapons, untrained for such combat conditions, unfamiliar with the tactics of open fighting, were thrown into advanced positions. . . .

A few who were lucky enough to incur disabling wounds, have survived. Most of the others perished in the battles near Volkovisk, Bialystok, and Lake Narev.[63]

This discriminatory policy was not a general one. After liberation, local partisan leaders usually established themselves as the government and improvised whatever policy they saw fit. The detachments cited above were active in the districts of Novogrudok, Pinsk, and Slonim.[64] Conditions were different in other places.[65] Yet the discouraging experience in the ranks of the partisans left a deep imprint on the Jewish survivors in White Russia and Western Ukraine. Most of them now felt like strangers in their native land. As soon as the Soviet government permitted repatriation to Poland, large numbers of these veterans of the guerrilla war, many of them decorated by the Soviet Union for valor, availed themselves of this chance to leave. The mood of these disillusioned men has been described by Kaganovich, himself one of them, as follows:

In the woods the Jewish partisan had had to fight . . . against antisemitically biased partisans. Not for a single moment was he able to forget that he was a Jew. . . .

Seldom has national awareness been as strong among Jews as it was among the partisans in the woods. It is no accident that the partisans were the first to register for repatriation—their thought was to reach Palestine, build a home of their hown, and if they had to give their lives, give them for their own people.[66]

Kaganovich has perhaps made too much of the determination of those fleeing the land of the Soviets to go to Palestine; many had only the vaguest notion as to their destination. But whatever its goal, this exodus of Jewish partisans who had fought on the Soviet side shows the profound effect the growth of antisemitism during the war and occupation had on the few Jews that survived.

NOTES

1. *Pravda*, November 1, 1939.
2. See Appendix to Part I.
3. From a collection of German documents (file Occ E 3a-2) in the YIVO archives, New York.
4. *Nazi Conspiracy and Aggression*, Office of U. S. Chief of Counsel for Prosecution of Axis Criminality, U. S. Government Printing Office, Washington, D. C., 1946, vol. VII, p. 979. This valuable collection of German documents suffers from wretched translation, so that the precise meaning has often to be guessed at. The spelling, especially of geographical names, has been corrected.
5. *Ibid.*, pp. 983ff.
6. After the pogroms carried out in the early days of occupation, German authorities proceeded to institute an organized system of extermination. Actual operations were entrusted to special detachments of the German Security Police, "reinforced by selected units—in Lithuania partisan detachments, in Latvia units of the Latvian auxiliary police" (*ibid.*).
7. *Nazi Conspiracy and Aggression*, vol. VIII, p. 101.
8. YIVO archives, file Occ E 3a-14. The report was passed on to the Reich Commissariat for the Eastern Areas by Major Doven, Chief of Staff to the Commander-in-Chief of the Armed Forces in the Eastern Areas (*Ostland*).
9. *Nazi Conspiracy and Aggression*, vol. VIII, p. 103.
10. *Ibid.*, vol. V, pp. 772–776.
11. *Ibid.*, p. 774.
12. One such instance does exist. Reporting on a three-week trip to the Ukraine and the Crimea sponsored by the Reich Ministry of the East in June 1943, Dr. Hans Joachim Kausch, a German journalist, mentioned the fact that 1,100,000 Jews had been "completely liquidated" in the Ukrainian *Zivilverwaltungsgebiet*, and that on his trip he had seen only four Jews (in a penal camp!); he then stated: "The Ukrainians displayed rather an indifferent [negative?] attitude towards the execution of Jews. In the course of the final executions last winter, resistance was put up by a few villages." This document (YIVO archives, file Occ E4-11) has so far found no corroboration in any Soviet document available outside of the Soviet Union.
13. *Merder fun Felker, Tsveyte Zamlung*, Moscow, 1945, p. 3
14. Independent Jewish Press Service, October 23, 1944.
15. *Merder fun Felker*, Moscow, 1944, p. 61.
16. Independent Jewish Press Service, October 23, 1944.
17. *Ibid.*, December 6, 1943.

18. G. Smolyar, *Fun Minsker Getto*, *Emes* Publishers, Moscow, 1946, pp. 77f.

19. It is inconceivable, for instance, that the wife should have been so careless as to attract the vigilance of the police by carrying parcels to jailed friends while her husband and father-in-law were engaged in important and dangerous underground work. Nor does the arrangement with the person in the city administration seem to make sense, for foundlings would normally be referred to Municipal Children's Homes, without secret pre-arrangement, password, or code. It is also hard to imagine that the smuggling-out of children should have taken place regularly over a period of weeks at the same place and hour without having been noticed. Ghetto conditions, as a rule, required greater inventiveness in finding ever changing ways of evading the watchfulness of the guards.

20. Grossman's reports on the Ukraine appeared in *Eynikayt* on November 25 and December 2, 1943 (and were later reprinted in several American newspapers). They were not, however, carried by *Krasnaya Zvezda*, the army newspaper whose correspondent Grossman was at the time, nor were they included in the bulky volume of Grossman's war dispatches and short stories issued (in Russian) in Moscow in 1945. *Eynikayt* discontinued the publication of Grossman's articles with the second one, though further installments had been promised.

21. *Eynikayt*, December 2, 1943.

22. In his highly informative book on the destruction of the Vilna Jewish community, Dr. Dworzecki, himself a survivor of the Vilna ghetto, though pointing out that only a small part of the population actively helped Jews, mentions seven professors of the University of Vilna who at great personal risk hid Jewish fugitives, supplied them with funds, etc.; the director of the Vilna Archives, a Lithuanian teacher, and a Polish nun who jointly hid and saved 12 Jews; several Polish women who each rescued scores of Jewish fugitives; former domestics of Jewish families who hid and saved the latter's children; a number of Catholic priests, Polish and Lithuanian, who helped Jews, hid them, and urged their parishioners to do likewise; the prioress of the Benedictine nunnery near Vilna, who concealed 17 Jews of the ghetto underground movement, and who also provided a meeting-place for conferences between Jewish resistance leaders and a Polish underground courier sent by the Jewish underground in Warsaw; numerous Poles who served as couriers of ghetto underground groups; and many others. Having recorded these instances—in Vilna alone—of which he had personal knowledge, Dworzecki added: "I imagine that the number of Poles, and of Gentiles in general, who hid Jews was considerably higher than we know. Rural Poles, incidentally, showed greater humanity than city-dwellers. Many more Poles would probably have given refuge to Jews if not for fear of discovery. The Germans hanged a man (a Jew) on Cathedral Square in Vilna, and announced in posters and newspapers that he was a Christian executed for having helped Jews; the corpse was left exposed to public view for several days." (Mark Dworzecki, *Yerushalayim d'Lite in Kamf un Umkum*, issued by the Jewish People's Union of France and the Jewish National Workers' Alliance in the United States, Paris, 1948, pp. 326ff., 335ff., 345f.)

23. A tortured lament over this attitude of indifference was written during the war by the much-commended Ukrainian Jewish poet Savva Golovanivskii. It was never printed in any Moscow publication, but more recently served as evidence of the poet's criminal "slandering" of the Soviet people. (See p. 359 below.)

24. A special organization for helping Jews was established by the Polish Underground Government in 1942, the Council for Aid to Jews (Rada Pomocy Zydom), in which all democratic parties participated; government funds and facilities were placed at its disposal. As in France, the Catholic Church took an active part in rescuing Jews, and many Jewish children were hidden in monasteries. See *In di Yorn fun Idishen Khurbn*, Undzer Tsayt Publications, New York, 1948, pp. 79f., 101f.; Bernard Goldstein, *Finf Yor in Varshever Getto*, same publisher, New York, 1947, pp. 373ff.; Betti Ajzensztajn, ed., *Ruch Podziemny w Ghettach i Obozach (Materialy i Dokumenty)*, published by Centralna Zydowska Komisia Historyczna w Polsce, Warszawa—Lodz—Kraków, 1946, p. 65.

25. YIVO archives, file Occ E 3b α-22.

26. *Ibid.*, file Occ E 3b α-63.

27. *Ibid.*, file Occ E 3b β-19.

28. *Ibid.*, file Occ E 3a-15.

29. *Ibid.*

30. *Ibid.*, file Occ E 3b α-45.

31. The YIVO collection, though of course incomplete, is comprehensive enough to serve as evidence. Other underground documents have been cited elsewhere. Moshe Kaganovich's book on the Jewish partisans (see n. 36 below) reproduced the February 17, 1944 issue of *Chyrvonnaya Zvyazda*, the underground publication of the Baranovichi district committee of the Communist Party of White Russia; it dealt with Nazi atrocities in Slonim and began with an article entitled "Gruesome Anti-Jewish Pogroms." This, however, was printed in 1944, at a time when the defeat of Hitlerism already seemed assured and Soviet policy no longer required that the Nazis' antisemitic misdeeds be eliminated from public discussion.

32. S. A. Kovpak, *Ot Putivlya do Karpat* [*From Putivl' to the Carpathians*], Moscow–Leningrad, 1945.

33. Petro Vershigora, "Lyudi chistoi sovesti" ["Men Whose Consciences Are Clear"], in *Znamya*, August 1945 and April–July 1946.

34. Kovpak's and Vershigora's memoirs best describe guerrilla action in the Soviet West, i.e., chiefly in the Ukraine west of the Dnieper and in White Russia. There was almost no partisan movement in the woodless Ukraine east of the Dnieper; in the Crimea and the northern Caucasus, where fewer Jews lived before the war, no problem arose in the ranks of the partisans.

35. Among contributions by Jewish writers, the following are fairly representative: Smolyar, *op. cit.;* M. Yelin and D. Gelpern, *Partizaner fun Kaunaser Geto*, Emes Publishers, Moscow, 1948; M. Lev, *Partizaner Vegn*, Moscow, 1948 (an inferior journalistic work).

36. Moshe Kaganovich, *Der Idisher Ontayl in der Partizaner-Bavegung fun Sovet-Rusland*, Central Historical Commission of the Partisan Federation PAKHAKH in Italy, Rome, 1948.

37. How much Polish material still remains to be digested can be seen from a catalogue of depositions compiled by Estera Goldhar-Markowa in "Materialy o udziale Zydów polskich w partyzant ce w Archiwum Z.I.H.," in *Biuletyn Zydowskiego Instytutu Historycznego pry C. K. Zydów w Polsce*, March, 1950, pp. 9–14.

38. Jewish partisans revenged themselves upon their oppressors by subjecting captive Germans to a "Jewish death." One can understand but not condone this. And one must certainly condemn a historian writing three years after the defeat of Hitler who, instead of seeking to explain such behavior historically and psychologically, glories in it.

39. Kaganovich, *op. cit.*, pp. 165ff.

40. *Ibid.*, p. 70.

41. *Ibid.*, p. 183. See also Tobya and Zusya Bielski, *Yehudey Yaar*, [*Forest Jews*], Tel Aviv, 1946, p. 164.

42. Kaganovich, *op. cit.*

43. *Ibid.;* see also Bielski, *op. cit.*, p. 220.

44. Kaganovich, *op. cit.*, p. 149.

45. *Ibid.*, pp. 149, 170, 177, 180f., 185.

46. *Ibid.*, p. 175.

47. *Ibid.*, p. 155f.

48. Corroboration of Kaganovich's observations can be found in reports collected by the Jewish Historical Commission in Poland (see the affidavits of the ex-partisans Lazar Bromberg, Benjamin Dombrowskii, Jozef Elman, Fima Gelfand, Abram Lerer, Yankel Reznik, and Izer Szwarc, on file with YIVO); in the testimonies published by the *Bulletin of the Joint Rescue Committee of the Jewish Agency for Palestine*, March 1945, pp. 19f. (ex-partisan R. K.); April 1945, pp. 9ff. (Yom-Tov

M.); August 1947, p. 13 (Tobya Bielski); and in the books already cited by Tobya and Zusya Bielski, Mark Dworzecki, S. Kaczerginski, and others.

49. Kaganovich, *op. cit.*, p. 143.

50. Kaganovich fails to mention even as much as the date of issuance of the order. Elsewhere (p. 188) he "quotes" an edict of the Presidium of the Supreme Soviet of the USSR purportedly issued "near the end of 1941" bearing the signatures of Kalinin and Gorkin and calling upon Soviet authorities to provide for the evacuation of Jews from imperiled areas. No such order was ever issued; the writer apparently was misled by an apocryphal document, which may also have been the case with the order concerning non-combatants.

51. Kaganovich, *op. cit.*, p. 151.

52. *Ibid.*, pp. 153f.

53. *Ibid.*, pp. 189ff.

54. Dovid Leibovich, "Bay Kossove in Polesye," in *Fun Letstn Khurbn: Tsaytshrift far Geshikhte fun Idishn Lebn baym Natsi-Rezhim*, Munich, no. 6 (August 1947), p. 50.

55. Kovpak himself (*op. cit.*, p. 126), while describing in detail the capture of Skalat, made no mention of Jews having been liberated by his detachment; nor did Fima Gelfand, a Jewish girl who spent two years with Kovpak's guerrillas and took part in their march from White Russia to Galicia (cf. her affidavit, No. 714, in Materials from the Lodz Archives, Documents of the Centralna Zydowska Komisia Historyczna w Polsce, on file with YIVO). According to Abraham Weissbrod, Kovpak's partisans upon entering Skalat seized the German depots, destroyed the buildings containing German offices, and blew up the bridges, actively assisted in all this by the local Jewish population. "When the partisans were preparing to leave, almost all the Jews asked to be taken along. But the partisans refused, saying that they needed soldiers, healthy men, and not Jews from the concentration camp who could barely drag their feet. Nevertheless, when the Soviet forces departed, they were followed by about 30 of the stronger Jews from the camp who refused to remain where they would meet certain death. The soldiers drove them back with sticks, but they continued to follow. After many trials several days later they were finally given arms and permitted to join the partisan detachment. Most of these young men from Skalat later perished in the great battle of the Carpathians." (*Es Shtarbt a Shtetl. Mgiles Skalat*, ed. I. Kaplan, Central Historical Commission of the Central Committee of Liberated Jews in the U. S. Zone of Germany, Munich, 1948, pp. 133ff.)

56. The Uncle Vanya detachment was mentioned only this once in Kaganovich's book. Thus it would seem that no former members of the detachment were among the partisans supplying information to PAKHAKH, and that Kaganovich got it secondhand.

57. Kaganovich, *op. cit.*, p. 189.

58. *Ibid.*, pp. 141f.

59. *Ibid.*, pp. 186f.

60. *Ibid.*, pp. 68f.

61. *Ibid.*, p. 280.

62. *Ibid.*, p. x.

63. *Ibid.*, pp. 281f.

64. *Ibid.*, pp. 25, 44, 55 and 144f. See also Bielski, *op. cit.*, pp. 194f.

65. Ex-partisans from the Vilna region had no knowledge of this type of discrimination when questioned by the present writer, except in one instance, in Oshmyany, where the commander ordering all Jewish veterans to the front was himself a Jew.

66. Kaganovich, *op. cit.*, p. 185.

CHAPTER VI

Demoralizing Effects of the War

Jewish Tragedy Shrouded in Silence

During the two years of Nazi-Soviet friendship (1939–1941), the Soviet press consistently refrained from discussing or even mentioning the German onslaught against the Jews. The outbreak of war brought scarcely any change in this. Although the fate of the Jewish population in the occupied provinces could not possibly have been unknown to the Soviet government, the press did nothing to strike back at the anti-Jewish heart of Nazi propaganda. Not only was there no discussion of antisemitism (this writer found not one article on the subject in this period), the very fact of the wholesale extermination of Jews was kept out of the Soviet newspapers.

During the first months of the war the Soviet press simply abstained from printing reports about the fate of Jews on the other side of the battle lines. Then, on January 6, 1942, in a note signed by Vyacheslav M. Molotov to all governments with which the Soviet Union maintained diplomatic relations, the government called attention to the "universal pillage" and "monstrous atrocities" committed by the "German authorities in Soviet territories seized by them."[1] The lot of the Jews was impossible to ignore:

> The German invaders stop at nothing to insult in every way the national sentiments of the Russians, Ukrainians, Byelorussians, Letts, Lithuanians, Estonians and Moldavians in the districts of the Soviet Republics they have occupied. Individuals of other nationalities encountered on their bloody path are subjected to similar outrages and violence —Jews, Georgians, Armenians, Uzbeks, Azerbaijanians, Tadjiks and others of the Soviet peoples closely united by ties of fraternal friendship and collaboration in the Soviet Union.[2]

The Jews, whose sufferings were immeasurably more terrible, were lost in this list. A second reference by the note to the Jewish minority was much the same:

> On June 30 the Hitlerite bandits entered Lvov, and on the very day staged an orgy of murder under the slogan: "Kill the Jews and the Poles." Having murdered hundreds of people, the Hitlerite bandits held an "exhibition" of the corpses in the city arcade.[3]

An enumeration of individual instances of German atrocities in Lvov and other places followed, and many victims were named, but none of the names was Jewish. Towards the end of the note a third reference to Jews was made:

Horrible massacres and pogroms were perpetrated by the German invaders in the Ukrainian capital, Kiev. Within a few days the Germans killed and tortured to death 52,000 men, women, old folk and children, dealing mercilessly with all Ukrainians, Russians and Jews who in any way displayed their loyalty to the Soviet Government. Soviet citizens who managed to escape from Kiev, give an amazing account of one of the mass executions: A large number of Jews, including women and children of all ages, was gathered in the Jewish cemetery of Kiev. Before they were shot all of them were stripped naked and beaten. The first persons selected for shooting were forced to lie face down at the bottom of a ditch and were shot with automatic rifles. Then the Germans shoveled a little earth over their bodies. The next group of people awaiting execution was forced to lie on top of them and was shot in the same way.

Many mass murders were also committed by the German occupationists in other Ukrainian towns. These bloody executions were especially directed against unarmed and defenseless Jewish working people. According to incomplete figures, no less than 6,000 persons were shot in Lvov, over 8,000 in Odessa, nearly 8,500 killed and hanged in Kamenets-Podolsk, more than 10,500 shot down with machine guns in Dnepropetrovsk, and over 3,000 local inhabitants shot in Mariupol, including many old men, women, children, all of whom were robbed and stripped naked before execution. According to preliminary figures, about 7,000 persons were killed by the German fascist butchers in Kerch.[4]

The holocaust depicted in the first paragraph was the infamous massacre of Babii-Yar, one of the most ferocious in the long tale of Nazi crimes. But even this naked singling-out of Jews for slaughter was described merely as part of a universal campaign of indiscriminate persecution directed against "Ukrainians, Russians and Jews who in any way displayed their loyalty to the Soviet Government." The facts, however, were so unequivocal that it was hardly possible to maintain this attitude. Molotov went on to tell of the extermination of Jews, as Jews, in Kiev, Lvov, Odessa, Dnepropetrovsk, etc.

Yet even then Soviet newspapers did not break their silence. The taboo placed on all discussion of the Hitlerite extermination of the Jews remained as much in force after as before the publication of the Molotov note.

In a second Molotov note of April 27, 1942, dealing with the "monstrous misdeeds, atrocities and acts of violence of the German fascist intruders in occupied Soviet areas, and . . . the responsibility of the German government and high command for these crimes,"[5] the extermination of Jews as the prime objective of Hitlerite policy was studiously ignored:

> The bloodthirsty, criminal plans of the fascists are bent on exterminating the Russians, Ukrainians, Byelorussians and other peoples of the Soviet Union. These monstrous fascist plans motivate the orders and instructions of the German command when it calls for the extermination of Soviet citizens.[6]

Whoever drafted the note could not have been unaware that Nazi policy, savagely though it dealt with Russians, Ukrainians, White Russians, etc., was not directed at their physical annihilation as national groups. This effort to make out the Soviet citizen as the target of the German fury perverted the note. The killings of "peace-abiding citizens" in Taganrog, Kerch, Vitebsk, Pinsk, and Minsk were mentioned in some detail. "Hundreds of thousands of Ukrainians, Russians, Jews, Moldavians and peaceful citizens of other nationalities," the note said, "perished at the hands of German hangmen in Ukrainian cities."[7] That most of the victims were Jews went unmentioned, and the preamble to the note misrepresented the goal of the Hitlerites as "the extermination of the Soviet population, prisoners of war and guerrillas through bloody violence, tortures, executions and mass killings of Soviet citizens, regardless of nationality, social status, sex and age."[8] The phrase, "regardless of nationality," unmistakably betrays the calculated lie.

Communist propaganda abroad, however, depicted the Soviet Union as the champion of persecuted Jewry, the best defender of the Jewish masses. All over the world, and particularly in the United States, a lengthy declaration issued by the Soviet government in December 1942 "on the implementation by Hitlerite authorities of the plan of extermination of Europe's Jewish population,"[9] was frequently cited by pro-Soviet writers.

At first glance, the statement of December 19, 1942 seems flagrantly to contradict the tenor of Soviet propaganda in 1941–42. Its purpose, however, can be understood only in connection with the joint declaration made by the United Nations on the "bestial policy of cold-blooded extermination" carried out against the Jewish people by the "barbarous Hitlerite tyranny" published the day before.[10] This declaration, which all the European nations aligned against Germany, including the Soviet Union, signed, and also the United States, said "that the German authorities, not content with denying to persons of Jewish race in all the territories over which their barbarous rule has been extended, the most elementary human rights, are now carrying into effect Hitler's oft-repeated intention to exterminate the Jewish people in Europe"; it also "reaffirmed" the signatories' "solemn resolution to insure that those responsible for these crimes shall not escape retribution and to press on with the necessary practical measures to this end." The Soviet statement of December 19, 1942 only reveals its true meaning against the background of this joint declaration by the Allies. It sought to blunt the pointedness of the Allied declaration, take away the special emphasis the latter placed on the persecution of the Jews as an essential part of Nazi policy and strategy.

The Soviet statement, while referring to the joint declaration of the Allies, said in the most general terms:

> Of late an intensification of the Hitlerite regime's bloody elimination of peaceful populations has been observed everywhere in European countries occupied by the German fascist invaders. . . . [The Nazis] are carrying out their bestial plan of physically exterminating large sections of the civilian population in German-occupied territories, utterly guiltless people of various nationalities, social rank, creeds and beliefs, and of all ages.[11]

However, to continue to maintain that the Jews were not being singled out by the Nazis would have contrasted too strikingly with the joint declaration of which the Soviet Union was a signatory. Along with the physical extermination of "large sections of the civilian population," it was admitted that the Nazis pursued "a special plan for the total extermination of the Jewish population in Europe's occupied territory . . . and also in Germany proper." Hair-raising details were given and the individual countries were listed in which anti-Jewish astrocities took place: Germany, Hungary, Rumania, Poland, Czechoslovakia, Austria, France, Belgium, Holland, Norway; in these countries only, according to the People's Commissariat for Foreign Affairs, was Hitler's "special plan" being executed. "German-occupied territories" of the Soviet Union were not included; the statement explicitly distinguished between "Europe's occupied territory" and Nazi-held "Soviet areas," apparently with the inference that in the latter the victims of Nazi antisemitism were foreigners, that is, Jews brought there from Central and Western Europe:

> Reports coming in from Soviet areas temporarily taken by the enemy . . . supplement information on the Hitlerites' bloody elimination of the Jewish population of Europe's occupied countries. Bestial atrocities committed against Jews brought from Central and Western Europe also are reported from Minsk, Bialystok, Brest, Baranovichi and other cities of the White-Russian SSR.

The killing of Soviet Jews was of course not denied, but this was made to seem only part of a campaign of extermination directed against the Soviet population in its entirety:

The monstrous crimes committed by Hitlerite robbers, rapists, and hangmen against peaceful Soviet citizens already have been exposed to the scorn of the whole world. In their overwhelming majority the victims of these orgies of banditry and murder are Russian, Ukrainian, and White-Russian peasants, workers, salaried employees, and intellectuals. The toll is heavy among the Lithuanian, Latvian, and Estonian peoples, among Moldavians, and among inhabitants of the Karel-Finnish Republic. Considering its small numbers the Jewish minority of the Soviet population . . . has suffered particularly heavily from the bestial bloodthirstiness of the Hitlerite degenerates.

Very recently, over all the Soviet territory that they have seized, Hitlerite occupationists have intensified still further their bloody regime of mass murder, punitive expeditions, burnings of villages, deportations of hundreds of thousands of peaceful citizens into slavery in Germany. . . . Information has been received that in this atmosphere of mad frenzy the Hitlerites also [sic] include Soviet citizens of Jewish nationality in the execution of their plan of total extermination. Thus, intensification of the terror against the Ukrainian population last summer and fall was accompanied by a number of bloody anti-Jewish pogroms in several places in the Ukrainian SSR.

Details on the pogroms were furnished. When lifted out of their context and given all together, as for example in a JTA dispatch from Moscow on December 22, 1942,[12] these details indeed gave the impression that the Soviet government was vigorously striking out against the Nazis' persecution of the Jewish people. Actually, the statement concentrated on the terror directed against "Russian, Ukrainian, and White-Russian peasants, workers, salaried employees, and intellectuals," making the Jews' case seem of secondary importance. The Soviet government was still not willing openly and consistently to expose the anti-Jewish essence of the Nazi atrocities and the Soviet statement was not commented upon in the Soviet press, nor did the authorities ever refer to it again. It did not herald a more active fight against Nazi antisemitism.

Silence on the anti-Jewish terror was particularly striking in official releases dealing with Nazi crimes in different cities and provinces of the Soviet Union. These releases, lengthy and detailed statements for the most part, appeared at irregular intervals in the leading Soviet newspapers between April 1943 and May 1945; they were issued by the Extraordinary State Committee for the Ascertaining and Investigation of Crimes Committed by the German-Fascist Invaders, which had been set up in November 1942.[13] Throughout this period the Extraordinary State Committee released 17 such statements,[14] a report on the Oswiecim death camp[15] and several special documents which need not be discussed here.[16] An analysis of these releases from year to year shows the successive stages in the evolution of the Soviet attitude to the extermination of Jews.

In 1943 the Extraordinary State Committee issued 7 general releases, of which 6 did not so much as mention Jews. The report on Nazi misdeeds in the province of Stavropol (Northern Caucasus) was the exception. There the well-known writer Aleksei N. Tolstoi, a member of the Academy of Sciences and of the Supreme Soviet of the USSR, personally supervised the excavation of a ditch near the Mineral'nyye-Vody railroad terminal, in which the corpses of over 6,000 Jews were found, among them many scholars, university professors, doctors, and other outstanding intellectuals from Leningrad who had been evacuated to the Northern Caucasus with their respective institutions early in the war. Tolstoi was deeply stirred by what he saw; his article, "Bloody Delirium," appearing in *Pravda* along with the Committee's statement,[17] was an outcry against the Nazis' anti-Jewish savagery. It is presumably thanks to Tolstoi's great prestige and influence that the story of the extermination of Jews in Stavropol was included in the official release.

But even this isolated reference to the extermination of Jews was apparently frowned upon. In December 1943 Tolstoi had several articles published in *Pravda*, in which he commented on the trial of participants in the Nazi atrocities in Kharkov; in addition, *Pravda* printed the detailed charges and daily carried a comprehensive, almost stenographic, account of the court proceedings.[18] Not even the word "Jew" was mentioned. The extermination of the Kharkov Jews was referred to as follows:

> In November 1941 some 20,000 civilian inhabitants of the city of Kharkov were moved under Gestapo orders from their apartments in the city to barracks located in the area of the Kharkov Tractor Works. Later on, they were taken, in groups of 200 to 300, to the near-by scrap yard where they were shot.[19]

Although Tolstoi had been in court throughout the trial, he made no reference to Jews in his comments on the trial; it can safely be assumed that he had been told to avoid the subject, for we know the man's personal temper from an article, "Retribution!", dealing primarily with the extermination of Jews, that he wrote upon the conclusion of the trial. Judging from its style and presentation, the article had been written for a newspaper, presumably *Pravda*; yet it never appeared in any newspaper, being published, after much delay, in the out-of-the-way scholarly annals of the Academy of Sciences.[20] The Nazis' crimes against the Jews apparently could not be discussed in the daily press.

This silence was maintained almost without interruption until late in 1944. Among the surveys of atrocities printed in 1944, even reports on places such as Kiev and Odessa, centers of Jewish life before the Nazi invasion, omitted any mention of the Jewish victims. Only once in the

first half of 1944 did the Extraordinary State Committee, reporting on
the city and province of Rovno, another area with a large Jewish population, quote an eyewitness to the effect that he had "seen more than once
how the Hitlerites destroyed Soviet citizens—Ukrainians, Russians, Poles,
Jews."[21] Messages to Stalin from the population of this or that liberated
region followed the same pattern; no crimes against Jews were mentioned
in messages from such regions as Zhitomir,[22] Vitebsk,[23] or Vinnitsa,[24]
where Jews had been especially numerous before the war.

The veil was lifted once, when *Pravda* in August 1944 printed the
address of the citizens of Minsk to Stalin:

> Of the civilian population in Minsk, more than 150,000 were killed,
> cremated, or hanged by the Hitlerite executioners. Minsk is ringed
> round on three sides by the burial grounds of victims torn to pieces
> and tortured to death by the German degenerates. The Jewish popula-
> tion was exterminated completely. The German Fascist invaders had
> driven 50,000 people from Minsk and the surrounding districts into
> the so-called ghetto. In addition, over 40,000 Jews had been brought to
> the Minsk ghetto from Hamburg, Warsaw, and Lodz. The ghetto's
> entire population was bestially tortured to death by the German
> executioners. Indescribable torments and suffering were the lot of
> men of science and culture. After prolonged abuse, the German
> degenerates bestially killed Professor Sitterman, an outstanding physi-
> cian; Professor Khurgin, one of the best surgeons; Professor Dvorzhits,
> one of the greatest specialists on diseases of the eye; Professor Klumov,
> the gynecologist; one of the city's most popular pediatricians, Gurevich;
> and many others.[25]

Six weeks later a survey of the Minsk atrocities, more reticent about
the fate of the Jewish population, was released by the Extraordinary
State Committee.[26] While the Committee could not possibly ignore the
citizens' report to Stalin, it chose to shift the emphasis away from the
Nazis' Jewish victims. All individuals mentioned by the Committee as
having been killed or having miraculously survived bore non-Jewish
names: Savinskaya, Golubovich, Professor Anisimov, etc.; of the Jewish
victims listed in the citizens' message, the Committee mentioned only one,
Klumov, whose name is not a Jewish one.

Thereafter the anti-Jewish misdeeds of the Nazis were again shrouded
in silence. A release on Estonia dwelt in detail on the death camp in
Klogi, where thousands of Jews had been put to death, but Jews were
not referred to.[27] A statement on Lithuania painstakingly enumerating
and describing Nazi camps in the area, said that tens of thousands had
been killed there. "Scholars and workers, engineers and students, Catholic
and Greek-Orthodox priests, not only residents of Vilnius [Vilna], but
also people of other cities, market towns, and villages in the Lithuanian

SSR," were slaughtered in Poneryai (Ponary) near Vilna;[28] and "peaceful citizens from Kaunas" and "nationals of France, Austria, and Czechoslovakia" were slaughtered at the Kaunas "death fort"; but no mention was made of Jews.[29]

Not until the very end of 1944 did the Committee refer directly to the war of destruction waged by the Nazis against the Jews; the survey of events in Lvov gave a number of details on the extermination of Jews,[30] and a belated report on conditions in Latvia devoted a special chapter to the "Bloody Elimination of the Jewish Population of the Latvian SSR at the Hands of the Germans."[31] This did not herald an end of the policy followed by the Committee from its inception. Another month went by and the Committee released material on Oswiecim (Auschwitz), perhaps the most dreadful spot on the face of the earth in those years, where over four million human beings, the overwhelming majority Jews, were gassed, cremated, or beaten to death. But unbelievable though it may seem, the word "Jew" was not so much as mentioned in the report on Oswiecim.[32]

The Extraordinary State Committee's attitude was revealed in its selection of commissioners to conduct the investigations of Nazi crimes. The Committee itself had one Jewish member, Professor I. P. Trainin, who was chosen not because he was a Jew, but as an authority on international law. Representatives of the Jewish community were not invited to assist the local investigating commissions, which were made up of Soviet officials of different categories and a small number of well-known local citizens. In some places (Stalino, Novgorod, Odessa) representatives of the Greek Orthodox clergy served on the commissions, and in one case (Rovno) both a Greek Orthodox and a Roman Catholic priest together. No Jews were appointed to serve as commissioners, not even in Kiev, Rovno, Minsk, or Oswiecim; only in Odessa was the representative of the Extraordinary State Committee a Jew, the aforemential legal expert, Trainin. The absence of Jews among the investigators [33] is indicative of the government's reluctance to draw public attention to the catastrophe Nazism had brought down upon the Jewish population.

When the Supreme Soviet of the Ukrainian SSR convened for the first time after the liberation on March 1, 1944, the fate of the 1,500,000 Jewish citizens of the Ukraine was not alluded to in the keynote address by Nikita Khrushchev, chairman of the Ukrainian Council of People's Commissars and secretary of the Central Committee of the Communist Party of the Ukraine. Speaking at great length on the occupation, Khrushchev, with a great display of emotion, paid tribute to the memory of hundreds of thousands of men and women killed or tortured to death, and recalled the sufferings and privations to which "our people" had been subjected by the enemy. He omitted saying that a huge proportion—

probably the overwhelming majority—of the civilians put to death by the Nazis had been Jews.[34]

As a result of the official silence, there was nothing to oppose the spread of Hitlerite antisemitism. The motives of this policy, which of course was never acknowledged to exist, are easy to make out in retrospect. It is apparent that the Soviet leaders were swayed by the fear lest an open and relentless denunciation of the extermination of Jews facilitate the task of Nazi propaganda, which would seize on this to denounce the "Judaeo-Bolshevik tyranny." It can also be assumed that underlying such "strategic" considerations was a certain emotional predisposition to ignore the Nazis' anti-Jewish offensive; this grew out of that disguised and stealthy antisemitism which had penetrated the ruling class of Soviet society after the Great Purge and in the years before the outbreak of the war.

This silence on the part of Soviet propaganda had the effect of disarming the masses of the people, who were daily exposed to the influence of the Nazi antisemitic hysteria. It allowed them to believe that there was nothing particularly harmful in the anti-Jewish aspects of Nazi philosophy and action. Thus antisemitism spread like wildfire in Nazi-held territories and also far beyond the range of German conquest.

The Soviet government's failure to fight antisemitism also paved the way for an unexpected Nazi success. In the Ukraine antisemitism frequently served as a mask for anti-Soviet Ukrainian nationalism and separatism. In the long run this caused the Soviet Union a great deal of tribulation. It proved so menacing that after the liberation of the Ukraine, the Soviet authorities, in order to win over nationalist Ukrainian groups, felt compelled to offer a special amnesty [35] to Ukrainian nationalists who had fought against the Red Army and taken an active part in the extermination of Jews, either in overt collaboration with the Nazis or on their own. (The amnesty had little apparent success.)

The policy of silence, which had been intended to weaken the force of enemy propaganda, thus abetted it and proved self-defeating.

Wartime Antisemitism

The policy of secrecy observed by the Soviet Administration in regard to the extermination of Jews would seem to indicate their holding a rather pessimistic view of the state of mind of the Soviet people. Men in leading positions seem all along to have expected that disclosure of the Nazi crimes against the Jews, far from arousing indignation and protest, would be welcomed by large sections of the population. No one could have arrived at so gloomy a view who did not in the first place believe that antisemitism had a far stronger hold on the Soviet citizenry than has ever been admitted or even hinted at.

There are no Soviet sources from which one can quote to show the currency and intensity of wartime antisemitism. The whole subject is a closely guarded official secret. But there is enough indirect evidence to show that prejudice found acceptance among the people, and slowly but steadily penetrated the government machine. The tendency was to overlook its propagation and to ignore even overt antisemitic acts. It is quite characteristic in this respect that the Soviet press failed to refute the antisemitic arguments that wartime conditions caused to be spread about.

Nazi propaganda kept repeating that the Jews were slackers, that the "Jewish war" was being fought by dupes who shed their blood for the Jews' sake while Jewish warmongers were busy reaping war profits. There can be no doubt but that Goebbels' broadcasts and leaflets reached the audience for which they were intended—the Soviet army—who in turn repeated the Nazi tales to Soviet civilians behind the lines. The Goebbelsian concoction was of course made up of lies. In the spring of 1944 the number of Jews who had been awarded the highest Soviet decoration for military valor, the title "Hero of the Soviet Union," had exceeded one hundred, and the number of Jews upon whom military decorations and medals had been conferred since the beginning of the war had surpassed 32,000, according to a report submitted to the Third Plenary Session of the Jewish Antifascist Committee in the USSR by Shakhno Epshtein, the Committee's secretary.[36] At the same session, the actor Solomon Mikhoels, chairman of the Committee, disclosed that Jews ranked fourth among Soviet citizens decorated for valor, and fifth among servicemen honored as Heroes of the Soviet Union at the Ukrainian front.[37]

The Soviet press not only ignored antisemitism, it minimized, if it did not conceal altogether, the presence and deeds of Jews at the front. This may seem hard to believe to anyone on whose memory are imprinted the frequent wartime dispatches of the Independent Jewish Press Service from Kuibyshev or Moscow with their many names of Jewish war heroes whom, the dispatches said, the "Soviet press" commended for their exploits, "specifically stressing their Jewishness."[38] It never was said what Soviet press was meant. In actuality, none of this appeared either in the Soviet government's *Izvestiya* or the Communist Party's *Pravda*, either in the Red Army's *Krasnaya Zvesda* or the trade unions' *Trud*. Only *Eynikayt*, the Yiddish-language publication, had anything to say about the military contributions of the Jews.

But if Soviet sources are lacking, there is another type of evidence of wartime antisemitism available: the testimony of people who lived all their lives in the Soviet Union—or at least spent the years of the war there—and who left the country at or shortly after the end of the war. This material consists of manuscripts, letters, depositions, and recorded interviews. Most of these expatriates are Jews; antisemitism to them was a grievous part of their lives and they may have exaggerated. Their testimony, moreover, has so far not been sifted or scientifically tested and evaluated and cannot be expected to contribute to the exact measurement of antisemitism's incidence or intensity; but these reports are nevertheless valuable for their description of the quality of Soviet antisemitism and can serve as the basis for tentative judgments.

Part of the large body of eyewitness testimony we now possess describes conditions in areas which had been occupied; after the liberation of these areas Jews who had fled or been evacuated began to return to them, in some cases as early as 1943. The Nazi occupation had left its heavy impress on these regions, particularly in the Ukraine, and returning Jews often met with a violently antisemitic reception.

A large part of the testimony, however, describes the antisemitism encountered in the interior of the Soviet Union, in the remote provinces of Kazakhstan, Uzbekistan, Western Siberia, etc., which were separated by thousands of miles from the battle area. Echoes of the Hitlerite propaganda, not always faint, reached these regions too, especially when wounded and disabled veterans began to flock to them. Another contributing factor was the transfer to these regions of large numbers of deported, evacuated, or fugitive Polish Jews whose alien appearance and ways aroused suspicion and hostility.

The Warsaw lawyer and socialist leader Dr. Jerzy G. Gliksman, a cautious observer not given to exaggerate, spent more than three years in Soviet prisons, camps, and centers for Polish deportees and refugees. He has this to say about the antisemitism which Polish Jews encountered in Soviet Central Asia:

> At work deportees met with the local population, Russian, Ukrainian, Tatar, or other, either free or also deported. They were often antisemitic. While working with Jews they tried to hinder their labor and molest them as much as they could. The comparatively poor output of the Jewish deportees—caused by physical exhaustion and lack of experience—was ascribed to their unwillingness to perform manual labor, which the local population took to be a typically Jewish characteristic. Such also was often the opinion of the managers and directors of the various enterprises in which deportees were employed. The high-ranking functionaries, recruited from the free Russian population, sometimes also comported themselves with undisguised unfriendliness towards the Jews and assigned them the hardest tasks.
>
> Even representatives of the NKVD, who are the most decisive and authoritative element in Soviet life, were not free of antisemitism, favoring non-Jewish refugees while at the same time unmistakably harassing Jewish ones.[39]

Hostility to refugees was widespread and from the start assumed a marked antisemitic character. The trading activities to which the refugees from Poland had to resort in order to keep alive and which stamped them as "speculators" did not improve matters. This clearly emerges from the statements of Displaced Persons—both Polish and Soviet Jews—questioned in New York in 1948 in connection with a study sponsored by the American Jewish Committee. A preliminary survey of the respondents' statements concludes:

> At first the Polish Jews sought to make a living as regular workers, in *kolkhozes*, industrial plants, and artisans' cooperatives. But they soon discovered that their earnings from such regular occupations were insufficient to keep them from starving. There was only one way to keep alive—the market, trade, "speculation." One of the interviewees related: "I went to work on a cotton plantation. After deduction of income tax, government loan bonds, war tax, and cultural fund contributions, my wages amounted to 150–180 rubles a month. You can live just about a couple of days on this. So I'd take on additional work at night. During the epidemics I dug graves, made coffins. Also I'd collect rags in the streets and sew them into shoes or slippers that I'd sell in the market."
>
> The "market" was not something Polish Jews had invented or brought to Russia from abroad; it was a genuine Soviet reality. Hunger, and a gnawing fear lest they grow too weak and sick to survive and go home, forced Polish Jews into market dealings regardless of whether they wanted to or not. Certainly they were eager to make as much money as they could. . . . The interviewees agree as to the lot of those among the Polish-Jewish refugees or deportees in the Soviet Union who did not find their way to the "market." They died of slow starvation.[40]

The native population showed hostility not only to the Polish Jews, who were obviously "foreigners," but also to Russian Jews who had been evacuated from invaded or threatened areas. In the malignant climate of want and of general deterioration of living conditions, ancient antisemitic arguments reappeared: "Jews were unjustly blamed for evading military service, and particularly for avoiding duty at the front. At that time cases occurred of Jews being insulted, assaulted, thrown out of bread lines, etc."[41]

The latent antagonism that broad sections of the provincial populations felt for privileged groups of the bureaucracy of the capital and big Central Russian cities flared up when central governmental institutions with most of their personnel were moved into their midst. The social contrast between the metropolitan bureaucracy and the provincial populace was blatant. These privileged groups, to be sure, were only a small minority of the mass of the evacuated, and Jews in turn were only a handful among the privileged. But when social resentment is permitted no direct outlet it naturally takes a devious path. Gliksman says: "Another group of Russian Jews, belonging predominantly to the bureaucratic class and having large financial means, aroused the hostility of the local population by sending up prices on the free market, which were very high at the time to begin with."[42] Other testimony confirms this.

The following statements are typical of the remarks heard by Jews in wartime Russia:

> The non-Jewish population in Tashkent did not greet Jewish evacuees from the Ukraine with particular cordiality. People would say: "Now look at those Jews who came. They all have plenty of money."
>
> At first we were well received in the *kolkhoz* we had been brought to. The *kolkhoz* farmers thought we were genuine Poles. But when they learned that we were Jews, they started a row: "Jews killed Christ. Jews don't fight in the war."
>
> In sheep-raising *kolkhozes* in the Astrakhan region, the members, above all the younger ones, would tell you they knew for sure that the Jews were to blame for the war.[43]

Much the same thing was said at the front, where resentment against "draft-dodgers," "war profiteers," and civilians in general was abetted by the continuous stream of Nazi propaganda. The following are verbatim quotations from interviews with Displaced Persons:

> My brother told me that the Russian soldiers in the front lines would often talk about how rich the Jews are, how they have plenty of money, and that all of them should be killed off.
>
> Russian soldiers young and old were at pains to convince me that there were plenty of Jews in Minsk and Moscow, but none in the front lines: "We have to fight for them." In a "friendly" way I was told: "You are a fool. All your people are safe at home—how is it that you are at the front?"[44]

The first statement was made by a woman medical officer whose brother was with a combat unit; the second by a Polish Jew who voluntarily went to the Soviet Union shortly after the occupation of Eastern Poland in 1939, subsequently enlisted in the Soviet Army, became an officer, was twice wounded, and at the last served with General Berling's Soviet-recruited Polish Army. Among other things, this man told of a conversation with an officer, whom he quoted as saying:

> You are a Jew—well, so am I. I am from Berdichev. I was given this Russian name in the Army. That's the way it's done now, because the authorities are afraid of antisemitism in the Army.[45]

This, too, has been confirmed by letters and depositions by former Red Army men, some of whom went so far as to say that commissioned officers known to be Jewish were in constant danger of being shot in the back by soldiers under their command. This, of course, may have been an exaggerated way of expressing the existence of antisemitism in the rank and file. Many Jewish ex-officers, however, reported that they had been advised by their superiors to drop their Jewish-sounding names, not because of the danger in case of capture, but because of the hostility in the ranks.

Many eyewitness reports agree in emphasizing an unexpected flare-up of antisemitism in the Ukraine immediately after liberation. General observations alternate with detailed stories of specific incidents. A Ukrainian Jew who left Kharkov in the Spring of 1944, and then the Soviet Union at the end of the year, and went to Palestine wrote this in a report to the Rescue Committee of the Jewish Agency for Palestine:

> The Ukrainians receive the returning Jews with open animosity. During the first weeks after the liberation of Kharkov no Jews ventured about alone in the streets at night. The position improved only after the intervention of the authorities, who reinforced the police patrols in the town. In many cases Jews were beaten in the market place, and once a Jew was actually killed by a Ukrainian. The peasants who were present during the attack in the market place began to quarrel with the police who were summoned on the spot. All of them, including the murderer, were arrested. In Kiev sixteen Jews were killed in the course of a pogrom which took place after the murder of a Russian officer by a Christian woman who was believed to be a Jewess.
>
> The Jews returning to their homes received no more than a small proportion of their property. Ukrainians summoned to court for possession of Jewish property were aided by other Ukrainians, who gave false evidence against the Jews. . . .
>
> The Ukrainian authorities are greatly antisemitic. Applications by Jews are not treated properly. When the Commercial Academy moved from Kharkov to Kiev several Jewish professors applied for permission to go there; but their applications were rejected. They addressed themselves to the chairman of the Ukrainian [Supreme?] Soviet, but received no response. The Jewish theater was not allowed to return to Kharkov, and broadcasts in Yiddish were not resumed. The official answer to all Jewish representations is that the antisemitism with which the population has been infected by the Germans can only be uprooted gradually.[46]

Similar observations were made in numerous letters addressed from Displaced Persons camps in Europe to the Union of Russian Jews in New York by former Jewish Red Army men; they had visited their Ukrainian homes in 1943–1945 and, finding the local population unsympathetic, made up their minds to leave the Soviet Union for good and go to Palestine or America.[47] Such was also the reaction of completely assimilated Jews neither especially sensitive to antisemitism nor inclined to make sweeping charges on the basis of isolated incidents. Some of these former Soviet officers, though anxious to arrive at a balanced judgment, wrote harsh things. Their statements cannot be accepted without reservation, but are nevertheless symptomatic. The following is an illustration:

> Captain I. G. . . . frankly admits that not before coming to Bucharest in 1945, where his attention was drawn by others to the strength of Soviet antisemitism, did he pay any attention to antisemitic incidents. Having now considered the matter, he expresses the opinion that "antisemitism in the ranks of the Soviet Army increased during the war."
> Another captain, formerly an active party man, thinks that "antisemitism in the Soviet Union is rampant to an extent that it is impossible for anyone never having lived in that accursed country to imagine." He says that many Jewish war heroes failed to be promoted or decorated because of the antisemitic leanings of some higher-ups, and that names of high-ranking Jewish commanders were not recommended for citation to the chairman of the Council of People's Commissars "because of the pernicious influence of the late Supreme Army Commissar Shcherbakov, member of the Politburo and secretary of the Moscow provincial and city committees of the Communist Party, a dyed-in-the-wool antisemite." . . .
> The writer is convinced that antisemitic influences do not originate at the top of the Soviet hierarchy, either civilian or military; he points to Shcherbakov as a more or less exceptional phenomenon. He contends that there are many more Jewish generals in the Soviet Army than is openly admitted, because the government, according to him, is afraid that publicity might kindle antisemitism, widespread as it is.[48]

This may have been simply the personal view of a disgruntled individual. But the bulk of the testimony makes it appear as probable that it reflects notions widely accepted in the Soviet Union at the close of the war and after. Information accumulated in recent years points to a steep rise in antisemitism. According to all available testimony, manifestations of antisemitism in daily life assumed a more aggressive character, were more frequent and more acutely felt during the war than even in the late 1920's.

NOTES

1. *Pravda*, January 7, 1942. The note was later included in *Soviet War Documents. June 1941-November 1943*, issued by the Embassy of the USSR, Washington, December 1943, pp. 85–99.

2. *Soviet War Documents*, p. 93.

3. *Ibid.*, p. 94.

4. *Ibid.*, p. 97.

5. *Pravda*, April 28, 1942. An abridged version of the note was published in *Soviet*

War Documents, pp. 100–127; the omitted passages are without significance here.

6. *Soviet War Documents,* p. 117.

7. *Ibid.,* pp. 119f.

8. *Ibid.,* pp. 100f.

9. The statement was released by the Bureau of Information of the People's Commissariat for Foreign Affairs and printed in *Izvestiya* and *Pravda* on December 19, 1942. Only a few passages of the statement were cabled overseas by the Associated Press (see *The New York Times,* December 20, 1942, p. 23).

10. See "11 Allies Condemn Nazi War on Jews," in *The New York Times,* December 18, 1942, pp. 1 and 10.

11. See n. 9 above.

12. *JTA News,* December 23, 1942.

13. Edict of the Presidium of the Supreme Soviet of the USSR of November 2, 1942, *Pravda,* November 4, 1942 (printed in English translation in *Soviet War Documents,* pp. 155ff.).

14. The following is a listing of these releases according to the localities referred to, the date in parentheses indicating the date of publication in *Pravda* and *Izvestiya:* (1) Cities of Vyaz'ma, Gzhatsk, and Sychevka, province of Smolensk, and city of Rzhev, province of Kalinin (April 7, 1943); (2) Krasnodar, city and province (July 14, 1943); (3) province of Stavropol (August 5, 1943); (4) Orel, city and province (September 8, 1943); (5) city of Smolensk (November 6, 1943); (6) province of Stalino (November 13, 1943); (7) Kharkov, city and province (December 13, 1943); (8) city of Kiev (March 1, 1944); (9) Novgorod, city and district, province of Leningrad (May 5, 1944); (10) Rovno, city and province (May 7, 1944); (11) Odessa, city and province (June 14, 1944); (12) Karel-Finnish SSR (August 18, 1944); (13) city of Minsk (September 20, 1944); (14) Estonian SSR (November 26, 1944); (15) Lithuanian SSR (December 20, 1944); (16) province of Lvov (December 23, 1944); (17) Latvian SSR (April 5, 1945). Items 1, 3, 4 and 6 were included in *Soviet War Documents,* pp. 158–165, 171–195.

15. *Pravda,* May 7, 1945.

16. These dealt with directives issued by the Nazi government and military command on the extermination of Soviet prisoners of war and civilians (*Pravda* and *Izvestiya,* March 11, 1944); the extermination of Soviet people through spread of typhus infection (April 30, 1944); the extermination of Soviet prisoners of war (August 3, 1944); the destruction of cultural treasures (June 25, 1943; August 30 and September 3, 1944). The last was a summary evaluation of the material damage caused by the occupying power (September 13, 1945).

17. *Pravda,* August 5, 1943.

18. *Ibid.,* December 16–20, 1943.

19. *Ibid.,* December 20, 1943. That the barracks in the area of the Tractor Works served for the detention of Jews seized by the Gestapo is apparent from documents reproduced by Ilya Ehrenburg, in his collections, *Merder fun Felker,* pp. 11ff.

20. *Vestnik Akademii Nauk SSSR,* 1944, no. 1–2, pp. 59f.

21. *Pravda,* May 7, 1944.

22. *Ibid.,* August 2, 1944.

23. *Ibid.,* August 6, 1944.

24. *Ibid.,* August 17, 1944.

25. *Ibid.,* August 5, 1944.

26. *Ibid.,* September 20, 1944.

27. *Ibid.,* November 26, 1944.

28. Ponary was the extermination center for the Jews of Lithuania and the neighboring Polish provinces.

29. *Pravda,* December 20, 1944.

30. *Ibid.,* December 23, 1944.

31. *Ibid.,* April 5, 1945.

32. *Ibid.,* May 7, 1945.

33. For sources, see nn. 14–16 above.

34. *Pravda*, March 16, and 17, 1944.

35. This amnesty was discussed in Khrushchev's speech before the Ukrainian Supreme Soviet.

36. Reported in *Izvestiya*'s account (April 12, 1944) of the JAC session, but not in *Pravda*'s (April 5, 1944).

37. See *Information Bulletin of the Embassy of the USSR* (Washington), April 11, 1944. The facts cited by Mikhoels were not mentioned in the reports of the JAC's session published in *Pravda* and *Izvestiya*.

38. See the Independent Jewish Press Service's dispatches from Kuibyshev of January 1, 8, 22, 25, and 29, and February 12 and 19, 1943, to mention just a few.

39. Jerzy George Gliksman, *Jewish Exiles in Soviet Russia (1939–1943)*, Part II, p. 6 [July 1947], unpublished manuscript on file with the Library of Jewish Information, American Jewish Committee.

40. Rachel Erlich, *Summary Report on Eighteen Intensive Interviews with Jewish DPs from Poland and the Soviet Union*, pp. 9f. [October 1948], manuscript on file with the Library of Jewish Information, American Jewish Committee.

41. Gliksman, *op. cit.*, p. 17.

42. *Ibid.*, p. 15.

43. Erlich, *op. cit.*, p. 26. The first statement was made by a Russian Jewish girl, a young intellectual; the second and third by Polish Jewish workers. The *kolkhoz* first mentioned was in the province of Kirov (former Vyatka). Of another *kolkhoz* in the same province a fourth interviewee, a Russian Jewish girl, said that her family had been well received by the farmers, who had taken them for Russians; but after a German plane dropped leaflets saying that the Jews had caused the war, someone hinted that the newcomers were Jews, and the friendliness turned into such outspoken hostility that the Jewish family had to leave.

44. *Ibid.*, p. 27.

45. *Ibid.*

46. *Bulletin of the Joint Rescue Committee of the Jewish Agency for Palestine*, March 1945, pp. 2f.

47. See A. R. L. Gurland, *Glimpses of Soviet Jewry: 1,000 Letters from the USSR and DP Camps. Report on Material Collected by the Union of Russian Jews, Inc.*, New York City, mimeog., on file with the Library of Jewish Information, American Jewish Committee [June 1948].

48. *Ibid.*, pp. 72f.

CHAPTER VII

Postwar Contradictions

All the available sources agree in pointing to a marked increase in anti-semitism in the Soviet Union during the war. This was caused by the specific wartime conditions discussed in the preceding chapter. After the war these specific causes gradually disappeared. Did the wartime anti-semitism disappear as well?

Abstractly considered, it need not have; once having reached a certain intensity and extent, it is conceivable that it might live on after the conditions begetting it have ceased to obtain. In the absence of an open, active, and persistent struggle against antisemitism and antisemites, this abstract possibility becomes a real likelihood. The secrecy and silence still maintained by Soviet domestic policy on antisemitism long after the end of the war, lead to the conclusion that the specific kind of antisemitism engendered by the war continues to influence the thoughts, emotions and actions of broad strata of the Soviet population.

The Situation in the Ukraine

It is possible to go beyond such general observations as these only in a very tentative way. Factual information that would permit an appraisal of the actual influence of antisemitism on Soviet life today is too meager to warrant definitive conclusions. We have seen that wartime antisemitism was particularly virulent in the Ukraine. Quotation was made from a detailed report describing conditions there in the early part of 1944. The subsequent course of events in 1944 and 1945 were illuminated by Hershel Vaynraukh in a series of articles published in 1948 in the *Jewish Daily Forward*, and additional evidence was supplied by Soviet Jewish Displaced Persons writing to the Union of Russian Jews from Italian and German camps. But the situation in the Ukraine has changed in some respects since 1944–45.

One piece of information, which at first sight would seem to have no bearing on the problem under consideration, opens a window for us on the Soviet Ukrainian scene. On the occasion of the thirtieth anniversary of the establishment of the Soviet Ukraine, the Presidium of the Supreme Soviet of the USSR issued a decree on January 23, 1948 conferring "decorations and medals upon personnel of industry, agriculture, science, culture, and the arts in the Ukrainian SSR."[1] Thousands of outstanding citizens awarded decorations and medals were listed together with their positions in the social and administrative hierarchy. Their first and last names and patronymics enable us to identify the Jews among them, and thus it can be determined in what fields Jews are prominent in the postwar Ukraine. In some cases, of course, one cannot tell.[2] But even so, the list of indubitably Jewish recipients of high honors is comprehensive enough to warrant some tentative conclusions.

The decree listed a total of 4,754 recipients of decorations, and 2,721 recipients of medals. Generally, medals were awarded to persons who recently earned promotion; and since the number of Jews in the Ukraine substantially declined during the war, there were few Jews in this category. By contrast, the recipients of decorations belonged to the old and established elite, mostly officeholders and public figures who had been evacuated (or gone underground) at the outbreak of the war and who had not resumed their positions in the Ukraine until after the liberation. By 1948 most of the evacuated had returned, and the list of awards reveals the position of the Jewish minority in the postwar elite. Of the 4,754 recipients of decorations, 102, or 2.1 percent, were easily identifiable as Jews. In addition, 47 individuals were listed who may have been Jewish; if these are included, the percentage rises to 3.1. When one allows for a certain number of Jewish recipients of decorations not identifiable by their names, the maximum percentage can be estimated at 3.5—a low figure when compared to the proportion of Jews in the urban population of prewar Ukraine (the elite was of predominantly urban origin), and even to the proportion of Jews in the Ukraine's total population (5.3 percent in the census of January 1939). Was this the effect of wartime decimation, or was there intentional discrimination? Both factors probably contributed in some degree.

In what occupational groups did these Jewish public figures fall? They were principally graduate engineers (especially managers of industrial establishments, most of them of lesser importance); some officials of the economic administration; physicians (among them 8 professors); party officials; and representatives of the arts (among them the chief conductor of the Symphony Orchestra of the Ukrainian SSR). It is difficult to overlook the fact that officials of the general Soviet administration, especially of the provincial and district executive committees, are almost completely absent.

The number of party officials was conspicuous—13, including Lazar M. Kaganovich, who for about a year (from March 1947 on) served as the First Secretary of the Central Committee of the Communist Party of the Ukraine. There were also two secretaries of party provincial committees (Moisei S. Spivak of Zhitomir, and Mark S. Spivak of Stalino), two

secretaries of district committees, three high officials of the central organization of the party in the Ukraine, etc.

From all this it would seem justified to draw the following conclusions:

(1) The policy pursued in the first days after liberation, the policy of
preventing the return of Jewish officials and dignitaries to the rabidly
antisemitic Ukraine, had obviously been abandoned, though it is impossible to say exactly when.

(2) While the Communist Party failed to fight Ukrainian antisemitism
openly, the danger was seen of nationalist anti-Soviet movements using
antisemitism as a mask behind which to advance themselves; step by step
the local population was conditioned to accept the presence of Jews in
high office, especially in the party. The enforcement of this policy may
in fact have been one of the special tasks entrusted to Kaganovich when
he was dispatched to the Ukraine.

(3) This official discouragement of antisemitism would seem to have
borne fruit in the field of industrial management, in the medical profession, in the arts, and elsewhere. It would not have been possible in 1944—
as is the case today—to have a Meier Leiba Aizikovich Kogan as chairman of the Provincial Planning Commission of the province of Kirovgrad,
and an Avram Gershkovich Kordon as manager of the Makeyevo Podol'sk
iron foundry.

(4) Antisemitism is still strongly entrenched; without being discussed
or referred to, it has to be taken into account. This is borne out by the
almost complete absence of Jews from the local Soviet administration.
Official discouragement of Ukrainian antisemitism thus has a somewhat
uncertain character. Antisemitism, though latent, remains a real danger
in the Ukraine.

Creeping Antisemitism in the Government

This decline in the Ukraine of one of the indices of antisemitism
reflected the influence of the Communist Party, which had political
reasons for fearing Ukrainian antisemitism. Elsewhere no such special
political reasons existed for party action against antisemitism.

Although antisemitism in the Russian SFSR never mounted quite so
high as in the Ukraine, only isolated Jews are now to be found as organizational leaders or ranking officials of the party there; this strikingly
contrasts with the situation in the 1930's. There has not been a single
reference in the press in recent years to Jewish individuals serving as
secretaries of the party committees in the RSFSR's many provinces. This
gives one more reason to believe that the appointment of Jews to party
positions in the Ukraine was the result of plan.

In the "home" provinces of the USSR wartime antisemitism might have
been expected to decline. The specific tensions of the war had subsided;

the evacuees had gone back to their homes; the Polish deportees and
refugees had left the Soviet Union; Hitlerism was dead. And since anti-
Jewish attitudes had never been deeply rooted in the popular masses,
the effects of wartime antisemitism could have been dispelled more
easily than in the Ukraine. But the Communist Party failed to act
against it, and it must be assumed that it will continue to persist for some
time.

That other, "new" type of antisemitism which began to make itself felt
in the late 1930's, the stealthy and ill-dissembled antisemitism of the
Soviet officialdom, is still present and seems to go unchecked. Owing to
it, Jews have been gradually relegated to the background of many
spheres of Soviet life.

How far this creeping antisemitism has advanced we can see from a
comparison of the membership of the Supreme Soviet of the Soviet
Union of December 1937 [3] with that of January 1946, the first to be
elected after the war. A total of 47 Jews were elected to the two
"chambers" of the Supreme Soviet in 1937, namely, 32 of the 569 members
of the Soviet of the Union (5.6 percent), and 15 of the 574 members of
the Soviet of Nationalities (2.6 percent); [4] the proportion of Jews in both
chambers was 4.1 percent. No such detailed data were released in 1946.
"The distribution of the representatives elected mirrors the multinational
nature of our state," was the vague statement of Nikolai S. Patolichev,
rapporteur of the Committee on Credentials of the Soviet of the Union;
he added, with equal vagueness, that "the nationalities inhabiting the
Soviet Union are fully represented." [5] Somewhat more specific information was furnished by Petr A. Shariya, rapporteur for the Soviet of
Nationalities:

> The distribution of the members of the Soviet of Nationalities
> vividly portrays the great comradeship of the peoples of the Soviet
> Union. Among the representatives there are Russians, Ukrainians,
> White Russians, Azerbaidzhanians, Georgians, Armenians, Turkmen,
> Uzbeks, Tadzhiks, Kazakh, Kirghiz, Karelians, Moldavians, Lithuanians,
> Letts, Estonians, Abkhazians, Osetin, Tatars, Komi, Buryats, Yakuts,
> Chuvash, Udmurts, Bashkirs, Jews, Mordvinians, Finns, Karakal-
> paks. . . . [6]

The list continues with a number of tiny ethnic groups. The order of
enumeration here obviously corresponds to the numerical strength of
the national groups in the Soviet of Nationalities. Jews in this listing
rank twenty-sixth. In contrast, Jews in the Soviet of Nationalities of 1937
ranked eleventh.

The Jewish population had of course been catastrophically reduced.
After having risen from 3,100,000 in January 1939 (when it ranked
seventh [7] among the nationalities of the Soviet Union) to about 5,000,000

(fourth or fifth [8] place) after the annexations of 1939 and 1940, it was reduced to something in excess of 1,800,000 [9] (ranking eleventh [10]) after the war. Whereas the Jewish population thus dropped from seventh to eleventh place, Jewish membership in the Soviet of Nationalities dropped from eleventh to twenty-sixth place.

In the Soviet of the Union, the situation was hardly different. In 1937 it had more than twice as many Jewish members as the Soviet of Nationalities. No official count was taken in 1946, but the names of the Jewish members can be got from the official roll of representatives, which gives patronymics as well as first and last names.[11] One cannot be sure of identifying all, since there might be a number of native (Oriental) Jews among the representatives of the three Transcaucasian republics (Azerbaidzhan, Georgia, and Armenia) and the five republics in Asia (Uzbekistan, Turkmenistan, Tadzhikistan, Kazakhstan, and Kirghizia), whose names are often indistinguishable from those of their countrymen. To avoid error, the entire representation of these republics (81 seats) should be eliminated. It then appears that in 1946 there were five Jews among 601 members of the Soviet of the Union, or less than one percent, as against 32 Jews among 569 representatives, or 5.6 percent, in 1937—a contrast even more striking than in the case of the Soviet of Nationalities.

Nationalism versus Cosmopolitanism

Although sometimes condoned by individual groups of officials, antisemitic tendencies until recently failed to find direct and open support in the government or the party. A spectacular change in the official attitude made itself felt early in 1949, when for the first time certain actions of the government began to betray a directly antisemitic character.

In recent years official Soviet ideology has borrowed increasingly from what in earlier decades was invidiously called National Communism. Soviet propaganda has been concentrating on the national, and specifically Russian, virtues and accomplishments of the Communist system. Stalin, it will be recalled, at a Kremlin banquet in 1945 singled out the "Russian people" as "the most outstanding of all the nations of the Soviet Union." This was contrary to all Communist tradition; in the 1930's it would have been regarded as "Great-Russian chauvinism," a criminal offense. Subsequent events, however, have shown that this was more than a slip of the tongue. Since 1946 the press, the radio, and the schools have been extolling the Russian people—not all the peoples of the Soviet Union together, but specifically the Russians—as "the most outstanding" among the nations not only of the USSR but of the world. Every triumph of humanity in virtually every field of knowledge and creative endeavor has been "proven" to have originated in Russia, thanks to the inexhaustible creativity of the Russian people. Any thought that the highest achievements of the human genius were made possible only by the creative efforts of many and different peoples has been denounced time and again as a piece of "cosmopolitanism"—the philosophy of people without roots or ancestry who deny their nationality as part of their "flunkey's adulation of the West."

The campaign against "cosmopolitans without ancestry" was broadened early in 1949 to take in the entire "front of culture and art," and rapidly passed from ideological admonition to "organizational action." A large-scale purge was carried out, engulfing scores of dramatic and literary critics, art scholars, musicologists, music critics, etc. Thus, Iogan Al'tman, for years one of the most authoritative Soviet critics of the drama, the chief editor of *Teatr* [*The Theater*], and author of several books (Lessing and the Drama, The Writing of Plays, etc.), was denounced as "an enemy of Soviet art" and "a diversionist on our ideological front"; the reason given was: "Al'tman hates everything Russian, everything that is Soviet; bourgeois nationalism and his loathing for everything Russian made him repeatedly and inevitably kowtow to the West."[12] Another, even more influential dramatic critic, A. Gurvich, was accused of "mocking the Russian people, the Russian man, Russian national traditions";[13] this after a decade of directing the taste of Soviet audiences. What this mockery consisted of can be seen from the indictment in *Pravda:*

> What can be A. Gurvich's notion of the national character of the Soviet Russian man when he writes that in the "kindhearted humor and naively trusting optimism" of Pogodin's plays, which allegedly express "the national character of the playwright's relation to the universe," the spectator, "joyfully experiencing [self-]recognition," saw himself as in a mirror, for "kindheartedness" supposedly "is not alien to the Russian."
>
> This slanders the Soviet Russian man. This is abject slander. And precisely because kindheartedness is utterly alien to us, we must expose this attempt to heap insult upon the Soviet national character.[14]

The "slander" that aroused the indignation of the leading party newspaper was merely an echo of the humanistic tradition of the pre-revolutionary Russian literature. To suspect the heroic Soviet man of kindheartedness was to wallow in the mire of loathsome bourgeois nationalism. Such charges, when preferred against persons bearing unmistakably non-Russian names (both Al'tman and Gurvich are Jews), had an obvious implication. Nor was it accidental that a writer was pilloried for having described "kindheartedness" and "trusting optimism" as characteristically Russian.

Another well-known literary figure, the Ukrainian poet Leonid Pervomaiskii (also a Jew), was bitterly attacked for having touched upon universal humanitarian ideas in a paper on a Ukrainian woman writer of the late nineteenth century, Lesya Ukrainka. In this paper, read at the jubilee session of the Ukrainian Academy of Sciences, Pervomaiskii was reported to have said:

> The humanism of classical Ukrainian literature thus extends its limits and grows deeper, supplementing Shevchenko's Promethean striving, his wrathful intransigence towards the enemies, and his love for his people, with Franko's broad-minded understanding and Lesya Ukrainka's shining humanity and devotion to the whole of mankind. Only in the creative work of Lesya Ukrainka does the national element for the first time in the history of our culture translate itself into the universally human.[15]

The paper was enthusiastically acclaimed by the members of the Academy in attendance, but this was before *Pravda* and the Communist Central Committee's *Kul'tura i Zhizn'* [*Culture and Life*] launched the anti-cosmopolitan campaign. Once the campaign was under way, Pervomaiskii was mercilessly denounced by L. Dmiterko, secretary of the board of the League of Soviet Writers of the Ukraine:

> Here Pervomaiskii has produced a perfected theory of cosmopolitanism. It now appears that Shevchenko, with his intransigence towards the enemies and his love for his people, was narrow-minded; whereas Ivan Franko, whose favorite supposedly was Heine [that forbear of all "cosmopolitans without ancestry"], broadened the "understanding of the world," and Lesya Ukrainka lifted Ukrainian literature up to "the humanity of the whole of mankind." This is accomplished cosmopolitanism. . . . Having sunk into the morass of bourgeois humanism, Pervomaiskii expounded corrupt cosmopolitan theories.[16]

Cosmopolitanism was really nothing more than loyalty to the humanistic tradition and recognition of cultural values of universal, and not narrowly national, significance.

To advocate cosmopolitanism was also to aid and abet American imperialism. The USSR's Deputy Minister for the Motion Picture Industry, V. Shcherbina, stated early in 1949:

> Cosmopolitanism is the banner of American imperialist reaction, which strives spiritually to disarm the nations of the world, to deprive them of the will to fight, to make them slaves of the Wall Street bosses dreaming of world domination. Gurvich, Trauberg, and Bleiman advocated essentially the same goal when they vilified Soviet art, held up to ridicule the national forms of our culture, and servilely expressed delight in American plays and motion pictures.[17]

To serve "American imperialist reaction" was, of course, tantamount to treason, and the guilty persons were publicly denounced as "diversionists" and punished accordingly.

Of the cosmopolitans thus unmasked as traitors in 1949, the great majority were Jews, and this fact stood out clearly in the limelight of the campaign.

Antisemitic Overtones in the Campaign Against Cosmopolitanism

Although Jews were relatively prominent among Soviet writers on literature, art, and music, they were still very much in the minority and their preponderance among the "cosmopolitans" was glaringly out of proportion to their number and importance. It should also be noted that most of these critics came from thoroughly assimilated Jewish people; their writings were in no way distinguishable from those of their non-Jewish colleagues. Why, then, did the purge of cosmopolitans concentrate primarily on Jewish critics?

It apparently had less to do with past performance than with a view to the future; once an aggressive policy of Russian nationalism had been decided on, the government might have assumed that Jews, whether assimilated or not, because of their origins and ideological traditions were not the best interpreters of the new official philosophy.

Jews not only constituted the great majority of the purged, but also the Communist Party and Soviet government were at pains to make this fact known to the population. The charges were presented in such a way as to call attention to the fact that the culprits had been using aliases to avoid detection, and that their true identity had at last been revealed. This is a familiar device in antisemitic campaigns the world over.

The first to use it was *Kul'tura i Zhizn'*, whose special task it is to enforce observance of the "party line" in cultural matters. In an article in January 1949 against "antipatriotic" dramatic critics [18] that followed up the first anti-cosmopolitan sally in *Pravda*,[19] the periodical stated that the unpatriotic writings appearing over the signature "Ye. Kholodov" had been written by a critic named Meyerovich. In a way this was a trial balloon. Shortly thereafter *Literaturnaya Gazeta*, the government's leading literary publication, followed suit and unmasked two more cosmopolitan critics, Yakovlev (Khol'tsman) and Mel'nikov (Mel'man).[20]

Throughout the month of February the names of Meyerovich and Khol'tsman were bandied back and forth. More disclosures were made in March. *Komsomol'skaya Pravda* revealed that Yasnyi was the pen name for Finkel'shtein, Viktorov for Zlochevskii, and Svetlov for Sheidlin.[21] A few days later the *Literaturnaya Gazeta*, attacking cosmopolitanism in Ukrainian literature, exposed the "true" identity of the writers Burlachenko (Berdichevskii), Zhadanov (Lifshits), Gan (Kagan), Martich (Finkel'shtein), Stebun (Katsnel'son), and Sanov (Smul'son).[22]

The public was thus given to understand that the unpatriotic critics, finally exposed as lackeys of the Soviet Union's enemies, had been hiding behind Russian and Ukrainian names, their real names being Jewish.

It is inconceivable that the government should have been unaware of the antisemitic consequences of its campaign. The Jewish minority as a whole was in effect being condemned in the eyes of the whole people.

At the same time there had been a shift in the Communist position on the Jewish problem, and it was now heretical to think that Jews in the Soviet Union could have any bonds with Jews in other countries; those who continued to maintain connections with, or to profess their kinship to "World Jewry" were automatically suspect. The official warning, sounded by Ilya Ehrenburg in September 1948,[23] caused shock and consternation among Jewish sympathizers with the Soviet Union throughout the world and particularly in the United States. As the drive against cosmopolitans gained momentum, the condemnation of Jewish nationalism grew more aggressive. The concept of an "international Jewish people" was denounced as subversive and treasonable. That Yiddish literature, for instance, transcended national boundaries and joined together Soviet Jewish writers with the "dyed-in-the-wool businessmen" of Yiddish letters in America, Palestine, etc., was a piece of unmitigated "bourgeois-nationalist cosmopolitanism" and served "the enemies of our Homeland."[24]

In the Ukraine antisemites among the Soviet elite who hitherto had been obliged to conceal their opinions now breathed freely. In the same article in the *Literaturnaya Gazeta* calling the attention to the Jewish cosmopolitans of the Ukraine, a Ukrainian poet, Savva Golovanivskii, also a Jew, was violently berated for having spread "nationalist slander" in a wartime poem, "Abraham," which had been inspired by the massacre of Jews in Babii-Yar, Kiev, in 1941:

> Golovanivskii is the author of a nationalist poem "Abraham" that is openly hostile to the Soviet people. In this poem Golovanivskii heaps terrible and unheard-of slander upon the Soviet nation, and lies brazenly by alleging that the Soviet people—Russians and Ukrainians—turned their backs on an old Jew, Abraham, whom the Germans marched through the streets of Kiev to be shot.
>
> This is a terrible defamation of the Soviet nation, which has succeeded, after a hard and bloody struggle and by dint of great sacrifice and effort, in upholding the freedom and independence of Soviet people of all nationalities.[25]

The attack was coupled with the denunciation of another Jewish poet, Pervomaiskii, for reprehensible "humanistic" leanings and also for "repeating Golovanivskii's defamation of the Soviet people."[26] All this amounted to giving the Nazi-contaminated strata of the population a clean bill of health. It was of this very article, which had so studiedly placed the Jewish names of those denounced as cosmopolitans in parentheses after their pen names, that the Sunday edition of the New York *Daily Worker*, in obvious confusion, wrote: "It is unwarranted to jump to the conclusion of officially-inspired antisemitism from this particular article, or the parenthesis [sic], which we in the capitalist world would react against very sensitively."[27]

The antisemitic overtones of the campaign against cosmopolitanism greatly embarrassed Communists and fellow travelers outside of the Soviet Union, who fell back on saying that it was customary in the Soviet Union to cite the original name of every person using a pseudonym. This of course was nonsense. In the first years of the Soviet era, a number of Communist leaders, Jews and non-Jews alike, did in fact append their real names to their famous revolutionary aliases when signing documents in their official capacity, as for example N. Lenin (V. I. Ul'yanov) and J. V. Stalin (Dzhugashvili). But as the Soviet system had greatly simplified the legal changing of one's name, and as, on the other hand, great prestige was attached to the pre-revolutionary aliases adopted to elude the Tsarist police, this practice soon ceased. Never, after the revolution, did either custom or law require pseudonyms to be followed by the real names of their bearers, which would indeed have made a pseudonym entirely pointless. This disclosing of original names was plainly an effort to discredit the cosmopolitans as non-Russian and alien.[28]

Jews among Holders of Stalin Awards

The uneasiness aroused abroad by the anti-Jewish overtones of the campaign against cosmopolitanism did not escape the attention of the authorities in Moscow. The denunciations were noticeably moderated after March 1949, and the divulging of the Jewish names of authors attacked as "foreign flunkeys" and "slanderers of the Soviet people" was stopped. Subsequently, to correct the bad impression made by the international discussion of "Soviet antisemitism," original names of non-Jews were revealed in the roster of recipients of Stalin Awards for 1948, made public in April 1949.

The fact that the prizes for 1948, as in the preceding years, had been awarded to a large number of Jewish writers, artists, scientists, and technicians did not fail to impress international opinion. Were not the reports of antisemitism in the Soviet Union exaggerated? In view of this, it is well to examine this matter of the Stalin Awards in detail. Since the authorities supplied no information on the nationality of the recipients of the awards for 1948, we must rely on the official lists, which gave first and last names as well as patronymics. Where doubt exists as to whether a name is Jewish or not, it has been counted as Jewish.[29]

The total number of Stalin Awards granted for 1948 was 302; but of these only 119 were conferred upon individuals, while 183 fell to groups of two or more honored for collective accomplishments, especially in the fields of technology, invention, the improvement of production techniques, and theatrical and motion picture production. A total of 1,033 persons received awards, of whom 107 were clearly Jews and 28 were doubtful. If thus 135 prizewinners are counted as Jews,[30] they come to 13.1 percent of all those receiving awards. Since the surviving Jewish postwar population accounts for no more than one percent of the total population of the Soviet Union, the proportion of Jews among Stalin prizewinners must be considered very high.

From the proportion of Jewish prizewinners in individual fields, we can see which still offer chances of advancement to Jews, and which are affected by discriminatory practices. In literature and the arts, there were 238 recipients of Stalin prizes, of whom 25 were certainly or possibly Jewish. The distribution by groups was as follows: stage and screen, 21 Jews of a total of 144; painting, sculpture, and architecture, 1 out of 38; music, 1 out of 17; literature, 2 out of 39. The overwhelming majority of Jewish prizewinners in these fields were in the theater and in motion picture production, all of them being recipients of collective awards. By contrast, the number of Jews awarded prizes individually was very small.

Prizes for scientific work were conferred upon 40 persons, of whom 6 were Jews. Only 2—Georgii Grinberg (mathematical physics) and Leonid Kantorovich (mathematics)—received individual awards. Those granted awards for technological inventions and improved production techniques numbered 755, of whom a large part—104—were Jewish; but only 2 Jews received individual awards. When all three principal divisions—literature and art, science, and technology—are added together, it appears that of the total of 1,033 prizewinners, 119, or 11.5 percent, were recipients of individual awards; but of the total of 135 Jewish prizewinners, only 7, or 5.2 percent, were recipients of individual awards. It can be seen from this that even in fields offering increased opportunities to Jews—industrial technology above all—recognition was rarely granted them as individuals; in general, a Jew was honored only as part of a team. In these fields, too, discrimination has begun to make headway. This trend was not reversed in the distribution of Stalin Awards for 1949 (made in March 1950).[31]

Discrimination against Jews was first felt in the spheres most closely allied with ideology and politics; conversely, those fields which are ideologically neutral have been the last to feel the influence of antisemitism. But even in neutral fields the tendency is to limit the participation of Jews. In this respect the change in the distribution of Stalin Awards in the last three years betrays a definite tendency.

The decline in the percentage of Jewish prizewinners calls for some comment. Of course, there is no reason why the percentage of Jews awarded prizes should remain unchanged over the years. The ranks of

TABLE X

DISTRIBUTION OF STALIN AWARDS, 1947–1949 [32]

Field of Endeavor	Year	Recipients	Thereof: Jews	
		Number	Number	Percent
Art and literature	1947	189	27	14.3
	1948	238	25	10.5
	1949	317	28	8.8
Science	1947	45	7	15.6
	1948	40	6	15.0
	1949	60	7	11.7
Inventions and improved pro- duction techniques	1947	476	89	18.7
	1948	755	104	13.8
	1949	1,210	145	12.0
All Fields	1947	710	123	17.3
	1948	1,033	135	13.1
	1949	1,587	180	11.3

the Soviet intelligentsia are steadily growing; the numbers of persons engaged in occupations requiring special skills and qualifications increase constantly. More and more young people from the "backward" nationalities are joining the intelligentsia every year. In the long run it is inevitable that the share of the "older nations" in the awards should decline. Yet in three short years the percentage of Jewish prizewinners dropped from 17.3 to 11.3, or more than one-third, the decline in the percentage of Jewish prizewinners being precipitous in every individual field: in science, one-fourth; in technology, over one-third; in art and literature, almost two-fifths. It would be hard to explain this decline by the advance of other minority groups. More or less it is the result of some kind of conscious or half-conscious and unacknowledged discrimination.[33]

Foreign Service

Similar changes gradually took place in other spheres of Soviet life. Perhaps the most characteristic was the almost complete disappearance of Jews from the agencies having to do with foreign trade, the diplomatic corps, and foreign service in general. In recent years the international press more than once reported rumors to the effect that the People's Commissariat for Foreign Affairs (now the Ministry of Foreign Affairs) was being gradually purged of Jews, that the institute for training men for the foreign service had closed its doors to Jewish applicants, etc. There is of course no way of verifying such rumors, for no listings of foreign service personnel or institute graduates are published in the Soviet Union. But while official information is lacking, certain things have been observed by foreigners in Russia. A former UNRRA official, for example, stated:

> In recent years Jews have been barred from recruitment into the Soviet foreign service, in which they once predominated because of their knowledge of foreign languages and the outside world.[34]

Another observer, a foreign correspondent inclined to minimize rather than make much of reports and rumors of antisemitism in the Soviet Union, remarked:

> It was . . . whispered that Jews were no longer being accepted by the Foreign Office in the diplomatic training courses. I do not know whether that is true or not. Three of the Foreign Office Vice-Commissars are Jewish, but I never saw a young Jewish attaché around the place, and I had a feeling that blond Nordic types were preferred.[35]

The correspondent, in speaking of Jewish Foreign Office Vice-Commissars (now Vice-Ministers), of course referred to Maksim M. Litvinov, Solomon A. Lozovskii, and Ivan M. Maiskii (a half-Jew). None of these three has so far been mentioned in the Soviet press as having been "released from duty"; but it cannot be entirely coincidental that for quite a while now none has been named in connection with an important assignment or function in the Foreign Ministry. And the reported absence of Jews among the younger Soviet diplomats is certainly in accord with reports saying that admission of Jewish applicants to diplomatic training schools has been suspended.[36] It is well known that after 1918 a large number of the Soviet diplomats had been Jews (Yoffe, Litvinov, Khinchuk, Umanskii, etc.); but there have been no Jewish names in Soviet diplomacy in recent years.

Much the same thing seems to have taken place in the Ministry (formerly People's Commissariat) of Foreign Trade. Not so long ago Jews had been numerous among the foreign trade officials, both in Moscow and abroad; today they are a handful. The monthly journal of the Ministry, *Vneshnyaya Torgovlya* [*Foreign Trade*], regularly lists officials authorized to negotiate on behalf of the Ministry or of its ancillary organizations. Occasionally the number of officials so authorized is as much as 30, 40, or more in a single issue. In May 1948, for example, 48 names were listed, of which only two were Jewish.[37] In January 1950, one of 22 names might have been Jewish; in February, perhaps one Jewish name out of 19; in April, one Jewish name out of 46.[38] Thus, in four months, of 87 officials named in the publication, three at best may have been of Jewish origin.[39]

This elimination of Jews from departments entrusted with the conduct of the Soviet Union's relations with the outside world is not principally inspired by antisemitism, but rather reflects a rise in Russian nationalist feeling, which is accompanied by a distrust of everything non-Russian in the narrowest sense of the word. It also indicates that the government, eager to frustrate the pernicious influence of "internationalism," is inclined to take for granted the fact that Jews are "internationalists." The upshot is anti-Jewish discrimination. And the authorities practising this discrimination inevitably succumb themselves to that stealthy and discreet anti-Jewishness which for years has been penetrating many spheres of Soviet society.

Stealthy Advance of Discrimination

As time goes by, Jews are eliminated from more and more fields. The latest Supreme Soviet elections are a case in point. As noted before, the proportion of Jewish representatives in both chambers of the Supreme Soviet had already been substantially reduced in the first postwar election in 1946. The process has advanced still farther, and the elections held on March 12, 1950 resulted in the almost complete elimination of Jews from membership in the Supreme Soviet.[40]

Of the 678 new members of the Soviet of the Union, only one—Lazar M. Kaganovich, from one of the Tashkent constituencies (Central Asia)—is known to be a Jew, and another—Mark S. Spivak, from Stalino—is presumably Jewish. At best 2 out of 678, or less than one-third of one percent (as against 5.6 percent in 1937)! In the Soviet of Nationalities, which has 638 members, there are two known Jewish members and one who is presumably Jewish, or less than one-half of one percent (as against 2.6 percent in 1937). The Jewish representatives elected were Ilya Ehrenburg the writer, from Riga (Latvia), and Dr. Rozaliya Gol'denberg, from the city of Birobidzhan, the only Jewish member elected from the Jewish Autonomous Province, which has five seats in the Soviet of Nationalities;[41] the member presumed to be Jewish was Anna E. Kaluger from Bessarabia.

In the Supreme Soviet as a whole, the proportion of Jews is less than .4 percent (as against 4.1 percent in 1937). Prominent Jewish members of the elite whose high position in the government hierarchy seemed fairly well established—such as Solomon A. Lozovskii and Maksim M. Litvinov in foreign affairs, the Minister of State Controls, Lev Z. Mekhlis, and the Minister of Industrial Construction, Semen Z. Ginzburg—all of whom still held office in the Supreme Soviet in 1946, are no longer members. A. Bakhmutskii, the secretary of the provincial committee of the Communist Party for the Jewish Autonomous Province, who represented Birobidzhan in the Soviet of Nationalities in 1946, was not reelected, and his name has not been mentioned in the central Soviet press for quite some time.

Since the middle of 1949 antisemitism in the USSR has shunned making any open display. But the stealthy variety of antisemitism, which, as repeatedly noted, has been gaining ground since the late 1930's, continues to exert its undeniable influence on Soviet society.

NOTES

1. *Vedomosti Verkhovnogo Soveta SSSR* [*Official Journal of the Supreme Soviet of the USSR*], February 13, 1948, Appendices 1 to 4.

2. Among those listed there were probably also Jews who had changed their names in order to conceal their descent; they were probably not many

3. Data from *Vybory v Verkhovnyi Sovet SSSR i v Verkhovnyye Sovety soyuz-nykh i avtonomnykh respublik, 1937–1938 gg. (Tsifrovoi sbornik)* [*Elections to the Supreme Soviet of the USSR and the Supreme Soviets of Union and Autonomous Republics in 1937–1938 (Statistical Résumé)*], Division of Information and Statistics, Secretariat of the Presidium of the Supreme Soviet of the USSR, Moscow, 1939, pp. 12f.

4. The Supreme Soviet is elected under a system that favors a strong representation, within the Soviet of Nationalities (but not within the Soviet of the Union), of national groups organized in Soviet Republics of their own (where, as a rule, the national group that gives the Republic its name constitutes the majority of the population). There were 16 Union Republics in January 1946, as aganist 11 in December 1937.

5. *Pravda*, March 15, 1946.

6. *Ibid.*

7. Based on data in S. Sul'kevich, *Territoriya i naseleniye SSSR* [*Area and Population of the USSR*], Moscow, 1940, p. 16.

8. Cf. data on Soviet population by nationalities at the outbreak of the war, as tabulated by Theodore Shabad, in Corliss Lamont, *The Peoples of the Soviet Union*, New York, 1946, pp. 212f. According to Shabad, who estimated the Jewish population at 5,300,000, Jews ranked fourth; but actually the Jewish population was closer to 5,000,000, that is, the annexations probably had moved it to the fifth rather than the fourth place.

9. See Appendix to Part I for statistics.

10. This assumes that no considerable changes have taken place in the relative sizes of the major national groups. At the time of the Soviet Union's entry into the war the group that ranked next below the two-million mark was the Moldavians, who then numbered 1,625,000.

11. *Pravda*, February 14, 1946.

12. G. Gurko, "*Burzhuaznyi natsionalist Al'tman*" ["Al'tman, a Bourgeois Nationalist"], in *Sovetskoye Iskusstvo*, February 19, 1949.

13. Konstantin Simonov, "Zadachi sovetskoi dramaturgii i teatral'noi kritiki" ["The Tasks of the Soviet Drama and Dramatic Criticism"], in *Literaturnaya Gazeta*, March 2, 1949.

14. "Ob odnoi antipatrioticheskoi gruppe teatral'nykh kritikov" ["An Antipatriotic Group of Dramatic Critics"], *Pravda*, January 28, 1949.

15. L. Dmiterko, "Sostoyaniye i zadachi teatral'noi i literaturnoi kritiki na Ukraine" ["The Present Situation and the Tasks of Literary and Dramatic Criticism in the Ukraine"], in *Literaturnaya Gazeta*, March 9, 1949.

16. *Ibid.*

17. *Sovetskoye Iskusstvo*, March 5, 1949.

18. "Proiski antipatrioticheskoi gruppy teatral'nykh kritikov" ["Machinations of an Antipatriotic Group of Dramatic Critics"], in *Kul'tura i Zhizn*, January 30, 1949.

19. See n. 14 above.

20. *Literaturnaya Gazeta*, February 12, 1949.

21. Boris Ivanov and Ye. Rodikov, "Burzhuaznyye kosmopolity v sportivnoi litera-

ture" ["Bourgeois Cosmopolitans in Sports Writing"], in *Komsomol'skaya Pravda*, March 6, 1949.

22. See n. 15 above.

23. Ilya Ehrenburg, "Po povodu odnogo pis'ma" ["On the Subject of a Letter"], in *Pravda*, September 21, 1948.

24. See I, Chap. 14, n. 41.

25. See n. 15 above.

26. *Ibid.*

27. Joseph Starobin, "Soviet Record Refutes Anti-Semitism Slander," in *The Worker*, April 17, 1949.

28. A Bulgarian visitor to the Soviet Union, Dr. Anzhel Vagenshtain, a Communist official in the Bulgarian motion picture industry, told a Jewish audience in Sofia—the Jewish Cultural Club—that in Soviet campaigns "it is always pointed out concretely who is the exponent of an enemy ideology." "Therefore if such an exponent has a Russian name and is a Jew, his Jewish name is put in brackets." In an attack on the supposedly pro-Zionist and anti-Soviet leanings of Jewish writers and film people, he added: "One has to say openly that the majority of the small group of cosmopolitans in the USSR were Jews." See "Kosmopolitizm't—Mezhdunaroden yezik na imperialistite" ["Cosmopolitanism, the International Language of the Imperialists"], in *Yevreiski Vesti*, organ of the Minority Commission of the National Council of the Bulgarian Fatherland Front, vol. VII, no. 260 (March 1, 1950), p. 4.

29. *Izvestiya*, April 9 and 10, 1949.

30. The number of Jewish prizewinners indicated by American pro-Soviet propagandists is less than that arrived at by the present writer. E.g., Moses Miller, in *Soviet "Anti-Semitism"—the Big Lie!* Jewish Life Publications, New York, n.d., p. 13, found "120 obviously Jewish names" among the recipients, while Tom O'Connor, in "Hoax of 'Soviet Anti-Semitism'—the Matter of Jewish Names," in *The Daily Compass*, May 26, 1949, p. 21 (reprinted in pamphlet form, as *The Truth about Antisemitism in the Soviet Union*, American Committee of Jewish Writers, Artists and Scientists, New York, n.d., p. 9), counted only 99 recipients as "unmistakably Jewish," *viz.*, 77 in technology and 22 in the arts. This did not prevent the author from stating that "almost 20 percent of Stalin prize-winners had Jewish names" (*ibid.*). Even assuming that he has omitted all the science awards, which would reduce the total number of recipients from 1,033 to 993, O'Connor's figures show 10 rather than 20 percent of all the prizewinners as Jewish.

31. As compared to the preceding year, the total number of recipients increased almost 53 per cent, that of Jewish recipients less than 32 percent. Of a total of 1,580 awards, 144 were for individual achievements, or 9.1 percent; but only 8 of the 179 Jewish prizewinners, or 4.5 percent, were honored for individual performance. The scholarly, literary, or artistic achievements of Jews found hardly more recognition than in the year before; in literature and the arts, the number of prizewinners rose from 238 to 310, a gain of 30 percent; but the number of Jews among them increased from 25 to 27, or only 8 percent; in science, a 50 percent increase in the total—from 40 to 60—contrasted with a 17 percent increase in the number of Jewish recipients—from 6 to 7. Of the overall increase in the number of awards to Jews, most were for industrial inventions and innovations; in this field 1,210 prizewinners were listed, as against 755 in the preceding year, a gain of 60 percent, and the number of the Jewish recipients of awards rose 39 percent from 104 to 145. (*Izvestiya*, March 4 and 8, 1950.) In the lists of prizewinners for 1949, the Communist press again found fewer Jews than this writer. Thus, *Morgn Frayhayt*, in its issue of March 19, 1950, counted only 110 Jewish prizewinners in scholarship and technology, as against our 152.

32. Data for 1947, from *Pravda*, April 2 and 21, May 30, and June 3, 1948; for 1948, from *Izvestiya*, April 9 and 10, 1949; for 1949, from *Izvestiya*, March 4 and 8, 1950; percentages have been computed.

33. According to reports by Displaced Persons and foreign visitors to the Soviet Union, a peculiar *numerus clausus* has been applied in recent years in institutions of

higher learning—not in the admission of students, but in the distribution of scholarships. Sporadic information on restrictions limiting the access of Jews to academic teaching points in the same direction. The following story was told by Edmund Stevens upon his return from the Soviet Union after serving many years as a foreign correspondent:

" 'Could you use a good secretary?' an old Jewish friend asked. 'How about taking on my son?'

"I was rather surprised at the suggestion. My friend knew as well as I that it was hardly discreet for a Soviet citizen to work for a foreign correspondent unless 'assigned' to the job. Moreover, his son recently had qualified for his master's degree in history with high honors, which should have guaranteed him a teaching post in almost any institution of higher learning. I said as much.

" 'That is what he thought,' my friend answered grimly, 'until he started making the rounds.'

"It turned out that wherever his son, who looked Russian, applied for a job he was received and told to fill out the application blank. But the moment his interviewer saw the word 'Jewish' he was politely told there were no vacancies—sorry. After months of this, the son was desperate for work.

"Our conversation took place early last winter. At first I discounted my friend's story, but soon I found corroboration from another source. The head of a department in a large educational institution told me he had received a directive to hire no more Jewish teachers and to dismiss those already on his staff whenever a convenient pretext presented itself." (*Christian Science Monitor*, January 10, 1950.)

34. John Fisher, *Why They Behave like Russians*, Harper Bros., New York—London, 1947, p. 108.

35. Harrison Salisbury, *Russia on the Way*, Macmillan, New York, 1946, p. 293.

36. Igor Gouzenko, who was on the Soviet diplomatic staff in Canada, said: "In 1939 we were privately and individually 'warned' at the Architectural Institute [in Moscow] that Jews in general were 'in disfavor.' We are told of a 'confidential' decree of the Central Committee of the All-Union Communist Party which had been passed about that time. The decree was sent out to all directors of educational institutions and schools throughout the Soviet Union. It established a secret quota of admission for Jews with a view toward curtailing their attendance at the Soviet educational institutes." This, of course, defies verification from Soviet sources. Referring to another secret anti-Jewish directive, the same author stated: "In the summer of 1945, Aleksashkin, chief of the secret division [of Soviet Intelligence], arrived at Ottawa and told us that the Central Committee of the Communist Party sent 'confidential' instructions to directors of all plants and factories to remove Jews from responsible positions and, under any pretext whatever, to place them in less important work." (*The Iron Curtain*, Dutton & Co., New York, 1948, pp. 157, 158.)

37. *Vneshnyaya Torgovlya*, May 1948, pp. 45ff.

38. *Ibid.*, January 1950, pp. 47f.; February 1950, pp. 45, 47f.; April 1950, pp. 46ff.

39. No appointments or transfers were announced in March.

40. *Pravda*, March 15, 1950.

41. In the Soviet of Nationalities of 1946, 2 out of the 5 representatives of the Jewish Autonomous Province were Jews.

Index

WORLD AFFAIRS: National and International Viewpoints
An Arno Press Collection

Angell, Norman. **The Great Illusion, 1933.** 1933.

Benes, Eduard. **Memoirs:** From Munich to New War and New Victory. 1954.

[Carrington, Charles Edmund] (Edmonds, Charles, pseud.) **A Subaltern's War.** 1930. New preface by Charles Edmund Carrington.

Cassel, Gustav. **Money and Foreign Exchange After 1914.** 1922.

Chambers, Frank P. **The War Behind the War, 1914-1918.** 1939.

Dedijer, Vladimir. **Tito.** 1953.

Dickinson, Edwin DeWitt. **The Equality of States in International Law.** 1920.

Douhet, Giulio. **The Command of the Air.** 1942.

Edib, Halidé. **Memoirs.** 1926.

Ferrero, Guglielmo. **The Principles of Power.** 1942.

Grew, Joseph C. **Ten Years in Japan.** 1944.

Hayden, Joseph Ralston. **The Philippines.** 1942.

Hudson, Manley O. **The Permanent Court of International Justice, 1920-1942.** 1943.

Huntington, Ellsworth. **Mainsprings of Civilization.** 1945.

Jacks, G. V. and R. O. Whyte. **Vanishing Lands:** A World Survey of Soil Erosion. 1939.

Mason, Edward S. **Controlling World Trade.** 1946.

Menon, V. P. **The Story of the Integration of the Indian States.** 1956.

Moore, Wilbert E. **Economic Demography of Eastern and Southern Europe.** 1945.

[Ohlin, Bertil]. **The Course and Phases of the World Economic Depression.** 1931.

Oliveira, A. Ramos. **Politics, Economics and Men of Modern Spain, 1808-1946.** 1946.

O'Sullivan, Donal. **The Irish Free State and Its Senate.** 1940.

Peffer, Nathaniel. **The White Man's Dilemma.** 1927.

Philby, H. St. John. **Sa'udi Arabia.** 1955.

Rappard, William E. **International Relations as Viewed From Geneva.** 1925.

Rauschning, Hermann. **The Revolution of Nihilism.** 1939.

Reshetar, John S., Jr. **The Ukrainian Revolution, 1917-1920.** 1952.

Richmond, Admiral Sir Herbert. **Sea Power in the Modern World.** 1934.

Robbins, Lionel. **Economic Planning and International Order.** 1937. New preface by Lionel Robbins.

Russell, Bertrand. **Bolshevism:** Practice and Theory. 1920.

Russell, Frank M. **Theories of International Relations.** 1936.

Schwarz, Solomon M. **The Jews in the Soviet Union.** 1951.

Siegfried, André. **Canada:** An International Power. [1947].

Souvarine, Boris. **Stalin.** 1939.

Spaulding, Oliver Lyman, Jr., Hoffman Nickerson, and John Womack Wright. **Warfare.** 1925.

Storrs, Sir Ronald. **Memoirs.** 1937.

Strausz-Hupé, Robert. **Geopolitics:** The Struggle for Space and Power. 1942.

Swinton, Sir Ernest D. **Eyewitness.** 1933.

Timasheff, Nicholas S. **The Great Retreat.** 1946.

Welles, Sumner. **Naboth's Vineyard:** The Dominican Republic, 1844-1924. 1928. Two volumes in one.

Whittlesey, Derwent. **The Earth and the State.** 1939.

Wilcox, Clair. **A Charter for World Trade.** 1949.